D1084553

C

Personal and Social Consumption in Eastern Europe

Bogdan Mieczkowski

The Praeger Special Studies program—
utilizing the most modern and efficient book
production techniques and a selective
worldwide distribution network—makes
available to the academic, government, and
business communities significant, timely
research in U.S. and international economic, social, and political development.

Personal and Social Consumption in Eastern Europe
Poland, Czechoslovakia, Hungary, and East Germany

PRAEGER SPECIAL STUDIES IN INTERNATIONAL ECONOMICS AND DEVELOPMENT

Praeger Publishers   New York   Washington   London

Library of Congress Cataloging in Publication Data

Mieczkowski, Bogdan, 1924–
    Personal and social consumption in Eastern Europe.

    (Praeger special studies in international economics
and development)
    Bibliography: p.
    Includes index.
    1. Consumption (Economics)—Europe, Eastern.
2. Europe, Eastern—Economic conditions.   3. Europe,
Eastern—Social conditions.   4. Marxian economics.

I. Title.
HC244.Z9C65   339.4'7'0943   75-6917
ISBN 0-275-05620-1

PRAEGER PUBLISHERS
111 Fourth Avenue, New York, N.Y. 10003, U.S.A.

Published in the United States of America in 1975
by Praeger Publishers, Inc.

Printed in the United States of America

To Adam Rudzki
a friend of people, books, and
ideas — and a respected
personal friend

CONTENTS

LIST OF TABLES AND FIGURE

LIST OF ABBREVIATIONS

AS	Annuarul Statistic al Republicii Socialiste Romania
Comecon	Council for Mutual Economic Assistance
DIfW	Deutsches Institut fuer Wirtschaftsforschung
DIfZ	Deutsches Institut fuer Zeitgeschichte
GNP	gross national product
GP	Gospodarka Planowa
GUS	Glowny Urzad Statystyczny
kg	kilogram(s)
KiW	Ksiazka i Wiedza
m	meter(s)
ND	Nowe Drogi
NEM	New Economic Mechanism
OP	Occasional Papers of the Research Project on National Income in East-Central Europe (New York: Columbia University, or Riverside Research Institute)
PWE	Polskie Wydawnictwo Ekonomiczne
PWG	Polskie Wydawnictwo Gospodarcze
PWN	Polskie Wydawnictwo Naukowe
RFE	Radio Free Europe
RPiG	Rocznik Polityczny i Gospodarczy
RS	Rocznik Statystyczny
SE	Statisztikai Evkonyv
SEzh	Statisticheskii Ezhegodnik

SG	Statisticki Godisnjak Jugoslavije
SJ	Statistisches Jahrbuch der Deutschen Demokratischen Republik
SR	Statisticka Rocenka Ceskoslovenske Socialisticke Republiky
ZG	Zycie Gospodarcze
—	(in tables) data not available
. .	(in tables) data nonexistent or negligible

International economic comparisons traditionally feature gross national product (GNP), its size and rates of growth, to provide an idea of relative economic successes of countries with similar or contrasting political and economic systems. Often rates of investment and its proportion in national income are cited, as well as growth of foreign trade, changes in trade balances, unemployment rates, and other statistics connected mainly with production. The purpose of the present study is to change that emphasis to the realm of consumption.

Production for its own sake seems devoid of sense, empty of purpose. It is only when one realizes that the ultimate aim of all productive activity is the satisfaction of our wants that production acquires a purpose and a sense, and ceases to be a goal in itself. Our wants are satisfied in the process called consumption. Concentrating our attention on consumption means focusing on the aim of economic activity rather than on the means of achieving it, which is production of goods and services. Logically, then, our focus seems more instructive and meaningful than a focus on production.

Production statistics are easier to come by, particularly in sources from Eastern Europe, than are statistics on consumption. That fact may explain, at least in part, the usual emphasis on production. Production signifies some potential, and that may lend it interest from the point of view of manufacturing, marketing, and defense establishments. Production, unlike consumption, is more palpable, easily quantifiable; its interrelations can be satisfactorily established; its results can be seen; it appeals more to the imagination. Evaluation of consumption, on the other hand, is surrounded by controversy, value judgments, doubts, even emotions. It is thus more difficult to handle analytically, and it generates more uncertainty.

While these reasons may explain the relative lack of interest in consumption problems, the central importance of consumption should make us willing to face the difficulties and come to grips with what is inherently more important: the satisfaction of wants, rather than preparation for that satisfaction in the form of production. As a criterion of performance of an economic system, consumption has a ring of finality to it. For what is a system worth if it cannot produce satisfaction among the population? And which system is not in the most understandably human sense "better" if not the one that secures a higher level of living for its people?

It has been assumed in the present study that consumption constitutes an ultimate desirable goal. Such an approach may be criticized as somewhat single-minded because it abstracts from social costs incurred in the production and use of more and more consumer goods, some of which costs have been expressed in terms of ecological damage (noted also in Eastern Europe); fostering of "money-grabbing" materialism to the neglect of higher human values; human wear-and-tear on the treadmill of getting more and more; and invidiousness that harms social cohesion. One could remember that an apparently viable alternative has been created within contemporary Chinese society, and that restriction of want satisfaction may become a necessity in the future. For the present, however, the pressures for higher consumption in Eastern Europe are strong, mainly because the current consumption levels there are relatively low while aspirations levels are much higher. Once the catching up process with the West is substantially advanced, the situation may change and consumption may lose some of its present luster.

The present study explains some of the main concepts in the area of consumption and traces its development in conjunction with important selected economic categories that influence the growth of consumption. There are no single "magic numbers" that emerge, but it is hoped that a broad assessment of consumption achievements in Eastern Europe will be possible on the basis of this study, as well as a better understanding of conditions that have shaped changes in consumption in the countries covered. Hopefully, the study also will stimulate further discussion and research in the field of consumption in Eastern Europe. This would help redress the one-sidedness of the usual production-oriented emphasis.

The 1960s witnessed the consumer in Eastern Europe emerge from his microeconomic obscurity and neglect, to assume a more important role in the scheme of things, including things political. Official statistics slowly started including more information on consumption, although the coverage has not by any means been uniform in Eastern Europe, and is far from comprehensive and continuous. Articles started appearing in professional journals; more recently, some books concentrating on consumption have been published. The present study includes the main aspects of the emerging East European discussion of consumption problems; in this way, it also fills in a gap in Western knowledge.

Insofar as the results of the research underlying this work point to greater practical concern in Eastern Europe with consumption and levels of living, they are optimistic for the future, since concern for people and their welfare may bring the peoples of the world closer together than any race for eminence in the production field ever could. Our results also point to an emerging concern in Soviet-type centrally planned economies with social compromises between competing goals, the chief pair there having been investments and consumption. In the past, investments were the unquestioned favorite of planners; by now the balance tends to be struck less unevenly. These and other developments outlined in this study tend to show that consumption will be more heard of in Eastern Europe in the future. And, it seems, all to the better.

The subject of consumption is a vast one, and much work has been going on. There are many aspects and results of calculations that could be added to the present study; given more time and resources at my disposal, they will eventually be added. The present study may hopefully serve as a framework for and introduction to future work in the area of consumption in Eastern Europe.

I have had the good fortune of receiving encouragement and constructive criticism from my friends. Po-chih Lee, Senior Economist at Bell Canada, assisted in computations on residual consumption utilized in Chapter 10. I am particularly indebted to Andrzej Brzeski of the University of California at Davis for his constructive criticism of the first draft of this study. I would like to thank Thad P. Alton for making available sources at his disposal and for his comments on several points. Stanley Zemelka of Bellarmine College; Stanislaw Gomulka of Aarhus University, Denmark; Gregor Lazarcik; Laszlo Czirjak; and George Pall offered valuable comments on individual chapters or parts.

Encouragement, help, and advice also are gratefully acknowledged from several colleagues and friends, especially Andrew Ezergailis, Frank Musgrave, and William E. Terwilliger of Ithaca College, and Marek A. Rudzki of the Planning Department of the Port Authority of New York.

I am indebted to my wife, Seiko, for her critical first evaluation of every emerging page, and for her steadfast faith. I am grateful to my young sons, Van, Ian, and Dean, for their interest in my work and their expressed desire to write books of their own some day. For many years, I received encouragement and source material from Adam Rudzki, to whom this book is dedicated.

THE THEORY AND
THE POLITICAL ECONOMY
OF CONSUMPTION IN
EASTERN EUROPE

1

THE IMPORTANCE
OF CONSUMPTION

In introducing the first United Nations study on levels of living, Dag Hammarskjold, then Secretary General of the United Nations, remarked: "The promotion of 'higher standards of living' is set forth in the Charter of the United Nations as a general goal of international economic and social activity" (United Nations 1954, p. iii). The U. N. Committee of Experts in its 1954 report groped for a general measure to be used in comparing the levels of living. It proposed the following as an

> acceptable international catalogue of the components of the level of living, although the precise connotation of each would to some extent be determined by national attitudes and standards resulting from peculiarities of environmental conditions, cultures, values and economic, political and social organization: 1. Health, including demographic conditions. 2. Food and nutrition. 3. Education, including literacy and skills. 4. Conditions of work. 5. Employment situation. 6. Aggregate consumption and savings. 7. Transportation. 8. Housing, including household facilities. 9. Clothing. 10. Recreation and entertainment. 11. Social security. 12. Human freedom (United Nations 1954, p. 26).

Most of the categories listed above are not easily subject to uniform quantification. The present study will be concerned primarily with item 6, aggregate consumption and savings, which is most amenable to quantitative comparisons, but it also will refer to other items, such as housing (item 8), clothing (item 9), recreation and entertainment (item 10), all three of which enter into consumption insofar as they are paid for out of individual incomes and, especially in the case of housing, subsidized out of public treasury and thus enter into social consumption. The present study also will make references to conditions of work and employment situation (items 4 and 5), and social security (item 11). Item 6, aggregate consumption and savings, includes the following elements:

(1) Proportion of national income spent on food. (2) Proportion of public expenditure spent on social services ([defined by the Committee of Experts to] include education, health services, social security, public assistance and special welfare services whether in the form of current expenditure, capital formation or transfer payments). (3) Public expenditure on social services as a proportion of national income. (4) Index of, and rate of change of, "personal consumption" per capita. (5) "Personal consumption" as a proportion of national income and index of changes therein. (6) Index of, and rate of change of, investment and savings per capita. (7) Investment and savings as a proportion of national income and index of changes therein. (United Nations 1954, pp. 38-39)

The present study will treat these subdivisions according to its own framework of reference, partly explained in Chapter 4, last section; social consumption will be treated in Chapter 2.

Further guidance and discussion of the problem of determining the level of living was provided by the United Nations in an ongoing series of publications (United Nations 1961, 1970, 1972a, and 1972b), and with reference to Poland was provided by a Western economist, Bohdan Brodzinski (1965). A short discussion of the United Nations guidelines was given in a Polish text on consumption, but only the first eleven of the twelve points cited above were listed there; item 12, human freedoms, was omitted. (Piasny 1971, pp. 98 n. 92, 95-100). However, an earlier Polish text on social consumption that listed the United Nations guidelines did mention "personal freedom" in place of "human freedoms" (Winiewski 1969, p. 24).

THE ROLE OF CONSUMPTION

The importance of consumption derives from the fact that it is the factor that determines the material level of living, which in turn is a factor, and normally the most important factor, in determining the overall level of living as defined by the United Nations. Variations in consumption will be therefore important in creating a picture of changes in the material well-being of the population. Rising per capita consumption normally will signify an improvement in the level of living, declining consumption a worsening level of living, and a near zero consumption would imply inability of the economy to sustain life.

In an economic system with less than full employment, consumption exercises an employment effect in that its rise leads to an expansion of employment. Economists talk in this connection about "the multiplier effect" in that, as the desire of the population to consume a certain proportion of national income rises, the national income and employment rise more than in proportion to the original shift in the consumption function. Additionally, a rise in consumption creates a need to increase the amount of capital (machinery, equipment, roads, communications) needed to produce the increased volume of consumer goods. Production of that needed capital, on top of the original increase in consumption, produces further expansion of national income and employment in what is called "the accelerator effect." An explanation of those two effects can be found in any textbook on principles of economics (for example, Samuelson 1973, pp. 220-32, 260-3). Thus, in an underemployment economy, consumption plays an important part in determining the equilibrium level and growth of national income and employment.

In a full-employment economic system, consumption obviously does not play that role. To the extent that the socialist economic systems are full-employment systems, consumption loses some of its importance as a determinant of the level of economic activity. However, the socialists stress that consumption is the true goal of all economic activity, apart from its role as indicator of the level of living and other functions discussed below.

All modern economic systems possess the institution of a market for labor, in the sense of a web of economic interrelationships on the basis of which labor is "sold" to an employer in exchange for payment, usually called wage or salary. That payment, in the hands of the employee, constitutes his gross personal income. After a deduction for all taxes, what is left is the disposable income, most of which is spent on personal consumption, while the residual constitutes saving. A relationship is thus created between the sale of labor on the labor market and consumption. To the extent that the employer — private or state — rewards greater productivity, or usefulness of labor to him, by payment of higher wage or salary, the employee finds that if he wants to consume more, he has to work more productively, which does not necessarily mean "harder." An incentive element is, consequently, built into the wage system, helping to maximize production by inducing employees to do their best to raise production and possibly improve its quality. Whether such an incentive system is actually operative, or how long it may remain operative, depends on many institutional factors, but the opportunity for its use is inherent in the wage system and in the fact that most of the wages received are spent on consumption.

To the extent that consumption is the last link in the incentive system, and to the extent that it helps to maximize output within a static system, consumption also improves the dynamic performance of the economy since every succeeding increment in output can start from a higher level of output than would have been true otherwise. A theoretical proof of this assertion is found in the Kalecki model (see Chapter 4, second section), or on the most general level in the synthesis of general theories of growth (Higgins 1968, p. 155), according to which:

$$\Delta 0 = a(\Delta Q) + (\Delta a)Q$$

where: 0 = total output
        a = output/capital ratio
        Q = the stock of capital

A higher level of national income, maximized thanks to the operation of consumption used as incentive, necessitates a higher level of capital stock, Q, and also allows more capital to be created, since it is easier to set aside more resources for investment—that is, for creation of more capital — out of a level of national income than would be true with a lower, not maximized, level of national income. On the basis of that larger amount of capital, Q, given other elements of the equation, the changes in output, $\Delta 0$, can also be larger. We conclude, therefore, that economic growth, measured in terms of changes in output, is speeded up with the use of consumption as an incentive to work.

The incentive function of consumption also may work in another way, namely, from the need for improved consumption to make the process of economic development a continuing one. New goods are invented, new processes created, in order to satisfy the consumer, who in the course of economic development acquires constantly increasing needs (Markowski 1972, p. 4). Consumers' wants appear in this context as a primum mobile, a force that propels the planners and producers to supply more and better assortments of goods.

Not the least important aspect of consumption is that it frequently is used as a basis for international comparisons, as indeed it will be used in the present study. Under conditions of (sometimes acute) international competition and rivalry among nations and economic systems of the cold war or cold peace era, the effort to gain people's allegiance, or even interest, goes on. Inhabitants of less developed countries may look for examples to follow among countries that are more developed, for a model to imitate. Among features sought in a model, they are certain to consider the level of consumption and the rate at which that level is raised. They also are likely to attribute the success or lack of it in the area of consumption to the economic and political system governing a given economy. As Abram Bergson pointed out: "comparative economic merits is an important issue, and beliefs about it are apt to be consequential . . . both for choices among economic systems, where such choices occur, and for choices among economic institutions within either system." (Bergson 1968, pp. 13-14.) For this reason, one-upmanship in the area of consumption is internationally inevitable, especially among the superpowers. Khrushchev's famous "We will bury you" directed at the Americans implied a conviction that the Communist system would bring "more and faster" in the area of consumption, and would catch up with the United States in per capita consumption by 1971. The inevitability of international comparisons make the study of consumption particularly important since such a study may supply answers to questions regarded as crucial in winning allegiance of third parties and enhancing a country's prestige. From the point of view of less developed countries, such answers may serve as a basis for policy guidelines. More generally, a study of consumption will provide us with some information about the results of economic policy that are deemed important by the population and should be considered as important by economic planners.

Bela Balassa, in discussing success indicators of an economic system, stated:

Three indicators can be said to contribute to consumer satisfaction: (1) correspondence of production targets to individual preferences, (2) correspondence of the actual saving ratio to the saving ratio desired by individuals, and (3) correspondence of actual work performed to individuals' preferences for work versus leisure. (Balassa 1959, p. 16.)

The first of the above-named factors is by far the most important in determining consumer well-being, and that factor is stressed in consumption studies. The other two factors, while of increasing importance from the individual point of view, are in a sense undesirable from the view of maximization of the growth rate because they constitute a constraint on economic growth. To the extent that individuals may want to consume almost all of their incomes and save little, there will be fewer resources freed for investment in capital to augment future production. To the extent also that people may expect more leisure, the output they produce will tend to diminish. Yet both these factors play an important role in consumer satisfaction, and both must be contended with in international comparisons of consumer well-being.

CONSUMPTION AND CONSUMPTION DATA IN MARXISM-LENINISM

Published statements in Eastern Europe accord to consumption the most important role. There are several reasons for this interest in achievements in the area of consumption, and the present section concentrates on exploring them.

Justification of the Socialist System

The first reason for the stress on consumption is the tradition rooted in socialist reaction to the appalling conditions of life among the working people in the early nineteenth century. For that reason, one can frequently find in Eastern Europe statements like the following: "It is an uncontroverted truth that in socialist countries all social and political activity aims at uninterrupted raising of the standard of living of the working people." (Knab and Pach 1968, p. 59.) "Social and political activity," like egalitarian policies or the sharpening of the class struggle, has obvious implications in the economic sphere. Some Polish economists who specialize in problems of consumption wrote:

> The goal of economic activity is a constant striving for increasingly better satisfaction of the wants of the society, or consumption. It appears from this that the ultimate goal of socialist production is not the whole of national income but that part of it which is consumed. (Piasny 1971, pp. 9-10.)

> All of economic growth serves to maximize current and future consumption that is the goal of socialist economy. (Hodoly 1966, p. 5.)

> Only in a socialist system does the maximum satisfaction of the wants of the society become the direct aim of production. (Pohorille 1971, pp. 21-22.)

> What in contemporary capitalist economy is, as part of "marketing," a modernized form of exploitation becomes under conditions of planned socialist economy an important element and a test of the realization of the humanist role of consumption. (Hodoly et al. 1971, p. 31.)

8

There is no doubt from these pronouncements that, at least in theory, consumption holds unchallenged primacy and plays a unique role in Communist countries. However, the traditional Communist approach to planning, as shown during the Stalinist period, was one of "primacy of production" and neglect of consumption. The "trial of the Central Statistical Office" in Poland in February 1948, which became the harbinger of Stalinization, featured accusations that the non-Communist Party staff in that office accepted the primacy of consumption. To the Communists this seemed, at the time, an unpardonable transgression, and the "trial" —held in the form of a two-day public debate—resulted in a wholesale reorganization of the Central Statistical Office and removal of the offending staff members. Studies of family budgets were discontinued, and statistical data became shrouded in official secrecy to the extent that policy decision makers were often deprived of relevant information on which to base their decisions (Drewnowski 1974, pp. 48-49, 53-60). A decline in per capita consumption followed in 1951-53, and the theoretical emphasis and economic policy had to await a slow change after 1953.

The new emphasis on consumption in Communist literature, noted inter alia by Brodzinski (1965, p. 5),* had to acquire official respectability by the usual invocations of Karl Marx (see Pohorille 1971, pp. 19-32; Hodoly 1966, pp. 18-19; Hodoly et al. 1971, pp. 19-31; Piasny 1971, pp. 21-28). The Marxian emphasis on production then became interpreted in the sense that production constitutes the most dynamic factor of development, which determines consumption; one should not juxtapose production to consumption since production is ultimately directed toward the satisfaction of consumers' wants (Pohorille 1971, p. 20). Consumption becomes, in this view, the final stage of production, and from consumption the Marxian process of production starts again. Consumption also acts as a stimulus to production, as well as being determined by production (Hodoly et al. 1971, pp. 19-20, 30-31; Piasny 1971, pp. 21-24). In their new interpretation of Marxism, the Polish economists came to a position where one of them proposed that "political economy should inquire not only into social laws of production and distribution, but also into economic regularities appearing in exchange and consumption of goods and services at different stages of social development." (Piasny 1971, p. 26.) This appears to indicate a new emphasis in Marxian economics, and there is a likelihood that this emphasis will be accepted as part of the received dogma.

---

*Maly Slownik Ekonomiczny 1958 did not yet include the concepts of consumption among its coverage on 1,019 pages, although it mentioned consumption on two separate pages as part of larger concepts.

A more traditional Marxian emphasis in connection with consumption is found in Marx's underconsumption–overproduction theory of capitalist crises, according to thich the insufficiency of consumption creates excess supplies on the market and causes depressions. Here consumption appears as a key element in Marx's theory. According to a socialist writer:

> Marx shows . . . what is the proof of the antihumanitarian character [of the capitalist economy], namely, the loss of human goals in the ceaseless pursuit of profit. (Pohorille 1971, p. 32.)

By implication, socialist consumption does serve human goals, has a humanitarian character, and would not create fluctuations in the economy.

To sum up, the above statements on the role of consumption are based on idealistic ideology; regardless of whether they are factually correct, their use seems unwarranted. Humanitarianism is stressed in those pronouncements, consumption is coupled to human aspirations, and it is averred that only under the unique social conditions created by socialism will consumption occupy its rightful place in the scheme of economic priorities, and that only under socialism will consumption be directed to proper satisfaction of human wants. The above statements also invoke, explicitly and implicitly, the authority of the founder (or in some cases founders) of Marxian thought, and thus belong to the Jesuitic tradition rather than to the open-minded tradition of scientific inquiry, where statements are weighed according to their own merit and not according to who made them.

Success Indicator

The second reason for the importance given to consumption in Eastern Europe is that it can be construed as a success indicator. Since improvement of the level of living is the stated goal of socialist economy, the results of the operation of that economy in the area of consumption indicate the degree of goal fulfillment. Thus, those results may be regarded as an index of success (Piasny 1971, p. 109). The general precept cited in this connection in socialist literature is "maximum satisfaction of needs" (Krzyzewski 1968, p. 52; Hodoly et al. 1971, p. 76; Piasny 1973, p. 21). Writing in the West, Bela Balassa cited consumption as one of the success indicators of an economic system (1959, p. 16), but none of the socialist writers has, to my knowledge, done so explicitly. An implied use of this concept is found, however, in the following quotation which refers to the Gomulka period in Poland:

[Consumption is] an area in which errors committed bring particularly negative results for the economy and the society. These errors may lie in an underestimation of consumption needs of the society, and in striving to balance the resulting economic disproportions exclusively by limiting the opportunity to improve consumption. (Markowski 1972, p. 3.)

In that view, consumption—when found inadequate—becomes a monkey wrench thrown into the economic mechanism, jamming it and producing general dissatisfaction with the working of the system.

Otherwise, publications in Eastern Europe are somewhat bashful in explicitly proposing the use of consumption as a success indicator. It may be that it is felt that such a proposition would be risky and might put the East European economies in an adverse light, in addition to restricting future policy choices.

International Comparisons and Propaganda

Consumption data also may be used for international comparisons. Some incomplete comparative data are found in various socialist publications on consumption, but comprehensive surveys are avoided. With regard to Western consumption, its negative aspects are stressed: unequal distribution, misinformation in advertising, creation of built-in and psychological obsolescence, artificial creation of wants, inadequate provision of collectively consumed goods (cf. Pohorille 1971, pp. 63-79; Markowski 1972, p. 143). These seamy aspects of consumption under capitalism are contrasted with the idealized picture of socialist consumption. When reference is made to under-achievement, it is oblique and either general or with reference to leaders who already have been removed from power. In connection with the gap between the percentage of the population with durable consumer goods in Poland and in other industrialized countries, one Polish author wrote:

It is obvious that that gap could have been, in many cases, decreased faster than it was. This was caused on one hand by errors in economic policy implemented in the last [Gomulka] period which underestimated the influence of an improvement in the level of living on increasing labor productivity and on the rate of economic development of the country, and on the other hand by the still unsatisfactory economic effectiveness shown, among others, by the excessive share of investments and employment in the increments of national income, by

11

the large use of raw materials, and by the irrational growth
of inventories that cannot find a buyer. (Markowski 1972,
p. 151.)

International aspects of consumption also are discussed in Eastern
Europe in terms of Western militarism that allegedly causes direction
of productive resources to armaments and destruction, and away from
consumption, although in the short run Western militarism, it is argued,
may help prevent depressions in capitalist countries. On the other
hand,

> In the socialist countries there are no internal social and
> economic factors which would operate in the direction
> of militarism. On the contrary, the economic interest
> of those countries mandates . . . disarmament because
> armament under full employment always creates the
> necessity to re-direct production to the disadvantage of
> consumption. That is why armaments hamper the
> realization of the basic aim of socialist production,
> namely, maximum satisfaction of the wants of the
> whole society . . . . (Piasny 1971, p. 174.)

Examples of Soviet "disarmament" are given, with references to the
Soviet Union being forced by U. S. militarism to "some increase of
expenditures on defense" (Piasny 1971, p. 176). Examples also are
given of potential increase in the supply of consumer goods in Eastern
Europe if defense expenditures could be eliminated.

At times, consumption statistics are presented in the guise of
propaganda designed to inculcate in the domestic population a feeling
of extraordinary achievement. This is done by several means:
(1) Consumption plans are presented in such a form as to intimate
near accomplishment in advance of the plan period. (2) International
comparisons of consumption achievements are offered selectively so
as to present own achievements in the best possible light.
(3) Consumption and consumption-related data are manipulated and
changed so as to reflect political requirements rather than reality.
(4) Ideological assertions, such as those cited above, are made in
place of statistical comparisons, removing international comparisons
from the area of facts and shifting them into the area of beliefs. The
aim of such propaganda is to quiet possible dissatisfaction about
actual consumption experience, and possibly to serve notice on those
who might protest lack of achievement in the area of consumption that
their protests would be contrary to the established doctrine and would
endanger their careers.

Efficiency Check and Tool of Social Policy

Consumption also provides a check on the efficiency of the economic system in its ability to reach the desired goals. This has been explicitly stated in connection with funds used for social consumption, an analysis of which, it has been postulated, should be included "in research on the effectiveness of economic administration" (Winiewski 1969, p. 144). This check can be made in terms of the investment-cost effect on consumption:

> We meet repeatedly with this question: Why, despite
> large investment effort made in our country for many
> years, it results in the form of a compound increase
> in consumption come clearly curbed and greatly delayed?
> To support the assertion contained in that question, one
> cites the fact that during the last twenty-odd years there
> were periods of serious slowdowns in the growth of con-
> sumption, and even an absolute decline in consumption.
> At the same time it is realized that, belonging to the
> groups of countries which engage [a large part of their
> resources] for investments, we are left behind by a
> number of countries — socialist as well as capitalist —
> with respect to the rate of growth of production and
> consumption. (Beksiak 1972, pp. 76-77.)

Obviously, a dissatisfaction with the cost-benefit calculus permeates the society which is told to postpone its consumption by diverting more of its resources to investments, and then finds that the results apparently fall substantially short of original expectations. Such disappointments reflect on the efficiency with which the economic system utilizes new capital created by current investments. In most cases, however, when consumption falls short of plans the failure of the system to deliver upon its promises is covered up, either by silence or by gloating over some unrelated successes, by blaming special conditions (such as the Korean War) or individuals (Gomulka in Poland in 1970) or natural forces (crop failures). A close parallel exists in this connection with the Soviet Union in the 1930s, as described by Roy Medvedev:

> The serious mistakes made during the collectivization
> and industrialization lowered the workers' standard of
> living, disrupted the supply of food and manufactured
> goods . . . . Strict rationing had to be reintroduced

in the cities. Discontent grew. It was hard to ascribe
all these shortcomings only to kulaks and "subkulaks."
Another scapegoat had to be found for Stalin's faults.
And such a scapegoat was found. . . . (Medvedev 1971,
p. 110.)

Consumption also has been used as a means of achieving social
goals posited by Communist ideology, whether egalitarianism, education, health, closer communal relations, or whatever. The easiest
way that can be accomplished is through social consumption, administered by the government. Such administration can regulate particular
components of social consumption with regard to their size, rate of
growth, and direction, but it also can determine relative size of social
consumption with respect to personal consumption. Official planners
also can change the distribution of incomes in the direction of greater
egalitarianism, or away from it. Through such redistribution of
incomes, they will affect the structure of consumption insofar as
different income groups are characterized by different consumption
patterns. Finally, planners can influence the composition and size
of personal consumption by virtue of their direction of production, out
of which consumption needs are satisfied. They can, for instance,
stress production of baby and juvenile articles, and hold down production of cars; they can increase production of some books and refuse
to produce blue denims. To the extent that consumer sovereignty is
rejected by party ideologues, such policy is not considered undesirable.

CONSUMPTION IN EASTERN EUROPE: SOME
INTRODUCTORY EXPLANATIONS

Any writer on consumption problems in Eastern Europe can easily
be accused of partisanship. Such a verdict may be prompted by the
politicized character of socialist systems, systems that are politically
oriented par excellence, ideologically motivated, and tend to be,
consequently, emotionally evaluated. Additionally, the international
rivalry in the era of the more or less cold war is conducive to the
making of invidious comparisons. The stronger the political interest
(Lenin's partiynost), the greater the proclivity to enter the realm of
invidiousness and competition, sometimes by juggling the figures
rather than by jogging actual consumption, or by engaging in impas-
sioned polemics rather than in nonpartisan measurements. Polemics
easily bring charges of partisanship; hence, such changes amount,
in the area of comparative economic systems, to a normal occupational
hazard. Accusations of partisanship also may be prompted by the subjective value judgments, possible preconceptions of the reader. Finally, they may be prompted by some verbiage used in this study.

In my approach to consumption, I do not follow Weber's postulate of Wertfreiheit in all respects. I confess to one preconceived notion, this being the importance of human freedoms, mentioned in the United Nations study cited at the beginning of this chapter. To the extent that such freedoms are severely curtailed in Communist countries by censorship, police, political restrictions, and dirigism in professional life and at places of work, the system may be considered inimical to fuller achievement of human well-being. In economic terms, under such political systems the Pareto optimum cannot be achieved in the sphere of noneconomic satisfactions. However, in the economic sphere, outside the area of human freedoms, I have no such preconceptions and I am ready to acknowledge the benefits of planning, direction, rationing, and social consumption, as long as it can be demonstrated that they are directed toward the aim of administration of scarce economic resources in such a way as to increase the sum total of satisfactions (utility or Pareto's ophelimity) and/or to maximize their growth.

The terms "socialist" and "Communist" are not used here as synonyms. Specific mention of East European economies is made with reference to their "Communist" system, to be understood as a system under which the Communist Party holds the reins of government, with all the resulting political, social, and economic consequences, rather than as the communist system in the meaning of Karl Marx and the ideologues of dialectic materialism. The term "socialist" is used as a generic term that embraces all possible kinds of socialism, from democratic or parliamentary socialism to its most authoritiarian form of "the dictatorship of the proletariat," "the Maoist system," or any other past, present, or future form of generic socialism. That is why an attentive reader will find the term "socialist" used more frequently in the first and theoretical part of this study, while the term "Communist" prevails in country studies in the second part. No value judgment is attached to either term. When the term "communism" is used without capitalization, it denotes the Marxist final stage of socialist development.

The term "Soviet-type economies" is used to cover countries of Eastern Europe that are governed by Communist parties and pattern their systems by and large on the Soviet model of central planning. The term covers the more rigid and traditional economic systems of Romania and Bulgaria, as well as the experimenting system of Hungary. However, it excludes the Yugoslav economic system, chiefly because of the political and ideological independence displayed by that country since its ousting from the Cominform in 1948. The term "Eastern Europe" is used to cover all European centrally planned economies other than the Soviet Union, and to include Yugoslavia.

The term "consumption" is used here basically to denote personal consumption, that is, consumption out of disposable incomes of the population. In order to engage in such consumption, individuals must obtain purchasing power, usually by selling their labor; they must find available products that attract them; and they must bid their money for those products at prices that either are regulated, as most prices in Soviet-type economies are, or are the outcome of market forces of supply and demand, as in a farmers' market. We may note, parenthetically, that "in Hungary about a quarter of consumer goods prices are determined in free markets, the proportion in Yugoslavia, Czechoslovakia and Bulgaria being over one-third, one-tenth, and one-tenth respectively." (Wilczynski 1970, p. 10.) These proportions have recently tended to increase.

The term "social consumption" is used basically to refer to goods and services that are not purchased on the market but are obtained free from the state.

This study concentrates on four East European countries: Poland, Czechoslovakia, Hungary, and East Germany. These countries provide the best, although not adequate, statistical coverage of consumption problems. They also constitute the economically most advanced bloc within Eastern Europe, fairly similar as to economic structure and problems, and not too dissimilar as to the level of consumption. Other East European countries —Romania, Bulgaria, and Yugoslavia —have been partly covered in this study, when information was available. (No satisfactory information was available for Albania.) Countries in this latter group have some similarities in their economic structure, relatively low level of industrialization, and low per capita consumption.

Several important topics concerning consumption have been omitted from the present study. Examples of such topics are: the structure of retail prices; relation between retail and wholesale prices; the problem of choice of a proper index number formula for calculating changes in consumption; choice of weights and changes in those weights as the consumption pattern changes; inclusion of new products into the index of consumption; efficiency in the consumer sector relative to that in capital goods sector; channels of influence between demand and supply; alternative models of adjustment of supply to changes in demand; advertising and the changing attitude toward it in socialist countries; elasticity of consumption; fringe benefits connected with work; consumption models generally. Some of those topics have been treated in other studies in connection with individual Communist countries (cf. Montias 1962, ch. 7; Hanson 1968, chs. 2, 6-8; Balassa 1959, ch. 4; Chapman 1963, ch. 3). Rather than repeating the treatment of these subjects, which can easily be found elsewhere, I decided to abbreviate my exposition and stress those topics that seem novel. I realize that covering all aspects of consumption is well-nigh impossible. My desire, therefore, is to highlight a few selected problems concerning consumption, to reflect on some crucial factors that have affected consumption, to provide quantitative illustrations, and thus, hopefully, to stimulate further interest in consumption problems in Eastern Europe.

It was tempting to include in this study calculations of elasticity of consumption. I hope to do that in a separate study in order to distinguish better, where possible, between price and income elasticities; some discussion of this topic is found in Chapter 6.

The sources used in this study derive mainly from East Europe, although many Western sources also have been used. In Part I, the theoretical portion of this study, reliance is mainly on Polish sources. Poland has recently published a large number of articles and books on consumption, and the spectrum represented in its economic literature is broadly representative of Eastern Europe and, in comparison with countries like East Germany or Romania, more advanced. In Part II, the country studies, national sources form the basis of information provided, with Western sources used for background and to provide independently derived estimates. It is hoped that such use of sources will help to assure consistency and fullness of treatment, while avoiding duplication.

Polish experience has been treated in somewhat greater detail than that of other East European countries. Similarity of problems encountered by countries developing under the system of Communist central planning would render detailed descriptions repetitive; thus, the description of Polish consumption problems may serve as partial background for the similar experiences in Czechoslovakia, Hungary, and East Germany. Chapters on those countries are therefore more sweeping, and they concentrate less on periodization of postwar consumption experience than does the chapter on Poland.

Some references to domestic currencies in Eastern Europe are made in the following chapters, in particular in connection with foreign trade. In order to provide a rough guide to the international values of those currencies their official exhange rates on U.S. dollars are quoted (The Official Associated Press Almanac, 1974, pp. 604, 498, 543, 531, 608, 480, 651, 618; cf. Marer 1972, p. 346):

Poland	zloty	15.9	= $1	
Czechoslovakia	crown	7.1	= $1	
Hungary	forint	29.9	= $1	
East Germany	DDR mark	2.22	= $1	(valuta
		mark 4.20	= $1	
Romania	leu	18	= $1	
Bulgaria	lev	2	= $1	
Yugoslavia	dinar	12.5	= $1	
USSR	ruble	.9	= $1	

It should be stressed that the official exchange rates in Eastern Europe are far removed from the purchasing power parity of respective currencies, and that the policy of Communist countries is to substantially overvalue their currencies. Two results are the emergence of multiple exchange rates on different transactions of the balance of payments, including black market rates, and nonequivalence between valuta, or foreign exchange currencies, and the same currencies used in domestic circulation (cf. Marer and Tilley 1974, pp. 763-6).

2

SOCIAL CONSUMPTION
IN EASTERN EUROPE

Statistics in Eastern Europe divide consumption into personal consumption (also called individual consumption or consumption from personal incomes) and social consumption (also called residual consumption, and earlier called collective consumption). Most of the present study is concerned with personal consumption, but the present chapter concentrates on social consumption, its concepts and trends. By and large, social consumption signifies consumption provided for by the society and not purchased individually in the market.

Social consumption is not unique to Soviet-type economies. In all countries there exist social wants that "cannot be satisfied through the mechanism of the market because their enjoyment cannot be made subject to price payments" (Musgrave 1959, p. 9).* The second "cannot" in the above quotation does not necessarily refer to physical impossibility but may also refer to conscious societal choice. For instance, under modern conditions, flood control, external defense, and internal maintenance of law and order cannot be provided through the market. The society as a whole has to decide upon, pay for, and administer the satisfaction of such wants. However, education, housing for low-income families, and some or all medical services may be provided either through the market or by the society at large. If the latter path is chosen, then "social consumption" in the socialist meaning takes place. Nonsocialist countries are, of course, also familiar with such social consumption, which comes in a variety of forms even though at least one leading Soviet economist, Stanislav Strumilin, asserted that "under capitalism . . . all goods and services indispensable to working people are . . . paid for" by the individuals (1959, p. 29, cited after Winiewski 1969, p. 31, italics added; cf. Due 1968, pp. 8-9, 22-27).

---

*Musgrave's concepts differ from those adopted in the present study.

Our normative concept of social consumption is related to its contribution to the level of living of the population, and to the question of whether expenditures on it have or have not been included in personal income. Any payment made for a service that does contribute to the level of living and that has not been otherwise included in the income obtained by the population for financing of personal consumption will be regarded as social consumption, unless such payment raises the value of services consumed in the sphere of personal consumption. In the latter case, such payment should be used to raise the value of personal consumption.

THE CONCEPTS

In socialist countries, several concepts can be differentiated in the area of social consumption, and different authors use different definitions. Figure 2.1 shows the relationship of the main concepts, the widest of which is that of "social consumption funds." In statistical coverage, this is termed "residual consumption" and is defined as covering

> use of materials and material services in enterprises and institutions belonging to the unproductive sphere, consumption by the population of material goods delivered to it without payment and —in net calculations—the value of amortization of capital goods in enterprises outside of the sphere of material production. (RS 1973, p. 117; labor costs are thus partly omitted.)

Official calculations of national income distributed may be described by the formula:

$$C_r = NI - C_p - A$$

where: C_r = residual consumption
NI = national income distributed
C_p = personal consumption
A = accumulation

Obviously, then, the concept of residual consumption includes government consumption and, in an open economy, net balance on current account of the balance of international payments. This conclusion is confirmed by Figure 2.1, where "social consumption funds" include "collective consumption," defined to include defense, administration, and services of local authorities (items A, B, and C). There are several reasons for finding such inclusion objectionable:

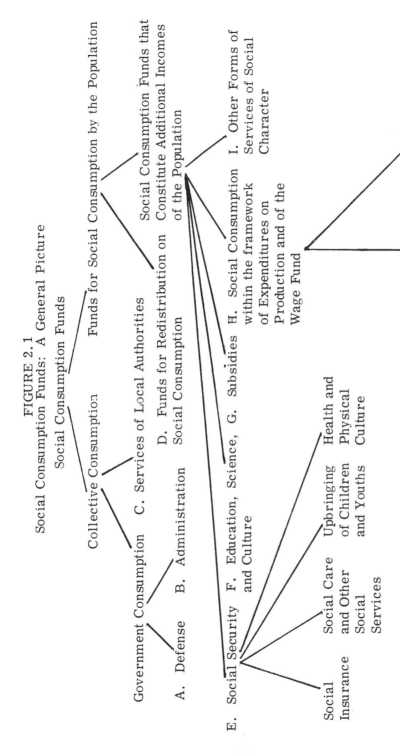

FIGURE 2.1
Social Consumption Funds: A General Picture

Social Consumption Funds

Collective Consumption   Funds for Social Consumption by the Population

Government Consumption   C. Services of Local Authorities   Social Consumption Funds that
                        D. Funds for Redistribution on   Constitute Additional Incomes
A. Defense   B. Administration   Social Consumption   of the Population

E. Social Security   F. Education, Science,   G. Subsidies   H. Social Consumption   I. Other Forms of
                 and Culture   within the framework   Services of Social
                                                        of Expenditures on   Character
                                                       Production and of the
                                                       Wage Fund

Social   Social Care   Upbringing   Health and
Insurance   and Other   of Children   Physical
            Social   and Youths   Culture
            Services

Sick Pay from   Social Expenditures from
the Wage Fund   Enterprise Funds

Source: Winiewski 1969, p. 351 et passim.

21

1. Consumption by individuals has been linked by us to the level of living. There is no direct and apparent link between many of the expenditures on government consumption and the level of living, and consequently government consumption lies outside the sphere of our interest, which is consumption as a factor determining the level of living.

2. Even though some government expenditures may eventually affect the level of living, there is no necessary connection between them. Take, for instance, expenditures on defense. Theoretically, they are incurred to protect from external aggression the "human freedoms" listed by the United Nations as a component of the level of living. But armed forces also can be used, as they have been in all too many countries, to stifle domestic freedoms. Armed forces, when used for aggression, also may bring about a radical deterioration of the levels of living, both at home and abroad. A point in question are the expenditures on "defense" by the Third Reich preparatory to and during World War II, and the ultimate result of those expenditures.

3. Some expenditures on government consumption may have controversial impact on the level of living. For instance, it may be asked whether expenditures on government censorship, on administrative suppression of handicraft services, or on regimented meetings and "spontaneous demonstrations" raise the level of living. Only a person biased against human freedoms would give an affirmative answer.

4. There is no necessary coincidence between the scale of preferences of governmental planners and that of the society as a whole, and consumers in particular. Under such conditions, even if government expenditures satisfied some wants of the population, they would be unlikely to maximize want satisfaction and hence would make a very imperfect indicator of contribution to the level of living.

5. Western social accounting practice does not include government consumption under consumption of households (cf. Alton et al. 1962, pp. 11-21; Alton et al. 1963, pp. 13-21; Alton et al. 1965, pp. 13-32), and for reasons of international comparability such inclusions should not be made. We may mention that, strictly speaking, military pay in kind (the value of food consumed by soldiers) should be added to consumption. East European statistics on consumption of foodstuffs by the population do, however, include food consumed by the military.

The component of collective consumption that has a closer connection with the level of living than defense and administration is "services of local authorities" (item C). This includes maintenance of housing, urban transport, water and sewer systems, parks, and streets. Such services are either only partly paid for by individuals (housing and transport), with the rest of the cost coming out of local government subsidies, or are customarily free (parks, streets). The communally paid for part of such services might properly be included under social consumption, on the ground that they add to human welfare, were it not for the fact that they are not felt as an augmentation of individual income, that most such expenditures would be resented and possibly avoided if required of individuals, and that some may be regarded as part of the social cost of production, as best exemplified by urban transport, which serves mostly to get people to and from work. A socialist economist concluded that these services "in some degree . . . exert an influence on the level of living, but their influence on the standard of living . . . is impalpable and not easily measurable" (Winiewski 1969, p. 85). Table 2.1 shows some indicators of urban utility services in Eastern Europe. Although interesting, the indicators shown do not reveal actual comparative volume of services per urban inhabitant since they do not take into account the density of urban population.

Funds for redistribution on social consumption (item D) only partly include expenditures on social consumption, with part directed toward production (Winiewski 1969, p. 97). These include expenditures on construction of schools, which should more properly be included as part of accumulation. On the other hand, some expenditures on social services increase the real income of the population and tend to raise its level of living. On the whole, it seems that function may be of lesser importance than the production function of these expenditures.

Out of expenditures on social security (item E), social insurance is by and large paid for through insurance contributions. For instance, in Poland in 1972, out of the aggregate expenditures on social security only 30 percent was contributed from the budget, the rest being contributed by various social security funds. But one of these funds had

TABLE 2.1

Some Indicators of Provision of Urban Utilities in Eastern Europe
(length of relevant network in meters per urban inhabitant in 1960)

	Water Mains	Sewers	Gas Mains
Poland	1.13	.89	.58
Czechoslovakia	2.32	1.30	1.0
Hungary	2.36	1.03	.71
East Germany	2.41	1.56	1.16
Romania	.87	.61	.25
Bulgaria	1.32	.45	. .
Yugoslavia	1.27	.61	.21

Source: Ginsbert 1965, reproduced after Winiewski 1969, p. 261.

23

an officially reported net surplus of contributions over expenditures (RS 1973, p. 577), while another was reported to have been in a similar financial situation, which further reduced the net contribution from the budget. The net effect of social insurance is not likely, therefore, to put real income into the hands of the population.

The second subdivision of expenditures on social security is "social care and other social services" which, unlike social insurance, are unconnected with work but depend on special circumstances and are charitable in character. Social care may be rendered in special institutions (for the blind, deaf-mute, invalids, mentally retarded, and insane) or by payments or help in kind (Winiewski 1969, pp. 210-14).

The third subdivision is "upbringing of children and youths," and it involves financing of day care, nursery schools, rooming houses for pupils and students, summer camps, and scholarships. Almost all these expenditures are financed from the budget, except some funded scholarships paid for by prospective employers.

Finally, the fourth subdivision of "social security" is "health and physical culture." The coverage of health insurance has been steadily increasing in socialist countries. For instance, in Poland it has increased from 15 percent of the population before World War II to 45.7 percent in 1950, 63.7 percent in 1965 (Winiewski 1969, p. 200), and substantially more in 1973, by which time coverage had been extended to individual farmers. Even for those not insured, all medical payments are below cost; in hospitals less than one-half of actual costs (Winiewski 1969, pp. 200-1). The volume and quality of health service has gone up substantially in comparison with the pre-World War II period. Table 2.2 shows some international comparisons of selected personnel in health service per 10,000 inhabitants. The number of nurses and doctor's aides per 10,000 inhabitants showed a still greater increase, and there has been substantial expansion of supporting personnel such as laboratory and dental technicians. In Poland, an "overproduction" of some health personnel has been observed, with some medical doctors leaving to practice in East Germany, Morocco, and sub-Saharan African countries (personal observation and reports from other travelers). As the result of vastly improved medical help, the mortality rates (the number of deaths per 1,000 inhabitants) declined in Poland from 13.9 in 1938 to 11.6 in 1950 and 8.0 in 1972, the decline being partly due to changed age structure (Winiewski 1969, p. 208; RS 1973, p. 96). Similar declines in mortality rates took place in other East European countries.

Table 2.3 provides an international comparison of infant mortality rates (mortality rates per 1,000 live births within the first year of life) and their dramatic decrease in Eastern Europe. Life expectancy at birth also increased with the decline in mortality and some morbidity rates, particularly striking in the case of tuberculosis (Mieczkowski 1972; GUS 1972, pp. 23-28, 48-52).

24

TABLE 2.2

Selected Health Personnel and Facilities in Eastern Europe
(per 10,000 inhabitants)

	Year	Medical Doctors	Dentists	Pharmacologists	Number of Hospital Beds
Poland	1938	3.7	1.1	1.1	21.8
	1971	15.6[a]	4.3	3.9	74.3
Czechoslovakia	1936	7.4	2.1[b]	..	54.0
	1971	21.1	2.8	3.8	102
Hungary	1936[c]	11.2	..	..	53.2
	1971[c]	20.5	2.5	3.9[d]	77.2
East Germany	1937	7.3	2.1	1.3[d]	98.2
	1971	16.4	4.3	1.7	110
Romania	1962	13.4	.9	2.5	52.8[e]
	1971	13.1	2.1	2.4	82.2
Bulgaria	1936	4.5	..	..	19.8
	1971	18.9	3.7	2.9	79.1
Yugoslavia	1936	3.7	..	..	18.1
	1970	10.0	1.5	1.8	56.5
USSR	1934	5.0	..	..	28.0
	1971	24.5	3.8	2.1	111

[a]Including interns.
[b]1950.
[c]State health service only.
[d]Includes trainees.
[e]1958.

Sources: Winiewski 1969, p. 206; RS 1973, p. 720; SR 1959, pp. 54, 433; Statistisches Jahrbuch fuer das Deutsche Reich, 1937, pp. 5, 542.

TABLE 2.3

Infant Mortality Rates and Life Expectancy at Birth in Eastern Europe

	1935–39 (average)	1950	1960	1970	1971	Life Expectancy at Birth[a]
Poland	139.2[b]	111.2	54.8	33.4	29.7	66.8
Czechoslovakia	111.4	77.7	23.5	22.1	21.6	67.3
Hungary	133.5	86	47.6	35.9	34.9	66.6
East Germany	66.3[c]	72	38.8	18.8	18.0	69.2
Romania	179[d]	117	74.6	49.4	42.4	65.5
Bulgaria	146.4	94.5	45.1	27.3	24.9	68.8
Yugoslavia	138.8[e]	118.4	87.7	48.9[f]	..	64.3
Albania	100.8	121.2	83.0	86.8	..	..
USSR	184[g]	81	35	24.7	23.1	65

[a] Latest available figures, between 1965 and 1972.
[b] 1936–38 average.
[c] All of Germany.
[d] 1938.
[e] 1937–39 average.
[f] 1965.
[g] 1940.

Sources: RS 1965, p. 559; RS 1973, p. 644.

All these are signs of an important contribution to the level of living in Eastern Europe by state expenditures on health. In Poland, it is estimated that such expenditures equal 7 to 10 percent of the wage fund (Winiewski 1969, p. 210), which measures the approximate contribution of state-provided health care to raising the level of living.

Other expenditures in this subcategory of "health and physical culture" are on state-sponsored vacations, physical culture, tourism, and sports. The amount of state expenditures in this field is rather small. In 1972 in Poland, it was less than the amount spent on social care and constituted 5 percent of total budget expenditures on health, social care, and physical culture, with health taking 88 percent and social care 7 percent (RS 1973, p. 589), the total amounting to .46 percent of total budget expenditures, to .5 percent of the wage fund, and to .3 percent of the gross incomes of the population (RS 1973, pp. 589, 584, 568, 543). Apart from the quantitative insignificance of these expenditures, one can wonder how much the expenditures on conspicuous striving for more and more sport medals, or on subsidizing of vacations for selectively chosen employees, has contributed to want satisfaction of the population as a whole. Perhaps it did, but there is no demonstrated proof to that effect. There is little doubt, on the other hand, that expenditures on social care, upbringing of children and youths, and health did contribute to raising the level of living in Eastern Europe, and that in the case of health that contribution was indeed considerable. Its indication is that in Poland in 1972 the budget expenditures on health constituted 7.8 percent of all state budget expenditures, and amounted to 8.4 percent of the gross income of the population derived from wages and 5.7 percent of net nominal incomes of the population (RS 1973, pp. 589, 585, 568, 543).

Education, science and culture (item F) contributes to the level of living only in part, namely insofar as education, included in the United Nations list is concerned. Without state financing, much of the education would have been financed privately; hence, budgetary financing of education raises the real income of the population. Whether the rise in real income can be measured by the whole of the state expenditure may be controversial, as some educational expenditures are clearly production-oriented and might not have been privately incurred if state financing were not available, and as the mix of educational offerings apparently does not agree with preferences of the population since special emphasis is officially put on vocational training while the percentage of applicants rejected from institutions of higher learning has been increasing.

The size of public expenditures on education in socialist countries is considerable. In Poland in 1972, they amounted (together with expenditures on upbringing linked to education) to 19.7 percent of all

TABLE 2.4

Students in Institutions of Higher Learning in Eastern Europe
(per 10,000 inhabitants)

	1938	1964	1971
Poland	14[a]	74	106
Czechoslovakia	20[b]	103	89
Hungary	14	91	83
East Germany	11[c]	66	89
Romania	17	65	72
Bulgaria	18	101	112
Yugoslavia	11[b]	84[d]	137
Albania	..	68[e]	..
USSR	..	158	187

[a] 1937.
[b] 1936.
[c] For the whole of Germany, 1936/37.
[d] 1963.
[e] 1962.

Sources: Winiewski 1969, p. 245; RS 1973, p. 717; SJ 1965, pp. 4, 463; Statistisches Jahrbuch fuer das Deutsche Reich, 1937, pp. 5, 582.

budget expenditures (RS 1973, pp. 585, and 588). Primary education has been improved and expanded to eliminate illiteracy, which in prewar Poland amounted to 20 percent of the population over 10 years of age (Maly RS 1939, pp. 29, 323, after Winiewski 1969, p. 236), and secondary education has been expanded. Table 2.4 shows the expansion of higher education in Eastern Europe, the degree of which indicates considerable educational effort and achievement, even when it is realized that many students are in higher technical schools that may not quite measure up to university standards.

Expenditures on science do not directly contribute to the level of living and should not properly be included under social consumption. Expenditures on culture and the arts also seem controversial in their

---

*However, the share of education in the social consumption fund declined in Poland between 1965 and 1971; see Kasperek-Hoppe 1973b, p. 124.

impact on the consumer. Some may help to extend the impact of education (expenditures on reading rooms, public libraries, and museums); others, like those on protection of national monuments, do not do so; still others, like expenditures on radio and television, are in excess of revenues obtained through license fees for radio and television sets. Such expenditures may then be considered a subsidy for the propaganda element in radio and television, and may actually contribute to a lowering of consumer satisfaction insofar as such expenditures may be used to finance the expensive jamming of Western broadcasts.*

Subsidies paid by the government to keep certain prices low for social reasons (item G) may be given for production of producer goods, in which case they do not have any direct influence on the level of living, or for the production or maintenance of some goods or services used by consumers. In Poland in 1972, such subsidies, called "negative budget differences," amounted to 19.7 percent of all payments from the budget to the socialized sector, and to 14.0 percent of all budgetary expenditures (RS 1973, pp. 587, 585), but the overwhelming portion was spent to support production of producer goods. The part spent on consumer goods subsidized (1) some products (some foodstuffs and baby and child wear), (2) some urban services, already found under item C above, and (3) housing.

Subsidies paid to support production of consumer goods did increase the purchasing power of the consumer, although they tended to interfere with the free market principle for consumer goods, and hence may not have added to the level of living in proportion to their magnitude.

Subsidies given to housing, and mentioned under item C above, on the face of it raised the level of living, but they were linked to some adverse phenomena: (1) a precipitous decline in private expenditures on housing; (2) a disastrous decline in standards of upkeep of housing, which worsened perceptibly the quality of, and hence the satisfaction derived from, housing; (3) inequities in the distribution of available housing; (4) decline in labor mobility due to difficulty of obtaining adequate housing near potential new places of work; and (5) some deterioration in the standards of construction of new housing, due mainly to the adoption of faulty systems of incentives to labor.

---

*In Poland in 1972, expenditures on radio and television constituted the largest single item of expenditures on culture and arts, amounting to 38 percent of current expenditures on that account (RS 1973, p. 589). One would do well, however, to note information from "The Radio War," The Economist (London), 30 March 1974, p. 42: "Last September [1973] . . . Russia and the other east European countries had no fewer than 3,000 transmitters whose sole purpose was to jam western broadcasts beamed to the communist world. The transmitters . . . cost $250 m. to install and $100 m. a year to run. This is more than the Soviet government spends on its domestic radio network. . . ."

TABLE 2.5

Housing Conditions in Eastern Europe

	Average Number of Persons Per: Dwelling	Room	Average Number of Rooms Per Dwelling	Percentage of Urban Dwelling Units Supplied with: Running Water	Toilet	Bathroom	Gas	Electricity	Dwelling Units Given to Use in 1971 Per 1,000 Inhabitants
Poland[a]	3.9	1.4	2.9	75.2	55.0	50.4	48.3	97.8[b]	5.8
Czechoslovakia[c]	3.6	1.3	2.7	69.8	48.7	49.4	38.2	98.5	7.5
Hungary[d]	3.1[d]	1.2[d]	2.6[d]	65.3[e,f]	61.2	..[e,f]	..	96.7	7.3
East Germany	2.8	1.1[d]	2.7	80.0[e,f]	..	27.2[e,f]	..	..	4.5
Romania[g]	3.6	1.4	2.6[h]	..	..	..	..	..	7.3
Bulgaria[e]	4.0	1.7	2.3[h]	55.0	25.9	18.3	..	98.1	5.7
Yugoslavia[c]	4.4	1.6	2.8	42.4	..	22.5	..	92.7	6.1
USSR	4.2	1.5	2.9	78[d]	73[d,i]	65[d]	..	..	9.4

[a] 1970.
[b] 1960.
[c] 1961.
[d] 1971.
[e] 1965.
[f] Including rural dwelling units.
[g] 1966.
[h] Not including kitchens, except when also serving as living quarters.
[i] Sewarage.

Sources: RS 1973, pp. 714-15; Smith 1973, p. 417.

These disadvantages may explain a late tendency to rely more on cooperative construction of apartment houses. Table 2.5 provides some data illustrative of housing conditions in Eastern Europe. Endowment with sanitary conveniences still seems inferior, and lack of information for Romania and partly for the USSR is unlikely to have been the result of unavailability of data to national statistical offices.

As stated above in connection with item C, there are valid grounds for inclusion of housing subsidies in the totals of personal consumption rather than in social consumption. Our approach will be to provide a general picture of consumption, and no precise calculations of relevant totals will be attempted.

State enterprises have at their disposal the so-called enterprise funds, which are said to contribute to social consumption (item H in Figure 2.1). However, some expenditures from that fund have an incentive wage character, amounting to about 60 percent of total expenditures for that category in Poland (for example, prizes) (cf. Krzyzewski 1968, p. 32); others, amounting to about 40 percent of total expenditures, do have social characteristics (such as expenditures on housing, amounting to about 25 percent of total expenditures, and on employee vacations, sports equipment, clubs and reading rooms, and social arrangements for children). Part of the current financing funds of enterprises also can be used for the above aims.

Part of the funds accumulated in cooperatives is spent for social purposes, most of it in cash, which appears both as income of cooperative members and as their expenditures for goods and services. Consequently, those sources of social consumption in a socialist sense can be disregarded for our purposes. Sick pay paid by state and cooperative enterprises can be neglected for the same reasons.

Other forms of services of social character (item I) in Poland include the Central Fund for Tourism and Rest; the Dwelling Fund of National Councils; the Fund for Technical Progress; the Village Funds; funds for the so-called social tasks; and activities of institutions and organizations of social character (such as labor unions and the Polish Red Cross). Almost all such expenditures are on investments, while even the rest is not felt as income by the population (cf. Winiewski 1969, p. 289). Consequently, these expenditures also can be disregarded. So can the winnings from state lotteries and payments from mutual insurance, both of which have an income-redistributive character described technically as transfer payments.

To summarize the conclusions from the present section, many of the expenditures regarded in Eastern Europe as social consumption in the broad sense do not contribute to the level of living and are government consumption, or part of enterprise costs, or even take on, on closer inspection, an investment character. Expenditures that more properly qualify for inclusion under social consumption, sensu stricto, are for social care, upbringing of children and youths, health (see item E), and education (see item F). Personal consumption should be raised by subsidies given to housing and public transportation (see item C).

Most of what is regarded as social consumption, sensu largo, in Eastern Europe can thus be disregarded in our normative understanding of that concept. To indicate the degree of quantitative difference such exclusion makes in the estimate of social consumption, we may note that while estimates of the official concept of social consumption in Poland amount to 32 to 39 percent of aggregate consumption (Winiewski 1969, p. 123), our concept of social consumption constitutes approximately 8 to 12 percent of aggregate consumption. Andrezej Brzeski estimated it for Poland as 5 to 6 percent of aggregate consumption (1964, p. 29). It should be noted that the coverage of social consumption differs as between different socialist authors.* A narrower and more acceptable definition of social consumption has been proposed jointly by several authors as covering goods and services transferred to the population without payment and bypassing the market.[†]

For general orientation, the relative magnitude of social consumption may be instructive. According to country official statistics, that consumption amounted in 1971 to 10. 9 percent of national income in Poland (RS 1973, p. 128), to 13. 7 percent of social product in Czechoslovakia (SR 1972, pp. 159, 461), to 8. 9 percent of domestically used national income in Hungary (SE 1972, p. 68), to 9. 6 percent of national income in East Germany (SJ 1972, p. 42), to 29. 3 percent of budgetary expenditures in Romania (AS 1973, p. 483), and to 9. 7 percent of national income in Yugoslavia (SG 1973, pp. 112, 122). In Bulgaria, social consumption amounted to 20. 2 percent of national income in 1970 (SEzh 1971, pp. 57, 281).

---

*Hodoly 1966, p. 219, estimated social consumption in Poland in 1964 at 11. 8 percent of aggregate consumption. The same author (1966, p. 227) estimated the share of social consumption in aggregate consumption fund in 1962 at 8. 6 percent for Poland, 10. 1 percent for East Germany, 25. 6 percent for Yugoslavia, and 10. 7 percent for USSR, while in 1955 this share was 16. 7 percent for France, 17. 2 percent for West Germany, 18. 2 percent for Italy, 14 percent for Belgium and Luxembourg, and 19. 9 percent for Holland. Winiewski 1969, p. 324, estimated social consumption at about 20 percent of aggregate consumption in Poland. Markowski 1972, p. 15, estimated social consumption in Poland at 14. 0 percent of aggregate consumption in 1970, after a steady rise from 9. 5 percent in 1955.

[†]Hodoly et al. 1971, p. 65. Krzyzewski 1968, p. 20, added to this definition "that part of the value of goods and services partly paid for which is covered by the society and not by the consumer." My preference, as stated above, is for inclusion of that element in personal consumption.

AN EVALUATION OF SOCIAL CONSUMPTION

Social consumption is endowed in Eastern Europe with ideological and practical importance not ascribed to the same social consumption when encountered in capitalist countries. It is instructive to confront various ideologically motivated claims ascribed to social consumption with actual experience in socialist countries, and for that purpose we may try to separate the various claims made in Eastern Europe concerning social consumption and consider their merits.

Ideological Importance of Social Consumption

Ideologically most important is the concept that one partakes of social consumption according to need. This renders social consumption an important step toward fulfillment of the communist goal of distribution according to rationally determined needs (cf. Krzyzewski 1968, p. 25), although one student of this problem ventured the opinion that

> social consumption is a form of distribution in which the labor input is disregarded. However, apart from wants there are other economic and social factors that are taken into account, and the want itself is satisfied at a level that in many cases departs markedly from requirements of social rationality. (Krzyzewski 1968, pp. 26-27.)

Social consumption is then an approximation toward communism, but it does not yet, of itself, represent the idealized communist conditions. Soviet opinion in this respect seems less critical. Stanislav Strumilin stated that social consumption represents a postponed part of the wage that could be called the socialized part of wages and that "corresponds already to the communist rule of 'to each according to his needs'" (Strumilin 1962, pp. 251-2 cited after Krzyzewski 1968, pp. 28-29; cf. Mstislavskii 1961, p. 101).

Such ideological superiority of social over personal consumption might indicate an imminent demise of the latter, but such is not the case despite its, on the whole, slower growth in Eastern Europe over the postwar period. Two factors are said to determine the relative magnitude of both forms of consumption, the first being the desirability of maintenance of market equilibrium. Social consumption affects the market situation by satisfying wants without payment, and consequently by leaving more purchasing power in the hands of consumers to be spent on satisfaction of alternative wants. A simple solution might be to reduce wage payments while increasing the relative scope of social consumption. But here the second factor governing the relative magnitude of social consumption enters the scene, namely, the need to maintain incentives by means of a continuation of the causal link between effort and consumption through wage payments. It is realized that "undue" (however that is defined) growth of social consumption in relation to personal consumption would be destructive of such incentives, and that it might furthermore make people take social consumption for granted, might make them less mindful of the need to economize in their consumption and thus lead to waste, as well as might lead people to make invidious comparisons about the, admittedly unequal, distribution of social consumption and hence make them dissatisfied (Krzyzewski 1968, pp. 36-44, 91-93; Hodoly et al. 1971, p. 70; Winiewski 1969, pp. 130-3).

In defense of social consumption, however, it is maintained that such consumption does play some incentive role. Those benefiting from it feel a more proprietary (the term has been used!) interest in socialized property; they feel closer bonds with the society at large and with their enterprise in particular; they begin to feel more responsible for the results of economic activity; they are inculcated with the "spirit of cooperation and solidarity" with other members of the society; they are less subject to the pull of their private and individual interests and thus become more socialized; and they begin to associate satisfaction of their cultural and social needs with the socialist society (Hodoly et al. 1971, pp. 68-69; Krzyzewski 1968, pp. 80-90). This attitude may express more the normative feelings of party ideologues than the normological description of nascent societal trends, if we are to judge from various unofficial reports from Eastern Europe.

Economic Role of Social Consumption

It is argued that social consumption secures a scientific basis for the direction of consumption and helps in economizing consumer goods. This argument seems to have originated from a desire to have everything planned on a scientific basis, and from a faith in economies of large scale, both in production and use. Even socialist economists regard this argument as controversial (Mstislavskii 1961, p. 102; cited also and critized in Krzyzewski 1968, p. 53). That social consumption can be subject to planning is uncontroverted. That this planning may be rational, based on some scientific precepts, also is acceptable. However, it does not follow that such scientific basis for the direction of consumption necessarily results in a superior level of living or in improved economic and social standards. Consumption by its nature is more personal and volatile, and less susceptible to successful calculation, uniformity, and direction than is production. The larger the scope of social consumption, and the more it replaces personal consumption, the greater is the risk that planning may fail to produce the expected results.

Expectations of benefits from economies of scale in consumption may well prove illusory. Communal cooking may save some labor in the task of cooking itself, but it may result in dissipation of some satisfaction from the ability to choose and select individually, and in dissatisfaction from standing in line and waiting for service. Production of uniform "utility" goods in Great Britain, introduced during World War II, was discontinued soon after the war, despite the cheapness of such production. Few would willingly give up their family life in favor of "more efficient" arrangements of child care, choice of leisure, or use of living quarters. This fact is appreciated in Eastern Europe as well as anywhere else.

It also is claimed that social consumption can help free an enormous amount of labor, and in particular free women from household chores. This argument does not seem to recognize the need to provide for those for whom women care in their homes. For instance, if a woman goes to work, somebody has to take care of her child. If a nursery school teacher can take care of ten children, even though a net saving of labor seems to result, it is not costless to the society. Time and possibly public transportation must be used in delivering the child to and from school, the school must be built, some administrative and service (cooking, cleaning) personnel also must be provided. Surely the society does not acquire the woman's labor without any cost to itself. Similar considerations obtain if the woman has an infirm parent living with her. The social cost of following the above argument tends, therefore, to be underestimated (Mstislavskii 1961, p. 102; Krzyzewski 1968, p. 53).

On a practical level, it is maintained that the main function of social consumption is the shaping of consumption according to the postulates of the consumption model, one of the requirements of which is the furthering of egalitariansim (see below). This argument again imposes upon consumers the preferences of planners, possibly to the disregard of the former's own preferences. It poses the picture of a regulated consumption in a regulated society as the rational one. In terms of a generalized slogan, "Social consumption is . . . an instrument of realization of general social preferences in consumption" (Hodoly et al. 1971, p. 66). These social preferences tend to be both formulated and satisfied by the central planners.

An Australian economist, Jozef Wilczynski, raised the valid point that social consumption allows no consumer choice at all in certain cases while in others it is

> provided under conditions restricting the consumer's freedom of choice as to the quantity, variety, place and time. The inevitable red tape, inquisitive officials and apathetic distributing centers all reduce the consumer to an inferior position. The psychological

satisfaction that may otherwise be gained from the
freedom of personal selection is largely lost.
(Wilczynski 1970, p. 14.)

Thus, shaping consumption according to the postulates of a model,
however "rational," carries with it costs in terms of consumer disutility inherent in both the loss of freedom and the administration of
such consumption.

More specifically, it is claimed that social consumption serves
to fulfill "the basic humanistic functions of the socialist system" by
ensuring (1) that the population attain a high level of education,
culture, and health; (2) that science develop, thus assuring economic
and social progress; and (3) that its workers will be educationally well
prepared and thus will help further economic development (Krzyzewski
1968, pp. 68-69).

Egalitarian Influence and Failures

The most frequently stressed aspect of social consumption is its
function of decreasing the differentials in consumption levels between
households, and of bringing closer to realization the ideals of an egalitarian distribution of goods and services among members of society
(Krzyzewski 1968, p. 51). It is maintained that social consumption
benefits particularly the lowest-income groups, and thus narrows down
the range in the level of living within society (Krzyzewski 1968,
p. 70).

This argument seems to be borne out by statistics of income from
social services according to income groups, as shown in Table 2.6.
The lower the income group, the higher is the percentage of income
(except for the eighth group in column 1) derived in the form of social
consumption. A comparison of columns 2 and 3 shows that blue-collar
workers tended to get more money benefits than did white-collar
workers, partly because white-collar workers do not receive sick pay
from social insurance. However, it should be noted that my own estimate yielded approximately equal absolute contribution per household
group in column 1, which on a per capita basis would tend to result in
a regressive scale due to a higher number of members per household
at lower income levels. Absolute figures on which data for columns
2 and 3 are based show a clear regression; that is, higher money
payments to households as their income increases. Thus, there was
a tendency for the absolute spread between income groups to widen
as the result of social services, although the relative spread between
them narrowed.

TABLE 2. 6

Contribution of Social Services to Household
Income by Income Group in Poland
(percentage of total income within each group)

Income Group	Share of Income from Social Services in Household Income[a]	Share of Social Payments in Aggregate Household Income of Employees in Socialized Sector Outside Agriculture[b]	
		Blue-Collar[c]	White-Collar[c]
Aggregate	8. 8	9. 9	7. 6
I	17. 7	17. 9	13. 2
II	13. 4	13. 0	12. 0
III	10. 7	10. 1	8. 8
IV	8. 8	8. 1	8. 4
V	7. 2	6. 8	6. 7
VI	6. 0	5. 4	4. 7
VII	5. 4	4. 3	4. 5
VIII	3. 2	—	—
IX	3. 6	—	—
X	3. 3	—	—

[a]Defined in terms of expenditures per member of household,
from lowest (group I) to highest (group X); in 1965.
[b]In 1963.
[c]Total divided here into seven groups.

Source: Winiewski 1969, pp. 130-31, 336.

That absolute differentials between income groups increase as
the result of social consumption is demonstrated by Table 2. 7, reproduced from the work of Michal Winiewski, a Polish expert on social
consumption. Absolute benefits from social consumption increase in
that table as income increases, and the correlation between both trends
is surprisingly high. On the other hand, however, the relative contribution of social consumption to household income, apparently in
terms of whole households rather than per household member (see
rows 3 and 4 in Table 2. 7), which would abstract from the effect of
smaller family size among higher-income groups, declines as incomes
increase, revealing an economically progressive character of such
contributions, and leading to a decrease in relative income differentials.

37

TABLE 2.7

Size of Income from Social Consumption Funds in Poland, and Its Share in Per Capita Income of Households Grouped According to Income Level in 1963

	Income Groups According to Annual Household Income Per Capita in Zlotys							
	Average	To 8,000	8,001–12,000	12,001–16,000	16,001–20,000	20,001–24,000	24,001–28,000	Over 28,000	Correlation Coefficient
Annual income in zlotys from social consumption fund, per capita, when households are grouped according to:									
Wage incomes	4,410	2,784	3,852	4,481	5,230	5,595	6,590	7,182	.99
Aggregate incomes	4,410	1,554	2,690	3,940	4,976	5,516	5,497	7,696	.97
Share of income (percentage) from social consumption fund in aggregate income, when households are grouped according to:									
Wage incomes	31.5	41.3	38.0	32.3	29.5	25.3	25.5	23.6	..
Aggregate incomes	24.2	23.6	26.1	27.5	28.1	25.0	20.7	23.2	..

Source: Winiewski 1969, p. 338.

It may be pointed out that the correlation coefficients between incomes and benefits from particular kinds of social consumption are less than for the aggregate, as in the relationship between educational benefits and household income, and in the case of social expenditures by enterprises. However, it is interesting that the correlation coefficient between household income and health services was calculated at 92, indicating that higher-income groups take greater advantage of free health care than do lower-income groups (Winiewski 1969, pp. 339-40).*

The impact of social consumption in Poland on households grouped according to size may be mentioned. The coefficient of correlation between family income and size is very high and negative (-. 95), indicating that the higher the income on the average, the smaller the family (Winiewski 1969, p. 340)†, an observation to which reference already has been made. Table 2. 8 reproduces from Winiewski's work the relationship between benefits from social consumption and family size. The correlation coefficients are high and negative (that is, the higher the number of family members, the lower the income per member of the family), with the correlation coefficient between family size and benefits from social consumption lower than the correlation coefficient between family size and full income per family member. This juxtaposition indicates that social consumption somewhat decreases the per capita income differentials between families of different size.

It may be pointed out again that calculations for correlation between family size and particular kinds of social consumption per family member yield a positive coefficient only for educational benefits; that is, as family size increases, each member tends, on the average (and including parents), to receive higher educational benefits. This is at least partly due to the fact that many smaller households consist of members who have passed the school age. The coefficients for social consumption other than education are negative (for housing and transportation, -. 85; for culture, tourism, and sport, -. 90), indicating that an average member of a larger family benefits less from social consumption than does an average member of a smaller family (Winiewski 1969, p. 342).

One may conclude that social consumption decreases, "although inadequately and unevenly, the differentials existing between families at different levels of income and of different sizes" (Winiewski 1969, p. 343). The inadequate contribution of social consumption to the

---

*It is interesting that U.S. data also point to greater use of medical services, connected with supplementary medical insurance, by higher-income groups than by low-income groups (U.S. Department of Health, Education and Welfare 1973, pp. 2-4).

†On the other hand, the correlation coefficient between family income and the number of income earners in the family was . 65; when money incomes only were taken into account, it was . 42.

TABLE 2.8

Size and Share of Benefits from the Social Consumption Fund in Income Per
Family Member According to Family Size in Poland in 1963

	Average	Members in Family						Correlation Coefficient
		1	2	3	4	5	6	
Full income per family member (zlotys)	17,345	27,680	21,362	17,840	16,607	10,642	10,265	-.96
Of which: from work of head of family	8,045	22,162	11,404	7,978	6,522	4,328	2,731	-.97
from work of other family members	4,890	—	5,429	5,675	5,100	3,538	3,881	-.69
from social consumption fund	4,410	5,518	4,529	4,187	4,985	2,776	3,653	-.74
Share of income from social consumption fund in aggregate family income (percent)	25.4	19.9	21.2	23.5	30.0	26.1	35.6	—

Source: Winiewski 1969, p. 341

lessening of differentials within the society was highlighted by the results of research by Andrezej Tymowski for Poland in 1969; he found that over 33 percent of four-member households and 14 percent of one-member households did not attain the minimum level of social consumption (Tymowski 1973, p. 90).

Certain elements of maldistribution of social consumption have been noted by Winiewski. For instance, social consumption enhances the inequality of per capita incomes between rural and urban areas, even though that influence seems to be diminishing. In Poland in 1950, an inhabitant of rural areas received on the average only 10.9 percent the social consumption of an urban dweller; that underprivileged relationship improved to a still very inferior 20 percent by 1965 (Winiewski 1969, p. 327).

One main tool in eliminating inequality is education. Yet, again, this part of social consumption has been distributed unequally between children of peasants and nonpeasants. Although in Poland peasants constituted about 33 percent of the population in the mid-1960s (RS 1973, p. 81), the proportion of peasant children in general-education high schools (licea) climbed to a bare 20 percent from the postwar low of 10 percent. In basic craft schools, they constituted 33 percent of all pupils; in advanced craft schools only 25 percent of pupils; and at institutions of higher learning only 20 percent of all students. The relevant figures for children of workers, whose number was smaller than that of peasants, and who tended to have fewer children, were higher by 50 percent, while the numerically smallest group of white-collar workers had the highest share (45 percent) of all students (Winiewski 1969, p. 329). Therefore, education as a form of social consumption has tended to exacerbate class distinctions in Poland; the tendency in other East European countries has been similar, although a gradual improvement has taken place (Winiewski 1969, pp. 330-31).

Rural areas also gain relatively less from state subsidies to cover low prices, and from enterprise and special fund sources of social consumption. It has been estimated that rural inhabitants obtain about one-fifth of all social consumption, much less than their share in total population, so that on the whole urban areas in Poland gain about five times as much from social consumption as rural areas do (Winiewski 1969, pp. 331-32), which is another way of expressing the 20 percent underprivileged relationship mentioned earlier. Therefore, a conclusion may be drawn that social consumption actually increases income differentials between socioeconomic groups, rather than decreasing them (Winiewski 1969, p. 335).

The gnawing realization of the inadequacy of social consumption in solving various problems of socialist societies, in particular the incentive and inequality problems, has led to a disenchantment with and a recent deemphasis of social consumption. Typical is the following statement:

It seems that, with the increase in the importance of
wages as basic remuneration, the social consumption
fund will in the long run show a decreasing tendency
since its excessive growth may not guarantee the
desired increase in labor productivity, and in some
cases could even lead to a waste of resources from
the social consumption fund (as for medicines). That
is why it is advisable to give preference to the growth
of remuneration closely tied to the results of work.
(Kasperek-Hoppe 1973a, p. 252.)

The tide seems to have turned. After some 25 years of preferential
treatment for social consumption, that consumption may now start
decreasing in relative importance.

3

PROBLEMS IN
EVALUATING CONSUMPTION
IN EASTERN EUROPE

Evaluation of consumption experience in Eastern Europe involves two separate parts: (1) a comparison between Communist and other levels of consumption and (2) determination of the growth of consumption in individual countries. The first part involves difficult problems of intercountry comparisons that are similar to interpersonal comparisons: How can one compare meaningfully whether individual A or individual B attained a higher level of consumption when it is known that their tastes, incomes, IQ endowments, rationality, and aims differ? Any such comparison necessarily involves an arbitrary judgment on the relative value of, for example, individual tastes, and on the relative importance of, for example, attainment of some level of material consumption versus satisfaction from the achievement of other goals. Similarly, customs, habits, tastes, aims, natural endowments, income distributions, and other circumstances differ between countries, and consequently their absolute comparison is virtually impossible. However, we can agree on some conventional scales of relative values and try to apply them to individual countries, albeit cautiously and with due explicit indication of the criteria used. We have explicitly mentioned criteria arrived at by the United Nations.

DIFFICULTIES IN ASSESSING CONSUMPTION
LEVELS IN EASTERN EUROPE

In discussing difficulties in attempting to measure the growth of consumption in the Soviet Union, Philip Hanson (1968, pp. 9-12) listed the following points, which are also relevant in Eastern Europe:

1. "The problem of the basic information on prices and quantities of products, wages and numbers of employees, size and number of

other incomes and size of population." The reliability of censuses, sample surveys, and official reports used in deriving official statistics is not assured, and it opens up what has been recently dubbed "credibility gap." In making their comparisons with prewar data, the Communist countries usually are blissfully oblivious of territorial changes. Data on nonwage incomes, especially the rather common incomes from moonlighting, are absent. Data on employment during the 1940s frequently are absent or sketchy; in Hungary, data on employment are absent for three years after the Hungarian Revolution; and coverage of employment data often shifts between "national economy" and "socialized sector." Encountering these and similar problems such as, discontinuities in coverage of statistical series—one by necessity becomes rather humble about one's conclusions.

2. "Concealment or falsification [of statistical data] by central Soviet authorities." This problem appears important in evaluation of data released during the Stalinist period in Eastern Europe (1949-54 in Poland, Czechoslovakia, and Hungary; earlier and later in East Germany). A recent example, proving that this problem has not disappeared, was reported in the Parisian Kultura: On December 19, 1968, Izvyestya reported that a new 500,000 kilowatt generator was put into service at Nazarov, but in mid-1973 (on an unspecified date) Trud stated that the generator in question had been burned out at factory trials. Officially, and as far as the public was concerned, however, the generator had been operative for five years (Kruczek 1973, p. 90) and contributed statistically to the satisfaction of some social needs; it may still be statistically operative.

3. "Differences between Western and Soviet concepts of national income. The difference that is relevant for our present purposes concerns the provision of certain commercial services to the population. Soviet figures of total personal consumption exclude the value of unproductive labour in such activities as house repair, passenger transport, laundries, and others. These figures will include the estimated cost of capital and materials used in these services, but not their labour costs. National income-type series for total consumption therefore are not comparable to our own." The "Marxist" concept of national income has been changing slowly in Eastern Europe to include more of the formerly "unproductive" services, recognized in the West as part of the national income. It is ironic as a historical observation that Vaclav Holesovsky, in a study on Marx and the Soviet national income theory, was led to the conclusion: "There is a good deal less conflict between Marx's writings and the Western concept of national income than there is between Marx and the Soviet theories on the subject." (1961, p. 325.)

4. To the extent that Soviet prices are regulated and do not reflect relative scarcities, and to the extent that dual price systems are not unknown—as in connection with agricultural products, black markets, and moonlighting of services—the problem of valuation is encountered.

It is particularly troublesome in evaluating housing services; some researchers, cited in Part II, have tried to solve this problem by estimating the value of housing at factor cost instead of at "market" prices. The latter connotes prices at which actual economic trans-actions took place, rather than some freely formed prices of housing that would then determine the quantities of housing supplied.

So much, then, for the difficulties connected with determination of the rate of change of consumption. Comparisons between countries raise similar difficultues, some of which influence the evaluation of growth rates of consumption. We will now turn our attention to these difficulties.

Differences in quality and in the rate of change of quality of con-sumer goods make intercountry comparisons not just difficult but downright obscure. Philip Hanson brought together some telling data on price discounts offered in Moscow to hard-currency purchasers to make Soviet wares competitive with Western ones (1968, pp. 62, 233). Existence of such discounts, of from 28 to 86 percent, points to sub-stantial quality differences, rendering qualitative comparisons of consumption less meaningful. (It also points to the overvaluation of the ruble.) Similar discounts were made on East European exports to the West (Burks 1974, pp. 61-62).

Changes in quality become especially important when they vary in the countries being compared. While consumer goods in Western coun-tries generally improve in quality, there were times in Eastern Europe when the quality of such goods deteriorated markedly. An official Hungarian source admitted to a 14 to 15 percent deterioration in the average quality of consumer goods between 1938 and 1955 (quoted in Holesovsky and Pall 1968, p. 9). Such an experience seems typical for Eastern Europe during the late 1940s and the 1950s. However, during the 1960s, and certainly during the 1970s, some improvements in quality were reported, partly in the wake of increasing volume of imports of consumer goods. This experience tends to depress the "true" consumption index during the time when per capita consumption was lagging or falling, and imparts to it an additional upward boost during a time when per capita consumption tended to rise, or rise faster. Again, however, quantification of this aspect of change in consumption is extremely difficult, in view of different and changing composition of consumption, as well as an inherent subjectivity in the evaluation of any, or at least most, quality changes. When the width of textile fabrics becomes narrower by 10 percent, we may easily agree that the consumption index of fabrics should be lowered by 10 percent. But when the proportion of wool in a woolen fabric declines from 90 to 81 percent, we cannot be certain that a similar 10 percent lowering of the consumption index of textiles is in order. And when it is realized that the above example concerns a simple commodity—very different from a TV set, car, or house—we begin to appreciate the quandary facing anybody making international comparisons of consumption trends. An additional problem involves shifts of consumption from goods whose quality declined to goods whose quality remained unchanged, which affects the weights attached to different commodities in the compilation of a consumption index. This problem is similar to one caused by relative price changes between commodities.

Differences in availability create another problem in that indexes of consumption volume, based on physical quantities, do not reflect the disutility in consumption represented by uncertainty of delivery, inconvenience connected with waiting in line, lack or limitation of choice, pressure at the counter to grab any proffered commodity without selecting the most desirable form, and so on. The degree of satisfaction derived from consumption departs from simple volume indexes under such circumstances, particularly when, within the coverage of the index, availability decreases and subsequently increases, as happened in Eastern Europe during the postwar period (cf. Wilczynski 1974, pp. 144–65).

Quality and availability of housing also change over time, creating changes in consumer well-being that may be of geometrically directly proportional nature, rather than of simple arithmetically proportional nature. Hanson made some perceptive comments on the problem of international comparison of housing services with respect to the Soviet Union (1968, pp. 65-70). Similar, although perhaps not as drastic, comments could be made about Eastern European housing conditions compared to Western ones. While the question "Is the bathroom free?" does not mean in Eastern Europe, as it does in Moscow, whether anybody is living in the bathroom (Hanson 1968, p. 66), apartments often are occupied in Eastern Europe by several families; heating problems are sometimes considerable; one may have to enter a new house underneath a net for protection from falling masonry; new houses sometimes have to be supported by others to keep them from falling sideways; a stench of urine pervades some staircases; elevators are absent or only partially operative for some tenants; and waiting for allocation of an apartment may take years. Under such conditions, an apartment in Eastern Europe is not the same good as one in Western Europe, and figures on per capita housing area do not fully reflect relative housing conditions.

Provision of social consumption and problems created by it were considered in Chapter 2. A mention should be made here, however, of state expenditures and activity that significantly affect material and/or psychic welfare but are not included in the usual narrow concept of social consumption. Examples are such municipal activities as sewerage, street lighting, and police protection; conditions regulated by the state, such as emission control, which determines maximum pollution level; activities and standards of branches of the state, including justice, labor standards, and labor protection. Hanson remarked in this connection, "In the Soviet Union the treatment by the state of all sorts of things —road surfaces, probation work, the shop network, free speech, public conveniences —shows a heroic disregard for human comfort and sensibility. But this is largely beyond the measuring rod of money." (1968, p. 74.) The last sentence in the above quotation indicates the reason for excluding those factors from any quantitative analysis. Nevertheless, mention of them should be made and they should be borne in mind when attempting a rough international comparison of welfare or levels of living.

What needs to be stressed in concluding this section is the unreliability of Communist statistics. Even economists in Eastern Europe do not always give complete credibility to official information, as shown by the Polish economists in 1955-56, Hungarian economists in 1956, and Czechoslovak economists in 1968. If, then, native economists are sometimes doubtful about consumption-related official data, it seems incumbent upon independent scholars to exercise some professional skepticism and independent judgment.

One of the fullest "inside" accounts of the unreliability of statistics published in Eastern Europe was given by Antoni Gutowski (1970), a Polish economist with considerable publication experience in Poland, and obvious "connections" and insights into the party apparatus, who emigrated to the West about 1968-69. Gutowski recounted how data on real wages calculated by the Central Statistical Office are changed upward by the political office of the Central Committee of the Communist Party, necessitating further revisions for the sake of consistency in other indicators published by the Central Statistical Office. Similarly, he recounted a conversation during which a "high dignitary" remarked that while officially the 1967 expenditures on defense amounted to 8 percent of the state budget, in reality they were at least twice as high. If that is so, then the actual budgetary expenditures on social consumption necessarily would have to be revised downward.

Gutowski also gave a thought-provoking list of discontinuities and gaps in official data reporting, including information on decorations awarded (with some political implications); data on minority groups (with ethnic and political implications); data on the Soviet Union (where international comparisons might not be too complimentary); data on employment, income, and services; and expenditures on safety in enterprises. He stated that there exists a systematic transmutation of the statistical base for comparisons in order to make objective comparisons impossible and thus to hide the actual state of affairs. The documentation of discontinuities in statistical reporting provided by Gutowski is solid and can be supported by this author's own experience with several official statistical yearbooks from Eastern Europe, although Gutowski's conclusion may be open to criticism on grounds that a new emigrant —eager to rehabilitate himself after extended activity in a Communist country, designed to support its political system —may be less than objective. On the other hand, however, Gutowski's statements do find corroboration in the findings of Western researchers (Mieczkowski 1971a, pp. 254-55).

In another article published in the West, Gutowski showed that
official statistics on growth in per capita consumption of meat in
Poland between 1958 and 1964 did not agree with other official data
that indicated a fall in per capita consumption of meat in urban areas
(1969, p. 105).

An example of contradictions within the data provided by official
sources of information in Eastern Europe was pointed out by a Western
economist, Bohdan Brodzinski, who in one speech by the Polish Communist Party leader, Wladyslaw Gomulka, delivered in March 1964,
found the following two statements: (1) that industrial production had
increased as compared with prewar by nine times and (2) that the value
of agricultural production before World War II was twice as high as the
value of industrial production, while in 1963 the value of industrial
production was twice as high as the value of agricultural production.
Since RS 1963 published information that agricultural production had
increased by 25 percent as compared with prewar, industrial production
could have increased only five times as compared with prewar (and not
the nine times indicated by Gomulka), unless some of the official
information was incorrect (Brodzinski 1965, pp. 12-13).

INDEPENDENT COMPUTATIONS OF CONSUMPTION
IN EASTERN EUROPE

Owing to the existence of problems of evaluation of Communist
consumption experience outlined in the preceding section, there arose
a need for an independent check on the veracity of Communist statistical data. These data are not verifiable at their source since no
independent scholar has, to my knowledge, had access to the raw
data at the various central statistical offices in Eastern Europe. In
the Soviet field, the Western pioneers in general computations were
Abram Bergson, Warren Nutter, Eugene Zaleski, and a number of their
followers. In the area of consumption, Western studies have been
made in the Soviet field by Janet Chapman (1963), Margaret Miller
(1965), Philip Hanson (1968), and in the East European field by Vaclav
Holesovsky (1963 and 1965) and this author, among others. Several
authors have published consumption data on East European countries
in papers submitted to the Subcommittee on Foreign Economic Policy
of the Joint Economic Committee of the U.S. Congress. In West
Germany, the Deutsches Institut fuer Wirtschaftsforschung also has
engaged in quantitative evaluation of East German economic growth,
including consumption.

The methodology of independent calculations is based on patient
collection of basic data in physical terms and then converting these
data into indexes with the help of a system of carefully defined weights,
sometimes using several stages of such conversion. A description

from an unpublished study by this author may be illustrative of procedures used in constructing an independent index of consumption.
My index of consumption was arrived at in three stages of aggregation,
starting with physical consumption series of narrow consumption
groups, for which data were obtained from official statistics. The
weights were based on 1956 or 1957 consumption patterns. This first
stage may be described by the formula:

$$i_{n.\ 1956} = \frac{\sum q_n p_{1956}}{\sum q_{1956} p_{1956}}$$

where i is the index of consumption groups obtained from aggregation
of primary quantity series (q), with the help of 1956 prices (p) or other
weight systems, depending on the availability of data.

The second stage of aggregation may be described by the formula:

$$I_{n.\ 1956} = \frac{\sum i_{n.\ 1956} Q'_{1956} P'_{1956}}{\sum Q'_{1956} P'_{1956}}$$

where I is the index of each of the groups of consumption derived in
the first stage, and Q' and P' signify the primary quantity series and
their prices, as used in the first stage.

The third stage of aggregation derived the aggregate consumption
index with the help of the formula:

$$TI_{n.\ 1956} = \frac{\sum I_{n.\ 1956} Q'_{1956} P'_{1956}}{\sum Q'_{1956} P'_{1956}}$$

where $TI_{n.\ 1956}$ is the index of aggregate personal consumption, and
Q' and P' are the sample expenditures for the consumption categories
derived in the second stage of aggregation.

An adjustment also was made for quality changes, and one for
changes in Poland's territory between prewar and postwar. Finally,
the index was recalculated to the per capita basis to reflect changes
in the level of living of individuals.

The results of such and similar research are useful for several
reasons:

1. They provide a check on the veracity of official statistics,
with credibility gap a not infrequent outcome.
2. They bring information on East Europe in line with that on
Western countries with respect to definitions, coverage, methodology,
and openness of derivation.

3. They enable a clearer assessment of the achievements of individual countries in Eastern Europe and their relative standing than would be possible on the basis of official statistics alone.

4. They may help make the leaders and planners in Eastern Europe more responsive to the true aspirations of their peoples, and thus may help increase the level of economic welfare.

5. They provide an indication of the economic, organizational, military, and perhaps even economic survival capacity of East European countries.

6. They provide an excellent training ground for economists interested in comparative economic systems.

7. For those who consider different economic policies and weigh their relative advantages, the results of independent research are similar to getting away from hard sales talk of systemic salesmen and being handed a consumers' guide that provides objective information. The reader can then make up his own mind without feeling the pressure of emotive appeals.

Like all other estimates, the results of independent research are only approximations and must be treated as such. They have the advantage of being explicit in their assumptions and methodology, and they offer flexibility for adjustments. They contain no ulterior motive and are solely the result of striving for answers that do not rely on the incontrovertible authority of the official source.

In Part II, many independently derived statistical series will be presented in addition to various official series. In the author's opinion, such independent derivations give a better perspective on actual changes in Eastern Europe than would be possible on the basis of official series only. However, a warning is in order: Credible and trustworthy statistical results may be applied improperly, producing wrong conclusions. It is the goal of this study to make explicit the limits in the application of independently derived estimates so as to reduce the chance of such pitfalls.

4

RELATION BETWEEN
CONSUMPTION AND
PLANNING IN
SOCIALIST ECONOMIES

THE FORMAL FRAMEWORK OF SOCIALIST CONSUMPTION

Socialist economists maintain that even the market-supplied part of consumption (as contrasted with social consumption) in Eastern Europe is different from that under capitalism since the socialist market functions within the framework of planned socialist economy (Hodoly et al. 1971, p. 40). The changes in consumer incomes, as well as prices of consumer goods, are formally the result of planned decisions (Hodoly et al. 1971, p. 44), in contrast to capitalist conditions. Within these parameters of incomes and of a set structure of prices there exist various degrees of scarcity created by producers, which impose a further limitation on consumer choice and consumer decision making. Thus some of the curtailment of consumer sovereignty is made by design, by planners' decisions, but some results from the peculiarities of socialist enterprise functioning and from maximizing decisions by producers which are independent of demand conditions (Zielinski 1973, passim; Mieczkowski 1954a, pp. 7-9; Mieczkowski 1954b, p. 57).

Consumption is formally recognized as the aim of economic activity, but in the view of planners it also becomes a means of attaining "the basic goals of the political system." Under socialism, it is contended, consumption should achieve such characteristics as would help maximize the goal of the development of society in the "desirable direction" (Hodoly et al. 1971, p. 55), this direction being decided upon by central planners. The ideological requirement made of planners is that they not be passive "in the face of individual consumption aspirations since many such aspirations have to be regarded as irrational from the social point of view, or as not attuned to socialist conditions of production, as conservative, inherited from previous [political] forms." (Hodoly et al. 1971, p. 103.) Following this requirement, the central planner becomes the spokesman for social forces (Hodoly et al. 1971, p. 103), and as such feels empowered to dictate the composition of personal consumption, although it is nowadays conceded in Eastern Europe that mutual influence does exist between the consumption model of central planners and that of the society at large, the latter conceived of here as "public opinion" rather than as the disembodied social aspirations and social good (Hodoly et al. 1971, p. 105). If that is true, there is or should be some give-and-take on the part of planners as well as consumers. But planners constitute the decisive decision-making element, and it may, at least at times, be hard to convince them that their particular priority scheme should be revised. Their natural tendency may be, and indeed has been, to seek recourse to slogans and generalizations that rationalize their point of view and impose their preferences on the society.

Consumer Preferences Versus Planners' Preferences

The dilemma between acceptance of consumer preferences and planners' preferences can be summarized as follows. If consumer preferences are not followed, then consumers may arrive at a negative evaluation of the functioning and efficiency of the economy—and possibly of the economic system itself—and the strength of economic incentives lessens since consumers do not see any satisfactory correlation between effort and eventual reward in terms of satisfaction of consumption aspirations. Furthermore, interest and participation in administering the enterprises and the economy become weakened and individual economic units may decide not to maximize the satisfaction of social needs, with the result of weakening the fabric of socialist society. Individual initiative, contrary or potentially contrary to social needs, may be at a premium, further disorganizing the planned economic system. On the other hand, if consumer preferences are followed, "attainment of basic goals of the construction of socialism" will be retarded, "conservative" and irrational traits in human psychology will become vested, and copying of material and cultural models or standards from rich bourgeois societies will spread (Hodoly et al. 1971, pp. 124-25).

In the above picture of undesirable consequences stemming from primacy of consumer wants, one can detect some intriguing assumptions, perhaps historically true but not logically necessary. One is the assumed necessary dichotomy between individual and planners' preferences. In a rational, educated socialist society, such a dichotomy seems curious to behold and inconsistent with the theoretical blueprint. Another interesting assumption is that, if left alone, the socialist consumer will necessarily follow bourgeois patterns, not only in his personal consumption but also in the—obviously "alien"—

cultural pattern he accepts. That in turn may imply either inherent inferiority of the socialist consumption and cultural patterns or a departure from the usual socialist assumption of rationality and educated social consciousness of people who live under socialism (Loucks and Whitney 1969, pp. 186-87). Such a departure also would be ideologically distasteful insofar as it is recognized that the demonstration effect leads to a waste of scarce resources on "luxury consumption" accepted as a model from rich capitalist countries (Chmara 1973, p. 125). The Marxian position is to reject the "natural trend" toward following the demonstration effect from outside, using as argument the criticism of technological determinism as mindless of social relations that were stressed by Marx, and using the Marxian criticism of the broader convergence hypothesis between capitalist and socialist societies as mindless of the ultimate goals of those societies (Chmara 1973, p. 125).

In the case of appearance of a dichotomy between consumers' and planners' preferences, it has been suggested that central planners resort to the "compensation principle" by offering to consumers, in compensation for socially undesirable goods they desired, other goods that are attractive but more conconant with the model of the central planners. For instance, instead of a private care the consumer may be provided with efficient public transportation or —at a further step in want satisfaction—good clothing (Hodoly et al. 1971, pp. 125-27). However, no utility equivalence is explicitly imposed on this compensation policy, its content being left to the decision of planners. Consequently, actual compensation offered may be less than full from the point of view of consumers.

The principle of consumer sovereignty is regarded by socialist writers as undesirable. They attribute the emergence of "consumption civilization" to artificial want creation and want manipulation by big business seeking maximization of profits. At the same time, however, socialist writers contend that market orientation under socialism would bring about a subdivision of large, centralized enterprises, leading to "weakening of the socialist economy and to chaos" (Hodoly et al. 1971, pp. 130-32; cf. Sokolowski 1973, pp. 251-55). A logical inconsistency is apparent in this argument: What is the apparent result of bigness under capitalism would, according to this reasoning, produce declining size under socialism.

In view of the above socialist argument the so-called "market solution" advocated by some economists is officially denounced. Yet there are voices heard in Eastern Europe in favor of such a solution of consumption problems (Kuron and Modzelewski 1966, pp. 28, 34, passim, circulated by samizdat in Poland and published abroad; Mieczkowski 1967a; Kurowski 1957a; Brus et al. listed by Mieczkowski 1971a, p. 14; cf. also Mieczkowski 1968b). Such voices undoubtedly seek the solution advocated in 1936 by Oskar Lange, who recognized a practically unfettered consumer sovereignty (1938, pp. 65-98). Under that solution, the socialist state would assure the citizen a given money income and authorize him to spend that income as he chose in buying commodities produced by the state. The Central Planning Board would set prices so as to cover full cost of production of given goods and then would adjust them according to relative market scarcities. Lange saw one major danger in the socialist solution: a bureaucratization of economic life, a somewhat prophetic insight. Once back in Communist Poland, however, Lange disavowed his earlier socialist solution and subscribed to the official one imposed by the Communist Party, which condemned consumer sovereignty.

The majority of East European economists would at present support the opinion that a "free, unfettered market, with which consumers' sovereignty is linked, cannot automatically replace the conscious process of development planning," adding that the consumers' market constitutes an important check on the functioning of a planned economic system (Hodoly 1970, p. 60).

Ways Planners Can Influence Consumer Preferences

In place of consumer sovereignty, consumer and market research is advocated in Eastern Europe. The results of such research "make possible formulation of structural regularities and developmental tendencies, as well as relations and dependencies between observed phenomena and processes [on the one hand] and the factors that determine them" on the other (Hodoly et al. 1971, p. 137; see also Regozinski 1973 and Los 1964, pp. 34-43).

East European planners also have come to appreciate the importance of advertising in shaping consumer demand to the extent that several Polish consumption experts recently stated, "It seems superfluous to provide grounds for the usefulness of advertising in the fulfillment of the consumption program." (Hodoly et al. 1971, p. 183.) Socialist advertising is, however, billed as informative in design, in contrast to advertising under capitalism, which is put down as competitive in character, persuasive in form, and disinformative in results (cf. Pohorille 1971, pp. 220-23).

The actual extent of advertising of consumer goods in Eastern Europe is severely limited, partly because desirable goods sell themselves, partly because growing consumer sophistication leads to rejection of undesirable, inferior-quality commodities churned out by the production apparatus without adequate quality control or adequate incentives to improve quality*—even if these commodities were heavily

---

*The poor quality of goods and resulting consumer resistance occasionally has led to bonfires of unsalable goods (Gutowski 1970, p. 85).

advertised, and probably in part because of the residual ideological phobia that used to condemn advertising as part and parcel of the "wasteful capitalist system" (Pohorille 1971, pp. 63-79, 127).

A less accepted mode of consumer guidance in Eastern Europe is consumer education, based on the premise of protection of consumer interests. There are ideologically inspired doubts whether such protection is necessary under conditions of socialism because of its "social consciousness" (cf. Hodoly et al. 1971, pp. 189-90; Nieciunski 1973, p. 1152). The need for consumer protection is not contested by East European economists where Western countries are concerned—be it in the form of Better Business Bureau, Consumers' Division of the Department of Labor, Consumers' Research, Federal Trade Commission, Bureau of Consumer Frauds and Protection of the New York State Department of Law, Consumer Union of the United States, the British Consumer Council, or any other form (cf. Roberts 1966). But arguments also are heard in Eastern Europe that the increasing complexity of consumer goods and scientific and technical information about health (example: cigarettes), safety (example: children's toys), and psychological aspects of consumption (example: noise) necessitate some type of rational consumer education. References to consumer education in the sense of showing a "more rational" pattern of consumption are found in East European economic literature, without specification as to the precise mode of such education. To the implied extent that such education would embody planners' preferences, it is without exception accepted as desirable.

Apart from consumer education, it is felt in Eastern Europe that consumer interests must be protected from illegal manipulation by individuals connected with, or employed in, domestic trade. Many ways of cheating the consumer exist in socialized trade, as shown by meat scandals in Poland, in which malversations amounted to millions of zlotys, as enumerated by a Polish author (Piasna 1973, pp. 173-79). Official sources usually blame individuals or private enterprise, and special control agencies have been entrusted with the task of protecting consumer interests. Recognition of this problem seems to have come recently, even though malpractices have existed since the beginnings of socialist trade (Piasna 1971).

In a more direct way than advertising or "consumer education," planners have an obvious ability to influence or determine the composition and quantity of collective consumption goods. They also can administratively influence consumption of particular goods by selecting the location and opening hours of particular stores. To prove the social desirability of such a policy, the example can be given of stores selling alcoholic beverages; such sales are banned on certain days or after certain hours. Sales personnel also can be used to advise consumers about particular goods (but the profit or sales turnover basis of premiums given to such personnel may create a conflict between interests of sales personnel and consumer interests); selected goods can be given prominent display; buying can be made less tedious by elimination of standing in multiple lines to make one purchase (self-service stores have been making their appearance in Eastern Europe but they are still far from widespread).

Ways Planners Can Influence the Market
in Consumer Goods

All these administrative means of influencing consumption are, however, marginal in importance compared to three traditional ones at the disposal of planners: (1) determination of the quantity and composition of output of consumer goods, (2) determination of consumer incomes, and (3) determination of prices. Determination of money incomes of the population takes place through the wage and employment policy; although it is not quite elastic downward, it may result in occasional wage declines. The usual change of money incomes is upward, and the rate of that change effectively serves as a regulator of consumer demand.

A small part of personal income derived from wages is taken by the government in the form of income taxes, accounting for a very small part of state revenue — 6.5 percent in Poland in 1972, which taxes constituted 6.8 percent of wages paid in that year and were less than savings deposited by the population during that year in savings accounts (RS 1973, pp. 586–87, 597, 543; the finer points of economic classification are omitted here). Another part of personal income is saved. In all East European countries, savings have been increasing greatly during the 1960s and 1970s, providing the state budget, into which they are channeled, with additional resources. The residual personal income is currently spent on goods and services. To the extent that planners determine income taxes and can create incentives for saving for a particular future consumption goal (a car, an apartment, or any other durable consumer good, not to mention the rate of interest paid on savings deposits or the kind of goods won in lotteries connected with saving deposits), they can influence the aggregate purchasing power left in the hands of consumers. This policy has been used by East European planners, but it can have, for all practical purposes, only a temporarily retarding effect on consumption.

The sinews of price policy include a general tendency to keep prices of consumer goods constant for extended periods of time, with such prices changed sporadically downward in order to encourage consumption (example: of radios) when production outruns demand, or changed upward when it is decided that consumption ought to be discouraged or demand reduced (as in the case of alcohol, meat, or cars). Chapter 6, section 1, provides a discussion of attempts in Poland to affect consumer demand through price revisions. Some prices are kept below their equilibrium level on grounds of general social policy, if the result of instituting equilibrium pricing would be inadequate satisfaction of wants. These wants are defined by Richard Musgrave as "merit wants" (1959, ch. 1); examples are housing and health needs (Pohorille 1971, pp. 187-88; Nieciunski 1973, p. 1151).

Prices also may be used to indicate social preferences in favoring consumption of particular groups in the population, as in the case of reduced-price theater tickets available to trade union members, or reduced-price railway and streetcar tickets available to certain categories. (To the author's knowledge, such practices have never been termed "price discrimination" in Eastern Europe.) In all these cases of lowering prices below normal equilibrium level, a certain redistribution of real income takes place and consumption tends to be encouraged as the result of sectional price rebates. Whether or not consumption actually will increase also depends on the ability of supply to increase when demand expands.

Studies of price and income elasticities of demand are made in Eastern Europe to provide a guide to production of different goods when income increases, and a possible guide for price formation designed to achieve market equilibrium.

Planners also can affect consumption by changing the distribution of income; studies in the pattern of expenditures by different income groups indicate interest in this means. Planners also can direct producing enterprises to regulate assortments of goods. The ensuing market scarcities and/or gluts can then sort themselves out by means of waiting lines or price changes. Apart from the obvious loss of utility to consumers, however, such a policy may result in additional higher social costs when, as frequently happens due to the incentive system based on physical weight of output, the commodities available on the market are more material-intensive than those the consumers would prefer (cf. Piasny 1971, pp. 128-29).

A Polish economist has said optimistically:

> Observations made not only [in Poland] but also abroad prove that the consumer . . . yields to the influence of economic and noneconomic stimuli. That is why — apart from some particularly drastic cases — actual consumption usually agrees with theoretical needs. This undoubtedly makes easier the rationalization of nutrition since one can expect that it will adjust itself to supplies, if a proper set of prices and an educative action will be secured . . . . The ability to overcome the tastes and traditions that impede a rationalization of nutrition constitutes today one of the more important instruments of nutritional policy. That ability is particularly useful when it comes to solving in practice the problem of "consumer sovereignty." (Los 1964, pp. 29, 37, italics added; cf. also pp. 31-32.)

This rather patronizing sentiment tends to show that planners, given proper tools and their judicious application, can achieve any desired "rationalization" in consumption. One can well doubt whether that is possible even in a completely isolated society, much less in one exposed to the outside demonstration effect. The author just cited found, in regard to the stubbornly high and rising Polish demand for meat, that regulation of demand for particular products may prove less effective than regulation of aggregate demand (Los 1964, p. 43). One can, however, agree with the general statement by Janusz Zielinski that "by setting prices and incomes the Central Planning Board creates definite requirements on the part of the population and thus determines the consumption model" (1965, pp. 629, 633-38), even if the word "determines" seems too strong.

The Dilemma of Rationality

In conclusion to the foregoing, we can state that centrally planned economies reject the Latin maxim that de gustibus non est disputandum (tastes are not subject to being questioned). It is accepted that individual preferences are shaped as the result of social forces, and the socialist state undertakes to guide those forces in the direction that planners think desirable. It is, furthermore, accepted that in some cases the society, through its planners, may have a vested interest in regulating consumption of certain goods and that sumptuary laws, including tax laws, can be used on such commodities. Application of the instrument of sumptuary excise taxes, used in the West, is in its origin akin to that socialist stand (cf. Due 1963, pp. 312-13, and Pohorille 1971, pp. 128-29).

The ideologically correct picture of the consumer then becomes one of a person who ceases to be a "passive" recipient of ideas from outside and does not force the economic system to pander to his notions. Instead, the consumer takes on the socially loftier role of a conscious evaluator, as a member of society, of a socially desirable model of consumption, and of a participant in the process of approval of that model by society. The importance of that consumption model is greater the longer the time period over which it is intended to serve. The consumer then, in his private capacity as an individual consumer, selects a given mix of consumer goods in consonance with his individual preferences, while staying within the bounds prescribed by the social model of consumption (Pohorille 1971, pp. 130-31).

Such a role seems subjectively acceptable in its general outline, but in practice some citizens' votes may be in the Orwellian fashion "more equal than others" in determining the socialist model of consumption and in the actual administration of production in conformity with, or in disregard of, that model, as shown in the third section of

the present chapter. The subjective acceptability of the general outline of the new, double role of the consumer mentioned above is
supported by the conclusion of Kenneth Arrow that there is no method
of joining of individual choices that would allow determination of
collective welfare:

> If we exclude the possibility of interpersonal com-
> parisons of utility, then the only methods of passing
> from individual tastes to social preferences which
> will be satisfactory and which will be defined for a
> wide range of sets of individual orderings are either
> imposed or dictatorial. (Arrow 1963, p. 59.)

And rephrasing the above:

> If consumers' values can be represented by a wide range
> of individual orderings, the doctrine of voters' sover-
> eignty is incompatible with that of collective rationality.
> (Arrow 1963, p. 60.)

Yet the danger lies in the tendency of any body that may emerge—
whether it is the classical Spartan system of gerontocracy, the
Platonian system of rule by philosophers, or a socialist system of
rule by the political and economic planners—to substitute their own
ideological, power (personal or state), charitable, cultural, or other
preferences for both the individual and the moral normative social
preferences (cf. Arrow 1963, pp. 81-91). This is the danger that the
third section of the present chapter addresses.

Consumption as Related to Investments and Their Structure

In their formal approach to their task, the central planners contend
that the investments they decide upon serve to raise the future level
of consumption. In practice, however, consumption may be depressed
for short or even intermediate periods of time, depending on the rate,
composition, and effectiveness of investments. The formal framework
for such conclusion is supplied by the Kalecki model representing the
increment of national income, ΔY, as a function of investments and of
the level of national income in a given year (Kalecki 1972, p. 10):

$$\Delta Y = \left(\frac{1}{m}\right) I - aY + uY$$

or:

$$\frac{\Delta Y}{Y} = \frac{1}{m}\left(\frac{I}{Y}\right) - a + u$$

where: Y = national income
        m = capital/output ratio
        I = "productive" investments in capital equipment
        u = coefficient of organization and economic improvements
        a = parameter of depreciation

If the capital/output ratio, m, remains constant, then:

$$\frac{\Delta I}{I} = \frac{\Delta Y}{Y} = \frac{\Delta e}{C}$$

where: C = consumption

Thus there is a proportional growth of investments, national income, and consumption (this and the following formulas have been adapted from Piasny 1971, pp. 134-48). If the capital/output ratio increases, and if planners increase the rate of investments in order to keep the rate of increase in national income constant, then:

$$\frac{\Delta I}{I} > \frac{\Delta Y}{Y} > \frac{\Delta C}{C}$$

or the increment of investments becomes larger than the increment of national income, and that in turn is larger than the increment of consumption.* In order to counteract this undesirable effect on consumption, which in turn has undesirable economic and political repercussions, planners have been trying, particularly since the 1960s, to introduce a policy of economic intensification (Mieczkowski 1970). If, on the other hand, the capital/output ratio declines, the sign of inequality in the above inequality is reversed, and consumers find themselves reaping the harvest of economic improvements.

The minimum rate of growth of consumption and national income is equal to the rate of growth of the population, so as to leave income and consumption per capita at least unchanged. This condition is shown by the following inequality:

$$\frac{\Delta Y}{Y} \geqslant \frac{\Delta P}{P} \leqslant \frac{\Delta C}{C}$$

where: P = population

---

*A separate problem of maximization of consumption over a period of time was discussed by Kalecki 1962, pp. 706-08. The author concluded that the criterion of maximization of consumption over a period is not useful for undertaking of investment decisions by planners. (See also Czerwinski 1965, especially p. 52).

To the extent that the largest claimant on national product is consumption, with investment in capital equipment the second largest claimant, and since investment is usually assumed as the factor that causes national income to grow (see Kalecki's model above), the conclusion may be that consumption plays a role of limiting the growth of national income. Such an interpretation is, of course, "unfair" to consumption on at least three counts:

1. It casts consumption in the role of a villain for those who want economic growth maximized—and most people do want that. It also skips over views, including those of socialists, that consumption is the final goal of economic activity.

2. It abstracts from other claimants on national product, such as investments in inventories, exports, and government consumption.

3. It abstracts from the "intensive" factors of economic growth, such as better use of manpower and investments, improvement in economic organization, introduction of better incentives, better education, a more efficient fiscal system, and modernization of the economy (cf. Mieczkowski 1970). (Kalecki covered those factors by his coefficient u.) All these factors tend to lower the capital/output ratio.

On the other hand, the traditional strategy for development of socialist economies has relied on the forced development of producer goods and raw materials industries, where the capital/output ratio is substantially higher than in consumer goods industries. Such a policy then leads to a rise in the average capital/output ratio for the economy as a whole which, as explained by Kalecki's equation, retards economic growth. If the pull of planners' desires is strong enough, the policy of favoring producer goods industries could be pursued ad infinitum, without consumers ever reaping the advantage of their past sacrifices undertaken to increase the amount of capital through reduced consumption.

Apart from the preference shown by planners toward capital goods industries, some other factors seem to work in socialist economies to retard the growth of consumption. In socialist economies characterized by autarchic tendencies, consumption based on low import content is considered more desirable than consumption that causes imports to rise. Housing does possess such low-import quality; even so, housing standards in Eastern Europe are inferior, according to Western standards. Therefore, some other force must hold down the level of expenditures on housing, be it an unwillingness to give up some investment programs desired by planners or some other force.

One of the factors holding down the potential growth of consumption is the accumulation of unnecessary inventories. A certain normal relationship between rising production and accumulation of inventories exists insofar as higher inventories of raw materials and goods in the

TABLE 4.1

Growth of Inventories and Reserves in the Polish Economy
(billion zlotys; in current prices)

| Year | Growth of Inventories and Reserves | | |
	Planned	Actual	Excess of Actual Over Planned
1955	4.9	18.0	+11.1
1960	18.4	25.5	+ 7.1
1961	17.0	32.9	+15.9
1962	23.4	21.5	- 1.9
1963	18.1	34.0	+15.9
1964	24.4	36.0	+16.6
1965	29.1	44.5	+15.4

Source: Cholinski et al. 1967, p. 84, cited after Piasny 1971, p. 152.

process of production are necessary to maintain a higher level of production. Similarly, in order to dispose of a higher volume of output, whether for consumption or for productive purposes, a higher level of inventories of finished products is necessary. Consequently, planners normally envisage a certain growth of inventories to accompany their programs of expansion. However, actual increases of inventories in Eastern Europe have tended to be substantially larger than planned, as shown by the example of Poland in Table 4.1. Similar experience has been reported from other Communist countries, including the Soviet Union. The result is that out of what statistics in Eastern Europe define as accumulation (synonymous with aggregate investments in Western terminology) a substantial percentage is taken up by the growth of inventories, leaving that much fewer resources for investment in the means of production, in the category that produces economic growth. An international comparison of the distribution of investments into productive investments and growth of inventories is given in Table 4.2. The table reveals a record of excessive accumulation of inventories, relatively three to five times higher than in the West. Such a practice, whatever its cause, constitutes a brake on economic growth by immobilizing resources in productively neutral or even negative stores of goods. Excessive inventories exist side by side with material bottlenecks, frantic searches for raw materials for production, an informal network of "fixers" who bring about swap transactions in inventories between enterprises, and other signs of economic wastefulness (Werewka 1969, p. 37; cf. Piasny 1971, pp. 148-55).

Another factor that holds down potential growth of consumption is defense spending, not a part of investments but classified in national accounts as "government consumption." Its official level is about 10 to 12 percent of budgetary expenditures, but due to concealment of much defense spending under other budget categories, the actual proportion is usually estimated at about twice the official one (cf. Gutowski 1970, pp. 73-74). That, of course, changes downward the amount actually spent out of the budget on social consumption.

Consumption is to a much smaller extent held down by the fact that it changes over time. Such changes usually necessitate expansion of capital equipment, and that requires some investments that, in turn, lay a claim on part of the national product produced and thus limit somewhat the amount available for consumption.

Thus investments and their structure, as well as government consumption, exert in the short run a depressing influence on consumption, and may do so even in the long run. This analysis, it should be stressed, does not consider the negative effect that depressed consumption may have on productivity, growth of national income, effectiveness of investments, and, in the final analysis, further prospects for improvement of consumption.

TABLE 4.2

International Comparison of the Proportion of
Growth of Inventories in Accumulation
(averages for 1955-60; percentages)

	Poland	West Germany	European Common Market	US
Gross investments	72.3	90.5	92.5	94.5
Growth of inventories	27.7	9.5	7.5	5.5

Source: Kuzinski 1962, p. 44, cited after Piasny 1971, p. 151.

PLANNERS' PREFERENCES AND CONSUMPTION

Discussion in Co-existence

The journal Co-existence, published at the University of Glasgow, carried in three issues in the early 1970s a discussion on planners' priorities in which this author participated (Zielinski 1971; Mujzel 1972; Mieczkowski 1973c; Zielinski's article was incorporated in his book, 1973, ch. 2.1). Janusz Zielinski of the University of Glasgow, who started the discussion, contended that consumers' preferences are one of the constraints on planners' preferences and that, at least in Poland (in my opinion this observation can be generalized to other East European countries), economic reforms up to 1970 did not result in a shift away from building up of heavy industry and toward better satisfaction of of consumer wants. Plan targets for increases in per capita consumption and in real wages showed a consistent pattern of decline, while plan fulfillment brought actual increases in consumption and in real wages to still less, except when political circumstances necessitated plan fulfillment in increases in the standard of living. The record has shown a tendency toward upward revisions and tightening of the economic plans, and subsequent breakdowns. (Roy Medvedev noticed the same tendency of raising the plan targets in the Soviet Union despite difficulties in meeting the basic—lower—plan targets; 1971, pp. 101-9.) Until 1971, planners refused "to take corrective measures when consumption targets [were] being systematically underfulfilled" (Zielinski 1973, p. 38). Zielinski concluded:

> The interests of consumers are best taken care of when
> political pressure on planners is strong and—according-
> ly—their hold on the population weak . . . . Immediately
> the pressure weakens—i.e. when the [Central Planning
> Board] considers the political situation under control—
> the rate of growth is raised again. The drastic nature of
> this increase seems to support the hypothesis that the
> consumer-oriented policy of the previous period was
> forced on planners by political circumstances, rather
> than as a reflection of their own preferences. The short
> life of the consumer-oriented policy points in the same
> direction. (Zielinski 1973, p. 39.)

A thoughtful analysis, in the course of which Zielinski disposed of the argument that planners lack the necessary information (cf. Ryc 1968, p. 296), led him to conclude that the Central Planning Board is "the main culprit" of the constant overinvestment policy. The causes of that deliberate bias are: (1) the Central Planning Board

"treats personal consumption as a cost of growth rather than the ultimate goal of growth" (cf. Ryc 1968, p. 321) and (2) "the overinvestment
policy may also be the result of a misguided effort of planners to fore-
stall the declining growth rates of socialist countries vis-a-vis their
capitalist adversaries" (Zielinski 1973, p. 43; italics in the original).
In order to satisfy their aspiration levels in the face of a declining
rate of performance of the economy, the planners decide to muddle
through by sacrificing consumption (and thus depriving themselves of
incentives as a policy tool that aims at increases in productivity) and
by increasing the tautness of the plan, which undermines the general
principle of economic calculus.

Zielinski's conclusions were controverted by Jan Mujzel, an
economist from the University of Lodz, Poland. He pointed to the
upgrading of labor in the Polish economy and, less correctly, to con-
cealed price rises, and putatively concluded: "Perhaps . . . Polish
economy could afford only to preserve the unchanged level of the real
wage rates" during the 1960s (Mujzel 1972, p. 160). Mujzel also
pointed to some official statistics of a late increase in the rate of
economic growth in Communist bloc countries, although at one point
he conceded that a deceleration of growth did take place in them
(Mujzel 1972, p. 163).

Mujzel ascribed the preference given by planners to investments
to the need to create jobs outside agriculture, to "urgent social needs
outside the productive sector," and to the need to strike a balance
between current and future consumption:

> In the socialist system, the relations between these
> values consist in the choice between some part of the
> potential current, "up-to-date" consumption and its
> growth in the next years. In every socialist country
> and in the country making up for the historical under-
> development in particular the one-sided preference of
> current consumption would have affected the basic
> interest of the society as a whole, its natural aspira-
> tions and needs of development. (Mujzel 1972, p. 161.)

What Mujzel left unmentioned, of course, was that it would be
the prerogative of the planners to decide how much to curb current
consumption in preference of future consumption, of the "interests of
the society as a whole, its natural aspirations and needs of development." He only asserted his faith that the expansionary orientation
of the Central Planning Board, its favoring of investments, satisfies

> the essential social interests. [Consequently] we
> should consider the political conditioning of [the
> Central Planning Board] not as a factor of its social
> alienation but, on the contrary, as the factor of sub-
> mission to society. (Mujzel 1972, p. 165.)

However, Mujzel acknowledged existence of errors in the period characterized by Zielinski (prior to December 1970), at which time worker discontent with Gomulka's consumption and wage policy removed him from power and brought in Edward Gierek:

> The relations between consumption and the growth of the national income were treated too formally and in a simplified way. [The Central Planning Board] did not take into consideration and did not want to make use of an important, though difficult to evaluate, favourable correlation between the growth of the current consumption, the growth of real wages in particular, and the growth of the occupational activity, productiveness and income. It did not pay attention to the influence which is exercised by the ambitious, consistently realized plans of the consumption growth . . . on people's attitudes and their willingness to save money. Important experiences were supplied here by the bold, "consumption oriented" economic policy of the new government in the country after December 1970. (Mujzel 1972, p. 163.)

In this way Mujzel actually confirmed Zielinski's thesis of political influence on planners' concessions to consumption.

My own comments in the Co-existence discussion concentrated on consumption issues. I applied to the Communist Party a statement by the leftist American economist, John Gurley, originally intended as criticism of capitalist institutions:

> Every ruling class describes its self-serving purposes in public-interest terms. Everything done is advertised as being in the national interest or even in the interest of the very class that is being hurt. (Gurley 1972, p. 20 n. 1.)

Inherent in the attitude synthesized by Gurley is an inclination to change the facts, particularly the inconvenient ones, while—we may add—inherent in the subordinate position of statistical offices in Eastern Europe is the ability of the ruling party to do so. Even without a conscious effort to change the facts, however, different economic systems impart varying degrees of deviation to quantitative measurements of their performance. For example, a study of Polish national income and product in which this author participated derived the share of personal consumption in Polish GNP by end use for 1954, 1955, and 1956 as 61.4 percent, 60.9 percent, and 59.5 percent, respectively, at market prices, while the minimal recalculation at factor cost yielded, respectively, 55.6 percent, 56.0 percent, and 56.5 percent, or markedly smaller proportions (Mieczkowski 1973c, pp. 178-79).

Against the Mujzel assertion that planners can evaluate consumer preferences independently of the ruling Communist Party apparatus, we may cite Harry Schwartz:

> Soviet planners make in advance the decisions—such as the division of national income between consumption and investment—that in a free enterprise society are simply the resultants of the independent decisions of competing individuals and groups . . . . we may point out the nondemocratic nature of this planning, the complete absence of . . . "consumers' sovereignty." Plans are drawn up on the basis of directives from the leadership of the Communist Party, which also controls the government . . . .
> Those who frame the plan directives can largely give second priority to consumer wishes.
> In short, the Soviet economic plan is a . . . comprehensive blueprint that attempts to govern the economic activities and interrelations of all persons and institutions. (Schwartz 1954, pp. 158, 178, 146, italics added; cf. Loucks and Whitney 1969, p. 486.)

Oskar Lange, the internationally known Polish economist, supported such an evaluation when he wrote that "the very process of socialist revolution" demands that the "regime exercise centralized control over the allocation and utilization of resources" (Lange 1963, p. 138, cited after Wilczynski 1972, p. 62).

Characteristically for the protagonists of central planning in Eastern Europe, Mujzel also showed a tendency to accept Communist goals as on the verge of fulfillment or actually accomplished, just on the strength of their being officially espoused. This tendency is particularly prominent in regard to levels of living. Margaret Miller observed the same trait in the Soviet Union:

> another Russian characteristic [is] the tendency to believe that what they want to be true in the future is already true in the present, and that any deviations of today are a betrayal of the desired tomorrow. (Miller 1965, p. 198.)

This strong conviction about the successes of today and the compulsive faith in tomorrow are probably originally based in the Communist doctrine of the mythical future that will result automatically from socialization. The doctrine contains the idea that "socialization will liberate man from the restrictions which nature and the economy now impose on him." This idea is contained in Engels, who wrote in "Anti-Duehring" that man will pass from "the realm of necessity" into "the realm of freedom" (Bochenski and Niemeyer 1962, pp. 61-62) Anthropologically, this tendency to accept goals as fulfilled facts seems akin to sympathetic rites prompting the advent of "the realm of freedom."

A confirmation of Zielinski's thesis of the influence of political pressures on consumption has been obtained from a study of Soviet consumption made available after the last contribution to the Co-existence discussion had been written. Two American researchers, in a study of Soviet consumer welfare during the Brezhnev era, noticed the following relationship between political situation and consumption:

> Under both Khrushchev and Brezhnev, the two welfare indicators [per capita consumption and per capita real disposable money income] grew much faster during the early years of their rule than during the latter years. The higher rates during the earlier years of both periods may reflect efforts by these leaders to consolidate their positions by currying favor with consumers. This is suggested most dramatically by the tripling of the rate of growth of consumption between Khrushchev's last 3 years and Brezhnev's first 3 years in power. (Bronson and Severin 1973, p. 377.)

Political pressures seem to produce the same effects in the Soviet Union as in Eastern Europe.

Planners and the Structure of Consumption

Beyond the Co-existence discussion, a new problem emerges in that one may question whether planners' preferences may not also dictate the structure of consumption. Maksymilian Pohorille asked that question in a book recently published in Poland (1971, pp. 154, 156-58) and, not surprisingly, answered that "this does not necessarily mean so." To him, the postulate of conscious and planned determination of the model of consumption implies (1) removal of "well-known disproportions" in the structure of production and consumption; (2) development of public discussion on the directions of satisfaction of wants of the society; (3) use of the communications media in accordance with the (otherwise undefined by him) interest of the society; (4) harmonization of efforts to satisfy the wants of the society to the fullest extent possible with the striving for the fullest development of human personality, and for the shaping of a new hierarchy of social values, including the new position of work and the working people in the socialist society. All this seems to amount to mouthing of slogans, without a logical and unequivocal answer to the question asked by Pohorille himself.

However, Pohorille's answer becomes more equivocal when it is realized that he agreed with a statement by another Polish expert on consumption problems, Janusz Los:

> It appears . . . that a thorough study of consumer pre-
> ferences . . . will allow such choice of the mix of
> foodstuffs which will make possible the preservation
> of basic assumptions of the plan without causing
> consumer dissatisfaction. If that is not the case,
> there will be need for an action of "consumer educa-
> tion." One has thus to envisage situations in which
> [the central planner], despite his best intentions,
> will not be able to take into account consumer prefer-
> ences. One will then have to direct the food policy
> so as to have the consumer abandon his point of view
> and accept that of the state, and in this way recognize
> the preferences of the state as his own. (Los 1964,
> p. 38; Pohorille 1971, pp. 162-63.)

One may well wonder how an economist who agreed with the above quotation could with any consistency say that planners' preferences would not dictate the structure of consumption, which is exactly what Pohorille did. A confrontation of such mutually contradictory statements may only create a feeling of being faced with a "double-think" of inter- esting proportions, particularly since these mutually contradictory positions were not taken at two different points of time, say before and after 1970 (under Gomulka and under Gierek), which under the politically fluid conditions in Eastern Europe might have been more understandable, but were enunciated in the same book, only five pages apart. * The case is an example of inconsistencies to be encountered in East European writings.

In an earlier contribution, Pohorille differentiated between a consumption model and a consumption plan, the former being shaped by the "habits and preferences" of consumers, while the latter was the result of economic exigencies that face planners (Pohorille 1966, pp. 291-92). But the consumption plan also was vested by Pohorille with a normative ("desiderative") element that works through income distribution and through investment planning, both of which affect future consumption. He posed a requirement for investment decisions to be autonomous, based on a "vision of the future society" (Pohorille

---

*Pohorille added to this approval of Los the latter's obiter dictum that one has to differentiate between long-term consumer education, to which Los referred, and expedient means of restoring market equilibrium, which addition may serve to obfuscate the issue but does not unequivo- cally determine the difference between the two situations.

1966, pp. 308-09), and concluded that the socialist system should use a mix of market mechanism and normative mechanism in adjusting production to social needs. The use of market mechanism would be predicated on consumer preferences not being in conflict with social preferences (Pohorille 1966, p. 309). In case of such a conflict, the social preferences would receive priority in the consumption plan. Thus Pohorille again showed himself in favor of planners' preferences dictating the structure of consumption, except of course where there is no conflict between theirs and consumer preferences.

A modificiation of this position is suggested in the writings of Jan Lipinski and Joan Robinson. Jan Lipinski, one of the edictors of the Polish Ekonomista, in advocating the percentage form of the turn-over tax, took a stand in favor of free choice of consumers within given categories of goods, untampered with by planners who, in his opinion, should not impose varying rates of a differential form of the turnover tax (1969 and 1972). However, such a stand still allows discrimination by planners between different categories of consumer goods, depending on their preferences. Nevertheless, Lipinski's explicit approval of a kind of "market solution" is an important departure from Pohorille's position.

An eventual market solution was envisaged by Joan Robinson, who urged that for the time being and before the standard of living rises to some level undefined by her, the "overall investment plan must continue to be made centrally" to assure the most economical use of resources. While implying the "market solution," she was satisfied with planners determining both the volume and direction of investments (Robinson 1965, p. 521, passim). These last two examples of social-ist thinking, Lipinski and Robinson, seem to indicate a measure of dissatisfaction with a solution that may override consumer preferences.

The discussion on the relation between planners' preferences and consumption may continue in Co-existence and other publications in the future, but some of its conclusions so far have an important bearing on consumption experience in Eastern Europe. The tautness in planning creates a sellers' market and a tendency toward deterioration of the quality of goods, especially in the sphere of consumer goods (cf. Ryc 1968, p. 309). The tautness is caused by a predilection of planners to favor investment goods, which puts consumption at a disadvantage. Only political pressures from society bring temporary relief from the discrimination against consumption exercised by planners, who, as a palliative, use slanted statistics to apply makeup to the picture of consumption. Finally, ideological fetishism seems to impede the chance for consumption to regain parity in the value system of Commu-nist planners.

One more consideration may be added to the foregoing. Central planners, despite their assertions, may not be representative either of consumers' interests or of society's long-range goals. There is no reason why that should necessarily be so, unless one assumes the

paternalistic stance that a person, or group of persons, "knows better."
This in itself seems presumptuous, and sounds more sloganeering than
the advertising adage that "Ford has a better idea." No advertiser
seems able to prove why Ford should have a better idea. And no
ideologue seems able logically to explain why planners should know
better.

In fact, one can suggest the hypothesis that planners are, by the
nature of their position, biased against consumers' interests to the
extent that those interests may diverge from those of the state and of
the perpetuation of Communist Party rule. The personal careers of
planners depend on the Communist Party, of which they are as a rule
members, and usually members in high positions. Consequently,
propagation of the supremacy of that party, of the hegemony of its
interests, and of the absoluteness of its rule are close to the hearts
of planners. But these are not criteria that would directly interest
consumers, who, we may assume, want to maximize their consumption
over a period of time. Therefore, this dichotomy of points of view is
bound to produce a divergence between policies likely to satisfy the
planners and the consumers.

One could perhaps argue that, in the interest of maintaining itself
in power, the Communist Party ought to seek popular approval, and to
gain that approval it ought to follow consumers' interests. Three
things may be wrong with this reasoning:

1. A monoparty rule, characterized by absence of alternative
political teams —but not necessarily by absence of alternative programs—may produce confidence that popular approval is not necessary.

2. The ideologues may inculcate the party apparatus with a conviction that, whatever the possible appearances to the contrary, the
party does ultimately seek the maximization of consumers' interests.
Popular approval, absent in the short or intermediate run, would then
follow in the long run, once the society sees the results of planned
policies, and may be achieved in the shorter period by proper education. In other words, the perceived, subjective interests of consumers
are secondary to the interests of consumers as visualized by planners.

3. Planners may not know, and indeed may not seek to learn,
about the aspirations of consumers, partly because of an a priori
assumption that they "know better," partly because of an absence
of a mechanism to gather and transmit the necessary information, and
partly because of a possible bias against any action that might create
the impression that consumers' preferences do count by themselves,
rather than through the interpretation given them by planners. Thus
the interests of the Communist Party may have a separate existence,
independent of consumers' interests.

FACTORS AFFECTING CONSUMPTION: AN ANALYTICAL
FRAMEWORK FOR COUNTRY STUDIES

Consumption experience of any country is influenced by two basic
sets of factors:

• Exogeneous factors that by and large change spontaneously and
are not easily subject to statistical evaluation. Examples of such
influences are tastes; new discoveries of natural endowments or their
depletion, pollution or loss through mismanagement of existing resources; change in the flow of information to consumers; change in income
distribution; changes in the attitude toward material consumption,
hedonism, income distribution, future consumption, or political,
economic, and social goals. These factors may be regarded by
statisticians as too esoteric, too difficult, not adequately defined to
be amenable to statistical analysis, too ideological in their content,
and — the last straw — inherently lying in the sphere of subjective
value judgments rather than objective, quantitative measurement.
Even though some of these factors could be quantified or set on a
comparative scale, the present study abstracts from them, leaving
this field to social and political theorists. However, to the extent
that these factors influence the level of welfare in the society, we
obviously are not in a position to make any firm declaration about
that level.

• Factors that constitute part of the economic ecology within which
consumption takes place and by which it is affected for better or for
worse. These broad economic factors will be discussed below, in
Chapters 5 to 9, together with consumption trends in the four countries
covered in this study. For the purpose of providing a schematic
framework, I have formulated here a list of factors particularly relevant to a discussion of consumption trends:

1. Planning exerts its impact on consumption through its system
of priorities that influence the direction of production and its expansion, as well as through its failures, both in terms of breakdown or
partial breakdown of such influence and in terms of an "unplanned"
influence — whether unforeseen and unintentional or resulting from
partial achievement of a given assortment of indicators. On a crude
level, we may assume that the actual economic changes had been the
planned ones; on that basis, we may blame or praise the planning
system for the consequences of given economic performances as they
concern consumption. But surely, this is not adequate for finer analysis
since economic performance does not need to be, and indeed usually
is not, completely in accord with the plan. Consequently, in the
chapter on Polish experience attention will be devoted to planning

and plan fulfillment. In the less detailed chapters on Czechoslovakia, Hungary, and East Germany, however, little attention will be given to ex ante planning and its influence on consumption.

2. Investments provide the basis and determine the direction of future expansion of production. Given the incremental capital/output ratio, and given full employment of resources, the larger the amount of investments, the greater the increments of output that may be expected in the future. The trouble is that, the larger the slice taken out of current national income to provide for investments, the smaller will be the residual that may be devoted to consumption. Thus a competitive relationship exists between current consumption and increases in future output; to the extent that future output may — but does not have to — be devoted to provision of consumer goods, this competitive relationship also extends to future consumption. Under free market conditions, the issue is determined by the propensity to save and the marginal efficiency of capital, but in Eastern Europe it is resolved by planners who, in this way, regulate current consumption.

Direction of future expansion of production is determined by sectoral disposition of investments. To the extent that planners in Eastern Europe tend to favor investments in capital goods industries, they create a precondition for faster growth of that sector over the consumer sector. In different periods, under political pressures, planners may at least temporarily change their sectoral preferences and may accord a higher share of investments to consumer goods industries. At other periods, when forceful industrial expansion is deemed paramount in importance, as it was during the Stalinist period in the East European countries covered by this study, investments in consumer goods will very nearly dry up while the capital goods sector will enjoy bountiful investments. Similarly, within the consumer goods sector, investments may favor agriculture or housing construction, or industry, services or social consumption. Their current direction will inherently exert its influence on the composition of future supplies of consumer goods and services. Thus a study of investments provides a useful indication of current economic policies that are bound to project on the future course of consumption.

3. Given a certain labor productivity, the volume of and changes in employment determine the quantity of output, among others of consumer goods (cf. Alton 1974, p. 287). Increases in labor force participation rates — that is, in the number available for work of every 100 persons of labor force age — therefore create favorable conditions for an increase in per capita consumption. Also, decreases in the dependency ratio — that is, in the average number of dependents not working per person employed, which is tantamount to increases in the number of persons working per 100 inhabitants (the rate of economic activity) — have a positive effect on increase in per capita consumption since an average household then has more members at work, bringing home

paychecks, and since greater employment results (the share of consumption sector remaining constant) in a greater output of consumer goods. Changes in dependency ratio result from changes in age distribution of the population (since that determines the percentage of persons within the labor force age); from incentives given to women to enter the labor force; from changes in health standards; from educational policies; from incentives given those of retirement age to postpone retirement; from changes in the proportion of the population in military service, and from changes in prison population relative to total population (cf. Denison 1962, chs. 5-9).

Labor productivity tends to rise in time with improvements in technology, education of the labor force, economic organization, and increases in capital employed per unit of labor. John Kendrick estimated that average growth in labor productivity in the United States between 1919 and 1957 was 2.3 percent per year, compared with 1.6 percent rate of growth during 1889-1919. (Kendrick 1961, p. 60). Between 1900 and 1960, increases in productivity contributed 44.1 percent to the growth of NNP (net national product), compared with a 17.3 percent contribution between 1840 and 1900 (Davis et al. 1972, p. 39). Under conditions of quick industrialization with borrowed technology, as in Eastern Europe since World War II, increases in labor productivity should be markedly higher. Given a certain dependency ratio, the higher the rate of increase in labor productivity, the higher is the possible increase in consumption, since part of the increased per capita output can be used for consumption.

4. Food is the most important single consumption category; consequently, agricultural production exerts an important influence on consumption prospects. A sequence of bad harvests may, unless relieved by imports of foodstuffs, spell difficulties in securing provisions. Plan-inelastic supplies of meat may mean upward price adjustments. Minor inconveniences may result from bad fruit harvests. Consequently, growth of agricultural production is one of the key indexes for determination of conditions under which consumption will develop. To the extent that agriculture also provides some industrial raw materials, its growth influences the growth of some other branches, the most obvious of them being the food industry, while some other examples are textiles (wool, flax), tobacco industry, leather industry, and vegetable oil, and byproducts such as those from slaughter houses. Agriculture, in turn, is dependent on output from other sectors, notably chemicals (fertilizers) and machine industry (tractors and other agricultural machinery). These input-output relations enhance the influence of agriculture on the economy.

Agriculture in Communist countries has not made a good showing, partly because of inadequate supplies of inputs from other sectors, but mostly because of the policy of forced collectivization, linked with expropriation of peasants under the euphemism of "agricultural reform," and a consequent destruction of incentives to produce. In some East

European countries, as in Poland and Yugoslavia, collectivization policy was abandoned and re-privatization of land was resorted to, both for political reasons and to promote agricultural productivity.

5. Foreign trade exerts an important influence on consumption in a multifarious fashion. Directly, it removes some consumer goods from domestic markets through exports, and supplements domestic markets with other goods through imports. The net result may be either augmentation of the aggregate volume of goods available to domestic consumers, as in an import surplus (negative balance) on the balance of trade in consumer goods, or a diminution of the volume of goods available to domestic consumers, as in an export surplus (positive balance) in the trade in consumer goods. Also directly, foreign trade affects the domestic market in services by engaging a larger or smaller part of the labor force and capital in service rendering to foreign countries (transportation and transit services; tourism).

Indirectly, economic relations with other countries help in adoption of more advanced technology, provide machinery and raw materials for industry from which production of consumer goods may ultimately result, provide a demonstration effect for consumers who are then likely to exert additional pressure for more and better consumer goods, and cause additional political pressures in favor of liberalization. Moreover, to the extent that foreign trade enables a country to reach a higher transformation curve—that is, to wind up producing and having at its disposal more commodities thanks to concentration of production in areas where it enjoys comparative advantage, the participant in international trade can afford higher consumption levels.

The usual problem in Eastern Europe is that foreign trade transactions on the balance of trade are measured in foreign exchange (devisa) units of national currency, with an indeterminate and variable relation to domestic value. Financially, differences between foreign exchange and domestic values are taken care of by positive (in the case of imports) and negative (in the case of exports) budget differences paid by, or to, enterprises engaged in foreign trade. But statistically there arises an area of doubt because, for instance, an import balance on the balance of trade does not necessarily mean that the same is true in terms of domestic values since exports and imports were recalculated into domestic values at different devisa–domestic–currency rates of conversion. Consequently, foreign trade statistics will be offered here as only proximate guides to the impact of foreign trade on consumption in Eastern European countries.

6. An increasing share of consumption consists of goods of industrial origin, with the steepest rate of growth among them being shown by durable consumer goods. Therefore industrial production of consumer goods is of great interest to our study of consumption. Furthermore, a comparison of rates of growth of output of capital goods with that of consumer goods reveals actual planners' preferences (barring objective difficulties in plan fulfillment), as distinct

from those announced in economic plans, and shows the working of political pressures at certain junctures of time.

     7. Distribution of income among different groups of population — rural-urban, white/blue-collar, high/low income groups — gives information on progress of egalitarianism in a given society, and on the ability of different consumer groups to satisfy their wants.

     8. Statistics of real wages are an important complement to consumption statistics, insofar as growth in the latter may have been achieved as the result of higher labor force participation rates. Information on work week, holidays, and legislation concerning leaves, also adds insight into the level of well-being.

The above schema, with certain variations, will be applied in Part II of this study, covering individual East European countries. Naturally, statistics concerning consumption itself also will be included. In this way, it is hoped, the reader will be better able to perceive the origins of given changes in consumption and to judge whether at any moment of time consumption was indeed maximized, at what cost a certain mixture of consumption and economic growth was achieved, and what the alternatives were to a given turn of events. Economists are fond of covering all these observations by a catch-all concept of opportunity cost. Thus our schema will explore the opportunity cost of the growth of consumption in Eastern Europe.

The approach used in the present study is thus to highlight the trends and factors relevant to the development of consumption. The alternative could be to present consumption data and explain them, possibly in econometric terms. However, it seems to this author that such an approach would be analogous to a military historian telling his readers who won a battle, with what casualties and what gains, while saying nothing about the disposition of forces, alternative disposition, movement of troops, other elements of strategy, armament used, and so on. It is my endeavor to provide here this kind of background information in the realm of consumption, so that the context within which consumption developed can be more easily perceived. Constraints of space forced omission of some factors of potential importance, including: industrial organization; system of incentives; education of the labor force; drainage of experts into areas nonproductive from the point of view of consumers (such as industries); labor relations; relative technological progress; development of the domestic trade network and the system of information used by that network; selection of partners in international trade; technological discoveries or absorption of such discoveries, whether foreign or domestic in origin, in the process Joseph Schumpeter called "innovation"; discoveries of new natural resources or their depletion or loss. Limitations imposed by the shortness of the human lifespan necessitate arranging one's activities with due regard for opportunity cost. Similarly, limitations of space necessitate some selectiveness in the material used in this book.

PART

II

**COUNTRY
STUDIES**

5

The raw material of a consumption study consists of the actual experience of consumers in a specified economic entity, or several entities. Accounts of such an experience can be evaluated, analyzed, and used as a basis for conclusions, but the experience itself constitutes the fulcrum of a consumption study. Consumption experience is subject to different interpretations, the more so the less reliable the statistics that form the quantitative indicator of consumption and changes in it. In order to narrow down the range of possible interpretations, therefore, it seems desirable to devote Part II of this study to a description of consumption trends in Eastern Europe, covering first Poland, and in the following chapters Czechoslovakia, Hungary, and East Germany.

THE 1945-49 PERIOD OF RECONSTRUCTION

During the 1939-45 wartime period, considerable ravages were inflicted on the Polish economy.* Poland lost about 11 million people, due to death, migration, and the loss of the eastern third of its territory. Many of the people thus lost were in their prime productive age, and many had above-average education and enterprise. Their potential contribution to postwar reconstruction would have been invaluable. The territorial loss of the eastern part of prewar Poland was partly offset by annexation of former German territories east of the Oder-Neisse line. These territories had been economically more developed

---

*The present chapter is based partly on the informative study by Ryc (1968). Individual references to that work and to numerous sources on which it was based are here largely omitted.

than prewar Poland, but they suffered considerable destruction during the last phase of World War II. Destruction of physical capital in postwar Poland amounted in aggregate to 38 percent of the total; in some sectors — transport, communications, trade, education, health, and administration — it eliminated between 50 and 65 percent of capital. Consequently, the first postwar task was to reconstruct the economy by building up its capital and reestablishing the productive network. Demographic losses were made up more slowly by the birth wave that lasted into the 1960s and by some migration of Poles from other countries, mainly the USSR (Kruszewski 1972, ch. 3).

Achievements of the Reconstruction Plan

During 1945-46, reconstruction was carried out mainly in a spontaneous effort of the population. The first formal plan, the so-called Three-Year Plan for 1947-49, utilized largely the same spontaneous forces and consequently was mostly a prognosis of the growth of production, national income, and the standard of living. The indexes of production approximately doubled between 1946 and 1949, as shown in Table 5.1. Per capita production increased considerably, and it was symptomatic of both the prognostic character of the Three-Year Plan and of the strength of spontaneous forces within the economy that plan fulfillment was substantially higher than plan goals, particularly in consumer goods, as shown in Table 5.2.

However, comparison with 1938 per capita production, particularly of consumer goods, is likely to have been exaggerated in this table, even if one takes into account possible divergence between production and consumption caused by inequality between imports and exports, and by accumulation of inventories. First, the index of unadjusted consumption per capita, calculated independently by myself and presented in the last section of this chapter, indicates a growth of less than 26 percent between 1938 (on prewar territory) and 1949 (see Table 5.49 below). Adjusted consumption per capita shows a slightly lower growth of less than 25 percent, while Table 5.2 indicates a rise of about 80 percent. Second, the index of real wages per capita was calculated by a Polish expert on consumption, Kazimierz Ryc for 1949 at 85, with 1938 taken as 100 (Ryc 1968, p. 32). Even with higher labor force participation rates in the later year, real consumption per capita could not have equaled prewar. Thus, before the war there was 1.44 dependant per worker, while by 1949 this figure fell to 1.19, indicating a decline of 10.25 percent in the number of persons depending on each wage earner and a consequent upward adjustment of the level of living. If this change is taken as representative also for white-collar workers and farm families, the index number of real wage of 85 in 1949 could be adjusted to 93.7 to indicate the standard of living index, 1938 taken as 100.

TABLE 5.1

Indexes of Growth of Production and
National Income in Poland, 1938-49

	1938	1946	1947	1948	1949
Gross production of industry and handicraft	100	70	90	120	148
Gross production of agriculture	100	47	60	75	86
National income	100	69	89	109	128

Source: Secomski 1950, pp. 31, 45, 66, after Ryc 1968, p. 19.

TABLE 5.2

Plan Fulfillment of the Three-Year Plan
on a Per Capita Basis
(1938 = 100)

	Plan for 1949	Fulfillment in 1949
National income	150	175
Production of consumer goods	125	184
Agricultural production	110	128

Source: Ryc 1968, p. 20.

81

An independent calculation by two Polish economists, each of whom provided part of the answer, was made in 1937 and 1961 prices (Zienkowski 1963, pp. 177-205; Zienkowski 1964; Ryc 1968, pp. 22-23). It resulted in an estimate of consumption per capita in 1949 of 142.6, with 1937 equal to 100, and of personal consumption of 132.1, with both index numbers obtained by use of 1937 price weights, in effect producing the Laspeyre's index. Using 1961 price weights, similar to the Paasche's index, although with an unduly late year chosen for the purpose of weighting, yeilded an index of 101.3 for aggregate consumption per capita and 102.9 for personal consumption per capita. The averages for those calculations are 117.6 for aggregate consumption and 131.4 for personal consumption. This compares with index numbers yielded from calculations by myself of 125.9 for unadjusted per capita consumption and 125.0 for adjusted per capita consumption, both compared with prewar territory.

To illustrate changes in consumption between 1938 and 1949, Table 5.3 shows changes in consumption in several main categories of the largest item in consumption: food. The growth of consumption of cereals indicates that an "inferior" diet pattern still obtained in 1949, while the growth of consumption of vegetables and fruits exaggerates the progress over the years since 1949 was a year of bumper crops, out of line with the trend of growth in the production of fruit and vegetables.

An author who in 1972 analyzed changes in consumption in Poland during the postwar period concluded that "changes in the consumption of individual products" in the period between prewar and 1969, which in some cases were faster in Poland than in other East European countries, "took place mostly during the period up to and including 1950, so that the increase of consumption in that period had a decisive influence" on the overall Polish performance in the area of consumption (Lewandowska 1972, p. 156). This hindsight view helps to assess the importance of the reconstruction period for personal consumption in Poland.

One has to realize, however, that the statistically satisfactory results of reconstruction were at least partly attributable to some external circumstances. First, the overall reduction in population allowed those who survived and remained in the postwar area of Poland to obtain a higher share of the product of that area. Second, Poland, as a result of the Yalta agreement, lost in the east a relatively poor area of lower-than-average per capita consumption while it gained in the west an area of substantially higher per capita consumption than that for prewar Poland, even though that same area was relatively poorer than prewar Germany as a whole. Thus, the westward shift of Polish territory tended by itself to raise per capita consumption. Third, the Polish postwar economy experienced a big shift to urbanization and commercialization that exposed to statistical measurement activities that previously lay within the subsistence agricultural sector and thus

TABLE 5.3

Per Capita Consumption of Selected Food Products, 1938-49

	Unit	1938	1946	1947	1948	1949	Index 1949/38
Cereal products	kg.	136	90	113	129	163.3	119.4
Legumes	kg.	3.0	..	1.0	1.9	2.8	93.3
Potatoes	kg.	275	175	218	233	273	99.3
Fruit and vegetables	kg.	70	..	59	66.4	97.8	139.7
Meat and fish	kg.	24	15.3	23.1	24.9	26.7	111.2
of that: fish	kg.	1.0	..	..	..	1.5	150.0
Fats, including butter	kg.	8.0	4.0	6.1	7.2	8.3	103.8
Milk and milk products	kg.	201.2	105.0	127.5	132.5	218.2	108.4
Eggs	number	114	90	71	97	116	101.8
Sugar	kg.	12.2	7.0	12.0	16.0	19.3	158.2

Source: Ryc 1968, p. 23.

83

TABLE 5.4

Agricultural-Industrial Price Parity, 1945-49
(April 1945 = 100)

	1945[a]	1946	1947	1948	1949
Agricultural production[b]	. .	47	65	77	91
Price parity between food- stuffs and industrial goods	84	58	56	55	66
Price parity of foodstuffs to dress and footwear	81	49	41	40	46

[a] From March to December.
[b] 1934-38 average equals 100.

Sources: RS 1972, p. 8; Ryc 1968, p. 30.

went unreported in statistics. Consequently, postwar statistics would have shown growth even without any increase in actual consumption per capita, just by virtue of the fact that more of the flows of consumer goods and services were going through the channels of trade.

In addition to these factors, one has to remember that, as shown in Chapter 3, Communist statistics are not entirely reliable. In connection with Table 5.2 above, it was noted that the growth of consumption between 1938 and 1949 was apparently statistically exaggerated.

The Three-Year Plan witnessed a comparatively rapid increase in agricultural production that, in conjunction with a buoyant market for industrial consumer goods and the difficulties connected with their production, led to a fall in the relation of food prices to prices of consumer goods of industrial origin, shown in Table 5.4. Such a decline in agricultural price parity was favorable to consumers but the trend was reversed in 1949 as a result of the policy of forced socialization that shifted into high gear in 1949. The socialization policy, begun with immediate post-liberation takeover of large industrial firms finalized in a law of January 3, 1946, continued with the declaration of the so-called "battle for trade" in May 1947, "won" by 1949, and achieved its traditional apogee in the forced collectivization of agriculture, started in 1949 and largely completed by 1953 (Wszelaki 1957, p. 352; Dolina and Mieczkowski 1957, p. 431; "Agriculture" 1957, pp. 297-98). Its results on agricultural production will be outlined below.

Real wages during the Three-Year Plan period grew substantially: in 1947 by 14 percent, in 1948 by 23 percent, and in 1949 by 13 percent.

During 1946-49 they approximately doubled (Beskid 1972, p. 65). However, because of the precipitous decline in real wages caused by the war, the estimate of real wages, with 1938 taken as 100, is as follows: 63 in 1947; 77 in 1948; 85 in 1949.

The level of living, however, tended to be higher than real wages, because of the higher labor force participation rates, an increase in the role of social consumption, and because housing conditions improved as compared with prewar when the average number of persons per room was 2.2, declining by 1949 to 1.7.

The postwar improvement in real wages was not evenly distributed. While real wages of blue-collar workers probably increased as compared with prewar by some 7 percent, white-collar workers experienced a decline compared with prewar. This relative shift is illustrated by a change in the ratio of white-collar to blue-collar wages, from 2.5 to 1 for prewar to 1.2 to 1 for 1949.

The change in the real income of peasants cannot be determined for lack of data and because of disparate movements of individual price relationships. Peasants, however, seem to have eaten better in 1949 than before the war, as shown by a comparison of their consumption of individual articles with 1936-37 taken as 100: cereals, 103; meat and fats, 130; potatoes, 98; eggs, 125; milk, 95; sugar, 190.

Reasons for Success

On the whole, several factors contributed to the success of the 1945-49 reconstruction and the 1947-49 Three-Year Plan. Some of them have been mentioned above, but they bear repeating:

1. The territorial shift exchanged the less economically developed areas of prewar Poland for the more advanced Western Territories obtained from Germany. To illustrate, out of total employment of 1.8 million workers in prewar enterprises employing more than 20 workers, only 225,000 were employed in the eastern areas lost to the Soviet Union. The Western Territories, on the other hand, immediately added 750,000 jobs in industry; added considerable productive capacity to the postwar economy, as shown in Table 5.5; contributed a more highly developed technology used by the Germans during World War II; added better although partly destroyed housing, government structures, and utilities; and brought into Poland an area with more intensive agriculture. The impact of territorial changes was reflected in an almost 10 percent reduction of population as compared with prewar Poland, a reduction of cultivable land by 20 percent, and an increase of jobs in industry by 31 percent. Such changes laid a foundation for the postwar reconstruction and development.

TABLE 5.5

Contribution of Western Territories to Gross Production
of Selected Products in Poland
(percent of total Polish production)

	1947	1948	1949
Coal	33	32	33
Lignite	99	97	97
Coke	51	45	53
Cement	27	30	32
Lime	68	55	58
Superphosphates	19	22	24
Radio sets	84	68	67
Cotton fabrics	27	25	25
Paper	28	32	33
Sugar	25	31	31

Source: Secomski 1950, p. 23, after Ryc 1968, p. 39.

2. Reconstruction by itself tends to be more productive than new development. The infrastructure of know–how, education, and skills is available; many auxiliary utilities are already in existence; productive organization is extant and consequently plants do not require lengthy warm–up periods; and investments can be concentrated on bottleneck sectors, thus giving rise to a high incremental capital/output ratio. This is why production in Poland picked up at a high rate after the first postwar renovation took place. Table 5.6 shows that investments during 1946-49 were highly concentrated, at first in transportation and communications, later increasingly in industry. Such an investment policy could not fail to maximize the results of reconstruction.

At the same time, however, investments were primarily directed to rebuilding rather than modernization. Such a policy contributed to lagging in labor productivity, and hence to lagging in potential rises of real wages. Table 5.7 reveals that average productivity in industry was lower in 1949 than in 1938. Other factors that contributed to this slow rise in productivity were low average qualifications of workers, many of whom were recruited from farms and other occupations; fluctuations in production caused by scarcity of raw materials and inferior organization of industry, with some former owners kept in managerial positions and inadequate incentives given to employees; and possibly some disruptions caused by progressing socialization.

TABLE 5.6

Structure of Investments, 1946–49
(percentages)

	1946	1947	1948	1949
Industry, mining, handicraft	29.1	35.4	36.2	41.2
Agriculture, forestry, fishing	15.6	15.9	12.9	12.2
Transport and communications	40.8	27.5	24.3	18.4
Trade	1.2	2.2	4.7	5.7
Social and cultural investments	5.0	6.4	7.7	8.2
Housing construction	4.3	8.5	9.2	7.5
Office construction	2.9	3.0	3.0	2.2
Utilities and miscellaneous	1.7	1.1	1.5	2.7

Source: Secomski 1950, p. 69.

TABLE 5.7

Employment and Labor Productivity
in Polish Industry, 1938–49

	1938	1946	1947	1948	1949
Employment (thousands)	834	1,202	1,445	1,562	1,701
Labor productivity (index)	100	54	66	74	85

Source: Calculated by the author on the basis of Ryc 1968, p. 48.

On the other hand, labor productivity in agriculture increased by 1949 by approximately 70 percent above prewar, partly as the result of a decline in the rural population from 24.4 million in 1938 to 16.1 million in 1946 and 15.7 million in 1949, and partly as the result of bringing under cultivation some formerly fallow land. Despite this favorable development, production per acre in postwar territory did not by 1949 reach prewar levels on the same territory.

3. The occupying Germans destroyed mainly handicraft and small-scale industry and had a policy of consolidating production in larger plants. During the postwar reconstruction, scarcity of raw materials and personnel did not allow handicrafts to regain their prewar position; this in turn increased the demand for industrial products and the profitability of industry.

4. Agricultural overpopulation declined, with the cultivable area per agricultural worker rising by 34 percent between 1931 and 1950. The average size of farms increased, and their demand for industrial products, including agricultural inputs, rose substantially.

5. The 1945-49 reconstruction utilized private initiative and private accumulation. Economic incentives, apart from patriotic zeal, reinforced the impetus of reconstruction, tended to reduce demand for consumer goods, and supplemented the resources used by the state to rebuild the country. The government consciously tried to encourage private initiative, at least for a time, and guaranteed its place by a law passed on September 21, 1946. This assurance greatly accelerated the settling of Western Territories. Table 5.8 shows the contribution of privately financed investments, but private initiative actually contributed far more than shown by that table on account of its characteristic decentralized initiative, resourcefulness, and drive. Ryc concluded ruefully:

> Liquidation of private industry conducted on a large scale in 1949 and achieved by administrative methods [by force] (and the earlier liquidation of private trade) contributed to premature . . . renunciation of benefiting from all possible means applied to reconstruction. (Ryc 1968, p. 47.)

6. Poland received valuable help from UNRRA (United Nations Relief and Rehabilitation Agency). Polish writers as a rule mention aid from the Soviet Union.* However, to the extent that the Soviet Union took a lot of equipment from the Western Territories as war

---

*I have in my collection a Polish publication which mentions the remarkable help given by the Soviets to Poland, including the USSR's gift of a radio station. Above that statement is a picture of a Red Army officer standing next to radio equipment clearly marked with the sign of RCA (Warsaw 1950, p. 30).

TABLE 5.8

The Role of Private Investments in
the Polish Economy, 1946-51
(billion zlotys at 1961 prices)

Year	All Investments	Investments in Socialized Sector	Investments in Private Sector	Private as Percentage of Total Investments
1946	15.5	8.6	6.9	44.6
1947	19.6	11.3	8.3	42.5
1948	23.9	15.7	8.2	34.4
1949	28.0	23.3	4.7	16.9
1950	38.6	34.9	3.7	9.6
1951	43.2	41.9	1.3	3.0

Source: RS 1965, p. 85.

indemnity and received additional "indemnity" from Poland in the form of coal shipments while tying exports to Poland to future imports from Poland, the value of that "aid" is controversial. Certainly, a Poland outside the Soviet orbit, participating in free world trade and in the Marshall Plan aid, would have been better off than the Poland of actual postwar experience.

Statistics collected by Paul Marer allow calculation of the balance of trade in international exchange in consumer goods. Such a balance, when positive, indicates exports of more consumer goods than are imported, and consequently a worsening of the position of domestic consumers as a direct result of foreign trade. (It should be noted that the total impact of foreign trade may still be favorable to consumption through importation of raw materials, new technology, machines that eventually will enable production of consumer goods, and so on. Marer gave statistics in terms of dollars at current prices and divided products into groups according to the Comecon Trade Nomenclature (Marer 1972, p. 2). Two of the groups comprise consumer goods: division III (foodstuffs and raw materials for foodstuffs) and division IV (industrial consumer goods other than food). Using those two groups, I calculated balances of trade in consumer goods as -$50.0 million in 1946 (reflecting part of UNRRA aid); -$2.3 million in 1947; $47.3 million in 1948; and $122.5 million in 1949 (Marer 1972, pp. 49, 58). Thus the direct impact of foreign trade on the Polish consumer shifted from favorable to unfavorable, but its initial beneficent effect was of utmost importance for the postwar level of living in Poland.

7. Coal during the Three-Year Plan consistuted 70 to 80 percent of Polish exports (some of it as forced indemnity to the Soviet Union). Coal prices tended to rise relative to other prices, thus improving Polish terms of trade.

It should be stressed that, on the whole, the success of the 1945–49 reconstruction laid good foundations for the future industrialization of the country.

THE 1950–55 INDUSTRIALIZATION PERIOD
OF THE SIX–YEAR PLAN

The reconstruction period restored and expanded the existing sectors of the economy without by and large changing its structure. It became the task of the following Six-Year Plan to accomplish a basic restructuring of the economy toward production of capital goods, so as to lay foundations for future expanded national growth and growth in consumption. In both areas — production of capital goods and production of consumer goods — a tendency toward autarchy was apparent in the parameters of the plan, whose emphasis was put on machine industry, chemical industry, iron and steel and steel-using industry.

Background and Reasons for Failure of Plans

In view of the planners' preferences, it was important to curtail purchasing power in the hands of consumers. Despite an initial monetary reform of January 1945 connected with conversion to a new medium of exchange (Mieczkowski 1954a, pp. 52–55), the amount of liquid reserves in the hands of the population increased greatly between 1945 and 1950, mostly as the result of deficit financing of the budget (Mieczkowski 1954a, pp. 55–56, 65). Consequently, as a prelude to a general retrenchment of the consumer sector, a new, stringent monetary reform was undertaken on October 28, 1950. It served several aims:

1. Economic: to stop inflation; to eliminate a large part of money holdings representing past savings, and to avert their being used to bid for resources that otherwise could be used for capital accumulation; to create conditions propitious for further planning; finally, to weld Poland into the ruble bloc.

2. Political: to penalize the remaining capitalistic elements in the economy; following the example of the Soviet monetary reform of 1947, to synchronize the Polish economy with that of the USSR in order to make them more interdependent (Mieczkowski 1954a, p. 68).

I have previously described the details of the reform (Mieczkowski 1954a, pp. 68-77), and they may serve as a general picture for the monetary reforms undertaken in other East European countries covered in this study, with only the particulars varying. From the time of the reform on, the planners could safely disregard the possibility of accumulated savings suddenly being bid on the market for consumer goods, thus creating unwanted inflationary pressures. The consumer sector was thus placed more firmly under planners' control.

The Six-Year Plan went through several versions, the first of which was published at the Communist Party Congress in December 1948. Compared with 1949, investments were to rise by the end of the new plan period by 130 to 150 percent, employment by 27 percent, national income by 70 to 80 percent, production in the socialized sector of industry by 85 to 95 percent, agricultural production by 35 to 45 percent. The rise in the level of living of the population was to amount to 55 to 60 percent, but no guidelines for the growth of real wages and real incomes in agriculture were included in the first version of the plan.

The second version, approved by the legislature in July 1950, was more ambitious. By 1955, investments were to rise as compared with 1949 by almost 140 percent, employment by 60 percent, national income by 112 percent, industrial production by 158 percent, and agricultural production by 50 percent. A somewhat wider band of 50 to 60 percent was set up for the rise in the standard of living, while real wages were to rise by 40 percent. While the first version was very ambitious and hence unlikely to be successfully completed, the second version was impossible, even by later Japanese standards, regardless of subsequent perfectionist rationalization that the industrial capacity utilization amounted at the outset of the plan to only 55 to 60 percent. *
Several factors were at work to prevent achievement of the ambitions incorporated in the plan:

1. As noted in connection with the 1947-49 plan, the average level of qualifications of the labor force was low, labor productivity was lagging, and incorporation of modern technology in production consequently proved difficult to achieve.

2. The plan listed as one of its goals a voluntary socialization of agriculture. Any knowledge of Soviet experience in this area, and of the "dizziness from success" experienced when socialization was

---

*Knyziak 1964, pp. 87-89, cited an estimate by W. Lissowski of a 65 to 70 percent utilization of capital in industry in 1950, and reduced it to 55 to 60 percent. During 1951-56, industrial production from older plants rose by at least 30 percent on account of fuller utilization of capital that existed before 1950. Less than full utilization of new capital equipment continued to be a problem in 1960s.

administered by eager, ruthless and basically all-powerful party
chairmen, would have led to a prediction of disaster in the fulfillment
of the plan for agricultural production.

3. The plan aimed at establishment of closer economic links with
other Communist countries, particularly the Soviet Union. This, in
conjunction with the outbreak of the Korean War and the reinforcement
of the Iron Curtain, meant the cutting off of Poland from advanced
technical information, from some raw materials and some foodstuffs
(example: citrus fruits), and from the true utilization of benefits
resulting from international exchange according to the principle of
comparative advantage.

4. The Korean War and the intensification of the cold war that
led to Poland's membership in the Warsaw Pact (the so-called Pact
for Mutual Assistance and Unified Command, signed on May 14, 1955)
forced Poland, as well as the other Communist countries, to shift
efforts to an additional expansion of defense industries. That expansion, begun in 1951, was particularly costly in terms of its preemption
of the best technicians, investment resources, and raw materials, as
well as in terms of a violation of previously set up interindustry links,
and consequent havoc perpetrated on the principle of balanced, planned
growth.

5. To the extent that the plan envisaged full utilization of all
existing equipment, much of which was superannuated, achievement
of higher labor productivity became more difficult and the use of raw
materials, including fuel, tended to become unduly high.

Ryc provided a good assessment of the difficulties encountered
in any evaluation of the achievements of the Six-Year Plan:

> Comparison of the aims and achievements of the Six-Year
> Plan is rendered extremely difficult because aggregate
> quantities used for comparisons are influenced by changes
> in the structure of production and in prices. Use of so-
> called fixed prices for comparisons did not constitute a
> good tool for characterization of the physical growth of
> production. New products that did not exist in the pre-
> war period were calculated in fixed prices, i.e., in
> prices of 1937. In this situation, when all indicators
> used to set the premiums for enterprises were based on
> gross production, calculated in fixed prices, there
> emerged a natural incentive to raise these prices by
> introducing frequently spurious changes in product
> characteristics. Independently of the rises in fixed
> prices made by design, counting in 1937 prices yields
> an index of Laspeyre's which in the case of substantial
> structural changes in production in the direction of in-
> creasing the share of industrial products yields a one-
> sided picture of high growth rate. In such a case one

TABLE 5. 9

Goals and Fulfillment of the Six-Year Plan in Poland
(1949 = 100)

	Plan for 1955	Fulfillment in 1955
National income	212	175
Aggregate investments	240	236
Employment	160	156
Consumption per capita	150-160	130-144
Real wages	140	104-113
Industrial production	258	270[a] 201[b] 210[c]
Agricultural production	150	113[a] 118[b] 117[c]

[a] Gross production.
[b] Net production.
[c] Gross net production.

Source: Ryc 1968, pp. 60-61.

should use an average of Laspeyre' s and Paasche' s
indexes. All these remarks pertain also to indexes of
aggregate quantities in the area of consumption . . . .
In the area of consumption problems, there is a poignant
gap in statistical data for the plan period. Research on
family budgets of workers and other employees was
suspended. Nobody can reproduce now the indicator
of the cost of living. In consequence, the basic data
on production and consumption can be derived only in
the form of estimates. (Ryc 1968, pp. 59-60.)

In addition, it can be said that plan indicators are subject to
ambivalent interpretations, as in connection with the concept of production. Ryc summarized his own estimates of plan fulfillment in two
tables reproduced here as Table 5.9. It is interesting to note that
while the cost of the plan—in terms of employment and investments,
or in terms of what the society had to sacrifice in the toil of its workers and in renounced potential consumption—were close to what had
been planned, its results in terms of national income, consumption,
and real wages were substantially below plan. As will be demonstrated
below, even the surprisingly candid estimates of Ryc are likely to
have been overestimates of actual achievements of the plan period.

Table 5.9 merits a more thorough discussion for the sake of
understanding its background as well as the overestimates it contains.
Starting with the index successfully completed, that of investments,

one has to note that the overall investment plan for all six years
(1950-55) was overfulfilled by 0.2 percent, while within that period
the early years saw substantial overfulfillment and 1955 saw underfulfillment of the plan. Apart from this maldistribution in time, there
also was a sectoral maldistribution insofar as investment outlays for
industry were surpassed by 8.7 percent and for construction by 3.5
percent, while investment outlays were inadequate for agriculture by
14.3 percent, for forestry by 19 percent, for transport and communications by 17.7 percent, and for trade by 14.5 percent. Within those
sectors there was a similar maldistribution from the point of view of
planned shares. Thus, heavy industry had been supposed to receive
76 percent of aggregate investments in industry but it actually got
85 percent of those investments, while food industry received only
5.9 percent and textile industry 3.7 percent. What is more, given
investment outlays failed to deliver planned objects, only 62 percent
of which were completed in industry, with similar results likely in
other sectors. This was due to cost overruns, familiar also under the
capitalist system, and to longer-than-planned gestation periods of
different investment projects (excessively long time elapsing between
the start of projects and their completion). In addition, increments
of output from completed projects proved disappointing.

Investments and Employment

Private investments dropped precipitously below their 1949 level,
mainly because of a substantial drop in investment in private farming,
discouraged as it was by the forced progress of collectivization.
Table 5.10 shows the investment data for the Six-Year Plan period.
Accumulation (outlays on new capital and growth of inventories)
grew during the plan period to about one-third of national income.
The trend in accumulation is shown in Table 5.11. The increase in
the share of accumulation in national income reduced the share of
consumption and contributed to the phenomena discussed below.
The second index in Table 5.9 whose fulfillment approximated
the plan was that for employment outside agriculture. A mass movement of young peasants into urban occupations was the primary vehicle
of this result. Some of the peasants were able to commute to work
from their villages and they formed the fast-growing group of "peasant-
workers." Additionally, labor force participation rates increased as
the low level of living, due to stagnant or declining real wages, forced
more family members to seek employment. Most striking was the
increase in labor force participation rates among women, whose
employment in the socialized sector outside agriculture rose during
the plan period by 84 percent. Also by 1959 the young generation,
which suffered heavy losses during World War II, passed into higher

TABLE 5.10

Investments in Poland, 1950–55
(million zlotys in 1955 prices)

Year	In Socialized Sector (net)				In Private Sector (gross)	
	Plan	Fulfillment	Percentage of Plan Fulfillment	Index 1949 = 100	Fulfillment	Index 1949 = 100
1950	18,593	20,150	108.4	136	2,745	79
1951	23,761	24,318	102.3	165	1,022	28
1952	28,665	28,650	99.9	193	1,163	33
1953	32,219	33,109	102.8	223	1,174	34
1954	35,095	35,117	100.1	237	1,680	48
1955	38,578	35,942	93.2	242	1,660	48
1950–55	176,915	177,286	100.2	—	9,444	—

Source: Ryc 1968, p. 63.

TABLE 5.11

Share of Net Accumulation in Poland's National Income, 1949–55
(percentages; in 1950 prices)

	1949	1950	1951	1952	1953	1954	1955
Share of accumulation in national income	22.7	29.4	28.8	32.0	38.2	32.8	31.2

Source: GUS 1957, p. 47.

TABLE 5.12

Growth of Employment in Poland, 1949-55

	1949	1950	1951	1952	1953	1954	1955
Average employment (thousands)	4,354	5,155	5,631	5,893	6,272	6,515	6,779
Index 1949 = 100	100	118	129	135	144	150	156
Annual percentage growth over preceding year	16	18	9	5	6	4	4
Employment in socialized sector (thousands)	3,966	4,885	5,463	5,748	6,149	6,397	6,671
Employment in private sector (thousands)	388	270	168	145	123	118	108

Source: RS 1959, p. 44.

TABLE 5.13

Changes in Employment in Representative Investment Industries in Poland, 1949-55

	Thousands of Workers			Indexes	
	1949	1953	1955	1955/49	1955/53
Total	617.5	1,423.8	1,397.5	226.3	98.2
In that:					
Construction material industry	89.6	138.0	149.6	167.0	108.4
Construction	307.5	770.6	730.2	237.5	94.8
Machine-making industry	220.4	515.2	517.7	234.9	100.5

Source: Karpinski 1958, p. 107.

TABLE 5.14

Changes in Employment in Representative Consumer
Industries in Poland, 1949-55

	Thousands of Persons			Percentages	
	1949	1953	1955	1955/49	1955/53
Total:	8,341.2	8,111.8	8,373.3	100.4	103.2
In that:					
Industrial branches producing consumer goods	750.7	972.9	1,043.7	139.0	107.3
Handicraft	340.5	123.9	129.6	38.1	104.6
Agriculture	7,250.0	7,015.0	7,200.0	99.3	102.6

Source: Karpinski 1958, p. 108.

age brackets and the younger age cohorts, not decimated by the war, entered the labor force in large numbers. The largest percentage increases in employment took place in the last year of the preceding plan period and in 1950, as shown in Table 5.12. It should be noted that employment in the private sector outside agriculture declined by 72 percent (Hodoly 1966, p. 103), causing substantial inconvenience to consumers since that sector, mainly handicrafts, directed its production to the consumer. By 1955, however, employment in representative branches serving consumption increased as compared with 1949, as shown in Table 5.13, but the increase amounted to a trifling 0.4 percent due to the fact that the increase in employment in industrial branches catering to consumers was almost completely offset by a decrease in employment in handicraft and agriculture. These results underline the emphasis placed by planners on the expansion of the investment sector, at the cost of consumption.

During the last two years of the Six-Year Plan, however, the relative emphasis changed somewhat away from investments, as visible in the last column of Table 5.13. The last column of Table 5.14 gives additional depth to this observation: While employment in representative consumer goods industries increased between 1953 and 1955, employment in representative capital goods industries declined in that period, after scoring substantial accretions in preceding years.

It has been estimated that half a million of those employed during the plan period, or 20 percent of the newly employed, were superfluous (Karpinski 1958, p. 123), with zero marginal productivity. No wonder, then, that labor productivity was lagging, although—due to deep-rooted secretiveness pervading that period and the consequent scarcity of data—no reliable index of changes in labor productivity is extant. A high estimate, obtained on the basis of L. Zienkowski (1959, p. 203), indicates growth of net labor productivity in industry of 30 percent during the Six-Year Plan period. Another estimate put the same growth at less than 20 percent (Wilczewski 1963, p. 750). It is possible that actual labor productivity in industry grew by 20 to 30 percent, probably closer to the lower estimate, as compared with the planned growth of 66 percent. In other words, labor productivity probably lagged similarly behind planned increases.

Agriculture, Foreign Trade, and Industry

Agricultural production rose during the Six-Year Plan period by 13 percent, while population increased by 12 percent, resulting in stationary agricultural production per capita. Labor productivity in agriculture increased, however, by more than 13 percent because agricultural population actually declined between 1949 and 1955, and so did the agricultural labor force. Since agricultural production is, under Polish conditions, the single most important determinant of consumption, stagnation in its per capita production could not but exert a strong retarding influence on the standard of living. The only positive development in that sector was a relative shift to animal husbandry, which tended to improve the qualitative composition of the diet. During the Six-Year Plan period, however, Poland became increasingly dependent on imports of grains, from 189,000 tons in 1949 to 1,365,000 tons in 1955.

Stagnation in agriculture was attributable mainly to the forced socialization in that sector, which discouraged the remaining private holders of land from improvements, investments, and indeed from paying much care, and also introduced a less productive form of land holding. Thus, although use of fertilizers per acre was more than twice as high in the socialized sector of agriculture than in the private sector, yields per acre were smaller. The socialized sector also benefited from various priority deliveries, including those of agricultural implements, while net investments in private agriculture were close to zero or even negative. These greatly reduced investments in agriculture are the second reason for stagnation in agricultural production per capita. Deliveries of agricultural inputs from industry were substantially below plan, deliveries of fertilizers running at 53 to 77 percent of plan.

Developments in the area of foreign trade also reflected planners' priorities. Ryc cited an example from 1953, when scarcities of consumer goods made the planners drastically increase prices of consumer goods in January 1953, causing a decline in real wages. In the same year, however, exports of foodstuffs and raw materials for production of foodstuffs increased by $23 million (in 1955 prices), while imports of the same products decreased by $34 million as compared with 1952. At the same time, imports of machinery and equipment reached an apogee for the plan period of $319 million. Thus, until 1954 there was no doubt as to where planners' priorities lay. Table 15.5 shows that the growth of imports of consumer goods was lagging behind aggregate imports for the whole Six-Year Plan period, and that in 1952-53 such imports were lower than in 1949. Until 1955, the growth of exports of consumer goods was, on the other hand, equal to or larger than the growth of aggregate exports. Therefore, Polish consumers, felt the direct impact of changes in foreign trade as a setback to their aspirations. It should be noted, however, that statistics collected by Marer (1972) supply a different assessment of the direct role of foreign trade for the Polish consumer.

As far as domestic industrial production is concerned, the Six-Year Plan was seemingly overfulfilled since gross production rose by 170 percent while planned growth was 158 percent. But the tendency to inflate the "fixed" prices and the use of the Laspeyre's formula make this result doubtful. Some real accomplishments in industrial

TABLE 5. 15

Consumer Goods in Polish Foreign Trade, 1949-55
(millions of dollars, in 1955 prices)

	1949	1950	1951	1952	1953	1954	1955
Total imports	630.0	704.8	801.0	775.6	770.9	900.9	931.7
Index of total imports	100.0	111.9	127.1	123.1	122.4	143.0	147.9
Raw materials for light industry	228.3	218.9	211.3	169.6	173.0	204.4	220.7
Raw materials for agriculture	17.3	22.9	33.1	25.6	31.2	31.4	27.2
Foodstuffs and food- stuff raw materials	60.0	64.9	61.1	81.6	47.7	116.7	121.3
Industrial consumer goods	23.4	35.5	43.0	31.0	19.8	30.3	40.4
Total imports for consumption	329.0	342.2	348.5	307.8	371.7	382.8	409.6
Index of total imports for consumption	100.0	104.4	105.9	93.6	82.6	116.4	124.5
Total exports	654.2	735.0	690.9	690.7	784.6	881.8	920.0
Index of total exports	100.0	112.4	105.6	105.6	119.9	134.8	140.6
Food and raw materials for foodstuffs	101.8	119.8	115.5	110.0	142.3	152.6	140.9
Industrial consumer goods	51.8	67.8	48.4	52.2	63.4	74.4	66.6
Total exports for consumption	153.6	187.6	163.9	162.2	205.7	227.0	207.5
Index of total exports for consumption	100.0	122.1	106.7	105.6	133.9	147.8	135.1
Balance of trade in consumption goods	-175.4	-154.6	-184.6	-145.6	- 66.0	-155.8	-202.1
Balance of trade in consumption goods on the basis of Marer[a]	122.5	133.1	71.5	83.7	176.1	84.4	45.7

[a] Current prices.

Sources: Calculated by the author on the basis of Karpinski 1958, p. 135, and Marer 1972, pp. 49, 58.

TABLE 5. 16

1950–55 Plan Achievements in Poland as a
Percentage of Planned Production

| | Production in: | |
	1955	Aggregate 1950–55
Pig iron	89	92
Steel	97	99
Coal	95	99
Electricity	92	95
Sulfuric acid	83	82
Cement	77	82

Source: Ryc 1968, pp. 86–87.

production are shown in Table 5. 16. Underfulfillment of the plan in
basic industrial raw materials, revealed by that table, indicates that
the plan was probably underfulfilled in the industry as a whole.

The growth of production in the consumer goods industry, with
1949 equal to 100, reached by 1955 an index number of 243. 5. Again,
however, objections similar to those pertaining to the all-industry
index may be registered, both of them probably stronger with regard
to this sector than with regard to the capital goods sector. In addition,
Ryc listed two other factors tending to deflate the above index figure:

1. The increasing degree of processing of products like meat,
butter, and milk added to their value and caused the index to rise
without adding to the quantity of basic foodstuffs.

2. The index number of 243. 5 for 1955 concerns the output of
socialized industry but during the Six-Year Plan production of consumer
goods from private industry and handicrafts fell considerably, so much
of the statistical increase represented only replacement of production
from the private sector by production from the socialized sector.
Table 5. 17 shows that even so, except for tobacco and sole leather,
the 1955 production of important consumer goods was below plan.
Foodstuffs made a bad showing because of setbacks in agriculture,
inadequate investments (including investments in food processing),
and disruptions caused by the changeover from private to socialized
ownership. Industrial raw materials for the production of consumer
goods (measured in physical terms to avoid one of the reasons for
exaggeration in official indexes) had, on the whole, less ambitious

TABLE 5.17

Production of Some Basic Consumer Goods in Poland
in 1955 Compared with Plan

	Index for 1955 (1949 = 100)	Percentage of Fulfillment of Plan for 1955
Meat	137.4	66.1
Animal fats	144.4	65.5
Sea fish (catch)	180.6	59.5
Milk for consumption	212.5	73.3
Butter	268.5	52.8
Milled cereals	197.2	73.3
Sugar	131.6	89.1
Beer	213.3	86.2
Industrial tobacco	190.6	103.4
Cotton yarn	127.1	88.1
Wool yarn	138.7	97.4
Paper	151.7	75.9
Hard leather	122.0	110.9
Soft leather	188.6	98.9
Dress	170	57

Source: GUS 1956, pp. 44-66, after Ryc 1968, pp. 88-89; the table covers socialized industry.

plan goals; hence their degree of plan underfulfillment was less than in the case of foodstuffs. However, their manufacturing into final consumer goods tended to be increasingly inferior; hence, the raw indexes provided in Table 5.17 tend to exaggerate the availability of consumer goods.

Changes in Consumption

Official statistics on the growth of national income and consumption are presented in Table 5.18. The increase in accumulation up to 1953 was higher than planned and contributed to the overfulfillment of the plan for that category for the plan period as a whole. Table 5.18 also reveals two distinct subperiods of the plan: (1) during 1950-53, accumulation was unduly high, which tended to curb consumption; (2) during 1954-55, accumulation actually decreased, allowing consumption to grow.

TABLE 5.18

Growth of National Income in Poland, 1949–55
(index numbers, in 1956 prices)

	1949	1950	1951	1952	1953	1954	1955
National income (distributed)	100	115	124	132	145	161	175
Consumption	100	108	117	121	125	147	161
Accumulation	100	153	162	193	261	240	252
Per capita:							
National income (distributed)	100	113	120	125	135	147	157
Consumption	100	107	113	114	116	134	144
Personal consumption	100	107.	112	114	116	134	143
Other consumption	100	109	121	116	114	134	162

Source: RS 1959, p. 58.

However, the mistakes of the first subperiod could not have been made up by the policies of the second subperiod.

It should be realized that the investment policy of the Six-Year Plan favored construction of new plants, resulting in increments of production lower than from equivalent investment on modernization or expansion of existing plants. Investments also were unduly spread out, which led to a high incremental capital/output ratio (Karpinski 1958, pp. 82-83, 88). Thus, when it came to expanding production of consumer goods in 1954-55, the productive potential of the existing facilities was less than it could have been. As a result, consumers failed to experience improvement in their level of living that could have been possible. Commenting on the growth in per capita consumption, shown in Table 5.18 as amounting to 44 percent during the Six-Year Plan period, Ryc voiced an opinion that such growth "is without doubt overstated" (Ryc 1968, p. 95). The overstatement was the result of assortment changes, hidden price increases, and an increasing degree of manufacturing of consumer goods (cf. Brzeski 1964, pp. 70-76).

The Polish Main Statistical Office undertook a recalculation of the index number of 143 for per capita personal consumption in 1955, with 1949 equal to 100, shown in Table 5.18. It took certain homogeneous foodstuffs and industrial goods that did not experience quality changes, and for which the income elasticity of demand was near average. It then found that the quantity index for these goods was about 10 percent lower than the index of consumption based on national income statistics. Correcting the 143 index figure by this percentage yields an index figure of less than 130.

To the extent that new products were not included in that recalculation, its result may be marginally lower than the "true" index. In order to give a better illustration of general consumption trends, I selected some important commodities for Table 5.19. Ryc drew the following conclusions from the same data:

1. During 1950-55, all important consumer goods showed substantial increase. Consumption of cereals increased comparatively little, indicating an improvement in the structure of consumption.

2. With the exception of cereals, consumption of all articles was higher than in 1949 throughout the Six-Year Plan period. Thus the improvement in consumption that took place in 1950 more than offset its deterioration in 1952-53 (cf. Przelaskowski 1960, p. 128).

3. Figures for individual products confirm the conviction rooted among the population that the standard of living declined during 1952-53. This contrasts with the official aggregate index of per capita consumption, shown in Table 5.18, which increased by one point in 1952 and two points in 1953. Such a comparison further tends to undermine the credibility of official aggregate figures.

TABLE 5.19

Per Capita Consumption of Some Basic Products in Poland, 1949–55

	1949	1950	1951	1952	1953	1954	1955	1955/49
Cereal products (kg)	163	166	160	161	163	166	171	104.9
Meat and fats (kg)	32.3	42.7	42.5	37.9	40.7	41.9	43.8	135.6
Milk and products (liters)	279	293	319	313	311	323	332	119.0
Eggs (number)	116	116	127	130	125	135	137	118.1
Fish (kg)	1.7	1.7	1.8	2.3	2.1	2.5	2.7	158.8
Sugar (kg)	19.3	21.0	24.9	22.4	19.9	22.4	24.0	124.4
Cotton fabrics (m)	13.3	14.4	16.1	15.7	15.1	16.0	16.5	124.1
Woolen fabrics (m)	1.8	2.1	2.2	2.3	2.3	2.2	2.5	138.9
Silk fabrics (m)	1.8	1.9	2.4	2.6	2.2	2.5	2.8	155.6
Footwear (leather tops, pair)	.5	.6	.8	.8	.8	.9	.9	180.0
Paper (kg)	9.8	11.1	11.8	11.6	10.9	11.9	12.9	131.6
Soap (kg)	1.7	1.9	2.3	1.9	1.8	1.9	2.1	123.5
Detergent (kg)	1.3	2.0	3.0	2.1	1.9	2.5	3.2	146.2

Source: RS 1965, p. 483.

Since the 1950-55 period witnessed substantial shifts of population from rural to urban areas and occupations, it is important to consider the effect of those shifts on consumption. Table 5.20 shows in part the estimate of the Planning Commission at the Council of Ministers of the division of the population between agricultural and nonagricultural. During the Six-Year Plan period, over one million members of the labor force left agriculture for nonagricultural employment, mostly in industry (Karpinski 1958, p. 118); the total shift, taking into account a higher birth rate among agricultural population, amounted to over 1.5 million.

The second part of Table 5.20 contains an approximative estimate by Ryc of the growth of consumption among both groups of the population, based on consumption of animal products. The table shows that consumption of food among the agricultural population experienced slower growth, although during the 1951-53 period the decline in food consumption also was lower among the agricultural population. However, the table, concentrating as it does on animal products produced by farmers, does not reflect the adverse effects of low-price compulsory deliveries from farmers, introduced in 1951 as a result of a decline in agricultural production. Nor does the table reflect the adverse effects of the price hike in consumer goods and agricultural inputs, with the latter increasing in price from an index number of 100 in 1950 to 240.8 in 1953. The peasants reacted to this price increase by decreasing their investments in order to maintain their level of consumption, and this fact explains the lesser effect on agricultural consumption of the developments in 1951-53.

It is instructive to calculate the effect of the population shift by itself on consumption. Ryc estimated that during the 1950-55 plan period consumption per capita in agriculture was an average of 30 percent lower than consumption outside agriculture. On that assumption, and using the population data from Table 5.20, I found that without any increase in per capita consumption within each group the consumption level for the population as a whole would have risen by 20 percent, and per capita consumption by 7 percent, just because of the shift of population from the lower-consumption group of agricultural population to the higher-consumption group of nonagricultural population. One should then decrease by this figure of 7 percent the 30 percent increase in per capita consumption derived above to obtain the estimate of 23 percent increase in per capita consumption within agricultural and nonagricultural population taken as an average of both. This figure may be regarded as average perceived increase in consumption per person although as noted above, the increase for the agricultural population tended to be lower while the increase for nonagricultural population tended to be higher. It also should be noted that the main beneficiaries of the improved level of living tended to be those very people who moved away from agriculture, particularly since the average number of dependants in that group was markedly lower than the average for the

TABLE 5.20

Agricultural and Nonagricultural Population in Poland,
and Growth of Consumption

(thousands of persons and index numbers in fixed prices)

	1949	1950	1951	1952	1953	1954	1955
Total population	24,601	25,039	25,512	26,007	26,510	27,020	27,580
Agricultural population	11,900	11,540	11,576	11,640	11,710	11,760	11,780
Nonagricultural population	12,701	13,499	13,936	14,367	14,800	15,260	15,800
Index of consumption of goods per member of non-agricultural population	100	123	112	110	116	121	..
Index of animal consumption per member of nonagricultural population	100	134	122	116	124	126	..
Index of animal consumption per member of agricultural population	100	107	104	105	108	108	..

Source: Ryc 1968, pp. 104, 110.

population as a whole. However, there was a group in the population that presumably suffered a noticeable decline in real earnings: the former participants in private crafts, professions, private trade, and private industry. Inclusion of that group in the index would tend to decrease it, but quantitative data for such an inclusion are totally lacking.

Changes in Real Wages

The trend of real wages outside agriculture is hard to estimate because the cost of living was not calculated during the Six-Year Plan; it is now difficult to reproduce such an index, if only because of changes in the structure of consumption, and hence in relative weights of different consumption categories, because of hidden price increases, influence of market scarcities on involuntary changes in the pattern of expenditures by the population, changes in the quality of goods, and changes in the degree of manufacturing (cf. Ryc 1968, p. 114).

An approximate index of real wages is nevertheless provided in Table 5.21. The table shows a decline in real wages during 1951-53, due basically to a drop in workers' purchasing power with regard to food. That purchasing power did not recover its 1950 level even by 1955, although it must be said that it did improve drastically in 1954 from its 1953 nadir. The purchasing power with regard to industrial consumer goods rose substantially, although the availability of those goods was highly inadequate. That availability was partly supplemented by sales in private stores and on the peasant markets, at much higher prices —for which an index is not available and presumably will never be reconstructed. The result of use of such an index would be to decrease the overall index of real wages. The index also omits purchases of services, housing, and utilities, whose impact on a more complete index is unknown.

An index of real wages published by Kucharski (without indication as to the methodology he used) is shown in Table 5.22. Applying it to an approximate chain calculation, with 1949 equal to 100, we obtain for 1954-55 a low index number of real wages of 99 and a high index number of 111. Ryc rejected the lower figure on the basis of a comparison between the increase in consumption by the population and the increase in employment. He assumed realistically that the margin of savings during the Six-Year Plan was negligible—that is, that wages equaled spending on consumption. He then recalled his estimate of the overall rise in per capita consumption to an index number of 135 for 1955, with 1949 equal 100, and to an index number of 130 for nonagricultural population, obtained from an adjustment for changed structure of agricultural to nonagricultural population. However, he then rejected the index figure of 130 as not reflecting the effect of rising employment and rising real wages on the ground that

TABLE 5.21

Ratio of the Index of Average Money Wages to the Index of
Retail Prices of Goods Bought by Households from
Socialized Trade in Poland, 1949–55

	1949	1950	1951	1952	1953	1954	1955
Total	100	112.0	111.6	108.7	104.8	119.5	122.5
Foodstuffs	100	113.4	116.1	103.8	91.2	101.8	106.4
Industrial goods	100	110.6	137.1	113.0	119.8	138.9	153.8

Source: Beskid 1962, p. 64, after Ryc 1968, p. 114.

TABLE 5. 22

Index of Real Wages in Poland

Year	Index
Over Two Year Periods	
1950-51	
(1949 = 100)	108-112
1952-53	
(1951 = 100)	80-84
1954-55	
(1953 = 100)	114-118
Selected Years	
1949	100
1952	96
1953	87
1955	109

Sources: Kucharski 1964, p. 372, after Ryc 1968, p. 115; Beskid 1972, p. 48.

in 1955 the share of the population engaged in the private sector was lower than in 1949 and that, consequently, more of the rise in consumption was attributable to the rise in real wages in socialized employment. On this point he seems to have neglected the fact that the part of the labor force employed outside the socialized sector in 1949 found later employment within that sector; such change therefore was reflected in employment figures for the socialized sector. Ryc then corrected the index number of 130 to 135 as showing the true rise in consumption outside agriculture due to the rise in employment and real wages. The growth of nonagricultural population, 1949 equal to 100, was by 1955 equal to 124. Multiplying both indexes, Ryc obtained an index of growth of aggregate consumption by nonagricultural population for 1955 as 167. 4. Since employment outside agriculture rose to an index number of 161, with 1949 equal to 100, and since a rise of 61 percent is thus attributable to the rise in employment, a small part of the rise in consumption is attributable to a rise in real wages, that part amounting to just under 4 percent. Ryc consequently accepted the index number of 104 as one that "indicates well the scale of increase in real wage" (Ryc 1968, pp. 117-18).

As indicated above, I regard part of Ryc's procedure as unwarranted. Apart from the objection listed in the preceding paragraph, Ryc used monthly or annual wage figures that do not reflect the impact of

rising overtime work; the incidence of such overtime, some of it
"voluntarily" unpaid, was rising during the Six-Year Plan period. If,
as seems preferable, an index number of 130 is used to reflect the
growth of per capita consumption between 1949 and 1955 (and arguments
have been presented here for using a lower index figure), then the
aggregate growth of consumption becomes 61 percent, which—with
the rise in employment of 61 percent—yields a zero rise in real wages.
I regard that as the upper limit of my own estimate. Indicentally, both
estimates, Ryc's and my own, indicate a relative improvement in real
per worker income in agriculture as compared with nonagriculture.

Both estimates also indicate that for the large majority of workers
the Six-Year Plan period did not result in an improvement in real wage,
but possibly the reverse. Any increases in real wages were due to
improvement in qualifications of the labor force thanks to a prodigious
educational effort, and to changes in the occupational structure away
from low-wage industries (such as textiles) and toward high-wage
industries (such as iron, steel, and machine making). It also may be
that average real wages seem to have risen in high-wage groups of
workers but fallen in low-wage groups. The former group influenced
the calculated average real wage index more than the latter because
of larger absolute numbers involved in the rise of its wages (Krencik
1961, p. 96, after Hodoly 1966, p. 110). The extensive policy of
growth adopted during the Six-Year Plan period undoubtedly contributed
to the stagnation of real wages. Productivity per worker was disappointing, and consequently the planners felt that no rise in real wages could
be afforded.

Households with an increased number of working members experienced an improvement in level of living, but those that relied on the
same number of breadwinners were likely to experience a decline.
These factors, taken in conjunction with exaggerated promises of a
40 percent increase in real wages made at the onset of the Six-Year
Plan, partly explain the general dissatisfaction among the population
with the achievements of the plan insofar as its impact on them. The
popular reaction was to seek relief in black market activity and in the
widespread theft from the state. One author, familiar with Polish
conditions, regarded "thieving [as] the functional disease of the
national economy" and thought that such thieving had been "raised
to the rank of a social institution" (Malecki 1960, p. 97).

Hodoly, an economist less independent of official statistics than
Ryc, concluded in his study on consumption: "The average real wage
was in 1955 only 13 percent higher than in 1949, and even that result
was achieved largely due to [increasing] overtime work. This was
the result of a fall of real wages during 1951-53. . . ." (Hodoly 1966,
pp. 108-09.) In a footnote, Hodoly explained that the indicator of 13
percent "corrected an earlier estimate by the Main Statistical Office,
according to which the rise in real wages during the Six-Year Plan was
supposed to have been 27.6 percent (on the base of 1949), which estimate evoked a general skepticism. . . ." (Hodoly 1966, p. 108 n. 88.)

As noted above, the Six-Year Plan envisaged a growth in real wages of 40 percent, the 27.6 percent figure having been announced as the realization of the plan. The correction of that official claim of plan fulfillment had a checkered history. Hilary Minc, the czar of Polish economy during the Six-Year Plan period, defended the official version of plan accomplishment before the party activ as late as December 1955. In February 1956, well into what was later described as "the thaw" period of questioning, criticism, and ferment that led to the Poznan uprising of workers in the summer and the changeover of the Communist Party leadership in October 1956, Wlodzimierz Brus, a noted economist, published in the daily Zycie Warszawy (February 2, 3, 5-6, 7, 9, 1956) a series of five articles under the title "About Real Wages During the Six-Year Plan" in which he articulately defended the official figure as resulting from "as scrupulous calculations as possible," although he did reduce the figure to 26 to 27 percent. At the end of the fifth article, the editors of Zycie Warszawy mentioned the large number of comments and questions evoked by the Brus series and expressed hope that their number would increase. Later, however, no comments or questions were published and the curtain of defense by silence was drawn around the Brus series. Despite this, Brus became the laughingstock of fellow economists; in his next contribution to Zycie Warszawy, in the form of an interview published on May 7, 1958, he showed himself sensitive to criticism when he remarked, "I see that I am again suspected of varnishing." (Italics added.) Parenthetically, the interview just mentioned was part of a cycle entitled "Legends and Reality."

The official claim was finally corrected by Andrzej Karpinski, who stated:

> Despite the 40 percent rise of real wages assumed in the plan, in reality no perceptive increase in real wages was achieved, and in comparison with 1949 real wages of certain groups of population suffered a certain decline. (Karpinski 1958, p. 7.)

The same author, in a book published six years later at a time when power was already firmly consolidated in the hands of Wladyslaw Gomulka, the new leader brought to power in October 1956, simply omitted that sensitive question, presumably in order not to undermine confidence in official pronouncements (Karpinski 1964).

It is possible that the estimate made by Ryc and discussed above contributed to the disappearance of his book from bookstores, conceivably even before its sale began, and to the fact that its re-publication is "not contemplated" (personal information).

The Six-Year Plan was, therefore, not successful in terms of promised changes in the level of living. Whatever achievements it did accomplish in the realm of changing the structure of the economy were obtained at a very high cost in terms of sacrifice of effort and forgone consumption. Consumption performed the function of a shock absorber. According to Stefan Kurowski:

> The level of living of the population was that "soft cushion" which neutralized all consequences, disturbances and errors of the system of administration of the economy . . . . And just the level of living of the population became the foremost test which showed that the economic experience of the period of the Six-Year Plan, experience with the system of administering [the economy], failed the exam. It ended with a glaring misfortune in the realization of the foremost goal of socialist economy. Lack of growth in the level of living of the population during six years that witnessed a two-and-a-half-fold rise in production . . . testifies to enormous social costs. . . . (Kurowski 1957b, pp. 290-91.)

This result may evoke some skepticism about forced, regimented industrialization of the kind that was prevalent during the Stalinist period of Polish economic history.

CONSUMPTION REVOLT DURING THE 1956-60 PLAN PERIOD

Several versions of the 1956-60 Five-Year Plan were worked out during the period 1955-57. The final guidelines for the plan were formulated during the Seventh Plenum of the Central Committee of the Communist Party in July 1956. The resolution of the Plenum stressed the goal of raising the standard of living. In view of the experience of the preceding plan, during which consumption was regarded as a "shock absorber in the economy," the resolution stated that, in case of a conflict between the postulates of increasing living standards and the other plan indicators, the latter ought to be adjusted to the former. The detailed work on the plan was based on this resolution, but before the final version of the plan was approved a political upheaval, often referred to as the Polish October Revolution, took place and forced its imprint on the plan (Secomski 1958, pp. 7-8).

The October Revolution had its roots in the post-Stalinist thaw of 1955-56, featuring intellectual ferment and expressions of widespread dissatisfaction with the level of living. (Lewis 1958, pp. 55-90, 139-62; Gibney 1959, pp. 88-121, 215-55). The Poznan popular riots by workers in June 1956 gave cause to much soul searching; in October of that year, under strong popular pressure, the leadership of the Communist Party was entrusted to Wladyslaw Gomulka, recently released from prison where he had been sent under accusation of

TABLE 5. 23

Plan and Fulfillment of Growth of National Income and
Production in Poland for 1960
(1955 = 100)

	Plan for 1960	Fulfillment in 1960
National income produced	145.7	137.4
National income distributed	144.7	139.3
Personal consumption	145.5	135.5
Other consumption	132.8	150.1
Accumulation	146.4	148.3
In that: net investments	155.4	154.6
increase in inven-		
tories and reserves	128.4	135.3
Gross production of socialized		
industry	149.0	159.4
In that: investment goods		
(group A)	150.6	166.3
consumer goods		
(group B)	147.4	151.9
Gross agricultural production	123.7	120.2

Source: Ryc 1968, p. 124.

"nationalist deviationism." The Communist Party apparatus, although
badly shaken and subject to some personnel changes, did not relin-
quish power; after a temporary spell of liberalization, it slowly tight-
ened its grip on intellectual and economic life. The 1956-60 plan
period witnessed these shifts, and they wrought their mark on its
course.

Considerable discussion on the model of the Polish economy followed the October events. It centered on the problem of improving
administration of the economy and on prices and their determination.
Dissatisfaction with the consumption performance during the Six-Year
Plan contributed significantly to the "model discussion," but the discussion itself had little effect on the determination of consumption
and its share in national income. Consequently, although the subject
is important from the point of view of its contribution to the theory of
socialist economy, it will be omitted from the present study (see
Montias 1962, pp. 272ff).

The final version of the Five-Year Plan was approved in July 1957,
a year and a half after its nominal start. By that time, events had
overtaken the planners and it had been realized that personal income

per capita would grow by 20 percent during 1956-57. However, the originally planned rise of 30 percent for the Five-Year Plan period was retained, imposing a much reduced rate of growth of personal income during the final three years of the plan. Much was made at the time, and for that matter until 1970, of the requisite to maintain market equilibrium. In the context of 1957, it was feared that the quickly expanding purchasing power would cause inflationary phenomena and jeopardize other plan goals.

Table 5.23 compares the goals of the plan for 1960 with actual achievements. It shows that the actual growth of national income, consumption, and investments was less than planned, and that inventories increased by more than planned. Among the indicators of production, it shows that the planned production of capital goods was overfulfilled while production of consumer goods was underfulfilled (a picture familiar from the preceding plan period), and that agricultural production was lagging behind plan. This performance pattern, despite the overall high rates of growth, seems unsatisfactory even in terms of official statistics, to which an independent check will be applied in the last section of this chapter.

Investments and Employment

The first two years of the plan period were dominated by a surge in consumption, continuing a trend established during the last two years of the preceding plan. Therefore, investments during those two first plan years were lagging. The year 1955 showed a small rise in investments in productive capital, as shown in Table 5.10 above, and total accumulation for the following two years was planned to be less than in 1955. However, in 1957, owing to a surge in inventories, accumulation showed an unexpected rise. Table 5.24 shows the course of accumulation during the plan period. It becomes apparent that investments show an increasing trend up to 1959. The drop in 1960 was associated with a decline in the growth of national income since, as shown in Table 5.24, the proportion of investments in national income did not decline and the proportion of accumulation increased. Some of that increase was in the form of unplanned piling up of inventories and reserves due to incorrect structure of production and low quality of some products.

Accumulation was higher than planned for the plan period as a whole, the excess mainly taking the form of unplanned increases in inventories. Within the category of investments, the relative emphasis changed as compared with the preceding Six-Year Plan, as shown in Table 5.25. Investments in capital goods industries showed a relative decline, investments in consumer goods industries a relative increase, and so did investments in construction and agriculture. A decrease in

TABLE 5.24

Plan and Fulfillment of Accumulation in Poland, 1955-60
(billion zlotys in 1956 prices)

	1955	1956	1957	1958	1959	1960	1956-60
Accumulation Plan	52.6	51.4	50.0	60.1	69.7	77.0	308.2
Fulfillment	51.7	50.8	63.0	65.0	71.3	76.6	328.7
Fulfillment over (under) plan	-.9	-.6	13.0	4.9	1.4	-.4	18.5
Net investment[a]							
Fulfillment	65.7	68.6	73.5	80.7	94.4	100.0	417.2
Fulfillment over (under) plan	-.1	-.1	2.2	-.6	1.7	-.5	2.7
Annual rates of growth of investments over preceding year (percent)[b]	4.0	4.7	7.8	10.3	16.6	5.9	..
Increase in inventories and reserves: Fulfillment over (under) plan	-.8	-.5	10.8	5.5	-.1	.1	15.8
Accumulation as percentage of national income[c]	23	21	23	23	23	24	..
Investment as percentage of national income[c]	15	14	14	15	17	17	..

[a]Socialized and private sectors, 1961 prices.
[b]Socialized and private sectors, 1971 prices.
[c]1961 prices.

Sources: Ryc 1968, p. 150; RS 1965, p. 89; RS 1972, pp. 126, 135.

TABLE 5.25

Gross Investments in Five-Year Plan, 1956-60
(billion zlotys, 1956 prices)

	Plan for 1956-60	Fulfillment in 1956-60	Percentage of Plan Fulfillment	Index number (1951-55 = 100)	Structure of Investment Outlays	
					1951-55	1954-60
Aggregate investments	300.2	308.2	102.7	146.4	100.0	100.0
"Productive" investments	205.3	212.2	103.4	138.9	72.6	68.9
Industry	120.0	128.0	106.7	132.9	45.7	41.6
Capital goods	100.9	105.8	104.9	124.0	40.5	29.1
Consumer goods	19.1	22.2	116.2	202.3	5.2	13.9
Construction	8.2	8.9	108.5	193.5	2.2	2.9
Agriculture	40.1	34.6	86.3	190.1	8.6	11.3
Forestry	1.1	1.0	90.0	125.0	.4	.3
Transport and communications	27.7	29.7	107.2	115.1	12.3	9.6
Trade	8.2	10.0	122.0	140.5	3.4	3.2
"Unproductive" investments	94.9	96.0	101.2	166.4	27.4	31.1
Local utilities	13.0	13.2	101.5	158.1	3.9	4.3
Housing construction	57.8	57.7	99.8	221.1	12.4	18.7
Social and cultural objects	19.7	20.8	105.6	185.7	5.3	6.7

Source: Szerwentke 1962, p. 29.

117

the relative importance of investments in trade, however small, did have a negative effect on the standard of living. On the other hand, increased relative importance of investments in utilities and local administration, housing, and social and cultural objects was, from the point of view of the level of living, desirable.

Desirable also was a new emphasis in the distribution of investments. Instead of the broad-front approach of the Six-Year Plan, the new plan concentrated on bottlenecks in production, and on machines rather than new buildings; both these policies tended to lower the incremental capital/output ratio. On the other hand, a somewhat retarding effect was exerted by the relative concentration of investments on primary industries—extractive industries and agriculture, both with high incremental capital/output ratios. Nevertheless, the overall effect was to lower the aggregate incremental capital/output ratio. However, serious shortcomings were present in the field of investments in the form of overly long gestation periods of projects undertaken, as well as 20 to 30 percent cost overruns. It has been estimated that, even though investment outlays in industry were almost 7 percent higher than planned, only 75 to 85 percent of planned increase in capacity actually was achieved (Ryc 1968, p. 156).

The planned increase in employment was not realized. Table 5.26 reveals that the employment plan was not fulfilled in all sectors of the economy, except for local utilities and the housing sector, where it was just achieved, and finance and insurance. According to Rajkiewicz this was primarily because the employment plan was overly ambitious in promising jobs to all those released from the armed forces and from security services after October 1956 (Rajkiewicz 1965, p. 135). However, the actual number of entrants into the labor force apparently was smaller than expected for several reasons:

1. A demographic low decreased the annual growth of the labor force from 140,000 in 1956 to 65,000 in 1958. Expected immigration from outside, mainly the return of Poles from the Soviet Union, was smaller than expected.

2. The increase in real incomes in agriculture diminished migration of labor from agriculture into other sectors, while the increase of real incomes in urban areas tended to abate the trend toward higher labor force participation rates among women.

3. An improvement in pensions, whose purchasing power had declined during the Six-Year Plan, enabled more persons to retire.

The demand for labor also was sluggish, for the following reasons:

1. A conscious effort was undertaken to whittle down the overgrown administration.

2. The overemployment of possibly half a million induced during the preceding plan period was, according to some, eliminated. Labor discipline was markedly stricter beginning with 1958.

118

TABLE 5.26

Plan and Fulfillment in Employment in Socialized Sector in Poland, 1956–60
(thousands of employees)

	Employment in 1955	Planned Increase in Employment	Employment in 1960	Achieved Increase	Actual Increase in Employment Over (Under) Plan
Total	6,498	1,273	7,103	605	-668
Agriculture and forestry	613	15	544	-69	-94
Industry	2,691	626	2,986	295	-331
Construction	730	107	788	58	-49
Transport and communications	562	136	655	93	-43
Trade	653	162	719	66	-96
Urban utilities and housing	132	78	210	78	0
Social and cultural objects	598	207	779	181	-26
Administration and justice	330	-42	231	-81	-39
Finance and insurance	52	-5	57	5	+10
Other	157	-11	134	-24	-13

Source: Rajkiewicz 1965, p. 143.

TABLE 5.27

Annual Changes in Employment Outside Agriculture
and in Labor Productivity in Industry, 1956–60

	1956	1957	1958	1959	1960
Changes in employment outside agriculture (thousands)	232	125	29	199	89
Preceding year = 100	103.9	102.0	100.5	103.2	101.4
Changes in employment in socialized industry, preceding year = 100	104.2	102.8	100.5	101.2	100.6
Changes in labor productivity in socialized industry, preceding year = 100	104.4	102.8	108.8	108.3	111.4

Sources: Ryc 1968, p. 162; Hodoly 1966, p. 98.

3. The basic work crews for plants completed during the preceding plan period had already been hired, so new jobs had to be created, by and large, through new investments.

4. According to some sources, fluctuations in production that characterized the earlier period, termed shturmovshchina in the Soviet Union, decreased as a result of improved deliveries of raw materials. (Personally I am skeptical about this point; see Mieczkowski 1967b.)

5. Labor productivity increased more than planned.

Table 5.27 shows annual changes in employment outside agriculture and changes in labor productivity in industry during 1956-60. The increases in employment are strikingly small compared to the preceding plan period (see Table 5.12 above). It also is interesting to note that in the socialized industry a smaller percentage rise in employment from 1958 onward was associated with markedly stepped up increases in labor productivity.

Labor productivity in industry rose by 1960 to an index number of 144 (133 for net production), with 1955 taken as 100, as compared with the planned increase to 127, and accounted for 83 percent of the rise in production. In construction, the actual increase was to an index number of 125 (132 for net production), compared to 124 planned, and it accounted for almost 50 percent of the rise in production for that sector. Average annual rise in net labor productivity was almost 6 percent in industry and construction; during the preceding plan period it was about 3.8 percent in industry. The small increase in employment, the tightening of labor discipline which started in 1958, and the comparatively large increases in labor productivity all form a consistent picture of the economy passing a somewhat chaotic early phase of expansion and settling down to a more ordered and efficiency-conscious growth. It also may be suggested that the increase in real wages and per capita consumption that characterized 1956 and 1957 helped to raise labor productivity by providing better incentives.

Agriculture, Foreign Trade, and Industry

Agricultural production staged a good performance during the 1956-60 period, as shown in Table 5.28. Especially worth noting in the table are the indicators of per hectare and per capita production, both of which rose markedly. The per capita production of crops, important as a determinant of per capita consumption, rose from a nadir of less than 92 percent of 1949 in 1955 to approximate equality with 1949 by 1960. It is possible that, had this result not been achieved, the dissolution of cooperatives and the re-privatization of land undertaken in 1956 would have been revoked. Good agricultural performance also was

TABLE 5.28

Gross Production of Polish Agriculture, 1955-60
(1949 = 100)

	1955	1956	1957	1958	1959	1960
Aggregate production	113.0	121.4	126.4	130.2	128.9	135.9
Per hectare of agricultural land	113.2	121.6	126.6	130.4	129.2	136.2
Per capita in population	101.1	106.6	109.0	110.4	107.6	111.7
Production of crops	102.6	110.9	113.0	115.3	113.7	122.7
Per hectare of agricultural land	102.8	111.1	113.2	115.6	113.9	122.9
Per capita in population	91.8	97.4	97.4	97.9	94.9	100.8
Animal production	133.1	141.6	152.3	158.8	158.4	161.4
Per hectare of agricultural land	133.4	141.8	152.6	159.1	158.7	161.7
Per capita in population	119.1	124.3	131.3	134.7	132.2	132.6

Source: RS 1965, p. 216.

121

TABLE 5.29

Changes in Poland's Foreign Trade, 1948-60
(in constant 1960 prices; preceding year = 100)

	Trade turnover	Imports	Exports
1948	154	144	163
1949	123	132	115
1950	120	115	124
1951	104	118	92
1952	99	94	104
1953	108	102	114
1954	109	117	101
1955	103	104	102
1956	104	110	98
1957	108	119	95
1958	113	104	128
1959	113	115	111
1960	110	105	116

Source: RS 1965, p. 334.

more likely than anything else to produce a modicum of
support for the Communist policies at home. The average
family in Poland devoted over 50 percent of its total budget
to expenditures for food: any shortage could have only
one effect, namely, an increase in passive resistance to
the Government. (Korbonski 1965, p. 300.)

An additional help to raising the level of consumption was received
during 1956-60 from the foreign trade sector. Substantial loans from
the United States for purchase of agricultural products under Public
Law 480 enabled Poland to supply increased foodstuffs to its consumers,
which contributed to raising consumption and maintaining market equilibrium. Table 5.29 compares the growth of imports and exports, for
the sake of perspective, over a longer period. The table shows that
during the first two years of the 1956-60 plan the tendency was for
imports to grow faster than exports, but that tendency was reversed
during the last three years of the plan period, leaving relatively fewer
goods for domestic use.

Table 5.30 shows the distribution of imports and exports between
the major categories. It reveals a major rise in food imports in 1957
and 1959, and a major rise in imports of consumer goods of industrial
origin in 1958. It also shows a decline in exports of food between
1955 and 1956-57, and a decline in exports of consumer goods of

TABLE 5.30

Polish Foreign Trade by Major Commodity Groups, 1955-60

(current prices; 1956 = 100)

	1955[a]	1956	1957	1958	1959	1960
Imports						
Machinery and equipment	121.4	100	87.6	96.5	115.0	119.4
Fuels and raw materials	97.4	100	133.8	133.2	138.7	154.9
Food and agricultural products	91.7	100	175.8	108.7	194.1	192.8
Industrial consumer goods	67.8	100	115.8	166.3	161.7	131.2
Total	103.0	100	122.5	120.1	138.9	146.3
Exports						
Machinery and equipment	79.6	100	126.7	184.6	195.8	241.3
Fuels and raw materials	108.0	100	94.7	85.8	89.3	92.5
Food and agricultural products	125.9	100	106.9	155.2	181.3	208.0
Industrial consumer goods	71.8	100	70.8	66.1	84.4	152.1
Total	102.4	100	99.0	107.6	116.3	134.6
Balance of trade in consumer goods on basis of Marer[b]	45.7	17.2	-104.0	-.7	-57.5	53.5

[a] 1956 prices.
[b] Millions of dollars at current prices.

Sources: RS 1959, pp. 251-52; RS 1965, pp. 335-36; Marer 1972, pp. 49, 58.

TABLE 5.31

Growth of National Income, Consumption, and
Accumulation in Poland, 1955-60
(constant prices; 1950 = 100)

Year	National Income	Consumption	Accumulation
1955	152	149	164
1956	164	164	161
1957	186	182	200
1958	192	188	206
1959	205	200	226
1960	211	204	243

Source: RS 1965, p. xxxiii.

industrial origin between 1956 and 1957-59. All these changes herald
a favorable impact of foreign trade on consumption, although by 1960
the situation changed again. The same picture appears from calculations
based on Marer's data, shown in the last line of the table. We also
may note that the increase in exports of machinery and equipment
throughout the Five-Year Plan period shows the results of industrialization of the Polish economy.

Table 5.23 above showed that industrial production of consumer
goods rose faster than envisaged in the plan. However, comparisons
of plan fulfillment with plan goals do not seem meaningful in view of
the delay in preparation of the final version of the plan. The indexes
of consumption of various industrial goods, presented below, show a
steady improvement in supplies.

Table 5.31 shows the growth in national income and in its two
main components, consumption and accumulation. It shows a decline
in accumulation in 1956 and its sudden rebound in 1957 as the result
of the fast increase in national income during that year. Thus consumption seems to have had a stimulative effect on national income, and
its growth did not impede growth of investments. In 1958-60, however,
consumption growth was small but accumulation increased out of proportion to the growth of national income.

Changes in Real Income of the Population

The fast growth of consumption in the early part of the Five-Year
Plan was caused by (1) an upward adjustment of wages, (2) a fast
increase in real incomes in agriculture, (3) an upward adjustment of

124

old age pensions and other social payments. The growth of wages during the whole 1956-60 period amounted to 61.5 billion zlotys, of which one-third constituted wage adjustments. The wage fund grew by 68 percent; if growth of social payments and the new lending to the population are considered, the growth of purchasing power in the hands of nonagricultural population rose by 71 percent, faster than the growth of final production outside agriculture.

The rise of incomes in agriculture was similarly higher than the rise in agricultural production because the new Gomulka regime tried to raise agricultural production by means of economic incentives, specifically by raising prices paid on agricultural products and by decreasing the regulated, low-price compulsory deliveries to the state. Incomes from agricultural production rose during 1956-60 by 30 billion zlotys, or over 80 percent, due partly to a rise in output but mostly to a rise in price received by farmers. In addition, consumption in kind by the peasant population grew during the Five-Year Plan by about 10 percent (calculated in 1956 prices; Szyndarczuk 1962, after Ryc 1968, p. 126). Total payments to the population in pensions, sick pay, and family allowances rose particularly rapidly in 1956-59, as shown in Table 5.32.

While incomes rose by 72 percent outside agriculture during 1956-60, and by 80 percent in agriculture, national income rose by only 39 percent. Hence a rise in prices was inevitable due to pressure of fast-rising purchasing power on the slower-rising output, even if account is taken of changing composition of that output toward consumption goods during the first part of that period. Consequently, real incomes rose slower than money incomes, but still faster than real national income (see Table 5.33). It should be pointed out that, while group B in the table (which may be taken as roughly equivalent to agricultural population) saw its real income increase substantially less than group A (roughly equivalent to nonagricultural population), its numbers remained unchanged during the 1956-60 plan period. The whole net increase in population took place in group A, so per capita changes in real income in both groups were much more nearly equal than would appear from Table 5.33. This is brought out in Table 5.34, columns 4 and 6.

As stated above, the rise in the incomes of the population in excess of the rise of national income took place during 1956-57 and was made possible by the decline in the rate of investments in national income, and by loans obtained from abroad to finance food imports. Growth of real incomes declined from an average of 13.6 percent in 1956-57 to 3.5 percent in 1958-60. However, during the latter period the rate of growth of national income also declined, again probably partly due to the slow disappearance of incentives. As a result, the growth of national income for the period as a whole was less than the growth of real incomes of the population.

TABLE 5.32

Payments to Population from Social Security in Poland, 1953-60
(billion zlotys)

	Sick Pay	Family Allowances	Pensions	Total Net Payments[a]	Total	Percentage Growth Each Year[b]
1953	1.3	4.9	2.4	8.2	..	..
1954	1.7	5.3	2.8	9.3	..	13.4
1955	1.8	5.6	3.1	10.2	10.6	9.7
1956	2.2	6.0	3.9	11.7	12.5	14.7
1957	3.2	7.0	5.5	15.1	16.0	29.1
1958	2.9	7.7	7.8	17.4	18.7	15.2
1959	2.8	8.0	10.3	..	21.6	15.5
1960	2.8	7.6	11.1	..	22.0	1.9

[a]Does not include administrative expenses.
[b]Includes current administrative expenses.

Sources: RPiG 1959, p. 737; RS 1965, p. 493; Winiewski 1969, pp. 173, 183, 190.

TABLE 5.33

Growth of National Income and Real Income of the Population in Poland, 1955-60

	1955 = 100				Preceding year = 100			
	National	Aggregate	In that:		National	Aggregate	In that:	
	Income Produced	Real Income	Group A[a]	Group B[b]	Income Produced	Real Income	Group A[a]	Group B[b]
1956	107	115	116	115	107	115	116	115
1957	118	129	131	122	110	112	113	106
1958	125	134	138	124	106	104	105	101
1959	132	141	151	122	106	105	109	98
1960	138	143	152	129	105	102	101	105

[a]Nonagricultural population, plus peasants working on state farms (PGRs).
[b]Agricultural population.

Source: Zienkowski 1963, p. 271.

TABLE 5.34

Use of Real Income of the Population in Poland in 1960
(1955 = 100)

	Aggregate		Group A: Nonagricultural*		Group B: Agricultural	
	Total	Per Capita	Total	Per Capita	Total	Per Capita
Consumption of goods	136-137	125-126	145-146	126-127	122-123	122-123
Investments	168-170	155-156	780	680	127-128	127-128
Services and other	195-197	180-181	200	174	171	171
Increase in money holdings	334	207	321	280	368	368

*Includes peasants working on state farms (PGRs).

Source: Zienkowski 1963, p. 265.

127

TABLE 5.35

Changes in Real Wages in Poland, 1955-60

	1955	1956	1957	1958	1959	1960
Index of real wages	100	111.6	120.8	124.8	131.1	129.1

Source: RS 1965, p. 489.

TABLE 5.36

Index Numbers of Real Income for Blue- and White-Collar Workers
Outside Agriculture in Poland in 1960
(1937 = 100)

	Blue-Collar Workers	White-Collar Workers	Aggregate
Per capita of the population	..	..	170
Per capita in labor force	230	85	173
Per employed person	175	74	136

Source: Kalecki 1964, p. 97; Hodoly 1966, p. 170.

As was shown in Table 5.24 above, the share of accumulation and investment in national income increased between 1955 and 1960. That this was possible despite an accelerated rise in incomes of the population is explained by Table 5.34, from which it appears that real consumption of goods rose during 1956-60 by 36 to 37 percent, while real incomes (as shown in Table 5.33) rose by 43 percent. Private investments, expenditures on services, and especially increased private savings account for the difference between the growth rates of real incomes and expenditures on goods. Private investment expenditures were mainly on housing, both cooperative and private, and on improvements of farms, including increases in herds. The importance of private investments during this period can be partly gauged by their contribution to total investments, which amounted to 12.9 percent (as compared with 4.6 percent during 1951-55). Private investments in housing contributed directly to an improvement in the level of living of the population. The pattern of change in the use of incomes shown in Table 5.34 is attributable to rising real wages. If incomes rose primarily as the result of increased employment, the rise of expenditures on goods would assuredly have been more pronounced. The rise in real wages is shown in Table 5.35, where it is shown that most of the increase took place during 1956-57, while 1960 brought a decline of two points.

The distribution of real incomes among the population changed by 1960 as compared with the prewar period. Michal Kalecki calculated the index numbers of real incomes of blue- and white-collar workers for 1960, with 1937 equal to 100. Table 5.36 shows Kalecki's results and indicates that white-collar workers fared substantially worse, both absolutely and relatively, than did blue-collar workers. The table also shows the effects of decreased unemployment (insofar as income per member of the labor force increased more than income per employed person); of increased labor force participation rates (insofar as income per member of the population increased more than income per employed person); and of the overall rise in real incomes, part of which is attributable to the territorial changes in postwar Poland. Kalecki estimated that the prewar ratio of an average white-collar worker's wage to that of an average blue-collar worker of 2.2 declined by 1960 to 1.12, indicating a substantial decline in income differences to the point of virtual disappearance of the difference (cited in Hodoly 1966, p. 171).

Changes in Consumption

The increase in consumption is shown in Table 5.37. The rise in the personal consumption fund in 1956 was as planned because the plan was made up in 1957. The negative differences between achieved

TABLE 5.37

Increase in Individual Consumption Fund and Per Capita
Consumption in Poland, 1956–60

	1956	1957	1958	1959	1960	1960/55
Individual consumption fund	110.8	110.5	108.3	104.2	105.5	146.0
Plan Fulfillment[a]	110.8	111.3	102.6	105.8	101.2	135.5
Difference in points[a]	–	.8	-5.7	1.6	-4.3	-10.5
Per capita individual consumption[b]	109	119	120	125	124	124

[a]Preceding year = 100.
[b]1955 = 100.

Sources: Rogozinski 1962, p. 7; RS 1962, p. 56.

TABLE 5.38

Per Capita Consumption of Some Basic Goods in Poland, 1955–60

	1955	1956	1957	1958	1959	1960	1960/55
Cereal products (kg)	171	151	154	142	144	145	84.8
Meat and fats (kg)	43.8	47.8	51.1	52.7	51.3	49.9	113.9
Milk and products (liters)	332	340	347	359	360	352	106.0
Eggs (number)	137	127	133	134	141	143	104.4
Fish (kg)	2.7	3.0	3.3	3.4	4.4	4.5	166.7
Sugar (kg)	24.0	25.2	26.5	28.5	29.6	27.9	116.3
Cotton fabrics (m)	16.5	17.8	19.2	19.6	19.6	17.9	108.5
Woolen fabrics (m)	2.5	2.7	2.7	2.6	2.4	2.2	88.0
Silk fabrics (m)	2.8	2.9	3.1	3.3	3.5	3.2	114.3
Footwear (leather tops, pair)	.9	1.0	1.2	1.2	1.3	1.3	144.4
Paper (kg)	12.9	13.7	13.6	14.2	15.5	16.0	124.0
Soap (kg)	2.1	2.3	2.2	2.3	2.6	2.6	123.8
Detergent (kg)	3.2	3.5	4.1	5.3	5.6	5.9	184.4

Source: RS 1965, p. 483.

TABLE 5.39

Polish Plan for Growth of National Income and
Consumption, and Its Fulfillment, 1955–60
(billion zlotys in 1956 prices)

	1955	1956	1957	1958	1959	1960	1956–60
National income produced							
a	236.6	253.5	262.2	290.0	315.7	344.8	1,466.2
b	235.6	252.1	279.2	294.6	310.8	323.7	1,460.4
c	-1.0	-1.4	17.0	4.6	-4.9	-21.1	-5.8
National income distributed							
a	236.4	254.0	272.4	300.9	320.9	342.1	1,490.3
b	239.1	257.7	292.9	302.2	323.4	333.1	1,509.3
c	2.7	3.7	20.5	1.3	2.5	-9.0	19.0
Personal consumption							
a	166.1	184.3	203.3	220.1	229.1	241.6	1,078.4
b	169.7	187.9	209.2	214.2	227.2	229.9	1,068.9
c	3.4	3.6	5.9	-5.4	-1.9	-11.9	-9.5
Other consumption							
a	17.7	18.3	19.1	20.7	22.1	23.5	103.7
b	17.7	19.0	20.7	22.5	24.9	26.6	113.7
c	—	.7	1.6	1.8	2.8	3.1	10.0

a = according to 1956–60 plan figures
b = plan fulfillment
c = difference between fulfillment and plan (b–a)

Source: Kucharski 1964, p. 371, after Ryc 1968, p. 150.

131

and planned increases in 1958 and 1960 are substantial. The index of per capita consumption shows a decline in 1960, in agreement with the decline in real wages shown for that year in Table 5.35. The average annual increase in per capita consumption was 4.5 percent for the Five-Year Plan, but in 1956-57 it was 9.1 percent and in 1958-60 it was only 2.1 percent, a trend that closely resembled the one in real wages.

Table 5.38 shows growth of consumption of some basic consumer goods. The improvement in the standard of living is revealed there in the changing pattern of food consumption, away from starches and toward more proteins, again with the exception of 1960. However, the plan was not fulfilled in the area of deliveries to retail stores: Deliveries of foodstuffs by 1960 rose by 45 percent as compared with 1955, but the plan envisaged a 50 percent growth. Deliveries of nonfoodstuffs rose by 72 percent, but the plan envisaged a growth of 100 percent. (Interested readers may compare Table 5.38 with Table 5.19 for consumption of the same products during the Six-Year Plan period.)

The quality of goods sold to the population apparently improved during the Five-Year Plan period, and so did the assortment, especially in the area of industrial consumer goods. Such an improvement, however, started from a very low initial level in terms of both quality and assortment.

The outcome of the above forces on consumption is summarized in Table 5.39. It is clear from the table that the plan was not fulfilled in growth of national income produced and personal consumption despite foreign aid that increased the national income distributed. It is also clear that the lack of fulfillment was caused by rather bad performance during the second part of the Five-Year Plan, and particularly its last year. It seems that, again, the overambitious growth of investments in the latter part of the period contributed to this result.

THE DISAPPOINTING DECADE OF 1960s

Characteristics

The 1961-65 Five-Year Plan did not contain the drama of the Six-Year Plan of industrialization, nor the excitement of the early period of the 1956-60 Five-Year Plan. Nor did it have the tragic fireworks that ended the 1966-70 plan period. It was simply a bridge between the periods of revolt, resembling somewhat the "stabilization" period of 1958-60. The same was true for the 1966-70 Five-Year Plan period, except for its last month, the pregnant and ominous December 1970. Because of this similarity and their transitional character, these two five-year plan periods spanning the 1960s and ending with December 1970

TABLE 5.40

Increases in Population in Productive Age in Poland
(thousands of persons)

	1951-55	1956-60	1961-65	1966-70
Totals for five-year periods	896	373	1,010	1,630
Annual averages	179.2	74.6	202.0	326.0

Note: Productive age defined as 16 to 59 for men and 16 to 54 for women.

Source: Ryc 1968, p. 167.

TABLE 5.41

Capital Goods in Polish Socialized Enterprises on January 1, 1961, by Age
(percentage structure in each category)

	Capital Goods Completed				
	Before 1921	1921-45	1946-49	1950-55	1956-60
Total capital goods	32.3	23.8	4.0	18.0	21.9
Structures	47.4	22.3	2.7	13.2	14.4
In that:					
Industrial buildings	35.7	26.1	3.6	16.8	17.8
Boilers and machines creating energy	15.3	30.5	4.1	25.5	24.6
Machines and equipment for general use	9.6	22.2	7.4	30.1	30.7
Machines and equipment for special use	13.6	25.8	5.6	21.3	33.7
Technical equipment	6.4	21.8	6.3	29.1	36.4
Transport equipment	4.4	13.3	5.1	27.4	49.8

Source: RS 1965, p. 104.

will be discussed together. There is no clearcut dividing line between them, and hence no difference in analytical evaluation. Both were part of the long-range plan for 1960-75, and that fact partly explains their similarity. Both plans stressed the doctrine of balanced growth, and both aimed at a rapid rate of growth. The outline features of both plans were similar.

First, they stressed the development of the raw materials base and energy production, partly to make up for imports of raw materials during 1956-60. The 1961-65 plan envisaged a gradual shift in favor of consumer goods, but that shift did not in fact materialize and production of consumer goods remained the planners' Cinderella for the rest of the decade.

Second, both plans had to contend with growing numbers of new entrants into the labor force. Table 5.40 shows that the postwar demographic wave, to crest during the early 1970s, started hitting the labor market during the 1960s. In order to accommodate the large group of young age cohorts entering the productive age, jobs had to be created, through investments, which provided additional pressure on planners to raise their investment goals.

Third, during both plan periods planners started showing an awareness of the backward character of industrial processes and capital endowment in Poland. Table 5.41 shows that in 1961 only a small proportion of buildings, machinery, and equipment currently in use was relatively modern, although even that picture does not reflect the technological obsolescence of equipment produced during the 1950s. Hence, modernization became one of the slogans of the five-year plans from 1960 onward.

Fourth, the balance of payments stimulation during 1956-60, when substantial imports were obtained on the basis of loans from abroad, forced planners to seek an improvement by raising exports. Modernization of production and improvement of the incentive system were some of the means intended to achieve that aim.

Fifth, a separate effort was directed, particularly in 1966-70, to stimulate lagging agricultural production. Investments in agriculture were to rise substantially, in 1966-70 by 66 percent. Use of fertilizers during the same period was to rise from 56 kilograms of pure content per hectare of cultivated land in 1965 to 136 kilograms in 1970. The reason for this emphasis was the rather inadequate growth of agricultural production during 1960-65 and the rising demand for foodstuffs, to be discussed in Chapter 6.

Investments and Employment

Investments for 1961-65 were to rise by about 50 percent as compared with the preceding plan period, equally distributed between

134

TABLE 5.42

Gross Investment Outlays in Poland, 1960-70
(billion zlotys, 1961 prices)

Year	Total Planned	Total Actual	"Productive" Planned	"Productive" Actual	"Unproductive" Planned	"Unproductive" Actual	"Productive" as Percentage of Total Planned	"Productive" as Percentage of Total Actual
1960	..	100.3	..	69.4	..	31.0	..	69.2
1961	106.4	107.8	74.8	75.9	31.6	31.9	70.3	70.4
1962	115.8	119.5	82.8	87.0	33.0	32.4	71.5	72.9
1963	125.4	123.0	88.9	90.9	36.5	32.1	70.9	73.9
1964	133.8	128.2	94.0	94.7	39.8	33.5	70.3	73.9
1965	142.7	140.8	98.4	106.2	44.3	34.6	69.0	75.4
1966	145.0*	152.9	..	116.1	..	36.7	} 76.1	76.0
1967	156.9*	170.3	..	130.6	..	39.6		76.7
1968	168.4*	185.1	..	142.1	..	43.0		76.8
1969	179.3*	201.1	..	155.5	..	45.6		77.3
1970	190.4*	109.7	..	160.4	..	49.3		76.5

*Prices of January 1, 1966.

Sources: RS 1971, p. 149; Dziennik Ustaw, 1961, no. 11, item 58, and 1966, no. 48, item 296.

"productive" and "nonproductive" investments. Actually, the former rose by 56.6 percent while the latter lagged behind with a 27.5 percent increase. Table 5.42 compares plan with plan fulfillment for the 1960s. Especially noteworthy is the excess of actual "productive" investments over planned investments, and the shortfall of "unproductive" investments compared to planned investments. The increasing share of the former in total investments, and the concomitant decreasing share of the latter also are symptomatic of planners' preferences.

In real (as contrasted with financial) terms, the 1961-65 plan fulfillment was quite inadequate due to higher planned costs of different projects, the cost overruns amounting on main projects to 10 to 12 percent (Monitor Polski 1961, no. 99; 1962, no. 89; 1963, no. 96; 1964, no. 87, after Ryc 1968, pp. 173, 173 n. 7, 186). A change made during the plan period — limitation of expenditures on investments in the "unproductive" sphere, and involving about 20 percent of investment outlays made during the last three years in the plan — had an obviously adverse effect on consumption prospects. These two trends continued through the second part of the decade.

Investments during 1966-70 were to be higher by almost 38 percent than those of the preceding plan period. Table 5.43 shows their sectoral distribution and the planned and actual increase above the 1961-65 plan period. It is apparent that all investment targets were overfulfilled, most of all in construction. Such an overfulfillment of investment imposed a heavy strain on the economy and could not help but adversely affect current consumption. Table 5.43 also reveals the relatively heavy emphasis on investments in the agricultural sector, designed to stimulate production of foodstuffs, which had become one of the main, if not the main trouble area of the Polish economy.

As stated above, however, completion of investment projects in real terms was lagging behind plan. Inadequate fulfillment of investment plans in real terms resulted in creation of fewer jobs than planned, and in bottlenecks that adversely affected the job situation. While the plan for 1961-65 envisaged an increase in jobs smaller than the expected growth of the labor force (Kuzinski 1962, p. 60, after Ryc 1968, p. 174), thus in effect planning for unemployment, the actual growth of employment in the socialized sector was nonetheless almost twice that planned, or 18 percent compared with the planned 10 percent. The reasons for this unplanned increase in employment were as follows (Rajkiewicz, no date, after Ryc 1968, p. 176):

1. Nonfulfillment of planned technological progress which, in order to achieve increases in production, necessitated expansion in employment. This situation held true for industry and construction.
2. Increases in the average length of paid vacations and in absenteeism.

TABLE 5.43

Distribution of Investments in Poland by Sectors, 1966–70

	Plan[a]			Fulfillment[b]
	billion zlotys	share	$\dfrac{1966\text{–}70}{1961\text{–}65} \times 100$	$\dfrac{1966\text{–}70}{1961\text{–}65} \times 100$
Total	840.0	—	137.6	148.1
Total without central reserves	816.0	100	133.6	..
In that:				
Industry	343.6	42.1	138.8	144.0
Construction	22.3	2.7	110.0	190.6
Agriculture	142.9	17.5	165.5	174.9
Forestry	2.8	.3	109.7	145.7
Transport and communications	85.5	10.5	134.6	160.5
Trade	24.2	3.0	134.3	166.0
Urban and utilities	29.1	3.6	125.3	142.0
Housing	115.7	14.2	111.3	128.4
Education, science, and culture	30.5	3.7	110.6	117.3
Health, social care, and physical culture	12.4	1.5	108.7	143.6
Administration, justice	7.0	.9	112.1	174.0

[a] In 1966 prices.
[b] In 1971 prices.

Sources: Ryc 1968, p. 223; RS 1972, pp. 140–41.

According to one author, Poland at the time probably had higher than optimal labor force participation rates (Rajkiewicz, no date, after Ryc 1968, pp. 176-77). The rate passed 80 percent in 1963, partly due to postponements of retirement, partly due to increased job seeking by women. Both these developments seemed to indicate that the growth of real wages, and the level of pensions, was inadequate to say the least, and that more work was the main, or the only, way to achieve an improvement in living levels. From this point of view, a parallel has been drawn between the Six-Year Plan of industrialization in 1950-55 and the 1961-65 plan. The parallel can be extended to the whole period of the 1960s.

The 1966-70 plan envisaged growth of employment in the socialized sector by 18 percent. Actual growth was 17.2 percent, with industry and transport showing higher than planned growth of employment and other sectors showing lower than planned growth (RS 1972, pp. 109, 351, 434). This development tended in practice to cut out the avenue of raising the level of living through increases in labor force participation rates because supply of consumer goods did not grow adequately.

The increase in labor productivity in industry, which was 7.5 percent annually during 1956-60, declined to 4.2 percent in 1961-65. In construction it fell from 4.6 percent during 1956-60 to 4.3 percent during 1961-65. Using the formula

$$S_p = 100 - \left(\frac{dN}{dQ} \times 100 \right)$$

where: S_p = share of change in labor productivity in the growth of gross production

dN = change in employment

dQ = change in gross production

the share of growth of labor productivity in the increase of industrial output was planned to amount to almost 84 percent during 1961-65 (Ryc 1968, p. 178). Actually, that share was below 60 percent. In construction the said share was planned to be 83 percent, while the achieved share was about 67 percent. Thus Poland's economic growth was much more extensive than planned, which had the effect of cutting down planned increases in real wages.

Agriculture, Foreign Trade, and Industry

Agricultural production was planned to rise during 1961-65 by 22.2 percent, but the actual increase amounted to only 14.5 percent as compared with 1960. The bad 1961 harvest set back animal husbandry and animal production rose less (by 12 percent) than production of crops (by 16 percent). The overall increase in agricultural production was less than in the preceding period, although the good harvest of 1960, used as the base for calculating the increase in production, may somewhat exaggerate this shortfall in accomplishment. Nevertheless, imports of grain were necessary throughout the 1961-65 period, and were higher in each year than the record 1960 level of imports of grain.

During 1966-70, gross agricultural production was planned to rise by 13.9 to 14.6 percent compared with 1961-65. Again, crop production was to rise faster than animal production. Two salient features stand out in the experience of this plan period:

1. After good harvests in the first three years, the last two years brought very bad harvests, which adversely affected the food situation.

2. The state was increasing its procurements of grain from farmers in order, perhaps ill-advisedly, to decrease Poland's dependence on imports. This policy, however, reduced the availability of fodder and thus adversely affected animal husbandry.

As a result of these developments, aggregate agricultural production by 1970 rose by only 9.6 percent as compared with 1965, while crop production rose by 10.5 percent and animal production by 8.1 percent, the latter having scarcely risen between 1966 and 1970 (RS 1972, p. 250). This setback in achieving plan goals had grave repercussions on the meat market; planners dealt with it by trying only to adjust demand rather than by stimulating supply, as will be explained in Chapter 6.

In order to rectify the balance of payments, which had become unbalanced by large-scale imports of grain, the 1961-65 plan envisaged growth of exports by 55 percent and of imports by 27.2 percent as compared with 1960. The actual fulfillment contrasted with that in agriculture in that exports rose in constant prices by 68 percent and imports by 57 percent. The equilibrium of the balance of payments was thus approached to a lesser degree than had been envisaged, while both exports and imports rose substantially above plan.

Foreign trade in the area of consumer goods showed the following changes:

1. The slight positive balance in agricultural products and foodstuffs increased markedly from 32 million devisa zlotys in 1956-60 to 1,082 million devisa zlotys in 1961-65, both expressed in current prices.

2. While trade in industrial consumer goods showed a negative balance in 1959, that balance became increasingly positive starting with 1960.

3. During the first three years of the 1961-65 plan period, there was a considerable decline in imports of some raw materials used in

industries producing consumer goods, and especially of textile raw materials and hides. This decline retarded the growth of light industry production, although during 1964-65 the above trend was reversed.

The 1966-70 plan set a comparatively moderate target of 30.6 to 31.0 percent growth in international trade turnover. The growth of exports again was to be higher than that of imports, 33 to 33.8 percent compared with 28.3 percent. The balance of trade was still to be negative, but the balance on current account, due to a positive balance in services, was to become positive. In the area of consumer goods, imports of foodstuffs were to decrease by 20 percent and exports of foodstuffs to decrease by 16 percent; for industrial consumer goods imports were to rise by 20 percent and exports by 86.4 to 92.8 percent (Dziennik Ustaw 1966, no. 48, item 296). Thus again, as during the Six-Year Plan of industrialization, foreign trade was slated to have the effect of reducing the domestic availability of consumer goods in Poland.

In actuality, foreign trade turnover, expressed in current prices, rose between 1965 and 1970 by 56.6 percent, exports rose by 59.1 percent, and imports by 54.2 percent. In the area of consumer goods, exports of foodstuffs rose by 18.1 percent while imports rose by 7.7 percent despite the earlier plan to lower them. Exports of light industry products rose by 89.6 percent while imports rose by 23.5 percent (RS 1972, pp. 395-96). Because of the disastrous 1969-70 harvests, the impact of foreign trade was to decrease the availability of consumer goods to less than originally planned for foodstuffs. The same general picture emerges from data in Marer's study (1972, pp. 49, 58).

Industrial production measured in net terms rose, on the average, faster during 1961-65 than during the preceding plan period, by 8.9 percent as compared with 8.2 percent. Table 5.44 shows the rates of growth of industrial production in gross terms and reveals that the sector of consumer goods became more underprivileged than in the preceding period (cf. Table 5.23 above), both in terms of the absolute gap between actual growth of producer goods production and that of consumer goods, and in terms of underfulfillment of planned expansion. Even the cautious Polish economist Andrzej Hodoly said this experience showed "alarming disproportions in the structure of production" (1966, p. 90). Since production of producer goods rose faster than planned, consumers received more purchasing power than they could spend on the market. That other sectors, besides industry, contributed to this adverse situation is shown by the following list of reasons for underfulfillment of the production plan on consumer goods: (1) underfulfillment of the plan goals for agricultural production; (2) reduction of imports of raw materials used for production of consumer goods; (3) delays in opening up of planned production of import substitutes, particularly in the chemical industry producing materials for the production of consumer goods; (4) incomplete fulfillment of investment plans in the area of consumer goods (Ryc 1968, pp. 185-86).

TABLE 5.44

Growth of Gross Industrial Production in Poland, 1961-70
(preceding year = 100; in constant prices)

	Gross Industrial Production[a]	Production of Capital Goods[b] (Group A)	Production of Consumer Goods[b] (Group B)
1961	110.2	111.8	108.3
1962	108.4	110.0	106.4
1963	105.4	107.5	102.4
1964	109.2	110.1	108.0
1965	108.9	109.8	107.7
1966	107.5	108.0	106.4
1967	107.9	109.1	105.3
1968	109.4	110.7	106.9
1969	108.8	110.0	106.9
1970	108.1	109.0	107.6
1965 } (1960 = 100)	149.6	159.9	137.4
1970 }	223.1	250.0	189.2
1970 (1965 = 100)	149.2	156.5	137.8

[a]Socialized and private industry.
[b]Socialized industry.

Source: RS 1972, p. 160.

    The 1966-70 plan assumed a 43.6 percent increase in gross indus-
trial production, or an average annual growth rate of 7.5 percent,
down from the average growth rates of the two preceding plan periods.
It was again posited that the rate of expansion of production of producer goods, at 8.2 percent annually, would be higher than the rate
of expansion of consumer goods production, at 6.4 percent (Dziennik
Ustaw 1966, no. 48, item 296; Feiwel 1971b, vol. I, p. 352). The
actual rise in gross industrial production amounted by 1970 to 49.2
percent, production of producer goods having risen by 56.5 percent
and production of consumer goods by 37.8 percent; the former was
higher by 49 percent than the latter, compared with the planned
margin of 28 percent (RS 1972, p. 160). Thus again consumers were
treated, both in the plan and in its execution, to the short end of
the stick.

Changes in Consumption and Real Income of the Population

The 1961-65 plan provided for an increase of 40. 6 percent in national income produced and of 33. 5 percent in national income distributed. The actual increases were 35. 2 percent (or 6. 2 percent annually) and 33 percent, respectively, with the underfulfillment due mostly to the failure of the agricultural plan. That failure also projected on the fulfillment of the consumption plan, which envisaged a rise of 30. 6 percent (personal consumption to rise by 32. 1 percent), while the actual rise was 28 percent (personal consumption by only 25 percent). Social consumption was to rise moderately by 16 percent but actually rose by almost 50 percent; this overshooting of the plan explained the relatively poor performance of personal consumption. The main shortfall in plan fulfillment occurred in 1964-65, when the plan envisaged an accelerated growth of national income and consumption, a growth that did not materialize.

The 1966-70 plan provided for an increase of national income produced by 34 percent and of national income distributed by 32 percent, with both figures slightly lower than accomplishment in the preceding plan period (Dziennik Ustaw 1966, no. 48, item 296). The actual increases were 33 and 32 percent respectively, again signifying a slightly lower growth rate than planned (RS 1972, pp. 121, 126).

Personal consumption was to grow by 1970 (as compared with 1965) by 27 percent and social consumption by 40 percent; these rates heralded a continuation of the stress on collective consumption begun during the implementation of the 1961-65 plan. Plan fulfillment, according to less than usually reliable official figures, was 37. 1 percent in constant prices and 158 percent in current prices (RS 1972, pp. 535, 539). Official data also suggest an improvement in consumption standards. During 1961-65, per capita consumption of starches went down and that of proteins increased (RS 1967, p. 528), while the endowment of households with durable consumer goods, (washing machines, sewing machines, refrigerators, TV sets) increased, in some cases considerably. Both these trends continued during the 1966-70 plan (RS 1972, p. 540). Table 5. 45 shows the growth in consumption of some basic consumer goods. It shows a decline in the consumption of inferior starch goods (cereals and potatoes), and an increase in the consumption of other goods. Between 1960 and 1970 per capita consumption of alcohol and tobacco increased; wine and mead showed the smallest percentage growth, and beer the highest. Consumption of soap and detergent apparently had reached a plateau.

Table 5. 46 shows the growth in real incomes of the agricultural population left for consumption and "nonproductive" investments during 1961-70. Relatively speaking, a smaller increase in agricultural incomes produced a rise in consumption equal to that of the urban population, due to the fact that the agricultural population was stagnant

TABLE 5.45

Per Capita Consumption of Some Basic Products
in Poland, 1960-73

	1960	1965	1970[a]	1973
Cereal products (kg)	145	141	132	125
Potatoes (kg)	223	215	197	183
Meat and animal fats (kg)	49.9	56.0	60.7	70.9
Fish and products (kg)	4.5	5.0	6.2	7.2
Milk and products [b] (liters)	352	356	397	412
Edible fats[c]	13.6	15.1	17.8	19.3
Eggs (number)	143	162	184	200
Sugar (kg)	27.9	32.6	38.9	41.6
Spirits (liters)[d]	2.4	2.6	3.2	4.2
Wine and mead (liters)	4.5	4.8	5.6	6.5
Beer (liters)	22.8	24.0	31.4	37.8
Tobacco products (kg)	1.6	1.7	2.0	2.3
Cotton fabrics (m)[e]	17.9	19.9	21.7	20.5
Woolen fabrics (m)[e]	2.2	2.3	2.4	2.7
Silk fabrics (m)[e]	3.2	3.1	3.7	4.7
Footwear (pairs)[f]	1.3	1.5	1.7	1.6
Paper (kg)	16.0	20.2	26.4	33.7
Soap and detergent (kg)	6.0	6.6	6.1	6.4

[a] Variant A.
[b] Recalculated in terms of milk.
[c] Recalculated into 100 percent of fat.
[d] Recalculated into 100-proof spirits.
[e] Including similar fabrics.
[f] Leather tops.

Source: RS 1972, p. 540; RS 1974, p. 146.

TABLE 5.46

Growth of Real Income of Agricultural Population in Poland
Left for Consumption and "Nonproductive"
Investments, 1961-70

	Annual Change	Index (1960 = 100)
1961	3.9	104
1962	-.7	103
1963	-1.5	102
1964	5.4	107
1965	5.1	112
1966	4.9	117
1967	.6	118
1968	1.5	120
1969	-5.0	114
1970	-.8	113

Sources: RS 1967, p. 296; RS 1972, p. 255.

TABLE 5.47

Changes in Real Wages in Poland During the 1960s

	1960 = 100	Previous Year = 100
1960	100	98.5
1961	103	102.6
1962	103	100.4
1963	105	102.4
1964	108	102.1
1965	108	100.0
1966	112	103.3
1967	114	102.5
1968	115	101.3
1969	117	101.7
1970	119	101.3

Sources: RS 1967, p. 522; RS 1972, p. 535.

or only slightly increasing during the 1960s, while the urban population was rising; still, the rise in real incomes seems negligible. The relative share of consumption directed to the agricultural population, as well as the relation of per capita agricultural and urban consumption, seems to have moved to the disadvantage of the agricultural population during the 1960s.

Real wages were planned to increase by 23 percent during 1961-65, or by the same proportion as per capita consumption. During the 1966-70 plan period, real wages were to grow more slowly, by only 10 percent (or about 2 percent annually), but employment was to increase, as indicated above, by 3.4 percent annually, or 18 percent in all. Official changes in real wages are shown in Table 5.47. Unaccountably, the index shows increases during 1969-70, when workers' dissatisfaction was increasing, to erupt in labor unrest in December 1970 and the following months. The aggregate wage fund increased much faster than wages due to increases in employment, characterized earlier in this section.

The two five-year plans that spanned the 1960s had as their goals development of the raw materials base, technological advancement, rapid rise in national income, and continued growth in consumption. In the implementation of the plans, it was found that these goals are not necessarily compatible. Technological advancement seems to have been a fiasco; labor productivity failed to show the expected improvement; growth rates of national income declined; and consumption rose less than planned. December 1970 revealed the depths of popular dissatisfaction with the economic achievements of the last two five-year plans, just as student riots of March 1968 showed political discontent with censorship and lack of human freedoms. The 1960s, therefore, can be classified as a period of unsatisfactory progress in the area of consumption, even in terms of official statistics.

INDEPENDENTLY CALCULATED INDEXES AND AN OVERVIEW

As stated in Chapter 3, the credibility gap in East European statistics has created a need for independent verification of official data. Therefore, the present section contains a general overview of independently derived estimates of the growth of these economic categories, which have been treated as relevant to the growth of consumption. The independent estimates can serve as corrections upon official data. In the preceding sections of this chapter, I have consistently used only data generated in Poland to provide for better internal consistency. These data can now be appraised in the light of independent estimates. In the following chapters, which provide a more synoptic review, independent estimates are placed side by side with the official figures.

TABLE 5.48

Calculated Indexes of Gross Investment, Industrial
Production, and Net Agricultural Production in
Poland, Prewar to 1970

| | Gross Investment | Production in Industry and Handicrafts | | Net Product of Agriculture |
		Calculated Index	Official Index	
1934-38	. .	. .	. .	89.3
1937	43.9	. .	. .	88.2
1946	25.3	. .	. .	31.7
1947	37.3	38.7	27.4	44.1
1948	47.4	46.3	36.7	57.4
1949	53.0	51.9	44.9	79.5
1950	58.8	59.4	53.1	91.2
1951	63.6	67.0	61.2	89.8
1952	70.5	71.6	69.6	87.5
1953	96.8	79.6	78.9	91.0
1954	94.8	86.2	86.2	93.7
1955	99.8	93.9	94.4	96.9
1956	100.0	100.0	100.0	100.0
1957	94.0	108.3	110.3	104.9
1958	107.7	116.3	119.3	110.5
1959	112.2	124.8	128.6	106.1
1960	133.9	136.1	139.6	111.1
1961	147.0	145.5	154.4	127.8
1962	144.5	155.3	167.7	105.0
1963	156.3	163.2	176.6	117.3
1964	186.2	176.4	194.6	116.8
1965	155.7	189.3	213.8	119.3
1966	203.1	200.0	228.6	130.3
1967	216.7	212.9	245.1	128.7
1968	235.6[b]	. .	268.1	136.2
1969	254.9[b]	. .	290.6	113.2
1970	265.2[b]	. .	310.4	116.0

[a] Income originating in industry and handicrafts.
[b] Official figures.

Sources: Korbonski, Wynnyczuk, and Znayenko, 1973, p. 2;
Wynnyczuk and Znayenko 1970, p. 2; Korbonski and Lazarcik 1972,
p. 4; RS 1973, pp. 139, 164.

TABLE 5.49

Calculated Indexes of Housing, Some Services, Some Elements of
Social Consumption, and Personal Per Capita Consumption
in Poland, Prewar to 1967

	Housing	Other Services	Culture and Arts	Education	Health, Welfare, and Child Care	Personal Per Capita Consumption
1937	79.9	169.6	53.6	60.9	. .	114.6[a]
1938	. .	. .	. .	. .	53.2	64.9[b]
1946	83.9	83.8	33.3	56.8	33.3	53.3
1947	85.8	101.9	38.5	65.2	40.4	64.0
1948	87.6	107.5	50.4	70.6	43.1	75.3
1949	89.5	112.7	61.3	75.9	53.5	81.1
1950	90.2	94.9	79.1	79.9	56.8	88.0
1951	91.4	90.9	81.0	84.5	65.9	89.7
1952	92.6	87.9	89.4	83.5	70.9	88.4
1953	94.1	89.7	88.5	86.4	76.9	87.3
1954	95.7	97.8	95.8	88.7	86.1	91.7
1955	97.8	100.2	97.6	93.5	93.5	95.4
1956	100.0	100.0	100.0	100.0	100.0	100.0
1957	103.0	99.1	101.5	102.9	107.8	107.1
1958	106.3	103.0	104.7	105.9	112.4	110.6
1959	110.0	109.1	107.0	112.4	118.5	111.1
1960	113.9	115.6	109.4	115.3	125.8	113.3
1961	117.0	127.9	115.0	122.2	133.6	115.5
1962	119.5	140.6	117.4	127.7	140.1	118.4
1963	122.0	152.6	112.2	134.7	145.3	122.2
1964	124.8	159.0	121.4	139.5	149.1	125.3
1965	127.8	164.3	124.2	150.9	154.1	127.6[c]
1966	. .	. .	. .	. .	. .	134.8[c]
1967	. .	. .	. .	. .	. .	137.5[c]

[a] Postwar territory.
[b] Prewar territory.
[c] Continuation of author's index, calculated at the Project on National Income in East Central
Europe and grafted on author's index.

Sources: Korbonski and Wittich 1968, p. 2, Mieczkowski 1969, p. 143.

147

Table 5.48 and 5.49 bring together estimates arrived at by several researchers, including myself. Comparing the independently derived indexes with the official ones, we arrive at the following observations:

1. The independent index of investments shows a lower rate of growth than does the official index of investment outlays in 1971 prices.
2. The independent index of industrial and handicraft production likewise shows a lower rate of growth than does the official index of income originating in industry and handicrafts.
3. Only the independent index of agricultural production shows a somewhat higher rate of growth than does the official index. Its authors noted that Polish agricultural production

> shows a more regular year-to-year pattern . . . than in some other East European countries (e.g., Bulgaria, Rumania, and Yugoslavia), where erratic weather conditions make large year-to-year variations in production more frequent. (Korbonski and Lazarcik 1972, p. 10.)

The index of housing in Table 5.49 can be regarded only as an approximation. Its authors found

> noteworthy discrepancies in the Polish data themselves. Specifically, the increase in occupied space implied by the 1950 and 1960 census reports is by no means accounted for by reported new construction. The gap is even greater if depreciation is taken into consideration. (Korbonski and Wittich 1968, p. 5.)

Polish economists have pointed to inadequate satisfaction of housing needs, and to Poland's lag behind other countries in the rate of improvement of housing (Rychlewski 1972, pp. 137-39; Lipinski 1964, p. 505; Dangel 1971, p. 349). One stated that the demand for housing was better satisfied in 1950 than in 1970 (Rychlewski 1970, p. 1172).

"Other services" in Table 5.49 covers banking and insurance, communal services, other socialized services such as barber and beauty shops, chimney sweeps, office help, and domestic help, as well as private services that include handicrafts and professional services. Owing to the importance in this index of the private services, which were discriminated against, the prewar volume of "other services" was reattained as late as 1965.

The index of culture and the arts implies a substantial increase in cultural and artistic activity and, presumably although not necessarily, a similar increase in the satisfaction of those who benefited from that activity.

The two indexes of (1) education and (2) health, welfare, and child care are the star performers in social consumption; they indicate substantial gains since World War II. On a per capita basis the improvement has been still greater, owing to a decrease in population from before the war, and it shows the considerable emphasis accorded those two areas by the administration.

The index of personal per capita consumption was computed by this author (Mieczkowski 1969). It shows the dramatic effect of inclusion into postwar Poland of the relatively affluent prewar German territory, while the most backward prewar Polish eastern territories were ceded to the Soviet Union. As the result, the prewar level of per capita consumption on prewar Polish territory was easily regained in postwar Poland as early as 1947-48, despite war-inflicted destruction, while the prewar level of per capita personal consumption on postwar Polish territory was regained only as late as 1961. The independently calculated index of personal consumption shows a markedly slower growth than does the official one.

The increase in real wages was slower than that of consumption because of increasing labor force participation rates which meant that even stagnant real wages would have resulted, ceteris paribus, in a rise in per capita consumption since a larger proportion of the population was working. Gross real wages per employed person, calculated with the use of Fisher's formula, increased between prewar and 1967 by 40.8 percent as compared with prewar Polish territory (on a net basis, including social services, they increased by 60.9 percent), but the increase was unevenly distributed since white-collar workers saw their gross real wages per employed person decline in that period by 11.2 percent (on a net basis, including social services, there was an increase of only 1.5 percent), while blue-collar workers experienced a 66.1 percent increase during the same period (an 89.9 percent net increase) (Beskid 1972, p. 32). During the postwar period, overall real wages declined in 1951-53, during the height of the forced industrialization period, and in 1960 (Beskid 1972, pp. 48, 54, 65). Since 1959, the process of equalization of the earlier blue/white collar wage differentials has been reversed, and white-collar wages started a relative increase compared to blue-collar wages (Beskid 1972, p. 55). It apparently was found expedient to provide greater incentives to educational achievement than the 1 to 1.06 ratio of wages (Beskid 1972, p. 55) achieved between blue- and white-collar workers in 1959.

Per capita consumption among peasants increased 3.2 times from the very low prewar level (Piasny 1970, pp. 287-88) by 1967, resulting in a narrowing of the gap between peasants and urban blue-collar workers to a relation of 1 to 1.1 (Beskid 1970, p. 82). Food consumption among peasants improved considerably as compared with prewar, but the structure of that consumption still differs considerably between rural and urban areas (Piasny 1970, p. 290). A sign of the still inferior situation of peasants, and possibly of different consumption traditions,

TABLE 5.50

Indicators of Change in Real Per Capita Consumption Expenditures by Households in Poland: 1968 Compared with 1937 or 1932

	Indicator of Expenditures Per Capita			
	Blue-Collar Households		White-Collar Households	
Category	1968 Prices	1937 Prices	1968 Prices	1937 Prices
Aggregate expenditures	2.0	2.5	1.3	1.4
Foodstuffs	1.7	1.8	1.1	1.1
Alcohol	2.2	2.9	.9	1.2
Tobacco	4.4	4.3	1.7	1.3
Clothing	2.0	2.1	1.4	1.7
Footwear	1.4	1.6	1.2	1.4
Housing	2.3	2.3	1.5	1.1
Fuel and light	2.4	3.7	2.4	2.7
Hygiene and health	3.6	3.7	3.2	3.3
Culture and education	10.1	11.0	1.9	2.1
Transport and communications	6.1	6.8	.9	1.0

Note: Figures are from 1932 for white-collar workers, 1937 for blue-collar workers

Source: Beskid 1972, pp. 89, 91.

is the fact that "income elasticity of demand for foodstuffs among peasant families is markedly higher" than in urban families (Beskid 1972, p. 163).

The structure of consumption changed in Poland between 1937 and 1968. When differentiated as between blue- and white-collar worker households, the main findings are as summarized in Table 5.50. As could be expected on the basis of information provided above on faster growth of blue-collar wages, consumption expenditures of blue-collar workers grew markedly faster. That white-collar worker consumption expenditures could grow, despite a decline in wages for that group, is due mostly to higher labor force participation.

Within the blue-collar group, food expenditures grew less than aggregate consumption expenditures, and so did expenditures on footwear and clothing. The fastest increase in expenditures was on culture and education, and transport and communications. Expenditures on alcohol and tobacco rose faster than the average.

A somewhat different pattern of changes in consumption expenditures emerges from data on white-collar workers. The lowest increase, in fact approximate stagnation, is shown in expenditures on alcohol and transport and communications, which were substantial consumption outlets among blue-collar workers. The highest increases were chalked up on health, then fuel and light, and then culture and education. Health consciousness among white-collar workers obviously is much higher in Poland than among blue-collar workers, which agrees with observations from other countries (cf. U. S. Department of Health, Education and Welfare 1973, pp. 2-4).

Table 5.51 compares the structure of per capita consumption expenditures of blue- and white-collar workers in 1968. Smaller expenditures on alcohol by white-collar workers are striking, while the higher share of expenditures on food among blue-collar workers agrees with their lower incomes. White-collar workers spend relatively much more on transport and communications, health, household furnishings, and culture and education, in that order. They spend relatively less, compared with blue-collar workers, on alcohol, tobacco, and food, also in that order.

Table 5.52 shows changes in the volume of food expenditures by blue- and white-collar workers between prewar and 1968. No declines were registered for blue-collar workers, but the smallest increases were on potatoes, cereal products, and meat and fats; by comparison, white-collar workers showed declines in expenditures on potatoes, cereals, and fats, and no increase in expenditures on meat. *

---

*Actually, per capita consumption of meat by white-collar workers' households declined by almost 50 percent, but consumption of meat products increased considerably. Aggregate per capita consumption of meat in white-collar households declined between 1932 and 1968 (Beskid 1972, p. 122).

TABLE 5.51

Comparison of Per Capita Consumption Expenditures by
Blue- and White-Collar Workers in Poland in 1968
(percentages)

Category	Blue-Collar Households	White-Collar Households	White-Collar Households as Percentage of Blue-Collar Households
Aggregate expenditures	100.0	100.0	132
Foodstuffs	51.4	44.3	113
Alcohol	2.2	1.6	93
Tobacco	2.1	1.7	107
Fuel and light	4.5	4.5	132
Rent	3.4	3.5	137
Household furnishings	5.5	7.0	172
Hygiene and health	4.3	6.3	190
Clothing and footwear	16.7	17.8	141
Culture and education	7.4	9.6	168
Transport and communications	2.5	3.7	198

Source: Beskid 1972, p. 95.

TABLE 5.52

Indicators of Growth of Volume of Food Expenditures in
Blue- and White-Collar Households in Poland
Between Prewar and 1968

	Blue-Collar Households: 1968 over 1937	White-Collar Households: 1968 over 1932
Aggregate foodstuffs	1.7	1.1
Cereal products	1.3	.7
Potatoes	1.1	.5
Vegetables and products	1.6	1.2
Fruits and products	3.1	1.6
Meat and products	1.4	1.0
Fats	1.4	.9
Fish and products	1.7	4.1
Milk and products, and eggs	2.0	1.1
Sugar and pastry	2.1	1.5
Other foodstuffs	3.5	1.0
Collective feeding	14.0	. .

Source: Beskid 1972, p. 93.

Largest increases in blue-collar worker expenditures were on collective feeding (cafeterias, restaurants), "other foodstuffs," and fruits. Largest increases in white-collar worker expenditures were possibly also on collective feeding (if information had been available), and on fish and fruit. For both groups, the category of fats showed a wholesome shift to butter and vegetable fats, and away from animal fats (Beskid 1972, pp. 93-94).

Between 1950 and 1968, per capita consumption of aggregate purchased foodstuffs increased by about 90 percent (Beskid 1972, p. 119). On the basis of a short period in 1963-68, it was calculated that the marginal propensity to consume was higher among white-collar households, while the marginal propensity to save was higher among blue-collar households. When growth of incomes stagnated during 1960-62, the marginal propensity to save became negative; that is, the amount of savings declined in order to provide for an increase in consumption (Beskid 1972, p. 115).

Finally, research on income elasticity of consumption expenditures yielded the following conclusions:

1. Income elasticity of consumption expenditures shows great stability over time.

2. Income elasticity of consumption expenditures does not differ appreciably between blue- and white-collar workers. It tends to be higher for blue-collar workers in the area of all basic needs. It tends to be higher for white-collar workers for expenditures on culture and education, and hygiene and health. However, these differences have tended to narrow down over time for expenditures on basic needs, and to be maintained for expenditures on culture and health.

3. Income elasticity of consumption expenditures is lower for all types of expenditures among higher-income groups as compared to lower-income groups (Beskid 1972, pp. 142-45; see also Bywalec 1972, pp. 121-38).

6

RECENT CHANGES IN CONSUMPTION PLANNING: THE POLISH CASE

Andrzej Brzeski recently stressed the uniformity of Soviet-type systems in Eastern Europe prior to the death of Stalin in 1953, and the economic reforms that have tended to heterogenize those systems since. Brzeski attributed to Poland the leading role in providng "a unique input into subsequent developments" in other East European countries (1971, p. 6; cf. Crawford and Haberstroh 1974, p. 46). With regard to policy toward consumers, Brzeski drew a comparison between the 1956 Poznan riots that served as a signal for changes in Poland and, with a delay, for changes in other East European countries, and the December 1970 Gdansk riots of Polish workers. In doing this, Brzeski showed that he expected the other countries in Eastern Europe to eventually be affected by the events in Poland. It therefore seems useful to analyze at greater length the recent changes in Poland, in terms of both the economic debate preceding them and the more empirically oriented policies that followed in the wake of the Gdansk riots. Like the great debate on the economic model conducted in Poland in 1956-57, these more recent changes are likely to influence official policies and consumers throughout Eastern Europe. The Polish case study presented here may therefore help improve understanding of changes in other East European countries. This procedure also is analogous to the overall presentation of the Polish experience in consumption in greater detail as a general illustration. Factual particulars are filled in separately for other countries in Chapters 7 to 9.

The Polish example is partly polemical in tone in order to bring out some uncertainties, dilemmas, and sudden turns in economic policy making, and to help the reader assess the views voiced by East European writers. The narrative is, consequently, different in style from other chapters of this study.

DISCUSSION ON CONSUMPTION PLANNING IN
POLAND IN 1968-70*

Background

Consumption in Poland did not grow rapidly during the 1960s.
According to Zygmunt Zekonski, writing in the official planning journal
Gospodarka Planowa, per capita personal consumption rose during
1960-68 by an average of 3.5 percent per year (1969, p. 6). Limitation
on the growth of consumption had been imposed by the emphasis on
producer goods as compared with consumer goods. In industry, production of producer goods rose on the average by 9.5 percent annually,
while production of consumer goods rose by 6.6 percent on the average.
A further limitation was imposed by the slower rise of agricultural
production, the gross output of which rose during the 1960s by about
2 percent per year, or by about 1 percent per person (Maly RS 1970,
p. 146); between 1960 and 1968, agriculture contributed only about
8 percent of the increase in national income while industry contributed
about 65 percent.

But the growth of per capita personal consumption of 3.5 percent
per year, if expressed in current prices, must be deflated for price
changes which averaged 1.2 percent per year during 1960-65, and
0.7 percent during 1965-67 (Zekonski 1969, p. 10), or about 1 percent
per year overall. (I assume that Zekonski took account of price
changes and that his figure does not require additional deflation.)

However, some price changes are not used as deflators because
they come in the "hidden" form of assortment changes. Zekonski estimated that these hidden price rises amounted to 1.6 percent per year
during 1960-65, and to 3 percent per year during 1965-67, or to 2
percent per year for the period as a whole, leaving only 1.5 percent
of average annual increase in per capita consumption. Writing in the
economic weekly Zycie Gospodarcze, W. Dudzinski described how
radical increases resulted from the substitution of new and more expensive goods for old ones. Between 1964 and 1968, textiles and footwear
increased in price in this way by 13.2 percent, material for dresses
by 20.8 percent, finished dresses by more than that, chemicals for
household use by 35.4 percent, durable consumer goods by 5.9 percent.
Dudzinski found it impossible to determine how much the average price
level had risen because, apart from the substitution of higher-priced

*This is a revised version of an article originally published in
Soviet Studies (University of Glasgow) 23, no. 4 (April 1971: 609-22).

brands on the market, there were some completely new goods and some improvement in quality of others (Dudzinski 1968). Adjustment for quality changes is not sufficient. An increasing proportion of total population was employed during the period, and this changes consumption rises expressed on a per worker basis. My own rough calculations indicate an approximate increase in the labor force participation rate expressed as a percentage of all population outside agriculture from 51.7 percent in 1960 to 59.6 percent in 1969. This increase was due mainly to the effect of declining birth rates, offset only partially by an increase in the proportion of the population past working age. If we calculate the number of persons in the "nonproductive" age groups (before 18 and after retirement) we find that there were, for every 100 persons of productive age, 83 "nonproductive" in 1960, 87 in 1963, and 81 in 1968 (Kawalec 1969, p. IX). This indicates that between 1960 and 1968 production per person should have risen in Poland by 2 percent simply because, on the average, more persons were in the working age groups.

This estimate assumes unchanged labor force participation rates, an assumption that is not quite correct. Direct figures on labor force participation were not available, but a substantial increase in the proportion of women in socialized employment (from 33.2 percent in 1960 to 38.6 percent in 1968) clearly occurred. There also was a rise in the percentage of women living in villages who worked outside their homes, from 48.7 percent in 1960 to 53.5 percent in 1966 (Kawalec 1969, pp. X-XI). While men living in the countryside showed a similar trend in labor force participation rates, no figures were available for men living in the cities and towns, where the rate declined somewhat, presumably because of longer education. Granted that the above percentages reflect the effect of changing age groups and changes in labor force participation rates, part of the annual rise in consumption may be attributable to these two factors. How big a part was indicated by Zekonski (1969, p. 6), who changed the aggregate increase in the real wage of over 5 percent on the average over the 1960-68 period to just 1.9 percent for each employed person, a change of over three percentage points.

If we added the 2 percent deflation for assortment changes to the 3 percent conversion factor for changes in labor force participation, we get a 5 percent minimum rate of increase in per capita consumption which, if realized, would leave the workers' real factoral reward unchanged. However, since only a 3.5 percent increase was actually reported, we may conclude that the level of living per worker declined on the average by 1.5 percent per year during 1960-68.

On the other hand, social consumption was rising at a faster rate than personal consumption increasing its share in total consumption from 5.9 percent in 1960 to almost 9 percent in 1968 (Zekonski 1969, p. 5). On this count, therefore, there seems to have been an increase in consumption per labor unit during the 1960s, even if it was rather small in comparison with the 1.5 percent decline estimated above. However, another author writing in the Communist Party ideological monthly Nowe Drogi, estimated social consumption as constituting between 15 and 25 percent of individual consumption, depending on whether depreciation is included in the estimate. If this estimate is correct, then a 10 percent rise in social consumption meant a rise of about 1.5 percent in individual consumption. Unfortunately, social consumption rose annually by less than 10 percent (Pisarski 1969, p. 115).

However, discussion in Poland in 1968-70 was not about whether to increase the share of social consumption in total individual consumption. That seemed a foregone conclusion, and there was no doubt that the trend would continue. The question was rather how to maximize personal consumption and the level of living, given the limited resources allowed for the consumer goods sector by planners. This became a matter of finding the investment mix in the consumer goods sector that would give the best consumption effect.

Arguments for Changing the Structure of Consumption

The income elasticity of demand for food is relatively high in Poland, while the incremental capital/output ratio in agriculture also is high. Thus, any rise in consumer purchasing power necessitates high investment outlays in the consumer goods sector. Jozef Pajestka, the leading Polish economist, complained about this in the party journal Nowe Drogi (1969a, p. 25; see also Markowski 1968). In a later issue of the same journal he became more explicit, citing the social costs per unit of market value of different product groups as 1.288 for food, 0.726 for clothing and footwear, 0.748 for durable consumer goods, 0.710 for chemicals, 0.791 for paper products, and 1.391 for transport and communications (Pajestka 1969b, p. 18). On this basis, Pajestka recommended expansion of production in nonfood products, mentioning, among others, cars, where the coefficient seems to be high, at least generically, but the pent-up demand is substantial.

In his article in Gospodarka Planowa, Zekonski elaborated in greater detail on Pajestka's proposals. Whereas Pajestka used figures for aggregate outlay content that take into account all costs, not just capital costs, Zekonski constructed a complete table of resource use, reproduced here as Table 6.1, to show that, except for transport, capital use in the production of foodstuffs was higher than in the production of manufactured goods. Zekonski's conclusions were similar to Pajestka's: "...with the same outlays on capital and labor we can, changing the structure of consumption, obtain a larger volume of the consumption fund, which . . . is not only desirable but socially necessary." (Zekonski 1969, p. 11.)

TABLE 6.1

Resource Use by Basic Elements of Individual Consumption
in Poland in 1970

	Use of Capital (K)	Use of Labour (W)	Import Content (M) (soc)	Import Content (M) (cap)	Aggregate Outlay Content (A)
Food	3.32	.628	.00397	.00430	1.288
Drink and tobacco	1.17	.155	.00295	.00452	.461
Dress and footwear	1.40	.310	.00587	.00644	.726
Durable consumer goods	1.66	.293	.00873	.00403	.748
Semidurables	2.22	.277	.00595	.00508	.801
Services (public transport)	5.82	.374	.00479	.00119	1.391

Note: Aggregate coefficients were estimated on the basis of detailed (commodity) indicators of outlay content for 1962, with weights derived from the structure of consumption in 1970. These coefficients represent the value of outlays for one unit of (market) value of consumption in a given group of products. The value of outlays was calculated as follows:

$$A = .16 + W + 13.5M_{soc} + 17.5M_{cap}$$

where A = aggregate coefficient of outlay content for a unit of (market) value of consumption

K = coefficient of capital use for a unit of value of consumption

W = coefficient of labor use for a unit of value of consumption

M = coefficient of import use for a unit of value of consumption

soc = M for socialist countries, using a factor of 13.5 for each devisa zloty

cap = M for capitalist countries, using a factor of 17.5 for each devisa zloty

Source: Zekonski 1969, p. 11.

Zekonski found two obstacles to such a policy. First, foodstuffs have a relatively high income elasticity of demand. The income elasticities of demand for 1955-67 were: for foodstuffs, 0.77 (of which meat, fowl, and products, 0.96); for clothing, textiles, and footwear, 1.18 (of which footwear and leather products, 0.22); for durable consumer goods, 2.92. Actually, the income elasticity of demand for foodstuffs for the last two years of the period, 1966 and 1967, was so much higher that it raised the coefficient from 0.69 for 1955-65 by 0.08 to the 0.77 shown above.

Second, prices of foodstuffs tended to rise less than average prices of consumer goods. The average annual increases in prices in the socialized retail trade were shown by Zekonski as in Table 6.2. However, as already indicated, some hidden price rises took place in Poland, in the form of changes in the assortment of products offered by the socialized trade to the consumer. Zekonski estimated them as shown in Table 6.3, where it appears that, except for alcohol and tobacco (for which overt price increases were offsetting the low hidden price rises), prices of foodstuffs tended to rise least. Consequently, both overt and hidden price changes during 1960-67 tended to make the prices of manufactured products relatively higher than those of foodstuffs, which tended to retard any switch by consumers from foodstuffs to manufactured products.

On the other hand, one factor tended to facilitate such a switch. As indicated clearly by various statistics on the educational level of the labor force (most comprehensive statistics are found in Kawalec 1969, p. 104; see also Zekonski 1969, Table 5), between 1958 and 1968 a substantial improvement in the educational qualifications of the Polish labor force took place. Statistics on consumption patterns of different income groups show that the higher the educational background of the head of the household, the lower the proportion of expenditures on foodstuffs (Zekonski 1969). Consequently, as time goes on and the educational level of the population improves, the share of food in the household budget decreases independently of changes in incomes. However, it should be remembered that Pajestka recommended a conscious, policy-directed relative shift from foodstuffs to industrial consumer goods, without relying on any autonomous tendencies in the same direction.

Pajestka's proposal for changing the structure of consumption was discussed mainly in the party theoretical journal Nowe Drogi and in the economic weekly Zycie Gospodarcze.*

---

*A useful list of articles in Zycie Gospodarcze is found in Dudzinski 1970, p. 4 n. 1. Miesiecznik Literacki and Polityka also took part in the discussion. Nowe Drogi 1970, no. 3, and Zycie Gospodarcze 1970, nos. 9, and 10, carried a panel discussion on the controversy, with eight participating economists. The main antagonists in the discussion were Pajestka and Jan Glowczyk, the latter the chief editor of Zycie Gospodarcze.

TABLE 6.2

Average Annual Increase in Consumer Goods Prices
in Socialized Trade in Poland

	1960–65	1965–67
All consumer goods	1.2	.7
Foodstuffs	.6	.2
Alcoholic beverages and tobacco products	3.5	3.7
Textiles, clothing, footwear, and leather products	.1	.1
Durable consumer goods	-.2	-.7
Other semidurable goods	4.6	.6

Source: Zekonski 1969.

TABLE 6.3

Estimated Hidden Price Increases of Consumer Goods in Poland

	1965		1967	
	1960 = 100	Average Annual Hidden Rise (%)	1965 = 100	Average Annual Hidden Rise (%)
All consumer goods	108.0	1.6	106.1	3.0
Foodstuffs	107.2	1.4	102.7	1.3
Alcoholic beverages and tobacco products	106.5	1.3	96.7	-1.67
Textiles, clothing, footwear, and leather products	105.8	1.1	112.7	6.3
Durable consumer goods	109.6	1.9	106.1	3.0
Other semidurable goods	109.6	1.9	125.0	11.8

Source: Zekonski 1969, p. 10.

The controversy dealt with (1) the price policy within the area of manufactured goods insofar as it influenced consumption and production and (2) the overall structure of consumption, and in particular the relative magnitudes of foodstuffs and manufactured products.

A Policy for Manufactured Goods

Consumer goods of industrial origin are burdened in Poland by a differential turnover tax, and provide widely divergent profit margins for manufacturing enterprises. The differential turnover tax is blamed for separating the stimuli to the producers from the market signals to the consumers. Neither of these two groups of participants in the production-consumption process can meaningfully adjust to each other so as to produce maximum satisfaction at minimum cost, since the factory prices and market prices are different. The most thorough and authoritative analysis of this problem was provided by Otton Niedzial-kowski (1969), who described the gradual and limited introduction of the percentage turnover tax in Czechoslovakia and referred to a general preference among Polish economists, including Pajestka, for the percentage form of this tax. The main disadvantages of the differential form of the turnover tax were given as follows:

1. The size of the differential form of turnover tax results from the difference between the levels of sale prices and factory prices. Consequently, it plays a passive role: It is limited to draining part of the accumulation for the state budget.
2. Tax rates show wide differences. This makes it difficult to calculate and compare the average tax burden for commodity groups, but economic planners must be able to make these calculations if they are to change prices. The diversity of rates makes it very difficult to compute the tax liability by enterprises producing a wide assortment of products, and makes the control of such payments virtually impossible.
3. Since the tax revenue depends on the composition of goods sold, the tax intake may show variations if the actual assortment of products is different from the planned one.
4. Unlike the percentage form of the turnover tax, the differential form cannot actively influence the prices of products and hence regulate the forces of supply and demand. The percentage form is easier to calculate and control.
5. The differential form of turnover tax fails to differentiate between goods produced at high cost and similar goods produced at lower costs.

161

Niedzialkowski stressed that some of the inadequacies of the differential form of the turnover tax result from incorrect determination of factory prices: These prices may be based on imprecise original cost calculations, inflated by producers anxious to increase cost estimates, and perpetuated by delayed revisions of factory prices. According to him, the percentage form of the turnover tax leads to wide variations in profit rates for different products produced by the same enterprise (given fixed sale prices), and for different enterprises producing the same products. Interproduct profit differentiation may lead to a product mix divergent from what the consumers prefer. Interenterprise profit differentiation may lead to pressures for additional taxes or subsidies. On the other hand, in an enterprise producing both profitable and deficit products, the deficits would be covered up and hence attract less attention.

Finally, Niedzialkowski was unwilling to accept the possibility that a tax might determine the final sale price of a product. He was opposed to a comprehensive one-step introduction of the percentage form of the turnover tax, partly because of fear that such a decision would result in increased prices, with the accompanying adverse social and political consequences. Instead, he favored the gradual, cautious introduction of the tax in conjunction with certain changes in the procedures used by the State Planning Commission, and after a reform of prices of intermediate goods. This was indeed the consensus of Polish economists at an earlier panel discussion (Nowe Drogi 1967; see also Mujzel 1969, p. 520).

A more forthright endorsement of the percentage form of the turnover tax was made by Mieczyslaw Rakowski (1970), who recommended neutrality of prices in order to make both factory prices and retail prices reflect the approximate cost of production. This would make it impossible for producers to change assortments without first considering the structure of demand. Instead, Rakowski proposed to take advantage of the "assortment revolution." Assume, for example (he wrote), the existence of two kinds of shirts, the traditional cotton one and one made of nylon. The cotton shirt costs 140 zlotys to produce, the nylon shirt costs 100 zlotys. The cotton shirt lasts 50 washings at 1 zloty a time and 50 ironings at 4 zlotys a time, while the nylon shirt lasts 300 washings at 1 zloty a time and needs no ironing. The cost of production and utilization of the cotton shirt is 140 + (50 x 50) = 390 zlotys, while the cost of the nylon shirt, which lasts six times as long as a cotton shirt, is 100 + (1 x 300) = 400 zlotys. This means that, in effect, per unit of time the nylon shirt is one-sixth as expensive as the cotton shirt. However, the high price set for the nylon shirts to discount their future value-in-use prevents the poorer consumers from buying them, so nylon shirts account for only a small proportion of shirt sales (this is summarized in Table 6.4).

In the "future case," an introduction of a percentage form of tax (represented in Table 6.4 by "profit") results in an increase in the sales of nylon shirts and a decrease in the sale of cotton ones, a

TABLE 6.4

Hypothetical Example of the "Assortment Revolution"

	Price Per Unit	Cost of Production	Profit Per Unit	Sales (million units)	Effect in Use (millions)	Total Value	Total Cost (million zlotys)	Accumu- lation
Present case								
Cotton shirts	200	140	60	10	10 x 1 = 10	2,000	1,400	600
Nylon shirts	400	100	300	2	2 x 5 = 10	800	200	600
Total				20		2,800	1,600	1,200
Future case								
Cotton shirts	245	140	105	2	2 x 1 = 2	490	280	210
Nylon shirts	175	100	75	6	6 x 5 = 30	1,050	600	450
Total				32		1,540	880	660

Source: Rakowski 1970.

163

60 percent increase in the effect-in-use for the consumers, a 45 percent decline in the expenditures on shirts by the population, a decline of 33 percent in the number of shirts bought, and a 45 percent decline in total cost of production and in accumulation. Even though the current practice in Poland is not to allow any decrease in the total accumulation, Rakowski argued that this would be preferable for three reasons:

1. A substantial improvement in the level of living of the population would occur.
2. The decline in accumulation would be substantially smaller than the increase in living levels. Consequently, the nominal wages would need to be increased less to yield the desired increase in the level of living.
3. The reduction in the cost of production shows that factors of production could be directed to increase production, consumption, and accumulation. In the particular case of shirts, another advantage would emerge: a reduction in imports of cotton.

In conclusion, Rakowski suggested a fairly speedy adjustment of prices to costs of production, allowing only a temporary delay for change in production capacity and new investments.
A similar argument can be used for declining costs, as with television sets or refrigerators, where again the pricing policy does not serve to maximize consumption effects. Both the above cases show that considerable improvement is possible within the sphere of production and distribution of industrial goods; the side effect, assuming an elastic demand for such goods, could be a drainage of purchasing power away from foodstuffs at least in the incremental sense. Thus Rakowski, although allowing for retardation caused by delayed investments and limitations in productive capacity, came out unequivocally in favor of the percentage form of the turnover tax, as well as in favor of uniform profit margins. However, he allowed for departures from this principle, based on social costs and benefits (Rakowski 1970).

General Structure of Consumption

Discussion of the overall structure of consumption abounded in misunderstandings, which will be omitted from the following recapitulation. Criticism of Pajestka's position concentrated principally on the following points:

1. Pajestka resorted to unwarranted aggregation and use of misleading indexes to support the assertion that consumption of food in Poland had reached a satisfactory level. Marek Misiak and

Ryszard Zabrzewski (1969) showed inadequate Polish consumption of many food categories; Jan Glowczyk (Nowe Drogi 1967) pointed to the misleading use of calorie intake as the sole index of the level of consumption of food; Boleslaw Przywara (1970), in defense of Pajestka, pointed to Poland's poor showing in the area of durable consumer goods. This part of the discussion engendered some general recommendations for improvement in the quantity and quality of products, and better assortment of products; for the use of advertising, improved sales techniques, and primary education to make the consumption pattern more desirable; and for a conscious use of price policy—with caution so as not to invoke the Giffen paradox. (According to the Giffen paradox, a rise in prices of foodstuffs could, by causing a reduction in the real incomes of consumers, increase the demand for foodstuffs, especially basic foodstuffs.)

2. A comparison of the aggregate outlay per unit of market value of different products is incorrect when it involves agricultural products on the one hand and manufactured products on the other. Under Polish conditions (in which farming is by and large under private ownership), accumulation, which increases market prices, takes place, and indeed should take place, only in the sphere of industrial products. The peasants contribute to state accumulation by purchasing their nonfood consumer goods and by buying increasing amounts of agricultural inputs. Consequently, the outlay coefficients used by Pajestka and Zekonski were misleading because the two price systems they straddle are incomparable. Under a price system ensuring an equal rate of accumulation in all product groups, the coefficients of total outlay and of capital use per unit of market value would be approximately equal (Rakowski 1970; cf. also Glowczyk 1970).

There is only a limited possibility of shifts in consumption since a given human want can be satisfied by a specific commodity or a set of directly competing commodities. If the structure of consumption were changed in any thorough way, in effect its assortment would become subservient to planners' choices rather than consumers' wants. According to the main exponent of this view, Jan Glowczyk, studies of "actual preferences" should be made with a view to determining social costs and benefits; no attempt should be made to select the cheapest way of satisfying a given quantum of consumption wants (Glowczyk 1969 and Nowe Drogi 1967). Most of the participants in the discussion, including Pajestka, agreed on the need for further study of the pattern of wants and factors determining them, although previously they had not been unaware of the sociological and psychological dimensions of the problem of formulating a model of a desirable consumption pattern (Kozminski 1969).

4. A hierarchy of social needs, representing a socialist model of consumption, must be set up. This suggestion by Wladyslaw Dudzinski (1970) was typical of the "traditional" approach, as was the stand taken by Andrzej Hodoly (1970), who opposed consumer

TABLE 6.5

Coefficients of Capital Intensity in Poland

	1965		1965-70:
	Direct	Total	Direct Incremental
Means of transport	.549	2.210	.660
Construction materials	1.733	3.448	2.092
Wood industry	.417	1.965	.652
Paper industry	.982	2.854	2.309
Textile industry	.508	1.897	.699
Clothing industry	.094	1.590	.092
Leather and shoe industry	.257	1.618	.469
Food industry	.305	2.610	.661
Construction	.292	2.393	.602
Agriculture	1.539	3.435	2.922
Transport and communications	6.945	8.029	3.684
Trade	.654	2.423	1.102

Source: Mazys 1970.

sovereignty and was critical of consumption patterns in capitalist countries. Hodoly extolled the conscious process of development planning. It allowed for improvement in the quality of consumption wants (presumably to bring them closer in line with the model), and for a conscious influence on these wants by the state, with a view to the cultivation of cultural values. In the sphere of production of consumer goods, this view stressed social rentability and intensification (raising productivity through selective growth, application of large doses of investment, and research and development), and strengthened labor discipline. In this way, a quantitative increase in consumption could be achieved. This approach rejected by implication Pajestka's acceptance of the desirability of maximizing consumption.

Finally, Kazimierz Ryc (1970a and 1970b) stressed the desirability of retaining a certain sort of egalitarian principle in consumption: Every consumer has the right to the same quantity of goods, but not to the same quantity of goods of the same quality. Thus, people with higher incomes would live better, in accordance with the slogan "equality in participation [in consumption], but difference in comfort." The slogan implies use of a peculiar quantitative measure of consumption. Furthermore, Ryc favored the dynamic growth of consumption, implying agreement with Pajestka's suggested use of incremental capital/output ratio and cost-benefit criteria. Ryc was, moreover, in favor of a critical adoption of some consumption patterns from advanced capitalist countries. Ryc's contribution may be regarded as an effort to reconcile the differences that emerged during the consumption debate.

5. Although not explicitly connected with the controversy, an article by Jerzy Mazys (1970) cast some doubts on Pajestka's conclusions. The author calculated capital intensity, defined as the average amount of capital per unit of production, for individual industrial branches in Poland, and came up with a table, a part of which is shown in Table 6.5. It appears that the agricultural sector is on the whole much less capital intensive than transport and communications (which puts seriously in doubt the economic calculus of Pajestka's advocacy of a "mass car," even though the coefficient for the production of means of transport is by itself lower than for transport and communications), and about the same as production of construction materials. Increasing agricultural production may not be as socially expensive as Pajestka seemed to think.

Observations

Four aspects of the problem of the structure of consumption were missing from the discussion in Poland. One is the obvious assumption of autarchy which underlies all the statements made, in particular Pajestka's and Zekonski's application of the aggregate resource-use coefficient. An alternative assumption of an open economy could radically change the coefficients, introducing a completely new dimension to the problem of maximization of consumption. Foodstuffs, when imported from countries with comparative advantage in their production, might prove relatively cheap.

Second, even within a closed economy, the resource-use coefficient for foodstuffs need not be regarded as a parameter in the planning process. In fact, Polish agriculture reveals considerable differences in the incremental capital/output ratios between different forms of property, even if one takes into account the fact that agricultural goods produced on socialized and private land are not equivalent. Table 6.6 showing the incremental capital/output ratios for two years illustrates this point. Even though the gap between the incremental capital/output ratios of the two main forms of property in agriculture is decreasing, alterations in the balance of the two forms of property would introduce some changes in the resource-use coefficient.

Third, one wonders whether Pajestka's use of the aggregate outlay coefficient was theoretically correct under Polish conditions. Even though it was not generally reported, and particularly not in a comprehensive single source, one could find sufficient information in Polish economic publications to suggest that several million people

TABLE 6.6

Incremental Capital/Output Ratios in Polish Agriculture

	1960	1965
All agriculture	6.41	6.50
Private peasants	5.88	5.96
State farms, including household plots	12.04	10.66
State farms, excluding household plots	14.60	12.14

Source: Strapko 1970.

were either unemployed or underemployed (Mieczkowski 1968a). Under these conditions, with hidden agricultural unemployment fairly prevalent, the social cost of labor —particularly in agriculture—was likely to be much lower than the accounting cost. Consequently, only capital and import use should be taken into account in making comparisons of per-unit cost of the main groups of consumer goods. Pajestka's conclusions would not be changed materially with this modification, but his approach would become theoretically more acceptable.

Fourth, although Dudzinski mentioned the economies of scale, no author developed the theme adequately. There obviously are substantial differences in the outlay-use coefficients within the main consumption groups, and it is these coefficients for particular products, rather than the aggregate coefficients, that should be compared. It may be that potato production, for example, is less resource intensive than production of buttons. Once these individual relationships are discovered, large-batch production could be planned, with lowered unit costs and reliance on international exchange to secure the domestically resource-intensive, high cost per unit of market value, commodities. Bela Balassa (1970) estimated that nonutilization of international specialization, which he termed "the inward-looking development strategy," results in static costs to some economies of over 10 percent of their national income. He added that, while no calculation had been made of the cost of such inward-looking strategy for Communist countries, "available information on the allocation process under centralized planning points to substantial inefficiencies." Thus, utilization of economies of scale, combined with international specialization according to the principle of comparative advantage, could substantially modify and increase the advantage of changing the structure of production. In light of this, one suspects that discussions of the structure of production—rather than discussions of the structure of consumption—would be more to the point.

To recapitulate, then, the relative resource intensity of foodstuffs as a group could be circumvented by recourse to international exchange; resource-use coefficients could be changed through institutional modifications; partial resource-use coefficients may be more properly used under certain conditions; and individual commodity resource-use coefficients may be utilized for policy decisions, with substantial elbow room for their decrease under conditions of large-scale production accompanied by international exchange.

The Polish discussion on the structure of consumption is probably far from closed. Everyone agrees on the desirability of further research into the problem, and most agree on the need for a quantitative approach to the planning of the future structure of consumption. This new approach may serve to maximize future gains in per capita consumption, as well as focus attention on the desirability of improving the level of living. It already has brought open and rational discourse on a subject heretofore handled in a propagandistic and axiomatic manner. Therefore, the discussion on consumption planning in Poland may be regarded as part of the rationalization process recently taking place in Eastern Europe.

EVENTS OF DECEMBER 1970

An outgrowth of the discussion on consumption planning was a decision to raise, without prior notice, prices of many basic consumer goods as of December 13, 1970. Coming at the end of a disappointing decade and just before the peak of the Christmas shopping season, this decision evoked considerable resentment. The total of price increases amounted to 17.1 billion zlotys (assuming the 1970 expenditure pattern*), or to 5.9 percent of the 1970 wage fund, but they were regressively distributed, concentrating on goods most important in low-income budgets, as shown in Table 6.7. Almost two-thirds of the cost of price increases to the consumer was concentrated in foodstuffs, of primary importance in low-income budgets; the others, including fuel, also were regarded by the population as of basic importance, especially in the middle of winter.

Some price decreases were announced simultaneously with the increases, their total amounting to 11.9 billion zlotys, or almost 70

---

*Official estimates may easily be criticized on the ground of the implicit assumption of zero elasticity of demand with respect to price. Estimates of the actual impact of price changes vary; cf. RFE, News from Poland, December 31, 1970, p. 3.

TABLE 6. 7

Share of Various Consumer Products in Price Increases
of December 13, 1970, in Poland
(percentages of total increase due to each category)

Category	Share of Increase
Meat, meat products, and fats	49. 7
Other food products	15. 4
Products of light industry	17. 7
Construction materials and wood products	4. 5
Coal and coke	5. 4
Other consumer goods	7. 3

Source: RPiG 1971, p. 456.

percent of the price increases. But most decreases were concentrated
in synthetic textiles (58 percent of price decreases; cf. pp. 162–63
above on the "assortment revolution") not yet in common use; in
durable consumer goods (16 percent of price decreases); pharmaceu-
ticals (10 percent of price decreases); and chemical products (8 percent of price decreases); and none were in foodstuffs (RPiG 1971,
pp. 456–57). Some additional concessions to the population—lowered
annual TV rates, somewhat higher family allowances, higher prices to
farmers for animals—seem to have been marginal, and they concentrated their impact on higher-income groups.

To add to the frustrations of working people, the government had
proposed introduction, at the beginning of 1971, of a new incentive
wage system that was widely expected to eliminate prospects for wage
increases (cf. Flakierski 1973). Therefore, the population assessed
the situation as one in which real wages and the level of living would
decline painfully, and this coming after a succession of several years
of what had been officially described as "stagnating real wages"
(RPiG 1971, p. 457).

It did not help the consumer to realize that the government, rather
than trying to accommodate consumer aspirations, tried to mold
consumption according to its own preferred pattern. On the day they
were introduced, the Communist Party daily, Trybuna Ludu, explained
the price changes as resulting from "the need to adjust demand for
foodstuffs, mainly meat, to the real possibilities of supplying the
market," and from "the necessity to adjust the system of retail prices,
and thus the consumption structure, to the developmental requirements"
of the Polish economy (December 13, 1970, after RFE, News from

Poland, December 31, 1970, p. 3). These "developmental requirements" were understood to stem from doctrinaire planners' preferences in favor of production of capital goods at the expense of consumer goods, preferences that during the previous two five-year plans had relegated consumption to the role of a "shock absorber," already well known and well resented during the 1950-55 Six-Year Plan.

There followed mass demonstrations started by the relatively well-paid shipyard workers in Gdansk, early changed into a brutal massacre by police forces. Five days of bloody disturbances in Gdansk resulted in several hundred deaths, never fully revealed to the public. Popular disturbances carried into another port and ship-building center, Szczecin, and continued in a series of strikes in other industrial centers in January 1971. The disturbances and their violence led late in December 1970 to the downfall of Gomulka, the First Secretary of the Communist Party since October 1956, and the choice of Edward Gierek as the new leader.*

Upon being installed in power, the new government rolled back the price increases effective March 1, 1971; called off introduction of the distrusted new wage incentive system; and promised a new era of consumerism, social justice, and quick economic growth. Obviously, a new and different economic policy was imminent, projecting particularly into the areas of consumption problems, incentives, and plan-making priorities.

CONSUMPTION BOOMS BEYOND PLAN IN POLAND

An official assessment of the last Polish Five-Year Plan under Gomulka (1966-70) as far as the standard of living was concerned was contained in a report by the Central Committee of the Communist Party published in the ideological monthly, Nowe Drogi:

> If the whole 1966-70 period brought only small and
> lower-than-planned results in the area of increase
> of real wages and of the improvement in living con-
> ditions of the population, particular difficulties arose
> in this area during the last two years of that period.
> (ND 1972, pp. 18-19.)

---

*Some unique documents on the December 1970-January 1971 events in Poland were published. See Kultura (Paris): 1971a and 1971b, Djilas 1971, Silone 1971, Mieroszewski 1971, Byrski 1971, Drewnowski 1971, Brus 1971, and Kultura: Dokumenty 1971. Cf. also Societe d' Edition, Librairie, Informations Ouvrieres 1972.

An editorial in the central planning journal, Gospodarka Planowa, stated even more strongly:

> In view of the impossibility of reaching the excessive
> number of goals, the level of consumption and the social
> situation suffered, and not only experienced lack of
> improvement but in some respects showed deterioration.
> A further consequence was the danger of a brake applied
> to the process of economic development. (GP 1972,
> p. 1.)

A foremost Polish specialist on consumption problems stated recently in the same journal that during the 1960s some social groups found their real incomes decreasing—which was a cautious way of indicating lack of improvement in real incomes (Zekonski 1974, p. 360).

The dissatisfaction caused by lack of progress in the level of living, and finally the decreed increase in food prices, led to the rise of Gierek, reputed as an efficient administrator with a good record of paying attention to workers' living standards in his former Silesian province. The purpose of the present section is to highlight the quantitative direction of policy changes instituted by Gierek, and the analytical conclusions reached by Polish economists on the results of the new policy.

Early Political and Conceptual Commitment to Consumerism

The outlines of Gierek's new economic policy were contained in his speech delivered during the February 6-7, 1971, Plenum of the Central Committee of the Communist Party. By that time some concrete policy decisions already had been made. These included improving living conditions for families with the lowest incomes and many children; raising the lowest pensions; freezing prices of basic foodstuffs at their pre-December 1970 level for a period of two years; gradually lowering prices of industrial consumer goods and increasing supplies; and fighting the hidden price increases that had plagued the Polish consumer during the Gomulka era. Therefore, the first Gierek moves were designed to alleviate the plight of the neediest and to prevent further sources of acute consumer dissatisfaction from arising again. These pragmatic concessions from previous hard-line programs were aimed at establishing an initial air of confidence in the new regime and preventing renewal of popular disturbances.

In his speech, Gierek also outlined plans to raise the production of meat, to import grain from the USSR, to seek new foreign loans, and to invest more resources in consumer goods industries. Housing construction was to rise, and the service and handicrafts sectors were, after a decade of doubtful growth, to be stimulated. Since the proposed new wage incentive system—developed in 1970 for introduction at the beginning of 1971—evoked widespread and just apprehension among workers, the scheme was abandoned and a new emphasis on basic wage, as contrasted with premiums, was adopted.* More powerful incentives to raise productivity were to be instituted, but workers were not to fear that unforeseen breakdowns in deliveries of raw materials to their factories would rob them of wages. The planned economic policies were thus designed to lessen possible mistrust and frictions between the party and the population.

For the time being at least, the party found itself hard-pressed by a tide of demands from the population. Some of these demands simmered among workers, some were expressed in graffiti on walls, but some found open outlet in the press, especially in the Baltic coast region, where the December 1970 workers' riots were most severe. (for a review of such demands from the provincial press, see RFE Research, April 14, 1971). The demands were obviously spontaneous, a reflection of deep-felt frustrations with previous maximum-exhortation and minimum-delivery policies. Their slogan was aptly noted by the London Economist (July 10, 1971, pp. 42-44) in a worker's answer to ideological tirades for more effort to raise GNP, strengthen socialism, and so on. The worker requested the party official to speak to his pocket because his ears were there. And Gierek did address himself to where the population could, or would, hear him: to their material interests. Where not "dangerously libertarian," he also courted the workers by providing them with greater representation of their own interests, as through the labor unions, which had been criticized for their frankly anti-worker role during the December workers protests (RFE Research, April 14, 1971, p. 16).

The courtship of the population also was evident in the selective promises of new benefits; for example, a promise of special housing construction for teachers was made by Gierek, obviously in the hope that better relations with educators eventually would result, through attitudes imparted to their pupils, in better relations with the educational system. This move is along somewhat the same lines as a

---

*The abandoned incentive system was criticized by one of the foremost economic writers on the following grounds: (1) it imposed a brake on the rise of wages by introducing an upper limit on the premium fund and paralyzing the promotion system; (2) the synthetic indicator of profit was limited to only 25 percent of the premium fund, while sectional (and haphazard) indicators were given an important role; (3) the system was highly complicated (see Fick 1971b). The transitional system, introduced in 1971, allowed wage increases, rewards for improved efficiency, and reduction of success indicators to at most five (see Fick 1971a).

more recent one by the Soviet government in its 1971-75 plan to take special cognizance of the welfare of the student population, student cafeterias, and students' food (Goldman 1971).

Part of the courtship by the new ruling group consisted in open critiques of the former government, with the apparent aim of at least partly bridging the confidence gap between the population and the Communist Party, and perhaps also allowing some excess steam of resentment and disillusionment to be released through the safety valve of open criticism. That denounciations of particular aspects of the now ancien regime of Gomulka and some party personnel were "in" was affirmed by Gierek himself in a February 1971 Plenum speech. He stated that it would be easy to blame the removed leadership for the December riots, but that the fault fell on everybody among the leading party members. Even though the new party boss hastened to add that the fault was not equally distributed, the sting of criticism stuck and put the apparat people on notice against again losing contact with the population and becoming mere arrogant bureaucrats. The hue and cry of reform-directed complaints voiced by lesser personages extended over both political and economic aspects of life in Poland, but the following review concentrates on the latter. The Polish press published a series of searching articles, as well as a number of discussions in which prominent economists explored what needed to be corrected in the economic system.

The Polish Economic Society passed in January 1971 a resolution that provided the conceptual underpinnings of the new policy:

> faster growth of consumption is currently and will be in
> the future a condition for attaining a faster role of growth
> of production. Without a proper growth of consumption
> the increasing capacity of the economy is not linked to
> the [ultimate] goal of production [that is, to consumption],
> and the mechanism of growth creates "production for the
> sake of production," which slows down the general rate
> of growth. (Ekonomista 1971, p. 354.)

The economists also reasserted that "the aim of the socialist economy is the full satisfaction of the needs of the population" (Wiszniewski 1971).

Various articles stressed the importance of building up an information system on the market for consumer goods, and the problem of guiding consumption into proper channels (Pawlowski 1971); within the field of consumption, authors urged expansion of services, and especially services that save the consumer's time. True, a Marxist hang-up had to be overcome, since the Marxist national income accounting practice excludes services, even though the recent trend in that area has been to include progressively more of the formerly "nonproductive" services among the constituents of national income (cf. Holesovsky 1961).

Mieczyslaw Rakowski (1971, pp. 448-54) estimated that the direct loss of (Marxist) national income resulting from expansion of time-saving services during 1971-75 would amount to 6.1 billion zlotys if an extra 200,000 persons were employed without additional investments in the area of services, or to 31,000 zlotys per person employed in services. Similarly, each zloty of investments in time-saving services causes a loss of potential national income of 0.33 zloty, leading Rakowski to an estimate of loss on account of investments of 6 billion zlotys from national income. Thus the aggregate loss of national income on account of additional employment and additional investment in the service sector was estimated at 12.1 billion zlotys. However, on the plus side of the ledger, the author estimated the value of the decrease in fatigue per person as a multiple of 20,000 zlotys, depending on the number of hours of household work saved by each hour of service rendering by commercial establishments. In addition, a substantial number of hours would become available for creative rest, free from the drudgery of household work. Decreased fatigue would raise labor productivity; this would then raise national income, without need for additional investments. This effect would offset, or more than offset, the loss of national income caused by additional employment and additional investment in services. Rakowski also observed that some women who otherwise could not be utilized in "productive" employment could be used in the expansion of new services; he thus arrived at an estimate of an ultimate rise in national income of 128,000 zlotys per person employed in services, or a net increase in national income of 25.6 billion zlotys. In addition, the average increase in free time per employed person resulting from the rendering of new services was estimated at 3.2 hours per week. Consequently, the total net effect on the economy resulting from additional rendering of commercial services clearly would be positive.

Abatement of Argument about the "Consumption Model"

The contention around the "consumption model" continued from the 1968-70 period into the early Gierek period. The main issue was possible direction of consumption and the means to be used in directing consumers toward purchases of goods with smaller capital content, to a large extent signifying a relative shift away from foodstuffs and toward manufactured goods. The emphasis given to social costs and benefits, and the manner of estimating them, also was discussed among economists at the time. Stefan Kurowski provided an analytical assessment of positions in that discussion, dividing the participants roughly into "economists," who wanted to utilize consumption as an incentive and tended to regard the volume of consumption as a success indicator of the system, and "planners," who wanted to preserve the status quo and limit consumption in order to accelerate the volume of investments and thus the growth of national income (Kurowski 1971). Kurowski's article evoked some dissent* but, for reasons stated below, the interest in the discussion soon abated. A pacifying note was sounded in the economic weekly Życie Gospodarcze in a call for reconciliation of individual and social consumption, for estimating future changes in consumption rather than dictating them, and for development of a theory of socialist consumption, the latter desideratum repeated in several articles (Kantecki 1972).

The stress in the articles shifted to adjustment of production to the preferences of consumers, with the following main reforms suggested: development of closer relations between trade and industry; integration of wholesale with retail trade; imports to follow consumer preferences; establishment of a premium fund for producers to reward better satisfaction of consumer wants; establishment of adequate profit margins for enterprises to make production for the consumer more profitable to them; and a reform of prices, the last point being a Communist perennial (Kierczynski 1971).

More basically, author after author hammered at the theme of consumption as the final goal of all production. Thus, for instance, Kazimierz Ryc opened a series of three articles on consumption, published in Nowe Drogi, by the statement:

> The thesis that production in a socialist economy serves the satisfaction of social needs has never been questioned. . . . productive effort of the society has as its goal supplying of increasingly abundant amounts of consumer goods. Besides, this is the final goal of all production. It should be noted that in a socialist economy — in contrast to systems based on private ownership of the means of production — it becomes a direct goal. (Ryc 1971a, p. 123.)

One of the chief central planners, Kazimierz Secomski, similarly reported conclusions reached by a number of experts that one of the two basic problems for the Five-Year Plan, 1971-75, was a radical improvement in the perceived level of living of the population (Secomski 1971, p. 205). That such consensus emerged as a result of disappointing past performance is shown by another statement: "Because a weak rate of growth in the level of living of the population was maintained from 1959, or for 11 years, a radical acceleration of that growth seems necessary during the current Five-Year Plan."

---

*For example, see Pohorille 1972. However, Pohorille did concede that the existing price system misinformed both producers and consumers.

(Krol and Drozdek 1971, p. 36.) The expectation of, or even demand for, a fundamental change in the policy toward consumption goods was raised by several writers. The mood obviously changed from one of considering whether and how to increase consumption to one of how far-reaching the increase ought or had to be. As it happened, however, a rapid, and higher than expected, improvement in the level of living pushed aside the importance of theorizing on how such improvement could be achieved.

Booming Consumption

Theoretical jostling of the late Gomulka and early Gierek period was soon submerged in the general euphoria over the obviously highly successful rising indicators of growth. The accouterments of that growth were such as to confound the "traditional" theory. During 1971-72, national income distributed rose by 10.2 percent annually* (compared with a 6 percent annual growth during 1966-70); real wages rose by about 5.8 percent annually (compared with a 1.8 percent growth rate during 1966-70[†]); at the same time, the consumption fund rose by 8.5 percent annually and the accumulation fund by an imposing 13.8 percent annually. It was an achievement in itself that while the ambition of the 1971-75 plan was to raise the rate of increase in real wages from the 11 percent for the whole preceding plan period to 18 percent, the first two years of the plan brought an increase of about 13 percent, despite a substantial rise in employment of about 800,000 persons. Yet investments rose at the same time by 27 percent, at a 13 percent annual rate, compared to the 8.2 percent annual rate during the 1966-70 period (Chelstowski 1972; cf. Nasilkowski 1973).

Between 1968-70 and 1971-73 the official annual growth rate in aggregate consumption increased from 4.5 percent to 9.1 percent; the rate of growth of personal consumption rose from 4.0 percent to 8.9 percent; while at the same time the rate of growth of investment rose from 4.5 percent to 20.7 percent. The symptomatic feature of that

---

*National income produced rose by 8.3 percent annually during 1971-72; the difference between the figures indicates running down of inventories and negative balance of trade with the rest of the world.
[†] The rate decelerated sharply in 1970: "for many groups of employees real wages did not rise at all, and in some cases even declined" (Zycie Gospodarcze 1971). The figures cited are official, and they are likely to represent an overestimate for the 1966-70 period.

acceleration, contrary to the rather static traditional socialist theory, was that while the growth of consumption (expressed here in overall and not in per capita terms) more than doubled between 1968-70 and 1971-73, the rate of growth of investment grew almost five-fold (Ryc 1974, p. 102).

In 1973 national income produced grew by 10 percent, and national income distributed by about 13 percent; the consumption fund grew by about 10 percent, while investments rose by 23 percent. The aggregate money incomes of the population rose by about 10 percent, and the wage fund by about 13 percent. Average real wages rose by 10 percent, while incomes of peasants used for consumption rose by 9 percent. The 1971-75 planned increase of real wages by 18 percent was realized by the middle of 1973. At the same time, a large increase in the total amount and assortment of consumer goods was planned, plus an increase in housing construction, in anticipation of the booming consumption based on that higher-than-planned increase in real wages (Gospodarka Planowa 1973, pp. 1-2; RFE Research March 27, 1974; Chelstowski 1974, p. 11; Biuletyn Statystyczny 1974, no. 1, "Insert," p. 1). Thus the original goals of the 1971-75 plan were expected to be overfulfilled by a substantial margin. Poland, according to the above figures, found itself among the fastest developing countries of the world. This, after the relative stagnation of the 1960s, must have come as a considerable surprise.

It should be noted, however, that despite this eminent success, the share of both personal consumption and aggregate consumption in national income (net material product) declined between 1970 and 1972, the share of social consumption having remained constant. This development differed from what took place at the same time in Czechoslovakia, Hungary, and East Germany (Alton 1974, p. 261). It was the result of very fast growth of national income in Poland and, to a smaller extent, of the considerable increase in personal savings that released resources from satisfying consumer needs. The widening import surplus also could have influenced this development in Poland, to the extent that the increase in imports favored accumulation (Alton 1974, p. 271). Personal savings, defined as increases in savings deposits and in cash holdings by the population, showed a substantial increase, from 2.44 percent in 1970 to 4.97 percent in 1971, 6.71 percent in 1972, and 8.37 percent in 1973 (Marczewski 1974, p. 9), contributing to avoidance of inflationary pressures in the Polish economy.

General Explanation of the "Consumption Miracle"

Normally, a consumption binge translates itself to a large extent into inflationary price increases, particularly when supply of consumer goods is, for one reason or another, restricted. However, it was noticed by 1971 that no such development had taken place, that "market equilibrium" was maintained. This fact was regarded as a paradoxical phenomenon, insofar as such equilibrium was achieved through an increase in the total purchasing power of the population, and despite the still inadequate (although rising) food deliveries, but with the help of fast-rising supplies of industrial products. The conclusion from such an experience was to strengthen the argument in favor of price flexibility and even in favor of some price decreases (Ryc 1971b, pp. 93-95). Consumption boomed without apparent increase in inflationary pressures, and without this being done at the cost of decreasing the investments — quite the contrary, in fact, with an unexpected rise in the rate of investments. Thus, voices were raised that the capitalist Keynesian model, which in its static form divides national income into consumption and investment, should be recognized as inapplicable to the socialist economy, where instead of planners' choice of devoting resources to either consumption or investment the real choice is for consumption and investment. Thus the theory of selective development was pronounced dead in socialist practice and a call was made for its theoretical correction (Krawczewski 1972). Such a correction could, of course, have been gleaned from capitalist theory where a clear distinction exists between a static model, with national income fixed and divided into consumption and investment, and a dynamic model in which mutual interaction between consumption and investment influences both the size and rate of growth of national income.

The most decisive step toward the new theoretical insight was made by Kazimierz Ryc, author of a study on the development of consumption in Poland that was apparently confiscated upon publication (Mieczkowski 1973b). Writing now obviously with the approval of party theoreticians, Ryc stated (1972) that consumption serves to increase investment rather than to add up with investment to national income. Hence no conflict between consumption and accumulation of capital need be postulated, but rather mutual stimulation. Ryc was careful to make a distinction between capitalist and socialist cases. While in the former increases in consumption lead to increases in national income through the interaction between the accelerator and the multiplier until all unemployed resources are employed and excess capacity is eliminated, potential increases of national income also can be vitiated under socialism, where no excess capacity exists since by definition there is no unemployment under socialism. This takes place when the policy of stabilization of the market leads to administrative limitation on increases in the wage fund and on increases in employment (still under the socialist assumption of full employment!), which limits production of consumer goods and hence limits the rise of national income. This brought Ryc to an analysis of the difference between Gomulka's and Gierek's consumption policies:

Manifestations of such a policy [of administratively imposed limitation of the wage fund] took place in the latter part of the 1960s. Limitation of growth of the wage fund and of the increase in employment, among others in order to slow down the extensive factors of development, unfortunately by administrative means rather than by social and economic methods, limited on the one hand the possibility of expanding production and on the other hand artificially constrained the domestic market. Thus, the increasing potential supply of many durable [consumer] goods was not utilized because of the unduly shallow market, resulting from the maintenance of high prices in relation to incomes of the less affluent part of the population, and [consequently] limited production because [lack of purchasing power in the hands of the population] decreased the opportunity to increase earnings and probably also to create additional financial accumulation of enterprises. (Ryc 1972, p. 102.)

Ryc concluded that it was a mistake to assume that one has to increase production before individual incomes can be safely raised. In actuality, the policy of limiting increases in incomes led to limiting increases in production. Consequently, abandonment of a deflationary policy can serve to dynamize production. And this is precisely what took place during 1971-72, when the scope for the expansion of production of consumer goods was broadened, while greater freedom accorded to enterprises in the management of their wage funds made for better adjustment of production to market demand by allowing more flexible expansion of the production of the goods desired most by the population. (This argument has to be understood, of course, as an impressionistic view of certain tendencies, rather than an assertion of absolute consumer sovereignty.) To allow a still greater degree of mutual accommodation between supply and demand, Ryc declared himself in favor of relative cheapening of the more highly manufactured industrial products, basically meaning durable consumer goods.

Consumption and investment in this view mutually interact and increase each other. They do so currently, without lags; that is, current accumulation raises consumption and vice versa. Consumption also is a factor that changes the structure of the economy through changes in the structure of consumer demand. Such a view seems to denigrate the absolutist approach to the role of planners as final deciders on the economy's development path. This impression is strengthened by a declaration by Ryc in another article:

a change in the rate of growth of production of consumer goods and of investment goods in favor of consumption is not . . . an act of planner's goodwill . . . but is the result of a long-lasting process of application of technological progress. (Ryc 1971b, p. 98.)

A similar limitation on planners' power was indicated by the Nestor of Polish economists, Edward Lipinski, who stated in a form that amounted to a confessio fidei of an old socialist: "all means of production serve in the final analysis toward production of consumer goods and services," adding that while central planners can favor or slow down some areas of consumption, they ought to take into account the side effects of their preferences (E. Lipinski 1972). These side effects obviously pertain to incentives to labor efficiency and the impact of changes in consumption on investments. Consequently, they closely follow Ryc's reasoning.

Finally, Ryc stated the obvious: (1) that consumption serves as an incentive to labor to increase labor productivity through premiums for more output, for better management, and for institution of labor-saving devices or organization; (2) as consumption increases, the standard of living rises and the quality of labor improves, thus leading to its greater efficiency; and (3) increasing levels of real income and consumption make for better satisfaction of needs in social consumption. The last point presumably indicates greater ease in increasing the services rendered by the state, which are part of the country's total production. This view was shared by Lipinski, who wrote:

Consumption becomes the most important productive force because just in the time free from work, from the direct rhythm of production, the development of the individual takes place . . . . The task of socialism is to imbue free time with meaning. (E. Lipinski 1972.)

Thus, Polish economists started to embrace an organic approach to the theory of growth, in contrast to the previously dominant mechanistic approach, according to which growth was simply the function of more and more investment in new productive capital. Growth of consumption, as in the Ramsey model of growth, finally became an integral part of the theoretical discussions in Eastern Europe (cf. Wan 1971, ch. 10; Zekonski 1974).

The New Stimulus to Foreign Trade

Revealing a tendency to replace the Soviet-type policy of autarchy that has led to a very low and declining Communist share in world

181

trade, * and as the result of adoption of new economic policies, Poland in 1971 started stressing the benefits of international division of labor.[†] It was revealed that in 1969 Poland and Romania showed the lowest share of consumer goods in their imports,[‡] while during the course of 1965-70 other Comecon countries increased, as compared to Poland, the share of consumer goods in their imports.

Examples of Hungarian prosperity and the Japanese economic boom became frequent subjects of articles in Poland, used to demonstrate that foreign trade can contribute to domestic economic development and well-being. There was a spate of reports on the mainsprings of foreign economic successes and the role of scientific and technological cooperation (Szeliga 1971; Rakowski 1971b; Gmytrasiewicz 1971; Metera 1971; Ptaszek 1971), and 1971 witnessed first changes in the treatment of consumer goods imports. The official allotment of foreign exchange for such purchases rose, such imports rose steeply by approximately 24 percent (my estimate on the basis of RS 1972, p. 395, by 30 percent according to Marczewski 1974, page 6), and the trend continued through 1972 (Kurowski and Plowiec 1972, pp. 896-97), during which overall trade turnover increased even faster than envisaged in the plan (by 19.3 percent) and imports of all goods rose by a very high 21.3 percent (Ciamaga 1973, p. 75). Imports of consumer goods constituted a rising share in overall imports, from 16 percent in 1970 to 18 percent in 1972 (Szyndler-Glowacki: 1974). This development, it may be pointed out, contrasted strikingly with the trend of planning in the Gomulka period. The original plan for 1971, worked out during 1970, envisaged a decline of 40 percent in imports of industrial consumer goods and a decline of 42 percent in food imports, while imports of such products as coffee, cocoa, and meat

---

*According to statistics from Vneshnaya Torgovlya, the share of Communist countries in world trade declined from 12.8 percent in 1960 to 11.7 percent in 1969. (Reported in RFE Research, March 19, 1971, and attributed to ideological direction of trade and bureaucratic regulation.) Poland had a per capita foreign trade turnover of only $215, much smaller than the turnover of other European countries (Kawalec 1971, p. 52). While Poland had about 2.2 to 2.5 percent of world industrial production (Kawalec 1971, p. 49), its share in world foreign trade turnover in 1971 was only 1.1 percent (RS 1972, pp. 688-89). Similar observations can be made about other East European countries (Fallenbuchl 1974, p. 92).

[†] The idea was not new, but previously it had been used only as a slogan. See Szeliga 1974, after RFE Research, April 2, 1974, pp. 1-2.

[‡] Chinowski and Stepniewska 1972, p. 149. Japan's share was still lower due to its almost total dependence on raw material imports and its own excellently developed consumer goods industry.

TABLE 6.8

Exports of Industrial Consumer Goods Within Comecon
(million rubles)

	1965	1970	1971	1971/65 (index)
Total	1,240	2,131	2,418	195
In that:				
Poland	149	378	389	261.0
Czechoslovakia	234	351	423	180.7
Hungary	192	240	358	186.5
East Germany	336	552	620	184.5
Romania	105	211	216	205.7
Bulgaria	120	229	224	186.7
USSR	102	166	179	175.5
Mongolia	2	4	9	450.0

Source: Jaroszynski 1973.

were to have been completely eliminated (Kosk 1972). In 1973, imports in value terms rose by 33.1 percent, and in real terms by 22.6 percent, while exports in constant prices rose by 11.0 percent (Szyndler-Glowacki 1974).

Some of the new emphasis on consumer goods naturally affected Poland's intra-Comecon trade. Overall turnover in that trade increased in current prices by about 8 percent in 1971, then 14 percent in 1972, and 13 percent in 1973, but imports of consumer goods from the Comecon countries rose substantially faster than overall turnover in 1971, slower in 1972, and declined in 1973 (RS 1972, pp. 397, 391; RS 1974, pp. 405, 411). It was pointed out that mutual exports of consumer goods of industrial origin also benefited the exporting countries in that they allowed utilization of economies of scale, allowed longer runs of production, and created jobs for new entrants into the labor force at a low cost in terms of necessary investment (Nowe Drogi 1972b, pp. 140-44). Overall statistics for exports of consumer goods of industrial origin from each Comecon country to all others are shown in Table 6.8.

Similarly, East-West trade was expected to benefit from both the creation of new markets for consumer goods in Poland and the faster growth of that country. It was asserted that socialist countries had started to regard foreign trade as a stimulant to economic growth, and that the new ambitious plans for growth of consumption had to rely increasingly on imports, in which the share of raw materials was likely to decline. Therefore, it was concluded, there were good prospects for a substantial increase in East-West trade (Ruminska 1972; Bozyk 1971). During 1972 overall, Polish imports from socialist countries increased by 10 percent, and overall imports from capitalist countries rose by 43 percent (Szyndler-Glowacki 1973). In 1973, in current prices, Polish imports from socialist countries increased by 12 percent, while imports from developed capitalist countries increased by 74 percent (RS 1974, p. 411). This trend seems encouraging, although it may not continue unabated.

It may be that the shades of the convergence hypothesis are becoming apparent in this general tendency to rely more on international division of labor. Ultimately, this new tendency is likely to force the Communist countries to realign their exchange rates to more realistic levels, to liberalize their trade, to scrap the present cumbrous system of positive and negative budget differences connected with foreign transactions (cf. Alton et al. 1965, pp. 128-34), and to multilateralize their foreign payments system.

Several Relevant Considerations

Each of the following subsections could be properly treated as a separate, more developed subject. They are treated here synoptically to provide the general panorama of changing economic climate in Poland insofar as it affected the consumer, and to throw additional light on the factors that contributed to the "consumption miracle."

Handicrafts

Between the end of 1969 and the end of 1971, the number of handicraft establishments declined in Poland from over 170,000 to less than 160,000, and employment in them declined from nearly 340,000 to about 306,000 (RS 1972, p. 440). Since handicrafts provide 50 percent of market services available to the population (Dlugosz 1972) and since the 1971-75 plan envisaged an expansion of handicrafts by almost 50 percent (Zycie Gospodarcze 1972; Graszewicz 1973 wrote about plans to nearly double handicraft production by 1975), some remedial measures obviously were called for. An analysis of the reasons for this decline showed lack of anywhere near adequate provision of raw materials at regulated prices, while handicraft products had to be sold at regulated prices; capricious administration of a peculiar form of income tax; competition from unlicensed moonlighters; an administratively imposed limitation on the market for handicraft products sold to state enterprises; and a pervading air of official suspicion that decreased the readiness of job seekers to engage in handicrafts (Dlugosz 1972).

As the result of such an analysis, a new law passed on June 8, 1972, provided for a fixed tax payment by handicraft, differentiated by craft and territory but fixed in advance to prevent administrative arbitrariness; for open registration into handicraft; and for territorial rather than central supervision. In response to this new policy, the number of handicraft establishments rose by almost 1,000 in 1972 and by over 8,000 in 1973, while employment in them rose by 8,700 during 1972 and by 20,000 during 1973 (RS 1973, p. 454; RS 1974, p. 455), proving that the new law did in fact encourage handicraft.

Services

The handicraft situation is part of a larger problem of supply of services. Comparisons with Western countries show that as income increases the share of services in the consumer budget rises. So far that share, due to considerable limitation of supply, has been low in Poland and has been rising only uncertainly; in 1965 it was 9.9 percent; in 1969 it was 10.9 percent; in 1970 it was 10.8 percent; and in 1971 it was 10.4 percent (Sopinski 1973, p. 127). Up to 1971 even the plans for the development of services, inadequate as they were to start with, were incompletely realized due to faults in planning and planners' preference for the sphere of "material production" (Niewadzi 1971, pp. 221-23).

During the 1971-75 plan period, expenditures on goods by the population were expected to rise by 41 percent, while expenditures on services could rise by as much as 62 percent, increasing the share of services in consumer expenditures to about 20 percent from the 10.4 percent share in 1971 (Niewadzi 1972). Consequently, opinions were being voiced that the planned expansion of services should be higher than that of goods (Rurarz 1972, p. 139), not only to help improve the level of living in most vital areas but also because much less capital is needed per worker in the service sector than in industry (Sarapuk 1972, p. 1118). Actual purchases of services rose during 1971-73 by 25 percent (Marczewski 1974, p. 8). From this point of view, expanding services constitutes an "inexpensive" way of developing the economy in that at the cost of relatively small investments many jobs are created and production grows relatively much. So far, no adequate improvement has been reported in services (RFE Research, March 29, 1974, p. 1), but their growth is stressed in economic publications (for example, Niewadzi 1974).

Housing

Supply of housing exerts a substantial impact on the level of living (E. Lipinski 1972). Yet in all Communist countries, and particularly in Poland, there exists a serious disproportion between the degree of satisfaction of housing and nonhousing needs of the population.

So far, Poland has shown a lower rate of improvement in that situation than other countries; it is expected that the supply of new housing will meet demand only by about 1989, and even then the total demand for housing will be greater than supply (Rychlewski 1972, pp. 137-42; Zarski 1972, p. 116). In all countries of Eastern Europe, the share of housing in GNP has declined since 1950 (Alton 1974, pp. 256-57).

The Gierek government seems determined to alleviate the situation, particularly serious in view of the entrance of the postwar demographic wave into the marriageable age—and consequently into the housing market (see speeches of party officials in Nowe Drogi 1972, no. 6). This, however, promises to be one of the thorniest, if not the thorniest problem awaiting solution by the new policy of consumerism.

Agriculture

Agriculture, which is largely private in Poland, showed good harvests after a couple of bad ones at the end of the Gomulka period. Agricultural production rose during 1971-72 at an annual rate of 5.4 percent, compared with a 2.6 percent rate during 1966-70 (Chelstowski 1972). This accelerated growth continued in 1973 (RS 1974, p. 292) and 1974 (current reports in Zycie Gospodarcze). Production of meat rose, and the main problem discussed was creation of an adequate food-processing industry (Mikolajczyk 1973). A substantial increase in the supply of fertilizers and other materials used by farmers was planned. Agricultural incomes rose during 1971-72 by 80 percent, leaving farmers with a 40 percent increase after purchases of materials needed for production (Chelstowski 1972). This trend continued into 1973 (RS 1974, p. 297).

Work Shifts

At one time it was thought that raising the so-called shift co-efficient (defined as the quotient of total workdays by production workers and the workdays worked on the largest shift), or increasing the number of workers on the second and third shifts, would result in an inexpensive increase in national income (Zycie Gospodarcze 1971; Pluta 1971). Recent statistics, however, reveal that for all practical purposes no change has yet occurred in the shift indicator.

Fluctuations in Living Standard

Soviet-type economies show more fluctuations in annual rates of change in the standard of living than do other economies. This phenomenon appears to be the result of treating consumption as an "amortizer of pressures" within the Soviet-type economy, whereby mistakes arising from faulty planning and faulty execution of plans in the area of investments in capital goods lead to constriction of consumption rather than to abandonment of some investment goals. This, in turn, leads to popular discontent, followed by a rapid improvement in consumption, and then a slide back into the original neglect of consumption (Hodoly 1966, pp. 131, 136-40; Ryc 1968, pp. 295-315). There is at least a possibility of continuation of such cyclical swings in the future; after the current exhilaration of consumption there may come a period of retrenchment.

Rent of Incompetence

An interesting point was raised recently in the weekly Polityka. It was contended that, while the consumer under the Communist system does not need protection from monopolists, as does the consumer in capitalist countries, there are enterprises in socialist countries which, by being the only sellers on the market (monopolists under Western definition), obtain a "rent of incompetence," or are protected from their own incompetence and manage to put the burden on the consumer, who ultimately pays its price (book review, Zycie Gospodarcze, 1972, no. 34; see also Mozolowski 1972). It seems that no protection from such "rent of incompetence" exists at present in Soviet-type economies.

Impact of Trade on Consumers

One of the most important factors that helped in the recent growth of consumption in Poland undoubtedly was the import surplus accumulated in the Polish foreign trade. Polish balance of trade deficits grew conspicuously from $60 million in 1970, to $165 million in 1971, then $400 million in 1972, then $1,400 million in 1973, and $1,550 million planned for 1974. These deficits were financed by foreign loans, those from Western countries amounting to $3 billion. In 1974, limitations on imports were announced, with priority given to imports of the "productive" kind (Neue Zuericher Zeitung, June 8, 1974). The likelihood was that, after a considerable improvement, the growth of consumption again would be retarded (cf. Wojcieszak 1974, pp. 192-94, 199-200).

Western help accorded consumption in Poland in 1971-73 was similar to that given in 1956-59, with similar results in terms of fast-rising consumption. It seems that whenever trade with the West is opened up, consumers are the main beneficiaries.

Poland has accelerated importation of foreign technology; mainly from the West. Its qualitative superiority, recognized earlier by Romania, helps in the drive toward "intensification" of the Polish economy. A recent book by Jozef Wilczynski, Technology in Comecon (1974), analyzes the manifold manifestations of this trend and its implications. Among the latter looms the dichotomy between accepted Communist dogma and the penetration by "capitalist transplants," leading to a hard choice between ideology and efficiency.

Domestic expenditures on research and development (R & D) have
shown considerable increase in Poland. Their share in national income
was 1. 1 percent in 1960, 2. 0 percent in 1970, 2. 2 percent in 1971,
and is planned to reach 2. 5 percent by 1975. Those expenditures are
planned to more than double between 1970 and 1975 (Jedrychowski
1974, p. 9), and they are part of the effort at "intensification" of the
Polish economy, described earlier by this author (Mieczkowski 1970).
Their effect is a stimulus to the growth of per capita production, and
hence also to per capita consumption.

A growing labor force does not by itself increase per capita consumption. It does, however, satisfy planners' priorities in the area
of investments more easily, and hence allows for quicker growth of
consumption conceived of as a residual (left over after the main
priorities of the planners had been satisfied). Since during the 1971-
74 period the cohorts belonging to the postwar demographic wave came
of age and entered the labor force in large numbers, such a situation,
to the extent that the new entrants were productively employed, did
indeed allow fairly substantial increases in per capita consumption
by itself.

CONCLUSIONS

The foregoing picture of a sharp improvement in consumer well-
being does not imply that a question posed by Gertrude Schroeder
(1973, p. 10) about the basic suitability of central planning for man-
aging a consumer-oriented economy has been answered affirmatively
in the Polish case. The "consumption miracle" in Poland is a recent
phenomenon, hardly tested by time. It reveals only a relative improvement in living standards, not yet assuring achievement of a high
plateau of consumer affluence. It seems to prove only that, given
application of suitable incentives and better utilization of foreign
trade, the consumer's lot under Communism could be substantially
improved (cf. Brodzinski 1973, pp. 126-27). It shows that the recent
Soviet experience with deceleration of the rate of improvement need
not have taken place. But it hardly assures continuation of the rapid
pace of progress. Keeping in mind the wide, politically induced
swings in economic indicators (and conspicuously in consumption)
that characterize Soviet-type economic systems, one can be allowed
some skepticism on that count.

One also may stop to reflect on the mechanism that brought about
the radical changeover in policy toward the consumer. It was not a
preconceived, planned decision by the managers of the economy, but
the wrath of the population and the eruption of serious rioting in
December 1970 that forced the change. Thus, the fountainhead of
the new consumerism was a popular swell of dissatisfaction with

living levels. However, the curious thing was that, once concessions were made to consumers, the results for the whole economy were so exhilarating that the planners decided it was, after all, a good thing. Furthermore, their pet area, investments in more capital goods, far from suffering was actually booming. Therefore, it may be that consumer complacency, apathy, or acquiescence in the decisions of planners may actually be harmful to both consumers' and planners' aims.

The planners, on their side, drew from the recent Polish experience a conclusion authoritatively stated by Jozef Pajestka: "All our economic policy is directed currently toward the realization of the thesis that a better satisfaction of human needs favors faster economic growth." (Pajestka 1973.) For the sake of consumers in Communist countries, let us hope that this lesson will endure. This is, however, not necessarily a foregone conclusion, as seems to be indicated by the following opinion:

> the mechanism of making basic economic choices is actually a political mechanism . . . search for improvement of the economic model must be supplemented by search for such relationships as would enable carrying of impulses not only between the consumer and the producer but also between the citizen and the state administration, in which field are concentrated decisions of primary economic importance. (Danecki 1972; italics in the original.)

One could, of course, interpret this quotation as an accurate description of the December 1970 riots and their aftermath. It is likely, however, that its author had in mind primarily carrying of impulses from the state administration to the consumer rather than the reverse, in which case it reflects the traditional thinking of Communist central planners. Old ideas die hard, and the contest for primacy in political acceptance and practical application is not yet over in Poland and the rest of Eastern Europe. This contest represents one of the most important issues facing contemporary Communism.

7

CONSUMPTION
EXPERIENCE
IN POSTWAR
CZECHOSLOVAKIA

The economic relationships between consumption on the one hand and investments, employment, productivity, agricultural production, foreign trade, industrial production, and national income having been explored in the preceding chapters, and the impact on economic well-being of changes in the distribution of consumption and in real wages having been indicated, this and the following two chapters will only briefly outline developments in those variables. Conclusions to these chapters will stress patterns of similarity within Eastern Europe. Intercountry comparisons will be provided in Chapter 10.

AN OVERVIEW

At the end of World War II, Czechoslovakia was the most indus-trialized country in Eastern Europe. It had achieved substantial industrial progress within the Austro-Hungarian Empire prior to World War I (Franzl 1924), and it continued, albeit uncertainly, its economic growth during the interwar period, achieving relatively high develop-ment in the following industrial sectors: textiles, footwear, china and glassware, sugar refining, beer production, machine making, and the automobile industry. Most of these sectors catered to consumer needs, and their growth was adversely affected by the depression of the 1930s and wartime priorities of the German occupation forces. However, heavy industry was expanded under German occupation and wartime damage was slight, particularly in comparison with other East European countries. Virtually no reconstruction was necessary in the Czechoslovak economy after the war, * and thus a relatively high per capita production was assured from the start of the postwar period.

As in Poland, socialization of the Czechoslovak economy started in 1945, and it accelerated after the Communist coup of February 1948 brought the country firmly within the Soviet orbit. According to official statistics, by 1955 some 90 percent of national income was produced in the socialized sector, as compared with 70 percent in 1948. By 1960, some 96 percent of national income was produced within the socialized sector (SR 1965, p. 139). Agricultural collectivization started in 1948, was renewed in 1956, and was almost complete by 1960 (Feiwel 1968, pp. 5-6). It progressed without setbacks, instead of experiencing the decollectivization witnessed in Poland in 1956-57, but then until 1968 Czechoslovakia had a firm-hand, orthodox Communist Party rule.

That firm rule under the party chief Antonin Novotny for a long time prevented political liberalization and a trend toward consumer orientation from taking roots in Czechoslovakia, although minor improvement in consumption took place during 1953-55 (Prucha 1972, p. 47). Tad Szulc (1971, ch. 7) described this post-Stalinist period as winter staying on in Czechoslovakia (the June 1, 1953, rioting of workers in Plzen was an isolated phenomenon). And again, the Czechoslovak reaction to the October-November 1956 events in Poland and Hungary was to tighten the hard line, perhaps as an instinctive reaction of any power elite that feels itself threatened.

The economic picture worsened in the early 1960s. A breakdown in labor discipline, resulting from high employment and a tendency to curb growth of wages, brought down the annual increases in labor productivity in industry from 7.7 percent in 1959 to 5.7 percent in 1961, and 3.1 percent in 1962. In 1963, Czechoslovakia became the first Communist country to attain the dubious distinction of achieving a decline of national income under a centrally planned system (Bernasek 1969). These problems

> were caused, inter alia, by [the previous practice of] fixing unrealistically high growth rates as a target; by adopting an inordinately taut and unrealistic development plan; and by overinvestment and the resulting strain and imbalances between the capacities of construction and

---

*Even so, material damage during World War II has been estimated as equal to Czechoslovak national income produced during the entire 1932-37 period (Prucha 1972, p. 40).

machinery industries, with accompanying organizational and foreign trade barriers and disparate rates of plan fulfillment in basic and processing industries. The planners seemed to have grossly underestimated the constraints (a meager raw materials base, a potential shortage of labor, and foreign trade barriers) on fixing excessively high growth rates. (Feiwel 1971, p. 366)

The deceleration of economic growth in the early 1960s also seems to have been caused by the low productivity of investments. Technical progress was handicapped by the disincentives built into the traditional planning system. Consequently, even though a high proportion of GNP was directed toward investments, the effects on output were relatively meager, providing no relief to the constrained consumption. Despite this obvious fact, some Czechoslovak planners attributed the stagnation of the economy to the fact that in the 1960s (except 1961) the rate of increase in personal consumption was higher than that of national income. This view was opposed by economists, who did not see a further depression of consumption as the way out of the difficulties but advocated instead direction of investments toward bottleneck areas. The debate became known as the "Are we living beyond our means?" controversy (Feiwel 1971, pp. 370-75). Alexander Dubcek later tried to solve this dilemma on lines that would not impinge on consumption.

The political floodgate opened with the 1963 report from the Kolder Commission, set up to study Czechoslovak purge trials. It "found that the trials had been frame-ups, and that the evidence had often been doctored or fabricated." (Szulc 1971, p. 181). There was a rebellion of the intellectuals in the wake of the Kolder report and a public disaffection toward the Communist Party. Early in 1964, Ota Sik was placed in the Central Committee's Economic Commission and started planning a reform of the battered economy. Yet for a time the hard-liners under Novotny held the tiller of power, despite student demonstrations in 1964, despite the ever-increasing intellectual ferment, and even in the face of the May Day, 1966, youth riots.

By the end of 1966, A Czechoslovak Academy of Sciences research team under Radovan Richta completed a study published under the title Civilization at the Crossroads. The study "pointed out that socialist countries had for some time tended to neglect the problems of post-industrial society" (Zeman 1969, p. 87), or what Zbigniew Brzezinski called "the technotronic age" (Brzezinski 1970). Czechoslovakia, the research team concluded, had been growing in an extensive manner by constructing ever more of the same factories, and had left largely unexploited the means of intensive development of the country. As the result,

automation of machine industry in Czechoslovakia is
3 to 6 times less developed than in America; the production of automation systems by the electronic industry
is 2 to 3 times lower than in advanced countries; in the
highest forms of automation, cybernetics, production in
Czechoslovakia is fifty times lower than in the U.S.A.
and 10 to 15 times lower than in England, France or
Sweden. The Czechs produce 3 to 4 times less plastic
materials than America or West Germany, and their
textile industry uses 4 times less man-made fibres
than Japan or France. (Zeman 1969, p. 89.)

The opportunities for extensive development had been exhausted in
Czechoslovakia by 1959, while labor productivity was two to three
times lower than in the United States, which pointed to an unfulfilled
potential for intensive growth and to the need to improve the quality
of the labor force.

A Czechoslovak economist, Otto Schmidt, (1968, after Zeman
1969, pp. 94–95), published his calculations of average wages in
Czechoslovakia, presumably in mid-1960s, compared with average
wages in some other countries, expressed in crowns:

Czechoslovakia	1,448
France	2,250
Austria	2,250
West Germany	3,560
United Kingdom	4,170
Sweden	5,900
U.S.	10,400

The average monthly wage for qualified technical and scientific
personnel at the same time was:

Czechoslovakia	2,000
France	12,900
U.S.	21,000

Zeman noted:

But the twist came in the comparison of participation,
between France and Czechoslovakia, in total world
industrial output. In 1962 Czechoslovakia's participation was 1.86 percent, that of France 3.86 percent.
France had 3.4 times as many inhabitants; Czechoslovakia therefore produced, in absolute terms, 1.75 times
more industrial goods [per capita]. One economist

attributed the discrepancy to the "pathological ultimate
ineffectiveness of our production, caused mainly by
badly qualified, dilettante management." (Zeman 1969,
p. 95.)

While Czechoslovak planners overly concentrated on increasing
industrial output, they neglected agriculture, services, housing, and
other sectors important to consumers. By concentrating on industrial
production the Czechoslovaks made themselves more dependent on
exchange within the Comecon, apparently to their own disadvantage,
due to unfavorable terms of trade. It should also be mentioned that
Czechoslovakia exported some industrial products on credit, thus
denuding the domestic economy of output that could have been otherwise used by the domestic consumer. These considerations, plus
the emphasis on the production of investment goods, explain the
unhappiness of the Czechoslovaks with their expanding industrial
production. The Czechoslovaks also believed that the foreign trade
system, especially in its relations with the Soviet Union, resulted in
a drainage of the Czechoslovak economy.
Such critical analysis led to the inescapable conclusion that
economic reform was imperative. Ota Sik's New Economic Model
formally went into effect on January 1, 1967, and it bore much
resemblance to the later introduced Hungarian New Economic Mechanism. Sik's model was subsequently given additional support by the
April 1968 Action Program, prepared for the Central Committee of the
Communist Party. The key aspects of the New Economic Model were:

1. Abandonment of the system of centralized allocation of
materials.
2. Increase in enterprise autonomy, with associations of enterprises that form individual industrial branches providing a guidance
element.
3. Greater flexibility of prices, to help utilize the profit motive
as the guiding arms of the system. Thus central planning would be
relegated to a less than previously overweaning role, and use would
be made of the market as the cheapest planner and controller (Holesovsky 1968; L. Urbanek 1968; Wheeler 1973, ch. 7).

The new model was described as favoring consumer sovereignty,
although such a view may exaggerate the planned departure from the
dirigistic system of traditional Communist economy (Selucky 1970,
p. 105). As it happened, Sik's model was given little chance or time
to prove itself. The apparatchiks were strongly entrenched in the
system and saw in the new program a threat to their interests. Powerful political currents diverted the attention of the country to a mes-
merizing extent and swept other problems into relative unimportance.

The Six-Day Mideast war of June 1967 and the anti-Israeli stance of the Novotny government caused widespread condemnation in the country. The Czechoslovak Writers' Union congress in Prague produced strong demands for abolition of censorship and for personal freedom, and the Slovaks were increasingly restive. The economy was limping badly, people had become cynical (thus, many of the people replied to a fake advertisement offering a Fiat 850 in exchange for a baby) (Szulc 1971, p. 240), there was angry vexation with constant inconveniences of life, and it was felt that the New Economic Model should be given more support than the regime was doling out. Novotny was removed from power in January 1968 and Dubcek was chosen as his replacement.

The well-known "Prague Spring" followed, with its advocacy of "socialism with a human face." Politically, it represented a spontaneous turn toward liberalization. Economically, it strived for practical introduction of the New Economic Model and abolition of autocratic central planning. However, between January 1968 and August of the same year, when Soviet tanks brought the new experiment to a halt, too little time had passed to give the Dubcek government a chance to make a definitive change in the institutional structure of the Czechoslovak economy, or to allow economic forces to produce any tangible results. The New Economic Model, therefore, remains basically a hope expressed on paper—and confined to it.

With the Soviet invasion of Czechoslovakia, reform stopped in its tracks. From April 1969, the new party leadership under the new First Secretary, Gustav Husak, started consolidating power in conservative, anti-reform hands. A new period of "normalcy" began in which, as earlier, "the hard-line party leaders and the administrative bureaucracy . . . formed a common front against pragmatic reformers" (Gamarnikow 1974, pp. 167, 201-4).

FACTORS AFFECTING CONSUMPTION

Investments and Employment

With the exception of the brief interlude of incipient reform during 1967-68, the planning system in Czechoslovakia was strongly centralized from 1948 onward. Even before that year arguments were made in favor of concentration of production on capital goods, for which the international market was expected to be much more favorable than the slumped interwar market for consumer goods that embraced the main exportable items of Czechoslovak production. But after 1948 a determined, planned effort was made to make Czechoslovakia into an

TABLE 7.1

Distribution of Czechoslovak Investments Between
"Productive" and "Unproductive," 1948-71
(percentages; in current prices)

Year	"Productive"	"Unproductive"
1948	68.0	32.0
1949	62.9	37.1
1950	71.0	29.0
1951	67.3	32.7
1952	65.3	34.7
1953	66.3	33.7
1954	60.6	39.4
1955	63.9	36.1
1956	63.5	36.5
1957	65.5	34.5
1958	69.0	31.0
1959	72.9	27.1
1960	73.0	27.0
1961	73.9	26.1
1962	74.3	25.7
1963	74.0	26.0
1964	74.6	25.4
1965	74.9	25.1
1966	75.9	24.1
1967	75.2	24.8
1968	74.5	25.5
1969	73.7	26.3
1970	69.9	30.1
1971	70.4	29.6

Sources: SR 1959, p. 110; SR 1965, pp. 46-47; SR 1972, pp. 24-25.

arsenal of capital goods for the whole Communist bloc. This policy was apparent in the pattern of investments made in the national economy, as shown in Table 7.1. Heavy favoring of investments in the area of capital goods production to the disadvantage of consumer goods is apparent from that table. It also shows that a decline in that favoritism occurred during the post-Stalinist period in 1954-57, and that another, relatively much weaker de-emphasis of capital goods took place during the ferment of 1967-68 and continued into the following period. These were, incidentally, also the periods of

TABLE 7.2

Average Employment in Czechoslovak Economy, 1948-71
(thousands of persons)

Year	Employ-ment	Population (end of year)	Employed as a Percentage of Population	Women as a Percentage of Employed
1948	5,545	12,339	44.9	40.1
1949	..	12,340	..	..
1950	5,577	12,464	44.7	..
1951	5,591	12,607	44.3	..
1952	5,600	12,754	43.9	..
1953	5,683	12,892	44.1	41.2
1954	5,850	13,024	44.9	41.6
1955	5,956	13,162	45.3	42.7
1956	6,047	13,296	45.5	41.8
1957	6,100	13,414	45.5	42.2
1958	6,105	13,523	45.1	42.2
1959	6,058	13,608	44.5	42.3
1960	6,063	13,698*	44.3	42.8
1961	6,159	13,824*	44.6	43.5
1962	6,260	13,902*	45.0	43.7
1963	6,311	14,004*	45.1	44.0
1964	6,374	14,107*	45.2	44.6
1965	6,477	14,194	45.6	44.8
1966	6,608	14,271	46.3	45.2
1967	6,686	14,333	46.6	45.5
1968	6,794	14,387	47.2	45.9
1969	6,919	14,443	47.9	46.2
1970	7,033	14,366	49.0	46.7
1971	7,125	14,436	49.4	47.0

*Figures for beginning of the following year.

Sources: SR 1957, p. 68; SR 1959, pp. 92, 54; SR 1961, pp. 60, 107; SR 1965, p. 84, 123; SR 1968, p. 132; SR 1972, pp. 22-23, 101, 131.

TABLE 7.3

Growth of Social Productivity of Labor in Czechoslovakia, 1949-67
(average growth per year in percentages)

Year	Annual Growth of Labor Productivity	Annual Growth of Labor Productivity Calculated to Reflect Quality of Labor
1949-53	9.2	7.3
1954-55	4.7	4.2
1956-60	7.1	5.1
1961-65	1.5	1.5
1966	8.5	6.7
1967	4.9	4.6
Average for 1949-67	5.8	4.7
Average for 1967-72	3.4	..

Sources: Nachtigal 1970, pp. 146, 153; Alton 1974, p. 279.

faster rates of increase in personal consumption, as shown in Table
7.10 below. It may be pointed out that during the second de-emphasis
on "productive" investments, even in 1970 when "productive" investments dropped to their lowest share in total investments, they did not
fall down to their 1948-49 relative level, much less to their nadir of
1954. Planners' preferences thus seem to have left a permanent
imprint on the relative share of investments in Czechoslovakia.

The growth of employment is shown in Table 7.2. It is interesting
to observe the trend to raise the proportion of the population in employment, undoubtedly influenced in part by the changing age structure of
the population since the main increase in that proportion took place
when the postwar demographic wave hit the labor market in the second
half of the 1960s. Before that, however, in the early 1950s, there
was no deep decline in this proportion, indicating economic and possibly other pressures toward acceptance of employment, especially by
members of households in addition to the main breadwinner.

The proportion of women in employment increased by about 7 percent during the postwar period, 1948-71, adding a total of 1,257,000
persons to the labor force, out of an increase in employment of
1,580,000. Thus women contributed 78.6 percent of the increase in
employment (SR 1961, pp. 106-7; SR 1972, p. 130), demonstrating,
as in other East European countries, the importance of this pool of
potential labor in Communist countries. Better provision of day care
and kindergartens, as well as provisions in the labor code protecting

198

mothers, helped in utilizing this source of additional labor (Lippold 1970, p. 97; cf. Burks 1974, p. 55).

Employment in agriculture and forestry declined from 2, 337, 000 in 1948 to 1, 280, 000 in 1971. As a proportion of total employment, it declined at the same time from 41. 5 percent to 14. 9 percent (SR 1957, p. 68; SR 1972, p. 130). Therefore, employment outside agriculture could rise, drawing on persons leaving agriculture as well as on the net increase in the labor force, mostly due to the economic activization of women. While total agricultural production rose by 63 percent between 1948 and 1971 from its low postwar level (see below, Table 7. 4), industrial and other production benefited from the influx of new labor. Czechoslovak national income could, consequently, show on the whole a good performance. The growth of the labor force and the decline in the dependency ratio in themselves signaled an opportunity for an increase in national income and per capita consumption. Therefore, part of those increases can properly be attributed to such developments.

Labor productivity grew in the postwar period at widely varying rates, as shown in Table 7. 3. There are striking fluctuations in the rate of growth of labor productivity, apparently not correlated with the growth of real wages, shown below in Table 7. 11 (cf. Alton 1974, p. 279).

Agriculture, Foreign Trade, and Industry

A comprehensive independent index of agricultural production for 1934-38 and 1946-61 was derived by Gregor Lazarcik, and it is used in Table 7. 4, with the official index (the base for which was the single year of 1936) grafted onto it from 1961 on. It can be seen from this table that only from the period of reform in the second half of the 1960s did agricultural aggregate production show any noticeable increase. Roughly the same period also witnessed a shift in the relative importance of agricultural production from crops to animal production, which is indicative of rising standards of living (cf. Lazarcik 1974, p. 386). However, the early postwar period until the mid-1960s was a time of lagging agricultural production; until 1960 the country was unable to regain its prewar aggregate production level. Such sluggish postwar recuperation obviously tended to limit the quantity of foodstuffs available on the market, particularly because the Czechoslovak population had been growing since 1946, and between the end of that year and the end of 1971 grew from 12, 075, 000 to 14, 436, 000, or by 19. 6 percent. Thus, per capita aggregate agricultural production increased between 1946 and 1971 by 40 percent,

TABLE 7.4

Indexes of Gross Agricultural Production in Czechoslovakia,
Prewar to 1971
(in 1956 prices)

Year	Total Crop Production	Total Animal Production	Total Agricultural Production	Sectoral Contribution of Agriculture to GNP
1934-38 average	100.0	100.0	100.0	118.4[a]
1946	83.6	64.7	74.6	..
1947	57.2	59.2	58.2	..
1948	85.9	66.3	76.6	81.1
1949	91.2	79.0	85.5	92.6
1950	88.2	86.6	87.5	100.1
1951	92.9	85.6	89.4	94.7
1952	83.6	89.6	86.5	95.5
1953	100.5	74.6	88.2	89.9
1954	89.9	81.7	86.0	90.9
1955	103.2	89.0	96.5	97.7
1956	103.7	94.1	99.2	100.0
1957	98.1	95.7	96.9	100.0
1958	101.9	96.8	99.5	107.9
1959	96.2	101.0	98.5	99.5
1960	106.5	101.0	103.9	106.0
1961	100.5	103.8	102.0	102.2
1962	88.5[b]	100.5[b]	94.3[b]	90.0
1963	100.2	96.1	98.1	89.1
1964	98.9	103.1	101.0	90.9
1965	84.7	106.3	95.6	84.0
1966	102.7	109.4	106.0	..
1967	108.1	115.7	112.0	..
1968	115.1	121.9	118.2	..
1969	116.1	123.2	119.7	..
1970	110.5	131.3	121.0	..
1971	113.7	135.9	124.8	..

[a]1937.
[b]Official index (1936 = 100) has been grafted onto Lazarcik's from 1962 onward in columns 1 to 3.

Sources: Lazarcik 1963, pp. 31-32; SR 1965, p. 252; SR 1972, p. 295; Lazarcik 1969, p. 8.

and between prewar and 1971 by about 23 percent.* Production per person employed in agriculture and forestry increased between 1948 and 1971 by 197.4 percent, due largely to a 45 percent reduction in agricultural employment during that period (SR 1957, p. 68; SR 1972, p. 128).

Column 4 of Table 7.4 shows the gross agricultural product (value added) as it contributed to national GNP, independently calculated by Gregor Lazarcik. Between 1937 and 1965 there was a decline of 29 percent in that product, whereas the hybrid Lazarcik–official index of total (gross) agricultural production shown in column 3 shows a decrease of almost 5 percent between the prewar 1934–38 average and 1965. The main source of the difference between the 29 and 5 percent declines so indicated probably lies in the difference in the prewar base and in a possible bias in the official part of the index shown in column 3. The concepts shown in columns 3 and 4 are not synonymous either; column 4 shows changes in value added by agriculture, net of all intermediate produce and net of purchases from other sectors and from the foreign sector.

Czechoslovak foreign trade value figures suffer considerably because of being published in devisa (foreign exchange) crowns, with the conversion rate from devisa to domestic crowns variable and ill-defined. The difference between the two rates was covered by positive and negative budget differences, variable in time and between commodity groups. Thad Alton et al. made this criticism in connection with the 1955–56 foreign trade data for Czechoslovakia:

> Official data are limited to the import and export of commodities, valued in foreign exchange crowns, that is, in import and export prices expressed in foreign currency multiplied by the unrealistic official exchange ratios between the domestic and foreign currencies. Invisible imports and exports go unrecorded, as do capital transactions . . . . The official method of valuation in terms of foreign exchange crowns has the consequence that foreign trade magnitudes are incommensurate with individual components of the GNP expressed in domestic prices. (Alton et al. 1962, pp. 44–45)

For this reason, the foreign trade figures and their impact on consumption, shown in the last column of Table 7.5, should be taken only as rough indicators of the direction of change. It seems that the

---

*Population in prewar territory was 14,412,000 in 1936 (SR 1959), p. 54). By 1973 per capita aggregate agricultural production increased by 47.5 percent over its 1934–38 base (Lazarcik 1974, p. 348).

TABLE 7.5

Czechoslovak Foreign Trade and Its Putative Impact
on Domestic Consumption, 1949–71
(millions of foreign exchange crowns; in comparable prices)

Year	Total Imports	Imports of Consumer Goods	Total Exports	Exports of Consumer Goods	Balance of Trade in Consumer Goods	(millions of current dollars)
1949	5,170	1,451	5,805	2,081	630	87.4
1950	4,603	1,280	5,608	2,134	854	118.6
1951	6,456	2,051	6,086	2,129	78	10.8
1952	6,307	1,818	6,294	1,631	-187	-25.9
1953	6,330	2,008	7,153	1,485	-523	-72.6
1954	6,716	2,365	7,238	1,639	-726	-100.8
1955	7,579	2,510	8,467	1,462	-1,048	-145.5
1956	8,537	2,373	9,988	2,278	-95	-13.1
1957	9,985	2,720	9,776	2,379	-341	-47.3
1958	9,772	2,599	10,895	2,779	180	22.0
1959	11,537	3,079	12,435	3,335	256	32.3
1960	13,072	3,306	13,892	3,563	257	24.4
1961	14,570	3,308	14,733	3,797	489	167.9
1962	14,904	3,412	15,793	3,819	407	56.5
1963	15,554	3,817	17,723	4,420	603	84.7
1964	17,489	4,095	18,545	4,198	103	14.3
1965	19,242	4,089	19,357	4,082	-7	-1.0
1966	19,699	4,381	19,764	4,132	-249	-34.6
1967	19,296	4,234	20,622	4,709	475	66.0
1968	22,155	5,056	21,638	4,936	-120	-16.7
1969	23,718	5,614	23,900	4,943	-671	-93.2
1970	26,605	6,266	27,305	5,579	-687	..
1971	28,870	6,450	30,095	6,709	259	..

Sources: SR 1958, p. 315; SR 1962, pp. 350–51; SR 1968, pp. 419–20; SR 1972, pp. 423–24; Marer 1972, pp. 46, 55.

late 1950s and the first half of the 1960s witnessed a negative impact of foreign trade on consumption, reversed in the more recent period.

However, it should be stressed that the overall impact of foreign trade was likely to be beneficial to Czechoslovak consumption insofar as new technology and international specialization (hopefully according to the principle of comparative advantage*) helped move the country's production possibility frontier outward. The service items on the balance of payments, not reflected in commodity statistics, also tended to benefit the population through travel, demonstration effect, and exertion of pressure on central planners. Thus, although the direct effect of foreign trade on consumption seems rather inconclusive, the overall effect was potentially favorable to an improvement in consumption levels.

The reservation that one might have with respect to the above conclusion concerns two problems:

1. There might have been exploitation of Czechoslovakia by the Soviet Union through rigging of the terms of trade to the disadvantage of Czechoslovakia; alternatively, there might have been exploitation of each Comecon member by other members, effectively reducing any possible advantage from international trade.

2. Czechoslovakia, on its own or under Soviet pressure, engaged in foreign aid to the less developed countries, thus at least temporarily denuding its own markets of scarce goods in order to achieve an export surplus on current account, a necessary condition for foreign lending. Apart from its direct impact on the domestic supply of goods, such a policy is believed to have caused the 1963 recession in Czechoslovakia, and thus could hardly have benefited that country.

Column 6 of Table 7.5 shows the balance of trade in consumer goods denominated in current dollars, based on Marer's work. It may be noticed that the results as shown in that column closely approximate the balance of trade as calculated by myself. The groups of products taken by me from Marer's work were division III (foodstuffs and raw materials for foodstuffs) and division IV (industrial consumer goods other than food), both according to Comecon Trade Nomenclature (Marer 1972, p. 2; cf. Montias 1974, pp. 664ff.). It may be pointed

---

*That trading according to the principle of comparative advantage may be difficult to achieve is shown by the following assessment: "Because of the autonomous system of domestic prices in each country, an automatic and purely internal character of the monetary system and arbitrary official rates of exchange which do not reflect relative values of currencies, it is impossible to compare prices and costs of production of particular commodities in different countries." (Kamecki et al. 1971, p. 242, quoted in Fallenbuchl 1974, p. 104)

out that the present study does not attempt to show the regional distribution of balances of trade in consumer goods, specifically with the Comecon area and with the West. Such regional balances may be interesting as an indication of relative dependence on different world areas for changes in consumer well being, but such balances also may be too tangential for our study.

Table 7.6 shows the rapid growth of industrial output. The discrepancy between the faster growth of producer goods and the much slower growth of the production of consumer goods is typical for the countries of Eastern Europe, and it persisted during the period of economic reforms in the second half of the 1960s. The Lazarcik-Staller independently calculated indexes point to the unreliability of official statistics. Between 1937 and 1965, the calculated index for industry without handicrafts (column 4) increased by 217 percent, while the official index (column 1) increased during the same period by 418 percent. Between 1948 and 1965, the calculated index without handicrafts (column 4) increased by 203 percent, while the official index (column 1) increased by 380 percent. Thus, the official index is almost twice as high (by 93 to 87 percent higher) as the independently calculated one, even without considering the upward bias imparted to the official index by the omission of handicrafts, as will be pointed out below. The unreliability of official statistics also was shown by Alfred Zauberman, who compared the official index of growth of industrial output in Czechoslovakia between 1937 and 1962, which was 470 with 1937 equal to 100, with two of his own estimates of 289 and 301 (Zauberman 1964, p. 120).

The Lazarcik-Staller independent calculations included handicrafts in one variant. Handicrafts were important in the provision of some consumer products, such as metalware, ceramics, textiles, clothing, shoes, and foodstuffs, but the new Communist government made, probably in 1948, a "decision to eliminate crafts as a form of organization for manufacturing activity . . . . By 1950, employment in the crafts sector dropped to one half, and in 1952 it was only twelve percent of the 1948 level." (Lazarcik and Staller 1968, p. 21.) Part of the earlier production in handicrafts was taken over by the industry; hence, the industrial production index should properly include handicrafts. Otherwise, an upward bias is imparted to the index, which becomes evident when one compares columns 4 and 5 of Table 7.6.

Lazarcik and Staller testify to the unequal treatment of consumption and capital goods in Czechoslovakia: "Between 1948 and 1965 . . . except for the clothing industry, output of consumers goods (textiles, shoes, provisions, soap) registered substantially lower growth rates" than did capital goods industries (Lazarcik and Staller 1968, p. 23). As the result of such unequal treatment, the structure of Czechoslovak industry changed:

> A clear shift can be distinguished in the output pattern,
> away from the consumers goods industries, for which

TABLE 7.6

Indexes of Industrial Output in Czechoslovakia

Year	Industrial Aggregate Output	Producer Goods	Consumer Goods	Lazarcik-Staller Calculated Indexes	
				Total Industry Without Crafts	Total Industry Including Crafts
1937	100	100	100	54.9	63.2
1947	..	..	..	47.7	..
1948	108	110	107	57.5	66.2
1948	100*	100*	100*	57.5	66.2
1949	114	114	114	62.3	68.9
1950	132	132	131	70.9	75.0
1951	150	156	144	74.8	77.1
1952	177	194	160	77.6	78.2
1953	193	219	166	78.5	78.9
1954	202	229	174	81.7	82.0
1955	224	249	197	91.8	92.0
1956	245	276	212	100.0	100.0
1957	270	304	234	110.2	110.1
1958	300	340	259	122.6	122.2
1959	333	383	280	132.5	131.8
1960	372	434	307	144.4	143.7
1961	405	473	333	153.7	152.9
1962	430	507	348	160.9	160.0
1963	427	502	348	160.0	159.2
1964	444	527	357	164.0	163.0
1965	480	576	378	174.0	173.0
1966	515	624	400	..	..
1967	551	671	426	..	..
1968	582	707	451	..	..
1969	613	749	471	..	..
1970	665	808	515	..	..
1971	711	867	548	..	..

*New series started.

Sources: SR 1958, p. 119; SR 1972, pp. 26-27; Lazarcik and Staller 1968, p. 18.

205

the country was known in international markets before the war, toward producers goods industries which serve the industrialization drive of the Communist bloc. The rapid increase in output was made possible both by preferential investment policies and by significant increases in industrial employment. (Lazarcik and Staller 1968, p. 26.)

Obviously, long-run emphasis on capital goods production does not bode well for the production of what is the basis for growth of consumption, namely, the increasing output of consumer goods. Certainly, such output can—or could—be realized, but increments in it were held back by Communist production priorities, with all the adverse effects indicated in Chapter 4. There seems no doubt that Czechoslovak industrial structure underwent a rapid change. Between 1948 and 1953 alone, the average annual declines in the shares of textile and foodstuffs industries in all industrial production were, respectively, 2.9 and 1.8 percent. For comparison, the corresponding declines for capitalist countries were cited as 0.9 and 1.0 percent (Goldman and Kouba 1969, p. 133).

Two further observations emerge from the official index of industrial production:

1. Prewar output was outstripped by 8 percent in 1948, markedly earlier than in Poland or East Germany, pointing to the lesser wartime destruction already mentioned. The small relative gain in the producer goods sector seems, in view of earlier observations, to indicate the possibility of statistical underestimation of the growth of industrial production between 1937 and 1948. Such an underestimate would be convenient for later propaganda purposes of improved achievement under Communist Party rule.

2. The 1963 decline in industrial production was concentrated in the producer goods sector, while the consumer goods sector showed only stagnation as compared with 1962. The recovery in 1964 was spearheaded by a determined effort to raise output of producer goods.

Table 7.7 shows the proportion of national income used for consumption. The share of consumption seems to have been to a large extent determined by the rate of growth of national income, in that when there was a decline or a slowdown in the growth of national income, consumption kept growing although at a slower pace than since 1959. On the other hand, acceleration in the rate of growth of national income did not tend to produce a proportional increase in consumption. Therefore, it may be asserted that consumption does not seem to have exerted a stimulating influence on economic growth in Czechoslovakia, but was rather a residual item, subject to a certain upward pressure and downward stickiness.

TABLE 7.7

Czechoslovak National Income and Consumption
(millions of crowns in current prices)

Year	National Income Distributed	Total Consumption	Personal Consumption	Social Consumption	Consumption as Percentage of National Income
1948	57,141	45,476	. . .	. . .	79.6
1949	72,167	56,107	. . .	. . .	77.7
1950	82,644	68,658	. . .	. . .	83.1
1951	101,459	78,956	. . .	. . .	77.8
1952	113,938	88,829	. . .	. . .	78.0
1953	126,673	95,109	. . .	. . .	75.1
1954	121,026	101,270	. . .	. . .	83.7
1955	131,163	105,576	. . .	. . .	80.5
1956	129,211	112,825	. . .	. . .	87.3
1957	139,547	118,237	. . .	. . .	84.7
1958	145,466	119,634	. . .	. . .	82.2
1959	148,076	121,385	. . .	. . .	82.0
1960	158,171	130,399	102,156	28,243	82.4
1961	169,610	134,878	104,454	30,424	79.5
1962	171,675	140,048	108,243	31,805	81.6
1963	165,724	143,454	110,545	32,909	86.6
1964	164,608	147,643	113,820	33,823	89.7
1965	169,587	154,169	119,154	35,015	90.9
1966	184,634	161,536	124,900	36,636	87.5
1967	224,771	174,070	131,649	42,421	77.4
1968	252,796	194,196	148,108	46,088	76.8
1969	285,227	214,345	164,904	49,441	75.1
1970	300,841	220,018	167,671	52,347	73.1
1971	313,613	233,511	175,350	58,161	74.5

Sources: SR 1965, p. 142; SR 1968, p. 148; SR 1972, p. 159.

It also may be noted that the share of social consumption in
Czechoslovakia tended to increase, in agreement with the general
tendency in Eastern Europe, from 27.6 percent of personal consumption
and 21.7 percent of aggregate consumption in 1960 to 33.2 percent of
personal consumption and 24.9 percent of aggregate consumption in
1971 (cf. Alton 1974, p. 261).

Changes in Consumption and Real Income of the Population

Although consumption declined somewhat as a share of national
income during the Stalinist period, that decline was not pronounced.
On the other hand, the decline that started in 1966 from an all-time
high of 90.9 percent continued right through the Prague Spring in
1968 and was arrested only in 1971, presumably as the result of the
Polish workers' riots in December 1970. This trend may indicate both
the economically fleeting nature of the Prague Spring and the determination of the Czechoslovak Communist Party to utilize part of the expansion of national income for investment priorities.

Table 7.8 shows the changing structure of food consumption. The
relative shift from starches to proteins after 1964 indicates rising
consumption standards, although at least the 1948 consumption of
fruit was not re-attained as late as 1970. The overall change in the
pattern of food consumption seems to have been in the same direction
as that observed in Poland during the late 1950s and the 1960s. However, when compared with Table 5.38, the Czechoslovak pattern of
food consumption appears superior in proteins (meat, fish, eggs) to
the Polish pattern. Clearly, the Czechoslovaks were on a higher
level of living than the Poles, owing largely to their earlier and more
advanced industrialization.

The structure of aggregate consumption in Czechoslovakia also
underwent some changes. During the period 1956-65, for instance,
the share of food in aggregate personal consumption declined by 6.2
percent, that of housing increased by 2.6 percent, and that of education increased by 1.8 percent. These and other changes are shown
in Table 7.9. The decline in the share of food is indicative, according
to Engel's law, of rising consumption levels, although the rather
substantial increase in the share of housing seems to contradict such
a conclusion. But then rents were regulated, and administered changes
in them affected the share of housing in consumer expenditures more
profoundly than changes in real income would have. The decline in
the share of tobacco, and presumably also alcohol, is interesting and
may reflect both rising levels of living and the concern about health
implications of such consumption. Increases in the shares of education, culture and recreation, as well as transport and communications
are in line with rising consumption levels.

TABLE 7.8

Per Capita Consumption of Selected Foodstuffs
in Czechoslovakia, 1936-70

	1936	1948	1957	1964	1968	1970
Meat (kg)[a]	34.0	28.4	51.0	59.1	69.0	71.9
Fish (kg)	2.1	. .	. .	4.5	5.0	5.2
Fats and oils (kg)[b]	14.1	9.8	17.4	20.0	20.6	19.9
Milk and products (1)[c]	205.4	124.9	133.7	175.2	193.0	196.2
Eggs (number)	138	95	174	203	248	277
Wheat flour (kg)	62.6	74.9	82.9	92.4	89.6	84.7
Rye bread (kg)	84.7	74.7	72.8	74.9	70.9	67.6
Sugar (kg)	23.2	22.7	33.5	37.4	39.1	37.7
Potatoes (kg)	118.9	95.2	131.7	118.9	112.2	103.4
Fruits, all (kg)	42.9	52.2	34.1	39.9	44.9	49.1
Alcoholic beverages (liters)[d]	3.4	. .	. .	6.3	7.2	8.4

[a]All meat in terms of carcass weight, including offal.
[b]Pure fat content.
[c]Milk products in terms of milk equivalent.
[d]In terms of 100 percent alcohol equivalent.

Sources: Zapotocky 1959, cited in Michal 1960, p. 202; other data from SR 1972, p. 462.

209

TABLE 7.9

Changes in the Structure of Consumption
in Czechoslovakia, 1955–65

	Shares in Percentages			Changes in Shares in Percentage Points	
	1955	1960	1965	1955–60	1960–65
Food	46.68	42.33	40.48	-4.35	-1.85
Clothing	11.17	12.29	11.75	1.12	-.54
Housing	13.39	15.34	15.97	1.95	.63
Education, culture, and recreation	10.99	11.66	12.76	.67	1.10
Health and personal care	6.41	6.41	6.93	.00	.52
Transport and communications	8.36	9.18	9.57	.82	.39
Tobacco	3.00	2.79	2.54	-.21	-.25
Total real income	100.00	100.00	100.00	—	—

Source: Z. Urbanek 1968, p. 120.

TABLE 7.10

Calculated Indexes of Czechoslovak Personal
Consumption, 1937 and 1948–65

	Consumption		Indexes of Aggregate Consumption	
	Excluding Housing	Housing	Market-Price Weighted	Factor-Cost Weighted
1937	91.5	109.1	91.9	94.7
1948	70.8	98.2	71.4	75.9
1949	77.1	98.4	77.6	81.0
1950	89.8	98.6	90.0	91.4
1951	90.2	98.8	90.4	91.8
1952	92.1	98.8	92.3	93.3
1953	88.1	99.0	88.4	90.1
1954	91.2	99.2	91.4	92.7
1955	95.6	99.4	95.6	96.3
1956	100.0	100.0	100.0	100.0
1957	103.8	100.9	103.7	103.3
1958	106.3	101.8	106.2	105.5
1959	108.8	102.3	108.7	107.7
1960	116.7	103.2	116.4	114.2
1961	116.6	104.2	116.3	114.3
1962	117.7	105.5	117.4	115.4
1963	119.2	106.9	118.9	116.9
1964	121.5	108.1	120.9	119.9
1965	125.5	108.5	125.1	122.4

Source: Holesovsky and Lazarcik 1968, p. 32.

210

Later data, presented in official statistics in a different format, show a further decline in the proportion of household expenditures for food, an increase in taxes paid, and an increase in the share of industrial goods (cf. SR 1966, p. 461; SR 1968, p. 460; SR 1972, pp. 468-69).

Table 7.10 reproduces the results of research by Vaclav Holesovsky and Gregor Lazarcik. It shows that the market-price weighted index of consumption may tend to overestimate the growth of aggregate personal consumption. The growth of that consumption expressed in terms of its cost to the society, or the factor-cost weighted index, rises slower than the market-price weighted index, mainly due to the undervaluation of the slowly rising housing services when they are valued at market prices. This phenomenon is common throughout Eastern Europe; it produces not only differentiation of indexes, depending on whether market prices or factor costs are used as weights, but also a characteristic lack of economic incentives to provide and maintain adequate housing for the population.

Housing services rose very slowly, and by 1965 still failed to recover their prewar level. Their 10 percent reduction between 1937 and 1948 also indicates a relatively small degree of wartime damage. By 1965 there were 294 dwellings per 1,000 persons in Czechoslovakia, compared with 335 in Austria and 515 in West Germany. However, most Czechoslovak dwelling units were small; dwellings with more than two rooms comprised 55.7 percent of Czechoslovak dwellings, while their proportion was 73.7 percent in Austria and 90.0 percent in West Germany. Only 33.3 percent of Czechoslovak dwellings had bathrooms (Sik 1972, p. 90).

Consumption other than housing declined relatively more during the war, dropping 23 percent between 1937 and 1948, but it also showed faster postwar progress, rising 77 percent between 1949 and 1965 while housing services rose by only 10 percent. The aggregate factor-cost weighted index rose during the same postwar period by 61 percent, and improved between 1937 and 1965 by 29 percent. There were two years during the height of the forced expansion, 1953-54, when the aggregate index (see Table 7.10, columns 3 and 4) dipped below 1952 as the result of a shortfall in consumption other than housing, an experience similar to the Polish one, although it occurred a few years later.

Table 7.11 reveals the cost of living index as declining on the whole in 19 years, even though the 1961-70 period witnessed creeping growth. (The official cost of living index, with 1937 equal to 100, also shows a surprisingly small increase to 160.8 by 1953, reduced to 131.5 by 1957; SR 1958, p. 328.) In consequence, the index of real wages increased faster between 1953 and 1971 than did the index of money wages. However, it should be realized that the latter index may be open to criticism from independent estimators. It shows between 1953 and 1958 a rise of 31.6 percent; an estimate by Jan

TABLE 7.11

Indexes of Nominal and Real Wages in Czechoslovakia

	Nominal Wages in Socialist Sector[a]	Cost of Living Index	Real Wages
1937	. .	66.1	. .[b]
1948	68.8	. . .	88.8[b]
1949	73.3	. .	. .
1950	80.0	. .	. .
1951	85.5	. .	. .
1952	89.2	. .	86.1[b]
1953	91.5	106.3	86.1
1954	97.5	102.8	94.9
1955	100.0	100.0	100.0
1956	103.8	97.4	106.5
1957	105.9	95.5	110.8
1958	108.1	95.3	113.3
1959	110.3	93.1	118.5
1960	113.7	91.2	124.7
1961	116.5	90.7	128.5
1962	117.3	91.8	127.7
1963	117.4	92.3	127.2
1964	121.3	92.7	130.9
1965	124.4	93.8	132.6
1966	127.8	94.1	135.8
1967	134.8	95.5	141.1
1968	145.8	96.6	150.9
1969	156.7	100.1	156.5
1970	161.4	101.8	158.5
1971	167.4	101.4	165.1

[a]Without cooperative farms.
[b]Michal 1960, p. 198; covers only blue-collar workers.

Sources: SR 1958, pp. 90, 328; SR 1960, p. 36; SR 1972, pp. 22-23.

Michal shows in a similar index—but excluding white-collar workers, which probably would have tended to show a faster growth—a rise of only 26.8 percent (Michal 1960, p. 198). Thus, the official index might have produced an overestimate of 18 percent or higher. It also may be noted that the Communist policy of holding down the growth of consumption below the growth of production, and in particular of holding the growth of real wages below the growth of labor productivity, started in Czechoslovakia earlier than in Poland, perhaps due both to higher absolute living levels in Czechoslovakia and to quicker postwar recovery in that country (Douglas 1953, p. 364).

Another indication of possible upward bias in the official index of wages is that, while it showed a 49 percent increase between 1948 and 1965, and while the number of employed rose during the same period by 17 percent (see Table 7.2), the market-price weighted index of aggregate consumption rose in the same period by 75 percent (see Table 7.10). But if the increased purchasing power in the hands of the population had all been spent, the consumption would have increased by 66 instead of 75 percent. (Incomes in agriculture, not included in wage statistics, probably rose less than wages, while other incomes, including black market and private, probably rose more.)

Column 2 in Table 7.11, the cost of living index, may require explanation. After the death of Stalin, resort was taken to a policy of selective lowering of prices, including some consumer goods prices. The impact of that policy, which lasted longer in Czechoslovakia than in Poland or Hungary, may have been exaggerated in official statistics. On January 1, 1967, an upward adjustment of producer goods prices took place in connection with the economic reforms of Sik's New Economic Model to put more money into the hands of enterprises. This had a slight effect on the cost of living index. A bigger upward push to the cost of living index was created by the Soviet occupation of August 1968 and the panic buying that followed it, and this is reflected in the rise of the cost of living index in 1969.

Table 7.12 shows the last two columns of Table 7.10 recalculated to per capita, instead of aggregate, personal consumption, using the population data from Table 7.2. It reveals that per capita personal consumption experienced a decline during the period of Stalinist industrial expansion, similar to that experienced during the equivalent period of Stalinist industrialization in Poland. The decline, which started between 1951 and 1953, was not made up until 1955 or 1956. A second decline started in 1961 and was not made up until 1963 or 1964. Again, there exists a similarity with Polish experience, as demonstrated in Tables 5.21 and 5.46 in Chapter 5.

The slowness of progress in living standards also seems striking. Between 1950 and 1964, per capita consumption rose by only 15.1 to 18.5 percent, or barely more (if at all) than 1 percent per year on the average. Another interesting observation from Table 7.12 is that

TABLE 7.12

Indexes of Per Capita Personal Consumption in
Czechoslovakia, 1937 and 1948-65

	Market-Price Weighted Index	Factor-Cost Weighted Index
1937	84.7	87.3
1948	76.9	81.8
1949	83.6	87.3
1950	96.1	97.5
1951	95.4	96.8
1952	96.2	97.3
1953	91.1	92.9
1954	93.3	94.6
1955	96.6	97.3
1956	100.0	100.0
1957	102.8	102.4
1958	104.4	103.7
1959	106.3	105.3
1960	113.0	110.9
1961	111.8	109.9
1962	112.2	110.3
1963	112.9	111.0
1964	113.9	112.2
1965	117.1	114.6

Sources: Tables 7.2 and 7.10; SR 1958, p. 55.

prewar per capita consumption levels within the present borders of
Czechoslovakia apparently were re-attained about 1949 or 1950,
again attesting to relatively small wartime destruction.

Table 7.13 gives some of the results of independent calculations
by Gregor Lazarcik on their relative magnitudes of changes in agricultural and nonagricultural incomes. It is apparent from the table
that agricultural per capita disposable personal income grew (except
for the period 1954-60) faster than nonagricultural income. Lazarcik
summarized his findings as follows:

The most striking finding of this study is that, contrary
to the general belief in the past, real income per employed
person and per capita in agriculture taken as a whole
tended to increase at a faster rate than in the nonagricultural sector in the postwar period . . . . In agriculture,

214

TABLE 7.13

Changes in Agricultural and Nonagricultural Income in Czechoslovakia
(in constant 1956 prices; billion crowns)

	Disposable Personal Real Income, Including Retirement Benefits		Per Capita Real Income, Including Retirement Benefits		Disposable Personal Real Income Per Employed Person in Agriculture as Percentage of Nonagricultural Income	Per Capita Disposable Personal Real Income in Agriculture as Percentage of Nonagricultural Income
	Agricultural	Nonagricultural	Agricultural	Nonagricultural		
1937	26.5	51.8	78.3	79.9	89.9	94.7
1948	19.9	59.0	74.2	102.6	55.1	69.9
1949	15.4	49.7	62.3	83.8	55.2	71.8
1950	16.5	54.2	68.3	88.3	58.1	74.8
1951	15.2	53.9	70.9	84.9	59.4	80.7
1952	15.9	48.8	75.4	75.2	72.6	96.9
1953	16.5	50.2	77.0	76.5	74.5	97.3
1954	19.5	57.6	90.1	86.9	77.2	100.3
1955	21.3	61.5	96.5	92.0	78.6	101.4
1956	22.9	67.2	100.0	100.0	81.6	96.7
1957	23.5	74.5	101.8	109.4	81.4	90.0
1958	20.5	77.0	90.6	111.1	72.1	78.8
1959	20.1	82.7	91.7	117.9	72.8	75.7
1960	21.9	90.2	109.3	123.1	83.4	85.8
1961	21.2	96.4	112.7	127.9	83.3	85.2
1962	19.2	99.0	106.6	128.8	77.3	80.0
1963	19.9	100.1	112.3	128.6	81.2	84.4
1964	22.9	103.7	132.7	131.2	93.6	97.7
1965	23.5	107.0	138.6	133.6	96.8	100.3

Source: Lazarcik 1968, pp. 22, 34, 31, 35.

215

the rate of growth of real income per employed person was higher than the rate per capita, while in industry and the total nonagricultural sector real incomes per capita were increasing at a faster rate than per employee. This divergent tendency can be explained by an increasing number of dependents per employee in agriculture due mainly to a rapidly aging agricultural population. In industry and the nonagricultural sector as a whole, per capita real income grew faster because these sectors had a declining dependency ratio and because the retirement benefits per retired person, not included in income per employee, increased 191 percent in industry and 93 percent in the general nonfarm sector. (Lazarcik 1968, pp. 36-38.)

CONCLUSIONS

The fact that Czechoslovakia started its postwar experience from a level of industrialization far superior to that of other East European countries, barring East Germany, makes its course under Communist central planning somewhat less typical. Still, Czechoslovakia does reveal several economic patterns characteristic of postwar East European experience. Among these are favoring of the capital goods sector; increasing labor force participation rates; fluctuations in the rate of change of economic indicators; less than impressive performance of agriculture (cf. Lazarcik 1974, pp. 384-86); an inconclusive direct impact of foreign trade; a tendency (although not quite clear in this case) for consumption to fall in the long run as a proportion of national income; and an improvement in the structure of food consumption and the structure of aggregate consumption. Personal consumption per capita experienced some setbacks, but on the whole it showed some, although rather slow, growth. The same can be said about real wages.

Czechoslovak experience in the realm of consumption is by no means impressive, even if one takes into account that its growth was rendered more difficult by the relative development of Czechoslovakia at the outset of the postwar period, and by its relative lack of war-inflicted destruction. The postwar period also witnessed considerable buildup of Czechoslovak industrial capacity, and thus of a potential for far greater improvement in consumption standards than was the case.

216

8

CONSUMPTION
EXPERIENCE IN
POSTWAR HUNGARY

The experience in Hungary is perhaps more typical of postwar Eastern Europe than that of Czechoslovakia, despite the tragic events of November 1956. The country was under firm Soviet domination from the outset of the postwar period, and it had to go through a process of industrialization, instead of a process of industrial expansion as in Czechoslovakia. Intensely patriotic, the Hungarians strived to build up their economy and tended to resent Soviet orders, Soviet troops, the joint Soviet-Hungarian companies which were believed to exploit the country for Soviet interests, the political sloganeering, religious intolerance, and all the other trappings of Communist Party rule.

The gradual stranglehold extended by the party over all aspects of life, the 1956 explosion of popular anger, the tragic despondency that followed, the grasping for roots of a new life in a reformed economic system eventually called the New Economic Mechanism—all these currents constituted the web on which the economic life of Hungary was woven. In Hungary, as in Poland, this web seems stronger and can be more forcefully felt under the patterns of economic life than is true for Czechoslovakia. However, as in connection with other countries covered in the present study, only occasional references will be made to noneconomic currents in Hungary. This does not mean that they were unimportant, but only that the focus of the present study leaves them by and large out of the picture, although the complex mutual interrelations between noneconomic currents and the living level cannot be denied.

AN OVERVIEW

"Prior to 1945 Hungary was an agricultural country in the process of industrialization" is the characterization by a foremost Hungarian-born economist in the United States (Balassa 1959, p. 25). This statement may not have done full justice to Hungary at the time. The interwar period witnessed an expansion in the share of industry and handicrafts in the national income, and a concomitant decline in the share of agriculture. By 1938, net value added in industry surpassed that in agriculture (Magyar Gazdasagkutato Intezet 1947, p. 6), while the 1941 population census showed 49. 1 percent of the population in agriculture (Czirjak and Marer 1973, p. 9). Further industrialization followed the pressures of World War II and the destruction wrought by the combatting armies and the Soviet "liberation." Reconstruction followed, and it used the forces of patriotic private initiative — as in Poland and Czechoslovakia — even though the process of gradual nationalization of industry, mining, and transportation was taking place at the same time, during 1945-48. A monetary reform of August 1, 1946, successfully stopped a rampaging inflation and resulted in confiscation of some liquid reserves accumulated during the war. At the same time as the reform, a planning office was formed, in charge of price control and rationing in addition to planning.

Meanwhile, the Communist Party was extending and consolidating its power. In the 1945 election the Communists received only 17 percent of the vote, but in the 1947 election they were able to weaken the opposition Small-holder Party and obtained 60 percent of the votes. (However, in 1947 the Hungarian Communist Party got only 16. 6 percent of seats in the Parliament, exactly the same proportion as in 1945; see Magyar Statisztikai Zsebkonyv, 1947, p. 216.) The Communist Party skillfully appropriated to itself the credit for the 1946 monetary reform and consequent stopping of inflation, for the 1945 land reform, and for other useful social measures that had widespread support, while at the same time blaming the opposition for all un-popular problems. After the 1947 election, its power became paramount. Having dealt by police methods with extra-party opposition, the Communist Party became involved in an intra-party struggle for control; characteristically, the anti-Rakosi losers wound up in prison and many of them on the gallows, the foremost of the latter being Laszlo Rajk.

The process of gradual Communist takeover was characteristic for the three Communist countries covered thus far in this study. The technique and the history of that takeover, while fascinating in themselves, lie outside the scope of the present study and are covered in other works (cf. Kecsekemeti 1961, chs. 1-2; Zinner 1962, chs. 1-6; Korbonski 1965, chs. 1-4; Szulc 1971, chs. 1-4). There are strong similarities, as well as some differences, in the timing of the takeovers in Poland, Czechoslovakia, and Hungary; in the treatment of political opposition; in the internal power struggle within the Communist Party; and in the economic programs copied from the Soviet Union. All these developments also carried the seeds of later rebellion, serious economic problems, and consumer dissatisfaction.

In 1947, the Three-Year Plan was launched, similar in its goals and methods to the Polish Three-Year Plan and almost coincidental with it. The plan's main goal was the reconstruction of the Hungarian economy. Nicholas Kaldor, a British economist, served as consultant in the formulation of the Hungarian plan, while in Poland the reconstruction plan was mapped mainly by socialist and non-party personnel who used a Western conceptual framework (Drewnowski 1974, pp. 48-60). National income was to increase in Hungary by 74.4 percent (1946/47 taken as base), and the level of living was to rise by 72.4 percent to achieve a level 3.4 percent higher than in 1938 (Balassa 1959, p. 27). The plan was successfully completed by the end of 1949, with investments 76.8 percent above the plan and GNP 7.8 percent above the plan (Eckstein 1954, p. 385).

Toward the end of the Three-Year Plan period, the signs of new trends loomed larger: an increase in central planning, a statistical blackout, almost complete nationalization in manufacturing, a rather inadequate recovery of labor productivity, and apparently exaggerated official claims of achievements. The official claim was that in 1949 real wages in manufacturing surpassed their 1938 level by 40 percent, while an independent estimate by Bela Balassa showed real wages in 1949 at only 98 percent of their 1938 level (Balassa 1959, p. 31). According to another independent researcher, Alexander Eckstein, personal consumption per capita in 1949 achieved only 96 percent of its prewar level, also contradicting official claims (Eckstein 1954, p. 387).

The period of accelerated industrialization started in 1950 in Hungary, as in Poland, with the launching of a new Five-Year Plan. The official share of investments in national income was to rise to 30 percent, and a higher proportion of investment funds was allocated to industry and less to agriculture; within industry, the lion's share went for the development of heavy industry. Also as in Poland, the new plan was shortly revised upward under pressure of ideology and the Korean War. The shortcomings of the accelerated plan soon became apparent and criticism mounted. Consumer goods industries apparently decreased production between 1950 and 1952; handicrafts declined even more precipitously than in Poland, leaving many wants of the population unsatisfied, particularly in rural areas. Agricultural production foundered as the result of forced collectivization and inadequate supplies of necessary inputs.

Despite promises of a steep rise in the standard of living (originally 35 percent for the whole plan period, revised upward to 50 to 55 percent), and early assertions of success in this area notwithstanding, the population felt a deterioration in living levels; Imre

Nagy, the then new prime minister, admitted this openly in 1953.
This admission was confirmed by the statistical yearbook for 1949-55,
which showed an 18 percent decline in real wages between 1949 and
1952 (SE 1949-55, p. 296). A qualification to this statement may
be added in the following quotation:

> Although it is true that day-to-day hardships growing
> out of the economic process were keenly felt, material
> deprivation had greater psychological than economic
> effects. In one way or another, families and individuals
> managed to get by. In 1951 and 1952, the cost of food
> and clothing rose sharply, but, at the same time, the
> earning power of families also grew. On the average,
> more members per family unit worked than ever before.
> What hurt, therefore, was not so much an absolute drop
> in purchasing ability as a relative impoverishment in
> terms of the equivalent effort needed to procure certain
> goods (and a deterioration in the variety and quality of
> goods available). The same is true of the hated system
> of norms. (Zinner 1962, p. 117.)

From the frustrations of the Stalinist era, the New Course was
born in the middle of 1953 with a program of removing the glaring
disproportions in the economy caused by the forced industrialization
period. Production of consumer goods was encouraged, as were
handicrafts. Measures were undertaken to stimulate agricultural
production (Balassa 1959, p. 37) with results satisfactory to the
recuperating levels of living. Social and cultural investments were
raised to increase social consumption. As a result of the New Course
policies, it was claimed that real wages rose by 6 percent in 1953 and
by 18 percent in 1954, while incomes of peasants rose by even more
(SE 1949-55, p. 296).

However, internal resistance from the hard-liners of the Matyas
Rakosi camp and apparent pressure from the Soviet Union managed,
about the beginning of 1955, to change this economic policy; there
was a reversion to the forced industrialization of the Stalinist mold,
which was to last until its reversal just before the 1956 Revolution.
Nagy was accused of subverting the law of socialist proportional
development. Nevertheless, it has been argued:

> The accusation that the rise in the standard of living
> outstripped the increase in production does not stand up
> in the light of the official data for the period of the Five-
> Year Plan as a whole. And only this can be the standard
> of comparison, since the policy of the New Course intended
> to remedy the reduction of the standard of living in the face
> of an increase in national income. Official pronouncements

allege that national income increased by 53 percent
in the Five Year Period, whereas consumption grew by
31 percent. If the upward bias of the two series should
be of similar magnitude, it can be deduced that the
rise in living standards actually fell behind the growth
of national income. (Balassa 1959, p. 41.)

The politics of retreat from the new industrialization period of
1955-56 went out of hand in the face of popular discontent and hatred
of Communist autocracy, and resulted in the Hungarian Revolution
of October-November 1956. The discontent was spearheaded by the
Hungarian intelligentsia and was first given shape in an October
1955 memorandum to the Central Committee of the Communist Party
from the leading members of the Writers' Association protesting the
government's autocratic cultural policies. The discontent was later
sustained by the Writers' Association and by the Petofi Circle of
technical intelligentsia. Political events that started with the removal of Matyas Rakosi from power in July 1956 then took over and
led to the October Revolution.

One ought to stress in this connection another similarity between
Poland and Hungary in 1956, and Czechoslovakia in 1968: the leading
role of the intelligentsia—especially writers in the first stage of
spreading discontent, and students and economists in the second
stage of widening discontent—in most but not all outbreaks of
popular discontent against Communist consumption and cultural
policies (some exceptions being the December 1970 Polish workers'
riots on the Baltic seacoast, the June 1953 Berlin riots, and the
June 1953 Plzen riots). In Poland, the intelligentsia (writers, students, and economists) led during the Polish Thaw of 1955-56, and
again in February-March 1968. In Czechoslovakia, the intelligentsia
(writers and students) led in late 1967 and early 1968. In Hungary,
writers and then students and the technical intelligentsia prepared
the ground for the October 1956 Revolution for at least a year
(Kecskemeti 1961, chs. 4-5; Zinner 1962, chs. 7-8). One should
remember in this context that in all three countries the intelligentsia
had helped in the survival of nationhood under foreign domination
until World War I, which explains the enormous prestige accorded
particularly to writers, who became traditional spiritual leaders,
substituting in Poland and Czechoslovakia for absent political leaders
(Gomori 1973, pp. 153ff; see also Mieczkowski 1973a). In Hungary,
the intelligentsia, with Kossuth as foremost earlier example of its
leadership, successfully established political and administrative
equality with the Austrians within the Hapsburg Empire under the
"dual monarchy" arrangement of 1867. Thus opposition by the intelligentsia had all chances of being embraced by the rest of the population, particularly since most people were acutely dissatisfied with
their level of living and hoped that a change in government would
lead to a higher rate of growth of consumption.

The October 1956 Revolution wreaked enormous human and physical damage on Hungary. It was followed by a crippling general strike, the first on record in a Communist country. The effects of the strike on economic activity carried well into 1957, although production of consumer goods, and hence consumption, was relatively little affected in the direct sense (see Table 8.5 below, where industrial production of nondurable consumer goods declined in 1956 by 12.5 percent below 1955, and rose in 1957 by 3.9 percent above 1955). The reconstruction under Janos Kadar was politically fairly mild* and designed to reduce the Communist Party's unpopularity. The byword of that period became "reform," as a process of long duration.

In one important respect, however, previous policies were unimproved, and that had an effect on consumption. The collectivization of agriculture started again late in 1957 and was virtually completed by 1961 (Ignotus 1972, p. 260). Later, in view of setbacks in plan fulfillment, some reforms were undertaken, starting in August 1965. As a result, household plots increased both their productivity and their size to the accompaniment of ideological approval (Ignotus 1972, pp. 275-76),† and collectives gained greater independence in management. However, growth rates for the economy as a whole were lagging behind those of the 1950s and it was felt that a radical alteration of the system of planning and management was necessary to lift the country out of an economic impasse (Schaffer 1970, p. 49).

A period of "positive work" followed, culminating in the adoption of the New Economic Mechanism (NEM), officially in January 1968, but in actuality piecemeal for several years before and after that date. The main characteritics of NEM were: decentralization of economic decision making to the level of the firm; reinstatement of the profit motive (the profit margin being proportional to the value of fixed and working capital involved in production) on lines of Evsey Liberman, and a general release of economic incentives; a freer, less rigid price formation with gradual loosening of price controls; emphasis on technocracy; more international division of labor and easier access to foreign capital; and incentives to private and cooperative construction

---

*There was, though, some (perhaps inevitable) retribution and "tightening of screws" (see Ignotus 1972, pp. 257-60). Still, ten years after the Hungarian Revolution the same writer was able to state: "The order of comparative liberalism may change from season to season; but that Hungary is ahead of most other communist countries can safely be stated." (Ignotus 1966, p. 120 n. 29; italics in the original.)

†By 1965, some 86 percent of Hungary's agricultural land was socialized, the rest being cultivated in private household plots that provided almost half the agricultural share of national income (Nagy 1969, p. 13; Kiss 1968).

of housing. However, NEM was cautious, especially if compared to the Prague Spring. It was primarily nonpolitical and pragmatic. Its goal was to move the country out of the economic doldrums while letting the Communist Party retain complete political sway (Ignotus 1972, pp. 277-82; Szabados 1968; Czikos-Nagy 1971, pp. 139-41).

NEM also had some welfare implications. An obvious one was that its undeniable success contributed to raising the level of living. The work week was reduced from 48 to 44 hours, and embraced an increasing portion of the industrial labor force. Individuals were given more freedom and opportunity to spend their money and leisure time according to personal preferences. Labor unions were directed to represent the interests of workers to a greater degree. Obviously, concern for improvements in welfare increased in Hungary, whatever the manifold political sources of that concern. This concern was evident in an early subjection of consumer prices to two criteria: (1) that inflationary tendencies had to be curbed and (2) that no decline in living levels could be permitted for any major segment of society. Neither eventuality apparently took place, but some apparent mistakes were observed in the staging and implementation of the economic reforms of NEM, ranging from the timing of its introduction to foreign trade (Buky 1972, pp. 33-37). The tentative evaluation of NEM already is inherent in the statistics for the period starting with 1968, which are discussed in the following section. By 1973, NEM was de-emphasized as a working policy and a blue-collar opposition to it arose on grounds that the market-oriented model tended to shift income distribution against them (Gamarnikow 1974, p. 195).

To provide a broad sociological outline, one should first note the growth of the middle class in Hungary to 15 percent of the population around 1968; before the war it constituted only 8 percent (Nagy 1969, pp. 13-14). The attitudes of the society shifted from prewar ascription toward achievement orientation, pragmatism, and expertise, to an extent that apparently worried the Communist Party. Its Political Committee passed a May 1967 resolution deploring that "in filling state and economic positions in a one-sided way, skill is the determining factor and political requirements are neglected . . . . state and economic leaders, exaggerating the demands of training, do not like to admit party members to their domain . . . . In some cases recently, experts who were not politically acceptable have been placed in leading positions." (Partelet, October 1967, after Szabados 1968, p. 18). An achievement-oriented system is, of course, more likely to result in higher productivity and better satisfaction of consumer wants, even though it also is likely to reduce the well-being of party apparatchiks.

FACTORS AFFECTING CONSUMPTION

Investments and Employment

As did other Communist countries, Hungary mounted a considerable investment effort during the postwar period. In 1955, gross investment amounted to the internationally extremely high 35.2 percent of GNP, and that proportion tended to increase over time (Czirjak 1973, pp. 5-6). Table 8.1 gives the picture of Hungarian investments as they affected consumption, namely, the index of official data on investments in current prices, the share of "nonproductive" investments (investments that benefited the consumer) in aggregate investments, and an independently calculated index of total gross investments (including net foreign investment, never included in East European official statistics of investment) in constant prices. A comparison of the official with the calculated index of investment (calculated index of gross investment in fixed capital, not shown in Table 8.1 and similar in coverage to the official index of investment, moved closely to the calculated index of total gross investment shown in that table) shows the influence of price changes and official exaggeration. However, even discounting official exaggeration, there emerges a picture of a prodigious investment effort that drew resources away from consumption and toward capital accumulation. Column 2 shows the decline in attention given to the consumer during the early 1950s until the early post-Stalinist period; then the Nagy period of consumerism and its reversal until 1956; a sudden improvement in 1957 that revealed an official desire to woe the consumer; and then a long downward slide, reversed by NEM.

From independent estimates in constant prices by Laszlo Czirjak one can calculate that between 1938 and 1967 personal consumption rose by 41.9 percent, government consumption by 126.5 percent, and gross investment by 389.5 percent. These figures reveal the enormous emphasis given to investments, as well as their opportunity cost in terms of retardation of growth of private consumption imposed by the ambitious investment program. Between 1949 and 1967, investments rose in constant prices by 244.3 percent; between 1949 and 1955 alone, they rose by 90.1 percent (Czirjak 1973, pp. 5-6). Such favoritism may perhaps explain part of the social dissatisfaction that sparked the Hungarian Revolution of 1956.

Table 8.2 shows the relatively slow growth of the Hungarian population (by 13.6 percent between 1938 and 1972) and a relatively faster growth of employment (by 27.6 percent between 1938 and 1972), indicating a rising degree of economic activization of the Hungarian population. This fact becomes apparent from column 3 of the table, showing the percentage of the labor force made up by women, which

TABLE 8. 1

Official and Calculated Indexes of Investment in Hungary

Year	Official Index of Investments in Current Prices	Share of "Nonproductive" Investments in Total Investments	Calculated Aggregate Gross Investments
1938	. .	. .	37. 0
1949	. .	. .	52. 6
August 1, 1947– December 31, 1949	. .	27. 1	. .
1950	86. 2	26. 0	76. 0
1951	117. 1	24. 4	95. 9
1952	142. 3	22. 3	89. 0
1953	150. 3	24. 7	99. 7
1954	105. 0	24. 5	82. 9
1955	100. 0	21. 8	100. 0
1956	103. 3	24. 1	53. 3
1957	100. 3	33. 1	100. 3
1958	204. 9	28. 6	93. 4
1959	286. 6	23. 5	109. 7
1960	334. 3	22. 8	109. 4
1961*	306. 8	21. 2	138. 4
1962	354. 7	20. 4	148. 2
1963	402. 3	19. 7	149. 0
1964	422. 0	19. 7	146. 2
1965	389. 7	20. 7	136. 0
1966	427. 6	20. 3	172. 4
1967	521. 5	19. 6	181. 1
1968	499. 8	19. 0	. .
1969	674. 1	21. 3	. .
1970	799. 0	21. 2	. .
1971	898. 8	22. 1	. .
1972	920. 0	23. 3	. .

*Start of a new official series covering only the socialist sector (but socialization of agriculture was virtually completed in 1961, and hence the difference in coverage with the preceding index covering the whole economy is relatively small).

Sources: SE 1960, p. 62; SE 1972, pp. 88; Czirjak 1973, p. 6.

TABLE 8.2

Population and Employment Date for Hungary
(including self-employment)

Year	Population at Mid-Year (thousands)	Employment on January 1 (thousands)	Women as Percentage of Total Employed	Number of Women Employed (thousands)	Employed as Percentage of Population
1938	9,167	3,948	27.8[a]	1,098	43.1
1946	9,024	..	..	..	..
1947	9,079	..	..	..	..
1948	9,158	..	..	..	..
1949	9,249	3,910[b]	30.1	1,177	42.3
1950	9,338	4,106.8[b]	30.5[b]	1,253	44.0
1951	9,423	4,225[b]	..	..	44.8
1952	9,504	4,306[b]	..	..	45.3
1953	9,595	4,349[b]	..	..	45.3
1954	9,706	4,400[b]	..	..	45.3
1955	9,825	4,470.0	..	..	45.5
1956	9,911	4,503[b]	..	..	45.4
1957	9,840	..	..	..	..
1958	9,882	..	..	..	..
1959	9,937	..	..	..	..
1960	9,984	4,735.0	35.1[b]	1,662	47.4
1961	10,028	4,626.1	35.8[b]	..	46.1
1962	10,061	4,543.6	36.2[b]	..	45.2
1963	10,088	4,569.3	37.8[b]	..	45.3
1964	10,120	4,634.7	38.1[b]	..	45.8
1965	10,148	4,649.2	38.8[b]	..	45.8
1966	10,179	4,665.5	39.2[b]	..	45.8
1967	10,224[c]	4,710.2	39.6[b]	..	46.1
1968	10,264[c]	4,767.3	39.7[b]	..	46.4
1969	10,303[c]	4,887.1	40.8[b]	..	47.4
1970	10,338[c]	4,980.2	41.7	..	48.2
1971	10,368[c]	5,010.3	41.9	..	48.3
1972	..	5,038.6	42.9	..	..
1973	..	5,061.2	42.9	2,170.2	..

[a] 1941.
[b] January 1 figure.
[c] Average of two adjacent January 1 figures.

Sources: SE 1949-1955, p. 57; SE 1960, p. 10; SE 1961, p. 3; SE 1963, p. 52; SE 1965, p. 52; SE 1966, p. 3; SE 1969, p. 83; SE 1970, p. 107; SE 1972, pp. 2-3, 111, 109.

rose from less than 28 percent in 1938 to almost 43 percent in 1973. While the total number of employed rose between 1938 and 1973 by 1,113,000, the number of women employed rose during the same period by 1,072,000. Thus only 41,000 (or 3.7 percent) of the total increase in employment was contributed by men, the rest (96.3 percent) being primarily the result of higher rates of employment of women, a picture similar to that in Czechoslovakia and East Germany.

Increasing labor force participation rates by themselves improve the opportunity for raising consumption levels, a topic that will be analytically developed in Chapter 10. The proportion of employed in the aggregate population increased from 43.1 percent in 1938 to 48.3 percent in 1971, indicating a 12.3 percent potential increase in consumption on account of a higher percentage of employment.

Agriculture, Foreign Trade, and Industry

Table 8.3 gives an independently calculated index of gross agricultural production (without forestry), one of net agricultural product, and an index of official net output of agriculture. The independently calculated indexes use the 1955 price weights; they were calculated by Laszlo Czirjak. Comparison of net product indexes reveals that the official index grew faster, and consequently is likely to have contained an exaggeration. Prewar gross agricultural output was achieved as late as 1958, and more consistently from 1963 on, but net agricultural product was below prewar during the 1960s. With the growth of population (shown in Table 8.2), such a performance did not contribute to improved chances for raising per capita consumption of food, although it should be remembered that prewar Hungary was a net exporter of agricultural products, and thus a relatively deficient agricultural production in the postwar period could have been made up for from the point of view of domestic consumption by a reduction in agricultural exports.

The retardation of growth in agriculture is striking in Table 8.3 (cf. Lazarcik 1974, pp. 384-86). Even according to official data, net output rose by a mere 3.9 percent between 1955 and 1972. The independent calculations show very mediocre performance during the 1960s. It is interesting to observe that agricultural production was booming right after the Hungarian Revolution, when private peasants were being wooed by official incentives. Once collectivization was virtually completed in 1961, the growth of production stagnated.

Table 8.4 shows that during the 1960s and early 1970s Hungary was a net exporter of consumer goods, which financed imports of other goods, and that the export surplus in consumer goods increased steadily (with minor setbacks in 1957 and 1970), indicating an adverse direct impact of the foreign sector on growth of consumption. Columns

TABLE 8. 3

Changes in Agricultural Output in Hungary

Year	Gross Output at Constant Prices: Independently Calculated Index	Index of Net Product: Independently Calculated	Index of Official Net Output Series
1934–38			
average	..	107. 9	..
1938	109. 8	110. 9	..
1946	62. 1	62. 1	..
1947	60. 6	60. 4	..
1948	77. 5	77. 5	..
1949	84. 9	84. 8	78. 9
1950	83. 6	83. 5	88. 2
1951	90. 6	90. 7	105. 0
1952	82. 7	82. 6	65. 5
1953	76. 0	75. 7	90. 9
1954	82. 4	82. 2	86. 7
1955	100. 0	100. 0	100. 0
1956	95. 5	95. 4	83. 3
1957	105. 5	105. 7	98. 0
1958	110. 1	110. 5	100. 8
1959	103. 1	96. 9	104. 8
1960	98. 8	84. 7	94. 0
1961	102. 3	87. 0	89. 6
1962	102. 1	85. 5	94. 4
1963	112. 7	94. 7	99. 1
1964	117. 1	97. 5	102. 0
1965	104. 3	85. 8	92. 5
1966	115. 2	..	101. 0
1967	122. 9	..	102. 0
1968	..	..	101. 0
1969	..	..	113. 4
1970	..	..	93. 4
1971	..	..	101. 0
1972	..	..	103. 9

Sources: Czirjak 1973, p. 3; Czirjak 1967, p. 41a; SE 1961, p. 43; SE 1972, p. 67.

TABLE 8.4

The Effect of Hungarian Foreign Trade on Consumption

Year	Index of Employment in Foreign Trade	Net Foreign Investment (million forints; constant prices[a])	Imports of Consumer Goods (millions of devisa forints)	Exports of Consumer Goods (millions of devisa forints)		Balance of Trade in Consumer Goods ($ million at current prices)
1949	100	660[b]	..	..	..	151.4
1950	100	962[b]	..	..	..	171.5
1951	100	623[b]	..	..	..	191.6
1952	100	185[b]	..	..	..	200.5
1953	100	310[b]	..	..	..	156.5
1954	120	30	..	..	..	149.3
1955	100	1,900	..	..	..	162.5
1956	120	300	..	..	..	143.0
1957	120	-4,972	..	..	..	59.2
1958	140	2,237	..	..	..	195.8
1959	140	23	..	..	..	211.7
1960	160	-3,519	1,765.7	4,138.8	2,373.1	206.0
1961	160	1,568	1,847.8	4,878.4	3,030.6	258.2
1962	180	-748	1,931.1	5,360.9	3,429.8	292.1
1963	200	-2,876	2,310.1	6,121.3	3,811.2	324.7
1964	200	-4,896	2,410.8	6,539.6	4,128.8	351.6
1965	220	1,620	3,186.7	7,866.1	4,679.4	428.2
1966	..	..	3,269.6	8,516.7	5,247.1	484.7
1967	..	..	3,968.2	9,328.3	5,360.1	456.5
1968	..	..	3,890.5	9,582.2	5,691.7	484.8
1969	..	..	4,218.6	11,131.0	6,912.4	588.8
1970	..	..	6,140.9	11,757.8	5,616.9	..
1971	..	..	6,908.4	13,667.8	6,759.4	..
1972	..	..	6,280.2	16,091.4	9,811.2	..

[a] Undefined.
[b] 1949 prices.

Sources: Czirjak 1967a, p. 8; Czirjak 1968a, p. 16; SE 1965, pp. 219, 220; SE 1970, pp. 68-69; SE 1972, pp. 328-29, 336-37, 340-41, 68; Marer 1972, pp. 48, 57.

TABLE 8.5

The Contribution of Hungarian Industry to Consumption

	Index of Official Data on Net Material Product	Independently Calculated Index of Gross Product	Independently Calculated:	
			Index of Some Industrial Consumer Goods*	Share of Those Consumer Goods in Total Industrial Output*
1938	..	56.4	55.4	25.0
1946	..	33.4	18.6	15.8
1947	..	29.5	34.8	32.2
1948	..	52.0	41.9	22.1
1949	47.7	56.0	48.7	22.1
1950	59.6	65.6	66.8	25.9
1951	70.2	74.2	75.7	29.4
1952	83.0	85.2	83.1	28.5
1953	92.3	89.8	84.1	25.2
1954	89.7	93.0	93.6	26.6
1955	100.0	100.0	100.0	27.4
1956	85.0	91.4	87.5	22.3
1957	102.9	101.4	103.9	29.0
1958	115.8	111.7	109.5	27.5
1959	125.3	120.2	116.9	24.8
1960	144.8	130.5	129.1	25.2
1961	159.9	142.2	141.3	25.3
1962	174.4	152.2	147.4	24.7
1963	181.5	159.5	154.0	24.6
1964	194.5	171.3	165.4	24.6
1965	203.1	181.0	169.6	23.9
1966	221.8	193.9	186.9	24.6
1967	242.0	200.9	200.0	25.4
1968	256.4	..	199.7	24.5
1969	267.9	..	..	..
1970	289.5	..	..	..
1971	305.4	..	..	..
1972	325.6	..	..	..

*Output of the following industries: paper; printing; textiles; clothing; leather and fur; miscellaneous; food, tobacco, and drink. Note that, the output of durable consumer goods is not included in the computation, those goods being found in the output figures of electrical and telecommunications equipment, and other industries, out of whose output exports take a high percentage.

Sources: SE 1961, p. 43; SE 1972, p. 67; Czirjak 1973, p. 3. Last two columns of the table were calculated by the author from a worksheet of Czirjak (1973).

3, 4, and 5 of the table, which lead to the balance of trade in consumer goods, were calculated by this author from official Hungarian statistics and are only approximative insofar as agricultural exports include some, unspecified quantities of fodder. What is important, however, is the general picture of the indicated trend toward widening of the export surplus in consumer goods, also supported by data obtained from Marer (column 6).

Column 1, the index of employment in foreign trade, shows that foreign trade increased considerably in importance for the Hungarian economy. Between 1938 and 1949, that index rose from 89 to 100, after a substantial postwar decline. Column 2 shows that over the longer period Hungarian foreign trade ran a negative balance of trade, underscoring the importance of net exports of consumer goods from the point of view of the Hungarian balance of payments.

Table 8.5 summarizes data on changes in industrial output (cf. Czirjak 1968). The official index of net industrial output shows faster growth than the calculated gross index, whereas the latter should normally show faster growth due to increasing amortization deductions on a higher level of industrial development. This, then, is another indication of a possible upward bias in the official index. The proportion of consumer goods in total industrial output, after the make-good postwar explosion, declined in 1948-49 but, interestingly, rose during the period of Stalinist industrialization, declining slightly toward its end, rising again as the result of Nagy's period of consumerism, declining in 1956, and rising again substantially during the early stabilization period of 1957-58, only to fall again to a 24 to 25 percent level from 1959 onward. Given a good growth performance of industrial output, such a stability in the proportion of consumer goods would, by itself, indicate encouraging conditions for improvement of consumption standards, were it not for an export balance of consumer goods, shown in Table 8.4.

The independently calculated index of production of some industrial consumer goods, excepting as it does durable consumer goods (see column 3 in Table 8.5), shows a very good performance over the postwar period as a whole and compares favorably with prewar. Again, however, many of the goods so produced were undoubtedly directed to export markets, where they apparently had a good reputation for quality.

Changes in Consumption and Real Income of the Population

Table 8.6 shows the index of official data on national income produced in comparable prices, an index of official gross domestic product in comparable prices, an official index of net material product, and calculated indexes of GNP produced, GNP on the use side, and

TABLE 8.6

Indexes of National Income, National Product, and Consumption in Hungary

Year	Official Indexes			Independently calculated indexes (in constant prices)		
	National Income Produced in Comparable Prices	GNP[a] Produced in Comparable Prices	Net Material Prices	GNP Produced at Factor Cost II Weights	GNP on the Use Side	Personal Consumption
1938	..	..	..	80.7	77.7	110.1
1946	..	..	..	51.6	..	..
1947	..	..	..	53.4	57.6	70.0
1948	..	..	..	66.8	63.7	78.1
1949	..	..	62.8	72.2	70.9	86.1
1950	..	..	75.8	76.8	80.9	87.7
1951	..	..	87.9	84.2	90.9	90.0
1952	..	..	86.4	87.0	88.4	85.9
1953	..	..	97.0	88.6	94.5	86.1
1954	..	..	92.4	91.7	92.1	93.6
1955	..	..	100.0	100.0	100.0	100.0
1956	..	..	88.6	95.5	88.1	109.5
1957	..	..	109.1	103.4	102.5	111.1
1958	..	..	115.2	110.3	102.2	113.4
1959	..	..	122.7	114.8	112.1	122.8
1960	100.0	100.0	134.1	120.8	113.4	124.0
1961	104.6	104.7	140.8	126.9	125.5	127.2
1962	110.9	111.1	148.9	132.2	131.8	129.8
1963	116.8	117.5	156.9	139.4	136.4	135.4
1964	121.9	123.0	163.6	147.3	138.0	140.1
1965	122.0	124.2	163.6	148.4	136.4	144.0
1966	132.0	133.4	177.0	157.6	157.0	147.8
1967	142.7	143.5	191.8	164.8	158.7	156.2
1968	149.9	150.6	..	168.9[b]	..	..
1969	161.8	160.9	..	175.6[b]	..	..
1970	169.7	168.4	..	183.3[b]	..	..
1971	180.8	180.0	..	195.3[b]	..	..
1972	189.9	189.9	..	203.4[b]	..	..

[a] Gross domestic product.
[b] Alton's index of real GNP grafted on.

Sources: SE 1970, pp. 68-69, 74-75; SE 1972, pp. 68, 73; Czirjak 1973, pp. 4-6, 8; Alton 1974, p. 270.

personal consumption—all in constant prices. The three official indexes moved closely together. In the period 1960-67, they grew respectively by 42.7 percent, 43.5 percent, and 43.0 percent, while the computed indexes grew by 36.4 percent in the case of GNP produced, and by 39.9 percent in the case of GNP on the use side. Similar discrepancy between official and calculated indexes continued during the 1967-72 period. The more comprehensive calculated indexes of GNP indicate exaggeration resulting at least in part from the official omission of services.

The index of personal consumption rose by 123.1 percent between 1947 and 1967, while the calculated index of GNP on the use side rose during the same period by 175.5 percent. The difference between these rates of growth, reduced though it was between 1955 and 1967, indicates the priority given to uses of GNP other than personal consumption.

Table 8.7 gives the relation between personal and social consumption based on official statistics. It is apparent that social consumption showed a higher rate of growth from 1960 on, while oral information obtained by this author points to a similar trend during the late 1940s and the 1950s. However, between 1963 and 1967 social consumption showed slower growth rates than did private consumption, and even posted a decline in 1965; as a result, its proportion to personal consumption, shown in column 3 of the table, temporarily declined. A belated influence of NEM may be indicated by a decline in that proportion in 1972.

Table 8.8 shows the structure of household expenditures on consumption as it changed from 1960 on. Food, while rising in absolute quantity, declined as a proportion of total household expenditures, indicating through Engel's law that an improvement in the level of living had taken place in Hungary.* The same can be said with regard to apparel. Housing remained constant as a proportion of total expenditures, being constrained by new housing construction. Other consumption categories increased their share in total expenditures, with transport and communications showing the highest rate of increase; expenditures on household furnishings were second. It is interesting to contemplate the third and fourth highest increases in household expenditures: beverages and tobacco. It may be that they were more accessible than other goods, or that frustrations of daily life drove people to alcohol and tobacco. The trend is similar to Poland and Czechoslovakia, and it does not seem to attest to enhancing social utility in consumption. On the other hand, further

---

*Andrzej Brzeski correctly remarked on this point (in private correspondence with the author) that the relatively less abundant supply of food might have produced the same result. Under Hungarian conditions, however, the decline in the relative importance of food seems more properly attributable to the operation of Engel's law.

TABLE 8. 7

Indexes of Personal and Social Consumption in
Hungary and Their Relationship
(in comparable prices)

Year	Personal Consumption	Social Consumption	Social Consumption as Percentage of Personal Consumption
1960	100. 0	100. 0	9. 4
1961	101. 1	113. 5	10. 5
1962	104. 6	147. 3	13. 2
1963	109. 5	151. 3	13. 0
1964	115. 5	159. 0	12. 9
1965	117. 1	150. 4	12. 1
1966	123. 0	152. 3	11. 6
1967	131. 0	159. 2	11. 4
1968	136. 9	182. 7	12. 5
1969	144. 9	201 3	13. 0
1970	156. 5	224. 3	13. 5
1971	165. 3	247. 2	14. 0
1972	171. 3	251. 9	13. 8

Sources: SE 1970, pp. 68-69; SE 1972, p. 68.

TABLE 8. 8

Structure of Household Expenditures in Hungary
(in constant prices; percentages)

	1960	1965	1971	1971/65 Index
Food	40. 6	37. 7	33. 0	119. 6
Beverages	10. 5	10. 9	12. 5	155. 6
Tobacco	1. 9	1. 9	2. 2	154. 7
Apparel	13. 4	11. 9	11. 2	128. 4
Housing	3. 5	3. 6	3. 5	131. 4
Fuel and power	3. 1	3. 5	3. 6	140. 0
Furniture	6. 8	6. 9	8. 0	160. 2
Health and personal care	5. 0	6. 0	6. 2	142. 6
Transport and communications	4. 2	4. 8	6. 1	173. 8
Education, culture, sport	8. 4	9. 8	10. 3	143. 8
Other	2. 6	3. 0	3. 4	153. 7
Total	100. 0	100. 0	100. 0	136. 5

Source: SE 1972, p. 383.

TABLE 8.9

Per Capita Consumption of Some Products in Hungary

Product	1950	1955	1960	1965	1970	1972
Meat and products (kg)[a]	34.3	36.9	47.6	51.6	57.6	61.7
Fish (kg)	.6	.7	1.5	1.6	2.3	2.3
Milk (kg)	99.0	86.7	114.0	97.1	109.6	114.0
Eggs (kg)	4.7	5.7	8.9	10.4	13.7	14.3
Fat (kg)	18.7	22.0	23.5	23.1	27.7	27.5
Cereals (kg)	142.1	151.7	136.2	139.2	128.2	127.0
Potatoes (kg)	108.7	102.1	97.6	84.3	75.1	70.0
Sugar (kg)	16.3	22.4	26.6	30.1	33.5	35.3
Vegetables (kg)	..	..	84.1	76.7	83.2	84.0
Fruits (kg)[b]	..	..	55.3	52.8	72.5	72.0
Cocoa (kg)	.054	.070	.355	.580	.857	..
Coffee (kg)	.057	.063	.143	.693	1.645	2.100
Tea (kg)	.010	.033	.034	.059	.072	.072
Wine (liters)	33.0	18.8	29.9	32.8	37.7	40.0
Beer (liters)	8.3	24.0	36.8	44.2	59.4	59.0
Brandy (liters)[c]	1.5	3.0	2.8	3.0	5.4	6.0

[a]Without fats.
[b]Including citrus fruits.
[c]50 percent alcoholic content.

Source: SE 1972, pp. 388, 389.

235

TABLE 8.10

Selected Durable Consumer Goods in Hungary
(per 1,000 Inhabitants)

	1960	1965	1970	1972
Refrigerators	3.8	25.1	102.7	148.7
Washing machines	45.2	114.3	178.7	200.8
Vacuum cleaners	10.7	45.1	99.0	122.1
Cars	3.1	9.8	23.3	33.1
Motorcycles, scooters	23.6	38.6	59.0	66.6
Radios*	222	245	245	244
Television sets*	10.4	81.8	171.2	200.5

*Number of subscribers.

Source: SE 1972, p. 389.

runners-up in rises of household expenditures—education, culture and
sports, and health and personal care—do seem to entail an element of
social usefulness and undoubtedly would be approved of by party
ideologues.

The low proportion of household expenditures on housing, characteristic of East European countries, is due to subsidization of that
sector by the government. Fuels, and transport and communications,
also constitute a relatively small proportion of these expenditures.

Table 8.9 shows per capita consumption of various foodstuffs and
beverages. What Khrushchev called "goulash Communism" is reflected
in the 80 percent rise of per capita consumption of meat between 1950
and 1972, although less significant if compared to 1938, when the per
capita consumption of meat was already about 40 kilograms (Holesovsky
and Pall 1968, p. 26). "Goulash Communism" also is reflected in the
relatively less important but substantial 280 percent increase in per
capita consumption of fish, a 200 percent increase in the consumption
of eggs, a 115 percent increase in the consumption of sugar, and substantial increases in the consumption of cocoa, coffee, and tea from
their very low levels in 1950. The social benefits of the 300 percent
increase in per capita consumption of brandy is somewhat more doubtful. It is interesting to observe a decline in the consumption of wine
between 1950 and 1965, followed by an increase in the latter part of
the period shown in the table to a level 20 percent above 1950. The

declines in per capita consumption of potatoes by 35 percent, * and
of cereals by 10 percent, reflect the Giffen paradox; they also are
indicative of improving levels of living (cf. Barabas and Nemeth 1966,
p. 218).

Table 8.10 shows the endowment of Hungarian consumers with
some durable consumer goods. Their availability increased from
extremely low levels, and therefore the percentage increase was considerable. One should keep in mind that the classifications given
are not strictly comparable to the Western ones, insofar as the quality
of Communist products is different: their refrigerators and cars are
smaller, their washing machines less automated, and so on. Nevertheless, an international comparison will be attempted in Chapter 10.

Table 8.11 gives two independently calculated consumption indexes
converted to the per capita basis. It appears from them that the prewar level of per capita consumption was achieved only as late as 1959.
Postwar recovery was slow and the indexes show stagnation between
1949 and 1953, during the forced industrialization period. The post-
Revolution Kadar era shows a steady, although not spectacular,
improvement in consumption.

Table 8.12 shows the official indexes of real per capita incomes.
During the 1960-67 period, which overlaps with the coverage of
Table 8.11, per capita personal real income rose by 31 percent,
whereas per capita personal consumption in Table 8.11 rose during
the same period by about 23 percent. Thus personal real income rose
faster than personal consumption. The reason for this discrepancy
lies partly in apparent official overstatement of the rise in real
incomes; partly in the difference between real income and real consumption, namely, in saving. Official data on savings are reproduced
in the first three columns of Table 8.13; the last two columns have
been used to calculate the average propensity to save by subtracting
dissaving in the form of borrowing from gross saving and dividing the
residual by money incomes of the population. Savings showed a
particularly steep increase during the 1960s, and the rate accelerated
during the NEM. The increase in savings was due both to the increase
in money incomes of the population (column 2) and to a substantial
rise in the average propensity to save to a level of 20 percent, which
looks almost like a consumers' strike or boycott. The possible
reasons for such a high average propensity to save are: unavailability
of the most desirable goods; bad assortments; bad quality; saving for
purchase of durable goods and/or for purchase of houses or apartments,
both of which might have seemed available in the future; and pre-
cautionary saving "for a rainy day." The result of this high volume

---

*The 70 kilogram per capita consumption of potatoes in Hungary
in 1972 was the lowest in Eastern Europe; cf. Table 10.4.

TABLE 8.11

Indexes of Real Personal Consumption Per Capita in Hungary

Year	Market Price Weights	Factor Cost Weights
1938	117.8	116.6
1947	68.1	72.0
1948	76.7	79.6
1949	85.1	87.0
1950	85.8	87.7
1951	92.7	93.7
1952	87.3	88.8
1953	86.6	88.2
1954	94.0	94.7
1955	100.0	100.0
1956	109.7	108.6
1957	112.1	110.9
1958	114.0	112.8
1959	123.6	121.4
1960	124.1	122.0
1961	126.9	124.7
1962	129.0	126.8
1963	134.6	131.9
1964	139.1	136.0
1965	142.8	139.5
1966	145.9	142.5
1967	153.5	149.5

Sources: Holesovsky and Pall 1968, p. 10; Bandor, Czirjak, and Pall 1970, p. 49.

TABLE 8.12

Indexes of Real Per Capital Income in Hungary

Year	Personal Real Income	Social Consumption Allotments	Total Real Income
1960	100	100	100
1961	101	103	101
1962	104	111	105
1963	110	120	111
1964	116	126	117
1965	117	130	118
1966	123	133	124
1967	131	139	132
1968	140	145	140
1969	148	153	149
1970	159	164	159
1971	166	174	167
1972	171	181	172

Source: SE 1972, p. 375.

238

TABLE 8.13

Savings of the Population in Hungary
(million forints)

Year	Gross Savings	Money Incomes of the Population	Credits to the Population	Net Savings	Average Propensity to Save (APS)
1950	289	..	..	..	..
1955	722	..	..	..	..
1960	5,542	118,518	1,450	4,092	3.5
1961	6,658	121,246	..	..	5.5*
1962	8,801	127,288	..	..	6.9*
1963	12,288	234,201	..	..	9.2*
1964	16,804	143,166	..	..	11.7*
1965	20,411	145,983	1,690	18,721	12.8
1966	23,029	156,986	..	..	14.7*
1967	24,797	167,918	2,394	22,403	13.3
1968	29,152	179,685	1,942	27,210	15.1
1969	35,097	193,666	2,220	32,877	17.0
1970	42,074	211,722	3,806	38,268	18.1
1971	48,398	226,838	4,554	43,844	19.3
1972	54,510	242,050	4,500	50,010	20.2

*Calculated on the basis of gross savings, without dissaving.

Sources: SE 1969, p. 368; SE 1972, pp. 377, 382.

TABLE 8. 14

Indexes of Nominal and Real Wages in Hungary

Year	Nominal Wage	Consumer Price Index	Real Wage
1960	100	100	100
1961	101	101	100
1962	103	102	102
1963	107	101	106
1964	111	101	109
1965	112	103	109
1966	116	104	111
1967	121	105	116
1968	124	105	118
1969	131	106	124
1970	139	108	129
1971	146	110	133
1972	153	113	135

Source: SE 1972, p. 376.

of savings was to free economic resources from current production of consumer goods and make them available for domestic investments, government consumption, and foreign investment.

Table 8. 14 shows official information on wages. Price increases during the NEM period were greater than during 1960-68, increasing the gap between money and real wages. A rise in real wages of 35 percent during the 13-year period shown in the table constitutes a good record. A comparison between Tables 8. 14 and 8. 12 shows that, over the 13-year period as a whole, real wages rose about half as fast as personal real income per capita. A small part of that difference can be explained by the increasing labor force participation, from 47. 4 percent in 1960 to 48. 3 percent in 1971. Another part might be explained by rising incomes of the agricultural population, but independent calculations show that disposable personal income in agriculture rose less steeply than disposable personal income outside agriculture (Czirjak and Marer 1973, pp. 12-13, 16-17). It seems, therefore, that the inclusion in Table 8. 12 of income from services and possibly estimates on various unofficial activities, such as moonlighting, account for most of the discrepancy between Tables 8. 12 and 8. 14.

CONCLUSIONS

Hungary shaped its postwar consumption history in the crucible of dramatic changes: the 1954 Nagy period of consumerism; the Rakosi hard-line policies before and after 1954; the Hungarian Revolution with its possible additional under current of consumer aspirations; Kadar's December 1961 "alliance policy" with the population and consequent flirting with consumers; and the NEM.

Behind these dramatic political changes lie economic forces that have determined the course of consumption: a high rate of investments, with investments directed to the areas of consumer goods playing the usual part of Communist Cinderella; rising labor force participation rates, particularly the higher economic activization of women; agricultural stagnation; loss through exports of many consumer goods that potentially would have been available to the domestic market; dynamic growth of Hungarian industry, with output of nondurable consumer goods by and large holding its own; fairly satisfactory growth of national income, with consumption constituting a declining share; consumption expenditures that attest to rising consumption levels; improvement in provision with durable consumer goods; rising per capita consumption; increasing savings, perhaps at an abnormally high rate; and rising real wages.

The emphasis on functionalism, the outward sign of which was the NEM program, generated some criticism. Part of this criticism was ideological and expressed in terms of ideological "impurity," "materialism," and "money grabbing" (cf. Robinson 1973, pp. 355-59). Some of it had consumption aspects:

> In addition to . . . outright opponents of the reform, one
> must consider those who do not reject the NEM per se
> but who criticize certain aspects or effects of it. The
> largest group of people in this category is to be found
> in the blue-collar sector, where egalitarian sentiments
> are widespread and often negate any attempt to implement
> the policy of wage differentiation. It is also here that
> one encounters the greatest dissatisfaction with the rate
> at which the living standard is rising, a phenomenon
> closely tied to the rapidly increasing expectations of a
> people who have finally been released from twenty years
> of austerity and imposed economic sacrifices. Such
> attitudes are expressed in various ways . . . but they

additionally find an outlet in the almost feverish determination that no one should rise financially too far
above the average. Jealousy, anger, and indignation
confront those who do . . . . (W. Robinson 1973, p. 358.)

Despite these and other objections, experiments in economic
reform continue in Hungary in a genuine search for efficiency, albeit
lately with an apparently diminished vigor. Whether the ultimate goal
of that quest is satisfaction of consumer wants or some other economic
or political aim is a matter for debate. For the time being, however,
one can make the observation that Hungarian consumers seem to have
benefited from the current phase of the search for economic efficiency.

9

CONSUMPTION
EXPERIENCE IN
EAST GERMANY

The German Democratic Republic (GDR, called here East Germany, in consonance with the appellation of other countries covered in this study) is perhaps least characteristic of East European countries in that it was the most developed region prior to World War II, and hence did not require prodigious industrialization to prove the superiority of the central planning system in raising a country to developed status. East Germany also constitutes the only East European exception to a basically full identification with national state; "basically full" because some ethnic minorities exist in all East European countries, including the Sorbs in East Germany (Hanhardt 1968, pp. 9-12), while Yugoslavia is a confederation of nationalities. On the other hand, East Germany allows the best comparison of relative development performance with another entity governed by a different economic system, namely, the Federal German Republic (FGR, henceforth called West Germany), which up to 1945 was on an almost equivalent, although possibly slightly higher level of economic development.

Despite the advanced economic character of East Germany, the Soviet model was uncritically applied to it, resulting in losses while learning how to adapt Soviet methods to East Germany conditions (Stolper 1960, p. 10). Those losses, plus reparation payments and other tributes remitted to the Soviet Union, could not help but adversely affect the standard of living. East Germany also suffered considerable war damage from Allied bombing as well as from ground fighting. In addition, it suffered from Soviet pilferage on both state (or "socialized") and individual (or "private") level. Therefore, considerable reconstruction effort was necessary to restore the country's productive potential. When one realizes that the reconstruction was carried on under the auspices of slavish acceptance of the Soviet model, with the added burden of reparations, it appears that the odds against East Germany were heavy indeed.

On top of these difficulties, East Germany has, as already mentioned, the West German measure against which its current economic achievements can readily be compared. The measure is not a nebulous state of socialist euphoria, present or future, so readily dispensed by the "publicity-agents of the Faith" (Lerner 1948, p. 502), but the actually existing economic system of West Germany. To the extent that East Germany has not measured up to the West German example, it has caused dissatisfaction among the population and, until the Berlin Wall was erected, drainage of people who decided to vote with their feet against the system that was less successful from the consumer's point of view. The possibility of such invidious comparisons between the two systems has created a considerable constraint on the economic and social policies of the East German administration. Without that constraint, East German policy assuredly would have been harsher and less mindful of the welfare of citizens. With that constraint, however, the level of consumption in East Germany has shown an improvement that seems at least adequate, even if one takes into account the disastrously low level of consumption at the outset of the postwar period.

AN OVERVIEW

Even as the Soviet armies battled their way through Germany, planeloads of Soviet-trained German Communists landed in the occupied territory, the first one bringing Walter Ulbricht and his team to Frankfurt on the Oder, another a group of Communist trusties to Dresden (Dornberg 1968, pp. 29-30). While the Soviet military administration ruled the country, foundations were laid for the new political orientation of the new administrative entity, under Communist domination of political parties, education, propaganda, local administration, and the shaping of a new value system (Hanhardt 1968, ch. 1; DIFW 1971, p. 25).

A land reform was carried out in September 1945, expropriating large farms and the Nazis; part of the land was redistributed and people's farms (state farms) were established with the rest (Hanhardt 1968, pp. 27-28). A monetary reform, undertaken partly to offset the successful monetary reform carried out in West Germany, was introduced on June 24, 1948. It resulted in partial confiscation of accumulated liquid reserves (Bundesministerium fuer gesamtdeutsche Fragen 1956, pp. 78-79, 82; Mieczkowski 1953, ch. 5, section 1-2), and in a socially desirable halt to inflation. However, full economic recovery was difficult because East Germany had been separated from the area of West Germany with which it had close links until 1945 (Hanhardt 1968, p. 115), and because of the heavy burden of reparation payments to the Soviet Union (Hanhardt 1968, pp. 34-35; Stolper 1960, p. 5), formally ended in 1953, in addition to which Soviet-East German joint

stock corporations had been set up to produce output exclusively for
Soviet use (Seume 1948, pp. 218-32). Joining with the better off West
Germany must have seemed generally and psychologically desirable to
most East Germans. The psychic aversion to the eastern orientation
of East German policy was summarized in muted tones by Arthur Hanhardt:

> Given the years of nazi propaganda against the Soviet
> Union and "the Slavs," the outcome of the war, the con-
> duct of Red Army troops, and the presence of expellees
> and refugees from East Europe, it seems reasonable to
> assume that the idea of identifying with the Soviet Union
> and the nations from the Baltic through the Balkans had
> limited appeal. In spite of the enthusiasm expressed by
> the communist political elite, the population generally
> looked eastward with some distaste—a feeling reinforced
> by mutuality and the memories of soldiers and prisoners
> of war who had experienced the eastern front. (Hanhardt
> 1968, p. 41.)

Regardless of these difficulties, the incorporation of East Germany
into the Soviet bloc continued relentlessly. East Germany became a
state in October 1949 and was granted formal sovereignty by the Soviet
Union in March 1954. Socialization of production proceeded quickly.
By 1950, a total of 59.4 percent of GNP was produced in socialized
enterprises; by 1962, this proportion rose to 85.0 percent, an additional 6.8 percent being produced in "semistate" enterprises, including
those producing on commission from the state. The share of private
enterprises in GNP declined from 40.6 percent in 1950 to 8.1 percent
in 1962 (Deutsches Institut fuer Zeitgeschichte 1964, p. 325).* On
the planning front, after a tentative Two-Year Plan in 1949-50, a new
Five-Year Plan of accelerated, Stalinist development was launched
for 1951-55. Its early results proved that the economy was responsive
to central direction. This, plus the political ambitions of the Ulbricht
government, which in the summer of 1952 achieved for East Germany
the status of a people's democracy and pined for full membership in
the Soviet bloc, led to new pressures to achieve faster growth at the
expense of workers. Ration cards were withdrawn from some groups,
affecting some 2 million persons. Production norms were drastically
raised in 1952 and 1953 (Baring 1972, pp. 13-22), creating dissatisfaction among workers that culminated in the June 16-17, 1953, Berlin
uprising, one of the first such spontaneous revolts of workers against
deteriorating living standards in Eastern Europe. (The Plzen workers'

---

*For participation in net product, see SJ 1972, p. 39; for
description of semistate enterprises, see Smith 1969, pp. 101-6.

riots of June 1, 1953, actually preceded the Berlin uprising but were
much less publicized.) A New Course policy of concessions to consumer aspirations was introduced in June 1953, but by summer of 1955
Ulbricht had proclaimed its official demise.

Despite a brief period of intellectual revisionism in 1956, East
Germany proceeded with ambitious plans for economic expansion, even
planning (after the model of Khrushchev's avowals to catch up with the
United States) to surpass West Germany in per capita consumption of
foodstuffs and other consumer goods by 1961. Like the Soviet declara-
tions, this one also proved unrealistic, partly because forced collectivization of agriculture from 25.2 percent of total arable land area in
1957 to 85.0 percent in 1960* resulted in a decline in agricultural
production.† After 1964, however, East German agriculture staged a vig-
orous improvement under the New Economic System, mentioned below.

During the 1960s, despite some intellectual ferment and oblivious
of the degree of cultural liberalization in Poland, Hungary, and Czechoslovakia, East Germany pursued its politically hard-line course. The
physical monument to it was the Berlin Wall, erected in August 1961
(Galante 1965, pp. 1-64). Its erection solved (from the East German
point of view) an economically and politically embarrassing situation.
About 2.7 million persons had left East Germany up to that time, some
60 percent of them members of the labor force and many of them highly
trained professionals, compelling East Germany to obtain its production
increases through increases in labor productivity. Since in Communist
countries about two-thirds of economic growth is derived from extensive
sources (Wilczynski 1973, p. 18), the increases in productivity were

---

*DIFZ 1964, p. 403. Socialized land amounted to 3.3 percent of
total utilized land area in 1952. One could be reminded that on July 1,
1945, Deutsche Volkszeitung, the leading organ of the East German
Communist Party, assured its readers that "it is obvious that private
ownership of peasants will not be touched" (Bundesministerium fuer
gesamtdeutsche Fragen 1956, p. 11). A land reform started shortly
thereafter, at the beginning of September 1945 (ibid., pp. 18ff; see
also Bundesministerium fuer gesamtdeutsche Fragen 1966, pp. 13-17).
    †Production, in kilograms per hectare of agricultural land, was
as follows:

	1950	1962
Cereals and legumes	422.5	304.5
Oilseeds	26.1	30.0
Potatoes	735.9	589.1
Sugar beets	831.9	707.0

However, area under cultivation rose in the same period; compare
Table 9.5.

not adequate to supply momentum for the desired growth. A sardonic comment on the workers' state was contained in the fact that some 23 percent of all escapees were industrial and handicraft workers. *

The political function of closing down the borders with West Germany was to strengthen the regime; the social function was to reconcile the population to Communist Party values and goals as those with which they had to put up; and the economic function was to stop the costly drain of labor, largely high-quality labor, and thus to lay foundations for "normal" economic growth, even though some disadvantages of the East German planning system had already been recognized. To cope with problems created by rigid central planning, the New Economic System for Planning and Directing the National Economy was introduced in July 1963. The earlier "ideology of the ton" was replaced by a profit-incentive system and by economic levers acting as macro-economic tools of policy. Instead of inflexible, detailed planning, the new system brought reliance on the market, cost-benefit calculus, managerial efficiency, and interest payments for the use of scarce capital (DIFW 1971, pp. 58-92). The results so far show that decentralization does not necessarily mean freedom from centralized decision-making (Hanhardt 1968, p. 98), and that greater freedom of enterprises does not imply greater freedom for East Germany or the East Germans. The latter point was illustrated by negotiations with the USSR on a trade agreement late in 1965, which apparently caused the suicide, on December 3, 1965, of the head of the State Planning Commission, Erich Apel, who objected to Soviet exploitation of East Germany. The retirement of Walter Ulbricht in 1971, and his death in 1973, seemed to reinforce the tendency toward political status quo. His followers do not possess his authority to lead East Germany through radical changes, even if they had a desire to do so. And that desire may be lacking in the face of apparent wide political acceptance of the regime,[†] substantial increase in the level of living, and an attitude of "If you have to live here, you can live here" (Schoenbaum 1972, pp. xiii, xii).

Another important East German achievement was to create an independent economic unit out of the truncated dependency that was the Soviet occupation zone in 1945. This reality poses psychological implications (a feeling that there really is a different Germany) as well as political implications (a recognition of at least relative

---

*DIFW 1971, pp. 31 n. 1 and 56. For the official East German view, see Bundesministerium fuer gesamtdeutsche Fragen 1956, p. 146, reproduced in English in Smith 1969, p. 89.

[†] Hanhardt 1968, p. 124, shows that the percentage of "loyal" citizens in population samples rose from 37 percent in 1962 to 51 percent in 1964 and 71 percent in 1966.

"permanency" of the present arrangement and former Chancellor Willy Brandt's recognition of East Germany) (Polikeit 1966, pp. 5-6; DIFW 1971, pp. 23-24). From an artificial creation of postwar politics, East Germany graduated into a self-contained country, second largest in the Soviet bloc in industrial output, the largest single trading partner of the Soviet Union (Marer 1972, pp. 128-41, 104-10), and the state with the highest level of per capita consumption in the Soviet bloc. At times, it has striven for a measure of independence from the USSR; its own interest, within the limitations of the Comecon structure and policies, seems to be fairly well understood among its Communist Party leaders (Hangen 1966, passim).

FACTORS AFFECTING CONSUMPTION

Investments and Employment

Official East German statistical series start mostly with 1950 or later. They show steeply rising investments, with a slowdown in the rate of their growth in the early 1960s and in 1971, as seen in Table 9.1. National income produced, shown in the same table, increased on the whole by half as much as aggregate investments, pointing to declining incremental capital/output ratios and to an increasing share of investments in national income. The latter phenomenon is shown in Table 9.2, which also reveals an increasing share of "productive investments" and an increasing share of social consumption. The main relative loser during the period shown in Table 9.2 was personal consumption. Both tables give a picture characteristic of East European economies: a steeply rising volume of investments, with construction smaller than investments in machinery and equipment; a high rate of growth of national income; a rising share of accumulation in national income and a declining share of consumption; and a rising share of social consumption in aggregate consumption. A trait found to a less prominent extent than in most other East European economies is shown in column 4 of Table 9.2: Except for a few years (such as 1950), the increase in inventories constituted a relatively small proportion of total accumulation. On the other hand, the preference given to the "productive" sphere in almost all years is characteristic, although one has to note that the degree of that preference declined in the 1960s.

Investments relate to what a West German author, Werner Obst, termed "the cardinal problem of the GDR economy" (1973, ch. 3). He noted the approximately equal rates of economic growth and of the rise in productivity in East and West Germany, while the economic useful-ness of progress, measured presumably in terms of consumer welfare, was clearly higher in West Germany (Obst 1973, p. 28). The

TABLE 9. 1

Official Indexes of Investments in East Germany
(in 1967 prices)

Year	Aggregate Investments	Construction	Machines and Equipment	National Income Produced (in comparable prices)
1950	100	100	100	100
1951	126	139	94	. .
1952	161[a]	158	157	. .
1953	194[a]	187	191	. .
1954	198[a]	181	203	. .
1955	226[a]	194	214	185[b]
1956	284	229	326	194[c]
1957	294	241	322	207[c]
1958	336	276	407	230[c]
1959	405	326	523	250[c]
1960	447	359	580	261[d]
1961	453	354	595	266
1962	463	368	609	273
1963	475	363	646	282
1964	520	389	727	296
1965	569	426	798	310
1966	610	440	884	325
1967	666	491	937	342
1968	735	545	1, 030	360
1969	848	630	1, 180	379
1970	911	661	1, 300	400
1971	911	666	1, 270	418

[a] Index of aggregate investments is higher than its constituent parts.
[b] 173. 2 according to SJ 1962, p. 161.
[c] Figures from SJ 1962 multiplied by the 1960 ratio of the indexes from SJ 1972 and SJ 1962.
[d] 242. 7 according to SJ 1962, p. 161.

Sources: SJ 1962, p. 161; SJ 1972, pp. 39, 43, 44.

TABLE 9.2

Domestic Use of National Income in East Germany
(in comparable prices; percent of total national income)

Year	Accumulation				Consumption		
	Aggregate	"Productive" Sphere	"Nonproductive" Sphere	Growth of Inventories and Reserves	Total	Personal	Social
1950	8.5	- 1.5	4.6	5.4	91.5	82.9	8.6
1951	9.7	3.4	2.4	3.9	90.3	83.6	6.7
1952	10.6	3.9	2.6	4.2	89.4	83.2	6.2
1953	12.3	5.3	3.0	3.9	87.7	81.3	6.4
1954	9.1	5.5	2.8	.8	90.9	83.0	8.0
1955	9.8	3.7	5.0	1.1	90.2	81.3	8.9
1956	15.7	10.2	3.8	1.7	84.3	76.5	7.9
1957	16.9	9.8	3.9	3.1	83.1	75.3	7.8
1958	20.1	10.5	3.7	5.8	79.9	72.3	7.7
1959	20.0	11.6	4.2	4.2	80.0	72.5	7.5
1960	18.1	9.0	6.0	3.2	81.9	73.7	8.2
1961	16.1	8.4	6.1	1.6	83.9	75.4	8.5
1962	19.0	8.0	5.9	5.2	81.0	72.8	8.2
1963	17.2	8.0	6.2	3.0	82.8	74.4	8.4
1964	18.9	8.8	6.1	4.0	81.1	72.8	8.3
1965	19.9	9.4	6.0	4.5	80.1	71.6	8.5
1966	21.1	9.7	6.2	5.3	78.9	70.4	8.4
1967	21.4	10.5	6.8	4.1	78.6	69.9	8.7
1968	19.7	10.9	7.8	1.0	80.3	70.9	9.4
1969	21.9	12.6	8.3	1.1	78.1	68.8	9.3
1970	24.0	12.6	7.7	3.7	76.0	66.8	9.2
1971	22.1	11.6	8.0	2.5	77.9	68.3	9.6

Sources: SJ 1962, p. 166 (for 1951–54 and 1956–59, apparently in current prices); SJ 1972, p. 42.

effectiveness of investment activity can be measured in terms of incremental capital/output ratios, and for that Obst supplied some interesting figures. During 1961-70 the incremental capital/output ratio, calculated on the basis of gross investments, was 5.04 in East Germany while in West Germany it was 3.34, or 34 percent lower than in East Germany. Also during 1961-70, the incremental capital/output ratio calculated on the basis of net investments was 3.69 in East Germany, while in West Germany it was 2.37, or 36 percent lower than in East Germany. The same indicator, calculated on the basis of comparative prices in order to avoid the effect of relative price differentials, becomes 4.50 in East Germany, while the West German one becomes 4.07, or 9.5 percent lower. Finally, when the cost of obtaining capital is added to the East German investment figures, the relationship of incremental capital/output ratios becomes something like 4.50 to 2.37, or 47.4 percent lower for West Germany. Thus every Deutsche Mark (DM) invested in East Germany gave only 52.6 percent of productive effect compared with the same DM invested in West Germany (Obst 1973, pp. 28-33). The incremental capital/output ratio in East Germany is relatively high, according to Obst, because "the strategy of [the East German] economy is directed toward ideological, political and social ends" (Obst 1973, p. 35). However, an improvement took place in the relationship between East German and West German incremental capital/output ratios in gross terms from 76.2 percent in 1960 to 85.7 percent in 1968 (DIFW 1971, p. 287). Nevertheless, despite such improvement, it still requires substantially more effort in East Germany to produce economic results equivalent to those in West Germany. Such greater necessary effort cannot but have an adverse effect on living levels insofar as proportionately more resources have to be diverted away from consumption and into investments in order to accomplish the politically paramount goal of economic growth.

Table 9.3 shows changes in employment in the East German economy. It reveals the very sluggish growth of the labor force, despite the increasing proportion of women in the labor force. In fact, one can calculate from Table 9.3 that the increase in the female work force between 1952 and 1971 amounted to 696,000 while aggregate employment between those years rose by only 533,000 indicating an absolute decline in the male work force of 163,000. This decline may have been due partly to drainage of men into military and paramilitary organizations, and partly to the demographic valley caused by lower births during World War II, but the main cause assuredly was the flight of East Germans to the West. Consequently, a substantial proportion of East German economic growth is attributable to intensive factors, in contrast to other Communist countries, as has been noted. Despite this reliance on growth in labor productivity, however, labor productivity in industry, measured in terms of gross output in West German productivity, from 33 percent to 32 percent of West German

TABLE 9.3

Employment in East German Economy According to Form of Ownership
(without apprentices; as of September 30, except 1952-59 when as of December 31; thousands)

Year	Total	State	Cooperative	Semistate	Private	Percentage of Women
1952	7,271	3,633	249	—	3,388	42.7
1953	..	..	..	—	..	..
1954	..	..	..	—	..	..
1955	7,722	4,167	466	—	3,089	44.0
1956	7,723	4,310	516	—	2,851	43.9
1957	7,810	4,445	534	..	2,777	44.4
1958	7,783	4,541	720	149	2,319	43.9
1959	7,820	4,695	879	293	1,905	44.8
1960	7,739	4,823	1,433	398	1,032	45.0
1961	7,787	4,892	1,551	382	961	45.7
1962	7,786	4,894	1,570	401	921	46.0
1963	7,646	4,868	1,488	405	884	46.0
1964	7,658	4,881	1,501	411	865	46.3
1965	7,676	4,930	1,498	468	781	46.7
1966	7,684	4,973	1,487	471	753	46.9
1967	7,714	5,021	1,485	477	732	47.2
1968	7,712	5,060	1,458	482	712	47.4
1969	7,746	5,101	1,468	490	686	48.0
1970	7,769	5,174	1,451	486	659	48.3
1971	7,804	5,249	1,438	481	635	48.7

Note: Statistical methodology apparently varies in different years.

Sources: SJ 1962, pp. 171, 175; SJ 1966, pp. 61, 65; SJ 1972, pp. 55, 59.

productivity (DIFW 1971, p. 287). That means that West German productivity further gained on that of East Germany, despite considerable absorption of untrained "guest workers" (workers from foreign countries) into West German industry.

Focusing again on the importance of the female component of the East German labor force, we may note that between 1949 and 1969 the economically active female population increased from 3.0 million to 3.7 million, while at the same time the number of women of labor force age declined from 6.6 to 5.0 million. These opposing tendencies were caused, in the latter case by westward migration, and in the former case by increased social consumption in the form of day care, kindergartens, and over-the-week houses for children, not to mention work cafeterias, effort to provide laundry services, and so on. Thus, for instance, the number of day care places for each 100 children under the age of three increased from 8.0 in 1955 to 23.7 in 1969. The number of places in kindergartens and over-the-week houses per 100 children between the age of three and the school entrance age increased from 14 in 1949 to 28 in 1955 and 55 in 1969 (Lippold 1970, pp. 97-98). Obviously, a conscious policy in the realm of social consumption, plus possible social and economic pressures, achieved the result of "liberating" some women from household drudgery and putting them, in factories. The effect of this on national income and household consumption was obviously gratifying. The effect on human welfare was more moot insofar as there was an inevitable loss of family cohesion, possibly psychological loss by the children, and possibly some loss in terms of greater human wear and tear.

The growth of state and cooperative sectors, indicated in Table 9.3, is characteristic for Communist countries; so is the decline of the private sector, although the said decline occurred to a relatively small extent during the Stalinist and early post-Stalinist period but gathered momentum after 1955. The emergence of the semistate sector, where the state is supposed to provide additional needed capital and assumes partial ownership, is unique to East Germany and explains some of the decline in the private sector.

A trend of importance for the standard of living was the steady increase in the proportion of dependents among the population between 1939 and 1960, as shown in Table 9.4. This trend was caused to a large extent by the departure of many persons of prime work age to West Germany, but it continued at least until 1968 (DIFW 1971, p. 31).

An additional factor that tended to decrease the real wage per worker was the steady reduction of the work week, although this factor tended to be offset to the extent that overtime was, or might have been, used more. The official work week was 48 hours in 1950, then 45 hours in most sectors in 1957. In 1966, the five-day work week was introduced, and in 1967 the work week was further reduced to 43.75 hours (42 hours in three-shift enterprises) (Staatliche Zentralverwaltung fuer Statistik 1969, p. 54). To offset the possible

253

TABLE 9.4

Proportion of Persons Outside Labor Force Age
in Total Population in East Germany
(percentages)

	1939	1950	1955	1957	1960
Outside labor force age	48.1	57.9	58.2	59.7	64.0
In that					
Children under 15	31.6	36.1	33.0	32.9	35.1
Retirees Age Group*	16.5	21.8	25.2	26.8	28.9

*Over 60 for women, over 65 for men.

Source: DIFW 1961, p. 140.

adverse effect of these reductions on production, the government increased its reliance on incentive wages. About 50 to 70 percent of income of workers in East Germany depends on the basis wage; the residual depends on selected success indicators. During the late 1960s currently paid work premiums increased from 4 to 8 percent in relation to the wage fund. In 1965-66, a new premium appeared, a year-end premium payable to any worker who had worked in a given enterprise for the whole year; it amounted to from one third to two times the monthly wage (DIFW 1971, p. 191). Apart from work incentive through participation in the enterprise profit, the year-end premium obviously is designed to reduce labor turnover, originally quite high in East Germany.

Once the East Berlin loophole in the East German border was closed, the East German government felt less threatened by invidious wage comparisons with West Germany. As a result, gross and net labor income rose substantially less in East Germany after 1960 as compared with West Germany, both in current respective Deutsche Mark (DM) and in constant purchasing power DM (DIFW 1971, pp. 192-207).

Agriculture, Foreign Trade, and Industry

Changes in East German agricultural production are shown in Table 9.5. Despite its depressed level in 1950 as compared with prewar, the rise in production was rather slow, the period 1955-63 evidencing stagnation in output. A 42 percent growth over a 22-year

TABLE 7.5

Agricultural Production in East Germany

	Product of agriculture and forestry			Stolper's indexes of aggregate agricultural production	
	Contribution to national income (million DM in comparable prices)	Index	Share of national income (percent)	in 1936 prices	in 1950 prices
1934-38	..	..	..	100	100
1950	8,904	100	28.4	72.5	74.0
1951	8,932[a]	100.3	..	85.2	87.5
1952	9,557[a]	107.3	..	98.6	103.5
1953	9,573[a]	107.5	..	85.0	88.0
1954	10,155[a]	114.0	..	88.1	91.3
1955	10,963	123.1	20.2	93.1	97.6
1956	10,850[b]	121.9	..	87.6	91.5
1957	11,299[b]	126.9	..	98.7	102.4
1958	11,617[b]	130.5	..	100.2	103.4
1959	11,758[b]	132.1	..	..	..
1960	11,991	134.7	16.4	..	..
1961	10,160	114.1	13.7	..	..
1962	10,101	113.4	13.2	.. } 100.4[c]	..
1963	11,106	124.7	14.0	..	..
1964	11,422	128.3	13.7	..	..
1965	12,147	136.4	13.8	.. } 122.2[c]	..
1966	12,733	143.0	13.8	..	..
1967	13,525	151.9	13.9	..	..
1968	13,422	150.7	13.1	.. } 130.2[cd]	..
1969	12,485	140.2	11.7	..	..
1970	13,188	148.1	11.6	..	..
1971	12,615	141.7	10.7	..	..

[a] Increase in gross production in current prices distributed in proportion to its 1950 and 1955 relation to the increase in net production figures in comparable prices.

[b] Same as under note a for 1955 and 1950.

[c] Lazarcik index.

[d] 1971-72.

Sources: Stolper 1960, p. 329; SJ 1966, p. 21; SJ 1972, p. 40; Lazarcik 1974, p. 337.

TABLE 9.6

Agricultural Production Per Hectare and Per Capita
in East and West Germany

	East Germany			West Germany
	1934-38	1955-59	1965-69	1965-69[a]
Hundreds of kilograms per hectare				
All cereals	20.6	24.3	30.0	33.7
In that:				
Wheat	24.6	30.3	36.6	37.4
Potatoes	173	159	180	270.4
Sugar beets	291	258	301	432.9
Kilograms per capita				
All cereals	400	341	407	283[b]
Potatoes	837	718	717	312[b]
Steer, live weight	..	71	101	87[b]
Eggs (number)	..	152	235	219[b]
Milk	..	304	404	360[b]

[a]Not quite comparable due to different statistical coverage.
[b]Crop years 1964/65 to 1968/69.

Source: DIFW 1971, pp. 143, 145.

period from 1950 to 1971 does not look impressive in view of the long-range opportunities open before East German agriculture after the war (cf. Lazarcik 1974, pp. 386-88). Wolfgang Stolper's index, showing that the prewar production level in agriculture was reached only as late as 1957-58, does not point to a notable achievement either. West German agricultural production, on the other hand, achieved its prewar gross output level in 1951, while income from sale of agricultural output was higher than prewar by 1950 (Statistisches Jahrbuch fuer die Bundesrepublik Deutschland, 1955, p. 136). On the positive side, although hardly complimentary to East German agriculture, there was a substantial reduction in the relative contribution of agriculture to national income, evidencing a fast rise of other sectors of material production and a change in the structure of the East German economy (cf. Boettcher 1956, pp. 94-98, 131).

Table 9.6 provides some agricultural comparisons with West Germany. It suggests that East Germany is less productive in output per unit of land, possibly partly owing to poorer Prussian soil, but that it is also more agriculturally self-sufficient because of smaller population density. By itself, of course, this fact is not disadvantageous to West Germany, which tends to rely more on international division of labor according to comparative advantage, and on making optimum use of its scarce resources.

Table 9.7 shows the latest independent estimates of agricultural production in East Germany made by Gregor Lazarcik. Using the 1965 East German price weights, his index yields results similar to those of Stolper (who used 1936 price weights and 1950 West German price weights), but with a more detailed background and carried to more recent years. The breakthrough to a higher plateau of production in 1965 is clearly discernible in the table (column 1), as is the higher development of animal production from 1961 onward, with crop production leading until 1955 (columns 2 and 3). This shift in the relative importance of major agricultural products indicates a pronounced improvement in food standards between those dates.

The index of output per person employed in agriculture (column 4) shows considerable increase in productivity of labor, statistically due partly to rising agricultural production but mostly to a decline in employment in agriculture from an average of 1.6 million during 1934-38, and 1.9 million in 1950, to less than 1 million by 1970 (Lazarcik 1972, p. 20).

Per capita agricultural output (column 5) shows that permanent recovery to prewar output levels was achieved in 1963 (1958 and 1960 having also risen above prewar), and that from 1967 on agricultural output per capita was about 20 percent above the prewar level. However, when the net contribution of agriculture to the economy was calculated after depreciation, and was divided by the number in the population (column 6), postwar production was found to have exceeded prewar in only two years, 1967 and 1968, which points to the costliness of the East German effort to raise agricultural production.

East German foreign trade statistics reveal very little about the possible direct effect on consumption. They show a pattern of growth of foreign trade usual for postwar Eastern Europe, but there is no indication as to the distribution of that trade between consumption goods and capital goods, and hence no information about its direct impact on consumption, except for my calculations shown in the last column of Table 9.8. One can speculate that expansion of foreign trade, through its effect on division of labor according to the law of comparative advantage, has contributed to increasing welfare. However, to the extent that one can suspect either exploitation of East Germany through trade by the Soviet Union, or mutual exploitation within the Comecon bloc (Pryor 1963, pp. 135-53; Wilczynski 1969, pp. 338-39), the conclusion on the direct impact of foreign trade on consumption becomes less certain. Table 9.8 shows the foreign trade statistics available from the official statistical yearbook of East Germany, with an apology for their inconclusiveness as far as

257

TABLE 9.7

Independent Estimates of East German Agricultural Production
(indexes; 1965 price weights)

Year	Output of Agriculture			Output Per Employed Person	Output Per Capita	Net Product Per Capita
	Total	Crops	Animal Products			
1934-38	100.0	100.0	100.0	100.0	100.0	100.0
1950	68.3	103.1	55.3	58.7	61.6	57.4
1951	82.1	105.2	73.5	77.7	74.2	70.0
1952	89.0	94.9	86.8	91.0	80.5	76.8
1953	82.5	92.5	78.7	85.3	75.2	69.1
1954	91.3	97.6	89.0	93.3	83.8	77.4
1955	90.8	90.1	91.1	88.9	83.8	75.9
1956	91.4	85.5	93.6	95.2	85.5	76.1
1957	99.9	102.5	99.0	107.4	94.5	84.3
1958	105.6	106.7	105.2	117.6	100.8	91.8
1959	102.7	87.9	108.2	120.5	98.4	88.5
1960	107.4	109.6	106.5	140.2	103.2	91.4
1961	97.2	79.3	103.9	129.6	94.1	79.4
1962	95.7	92.0	97.1	127.2	92.7	75.8
1963	103.5	92.3	107.6	140.5	99.9	84.7
1964	106.0	93.1	110.8	143.0	103.4	84.5
1965	115.6	100.0	121.4	158.2	112.5	93.5
1966	120.8	101.5	128.0	168.9	117.3	97.3
1967	125.5	113.4	130.0	178.0	121.7	101.8
1968	128.6	108.9	136.0	184.9	124.7	103.2
1969	124.1	95.1	134.9	203.8	120.4	97.1
1970	126.7	103.1	135.6	214.6	123.1	92.3
1971-72	130.2	104.9	144.0	231.1	126.5	90.1
1973	137.0	107.9	152.9	258.8	133.2	88.2

Sources: Lazarcik 1972, pp. 7, 20, 16; Lazarcik 1974, pp. 337, 348, 349, 371.

258

TABLE 9.8

Indexes of East German Foreign Trade
(calculated in devisa DM)

Year	Index in Current Prices	Index in Current Prices	Balance of Trade in Consumer Goods (in millions of dollars in current prices)
1949	15.0	14.3	. .
1950	18.4	21.4	−99.2
1951	32.3	27.7	. .
1952	33.5	35.2	. .
1953	43.8	44.8	. .
1954	58.3	50.1	. .
1955	58.6	53.7	−281.5
1956	64.1	61.0	. .
1957	83.1	74.5	. .
1958	86.7	77.6	. .
1959	97.0	91.9	. .
1960	100.0	100.0	−427.4
1961	103.4	102.6	−212.6
1962	107.4	109.7	−158.2
1963	122.9	106.2	−229.9
1964	132.8	120.2	23.8
1965	139.1	128.0	34.5
1966	145.2	146.5	61.1
1967	156.6	149.4	. .
1968	171.8	154.6	. .
1969	188.2	187.9	. .
1970	207.5	220.9	. .
1971	230.0	226.0	. .

Sources: SJ 1972, pp. 301, 302; Marer 1972, pp. 47, 56.

their effect on consumption is concerned. In some years, exports seem to have forged ahead of imports, thus decreasing national income available for domestic distribution in comparison with national income produced domestically; but on the whole, the growth of exports and imports was fairly well matched.

A putative indication of the adverse direct impact of foreign trade on domestically available resources, and hence on consumption, is contained in the comparison between national income produced and national income distributed. A positive difference between them indicates: (1) a surplus on current account of the balance of payments,

TABLE 9.9

Comparison Between National Income Produced and
National Income Distributed in East Germany
(millions of DM at current prices)

Year	National Income Produced	National Income Distributed Domestically	Excess of National Income Produced Over That Distributed
1950	29,109	28,157	952
1951	35,252	33,225	2,027
1952	40,130	38,575	1,555
1953	42,443	42,236	207
1954	46,066	44,770	1,293
1955	50,037	48,430	1,607
1956	52,288	51,246	1,042
1957	56,015	55,751	264
1958	62,011	62,790	−779
1959	67,488	67,858	−370
1960	70,520	70,393	127
1961	72,864	72,645	219
1962	74,448	74,898	−450
1963	76,749	74,898	1,851
1964	80,447	78,558	1,889
1965	83,148	81,937	1,211

Source: Schaefer 1967, pp. 45, 67, 88, 105.

(2) a rise in inventories, (3) statistical discrepancy, or (4) a mixture of those possibilities. Table 9.9 gathers the available statistics on this point. The excess of national income produced over national income consumed shown in that table seems rather large; that may constitute an indication, albeit an incomplete one, of some of the losses resulting to the economy from foreign trade.*

The last column in Table 9.8 shows the balance of trade in consumer goods, calculated on the basis of Marer's work. It indicates a positive impact on consumption (a negative balance of trade in consumer goods) for selected years until 1963, and after that a negative impact. As in Table 7.5 in Chapter 7, the balance was obtained from

---

*According to Snell and Harper 1970, pp. 568-75, the reorientation of foreign trade to the East has done greater economic harm to East Germany than did direct Soviet exploitation.

foodstuffs and raw materials for foodstuffs, and from industrial consumer goods other than food. It is hard to say whether that column, or Table 9.9, gives a better indication of the actual role of foreign trade in the area of consumption. One conclusion does seem obvious: Statistical coverage of foreign trade of East Germany is by no means satisfactory.

One also should mention here one of the most important functions of East Germany's foreign trade from the point of view of consumption: It provides a link with the West European Common Market through East German exports to West Germany, which are treated by the West Germans as intra-German trade (Gamarnikow 1974, p. 199). For East Germany, this has meant easy access to Western technology and hard currencies to finance imports, both of which have helped in raising East Germany's level of consumption.

Table 9.10 compares two official with two independently derived indexes of industrial production. It is apparent that the gross production index results in an (also "gross") exaggeration of industrial growth due largely to double counting. However, even the official index of net production (not reproduced here) is higher than the independently derived index, which conforms to the statistical experience in other East European countries (Ernst 1966, p. 879 and passim). It appears from the independent indexes that the prewar level of industrial production was reestablished by 1953, which is indicative of the degree of war and postwar devastation of East German industry. Prewar per capita industrial production was achieved later, in 1954 or 1955, indicating slow recovery of labor productivity, and due largely to the higher dependency ratios shown earlier in Table 9.4. From 1955 on, labor productivity in industry was rising at a fair rate, as shown in the official index (see Table 9.10, column 3). However, as indicated by the Czirjak-Dusek index, industrial production did not rise as much as shown in the official index, which also deflates the gains in labor productivity claimed officially. Between 1950 and 1967, the Czirjak-Dusek index rises by 202 percent; the official index rises during the same period by 345 percent. The independently calculated index also shows that as late as 1950 industrial production, due to dismantling and to a vengeful Soviet policy, was 30 percent below 1936. It must be remembered that between 1936 and at least 1944, a considerable increase took place in the German industrial production on account of total mobilization of German industry for the war effort. This means that, given a rise in output between at least 1947 and 1950, the decline in industrial production caused by war action and by the early Soviet occupation policy was indeed considerable. The prewar output level was reached in East Germany only in 1953; in West Germany it was reached in 1950 (Mieczkowski 1953, p. 123).

East German official indexes of gross industrial production are highly exaggerated, because of the increasing division of labor between enterprises and the increasing degree of manufacturing of

TABLE 9.10

Indexes of Industrial Production in East Germany

Year	Official Indexes		Stolper's Indexes of Industrial Production			Czirjak-Dusek Index of Industrial Production
	Gross Production	Labor Productivity for Whole Industrial Labor Force	in 1936 Prices	in 1950 Prices	Per Capita in 1950 Prices	
1936	..	..	132.8	149.9	100.0	59.8
1949	79	..	..	..	..	..
1950	100	..	100.0	100.0	58.6	42.1
1951	123	..	113.3	116.9	68.8	50.2
1952	142	..	126.6	128.2	75.4	53.7
1953	160	..	145.4	148.9	88.3	59.6
1954	176	..	159.0	161.9	96.6	66.6
1955	190	100	168.9	170.0	102.1	72.0
1956	203	107	177.8	178.3	108.5	75.3
1957	219	112	186.9	188.3	115.9	77.8
1958	242	122	197.6	199.0	123.6	83.6
1959	272	133	..	..	..	92.8
1960	294	141	..	..	..	100.0
1961	312	149	..	..	..	103.3
1962	332	159	..	..	..	108.4
1963	346	167	..	..	..	113.0
1964	369	178	..	..	..	115.7
1965	392	188	..	..	..	119.4
1966	417	200	..	..	..	123.0
1967	445	213	..	..	..	127.2
1968	471	224	..	..	..	..
1969	503	238	..	..	..	..
1970	537	253	..	..	..	..
1971	567	266	..	..	..	..

Sources: Stolper 1960, pp. 242, 243; Czirjak and Dusek 1972, p. 3; SJ 1972, pp. 114, 137.

TABLE 9.11

Indexes of Industrial Production of Consumer Goods in East Germany

Year	Official Indexes of Gross Production			Stolper's Calculated Indexes		
	Light Industry Without Textiles [a]	Textiles	Foodstuffs	Manufactured Consumer Goods	Food Industry	Nondurable Consumer Goods [b]
1936	96[c]	102.0	127	227.5	151.9	170.0
1946	42[c]	..	49	..	..	61.2[d]
1949	77[c]	..	77	..	..	75.7
1950	100	100	100	100	100	100.0
1951	..	..	..	122.5	127.9	123.0
1952	..	..	..	135.3	139.2	135.2
1953	..	..	..	147.4	155.0	148.5
1954	..	..	..	163.4	166.5	162.1
1955	159	174	217	165.4	174.2	163.3
1956	..	..	..	164.8	169.1	162.9
1957	..	..	..	170.2	181.2	173.0
1958	..	..	..	181.4	188.6	184.5
1959	..	..	..	..	..	197.6
1960	241	239	302	..	..	208.6
1961	258	242	313	..	..	215.3
1962	273	251	314	..	..	220.5
1963	267	252	326	..	..	218.1
1964	280	257	341	..	..	220.9
1965	291	271	354	..	..	227.1
1966	308	285	369	..	..	233.7
1967	326	298	384	..	..	242.7
1968	347	302	400	..	..	..
1969	368	311	417	..	..	..
1970	393	331	440	..	..	..
1971	403	343	451	..	..	..

[a]Without glass and fine ceramics.
[b]Calculated by the author from the Czirjak-Dusek study; includes textiles, apparel, leather and fur, paper, printing, food and tobacco.
[c]With textiles.
[d]1948.

Sources: Stolper 1960, p. 251; SJ 1066, p. 154; Czirjak and Dusek 1972, pp. 19-20; SJ 1972, p. 116.

goods. Both these factors tend to raise gross indexes more than the net ones, while it is the latter indexes that measure changes in output available to final users, including consumers. Consequently, official gross indexes can be used only as a rough guide to developing industrial production and its effect on consumption.

The development of industrial production of consumer goods is shown in Table 9.11. A juxtaposition between official and calculated indexes shows that according to the former, by 1950 the prewar level of production was reached in light industry, while food industry was still 21 percent below prewar gross production. On the other hand, Stolper's index shows that by 1950 both industrial branches remained substantially below their prewar output levels but the food industry had shown a relatively better recovery (output 34 percent below prewar) than had light industry (output 56 percent below prewar). According to Stolper, light industry had not reached its prewar output level as late as 1958, while food industry reached that output level by 1953. The discrepancy between these two sets of indexes is attributable to Stolper's index measuring net output, or value added, while the official index is in gross terms, with the disadvantages already alluded to. (Stolper 1960, pp. 235-59; official statistics also are inflated by increasing coverage—see ibid., pp. 236-37). Given the relatively slow recovery of production of industrial consumer goods, consumption standards could not have shown adequate progress.

The index of production of nondurable consumer goods (column 6 in Table 9.11), calculated by this author on the basis of a study by Czirjak and Dusek, closely agrees with the Stolper indexes and shows the official index to be substantially exaggerated. Obviously, industrial progress in the area of consumer goods was not as substantial as shown by official statistics. It should be stressed here that a production-based index of consumption, like the one in column 6, tends to overstate the actual growth of consumption, particularly in the case of East Germany, which exported many consumer goods, even though this factor may be partly offset by late fast growth of consumer durables, not included in the index. The result is likely to be a net overstatement of the growth of aggregate consumption.

Changes in Consumption and Real Income of the Population

Table 9.2 above showed the proportion of domestically available national income used for consumption. As stated above, that proportion experienced a decline, from 91.5 percent in 1950 to 77.9 percent in 1971. Characteristically for Communist countries, social consumption rose between the same years faster than either personal consumption or national income, increasing its share from 8.6 percent of national income and 9.4 percent of aggregate consumption to 9.6 percent of national income and 12.3 percent of aggregate consumption.

TABLE 9.12

Stolper's Calculated Indexes of Consumption in East Germany

Year	Real Consumption in 1936 Prices Deflated by		Per Capita Real Consumption Deflated by		Consumption as Percentage of GNP Deflated by Retail Price Index
	Retail Price Index	Cost of Living Index	Retail Price Index	Cost of Living Index	
1936	234.1	171.6	266.5	195.0	60.0
1950	100	100	100	100	32.6
1951	130.0	145.2	130.3	145.5	38.6
1952	161.0	175.3	161.8	175.8	44.4
1953	183.7	196.3	186.1	196.8	47.7
1954	218.3	231.5	222.7	235.6	52.9
1955	234.5	245.4	240.6	251.3	54.5
1956	236.5	247.8	245.8	257.1	53.1
1957	241.4	254.3	253.8	266.8	51.5
1958	258.8	270.9	274.5	286.9	53.1

Source: Stolper 1960, p. 434.

TABLE 9.13

Indexes of Retail Trade Turnover in East Germany

Year	Aggregate Retail Turnover	Foodstuffs, Tobacco and Alcohol	Industrial Consumer Goods	Aggregate Retail Turnover Per Capita
1950	100.0	100.0	100.0	100.0
1951	124.0	122.7	126.1	124.2
1952	144.9	145.4	144.2	145.3
1953	158.6	159.0	157.9	160.4
1954	172.2	166.6	181.0	175.4
1955	182.8	172.6	198.9	187.3
1956	189.2	178.5	205.8	196.5
1957	201.8	187.2	224.8	211.8
1958	221.1	206.0	245.0	234.2
1959	243.6	226.8	270.2	258.9
1960	260.5	236.2	298.6	277.7
1961	275.7	248.4	318.6	296.1
1962	273.9	252.3	307.9	294.5
1963	274.8*	255.6*	305.1*	294.5
1964	283.9	264.1	315.0	307.3
1965	296.0	173.7	330.9	319.7
1966	308.1	285.4	343.9	332.0
1967	320.1	297.6	355.4	344.6
1968	335.7	311.1	374.3	361.4
1969	355.7	327.5	400.1	382.9
1970	371.1	339.1	421.5	399.9
1971	385.6	348.9	443.3	416.0

*Start of a new series.

Source: SJ 1972, pp. 3, 287.

266

Table 9. 12 reproduces part of a table from Stolper, showing aggregate real consumption, real consumption per capita, and consumption as a percentage of GNP. The prewar level of per capita consumption was re-attained between 1953 and 1958. The postwar decline in the share of consumption is apparent from the table, as well as the relative stability of that share between 1954 and 1958. Stolper regarded the last column, consumption as proportion of GNP deflated by the retail price index, as the only acceptable one. He rejected deflation by the cost of living index as yielding too high a share, unrealistic because of the high percentage of rationed goods at the time, and because house rents were included in the cost of living index while the GNP estimate did not include them. Consumption as a proportion of GNP dropped precipitously after the war; even by 1958 it did not recover its prewar level, which had already been affected by the armament effort of Hitler's Third Reich.

Table 9. 13 is a complement to Table 9. 12, and is based on official sources. Comparing the aggregate index of retail trade turnover with Stolper's index in Table 9. 12, we find the latter higher. The explanation lies in Stolper's use of Laspeyre's formula; the official index used postwar weights, apparently adjusted at least twice. Laspeyre's formula typically results in higher index numbers than does Paasche's.

Industrial consumer goods in Table 9. 13 show characteristically higher dynamics than do foodstuffs. Deflation to a per capita basis also decreases, but not radically, the index of aggregate retail sales. It may be noticed that such deflation in Table 9. 12 actually raises the index, as it does in Table 9. 13 incrementally until 1964, due in both cases to declining population as the result of migration to West Germany. As stated in the preceding section, construction of the Berlin Wall plugged that hole in the population vessel.

Table 9. 14 shows the share of goods in individual consumption, and the relation of savings to consumption. The share of goods in consumption increased substantially, indicating both their increasing availability and the existence in East Germany of the usual problem of provision of services, which is the bane of Communist countries. It may be noted that trends concerning consumption in kind are not reflected in this relationship since consumption is taken as tantamount to consumption expenditures without any imputed values.

Savings have shown substantial growth, both absolutely and as a proportion of personal consumption, the result being a rapid growth of savings accounts. The permanent income hypothesis and the increasing marginal propensity to save as income increases seem to have found here a proof. However, the slowdown in the growth of consumption during 1962-63 (see Table 9. 13) apparently led to a considerable drop in the marginal propensity to save during those years, indicating existence of rising levels of expectations. Such a slowdown was, incidentally, much more feasible politically after the erection of the Berlin Wall since it did not result in increased westward migration,

TABLE 9.14

Goods and Savings in Relation to Personal Consumption in East Germany

Year	Share of Purchases of Goods in Individual Consumption (percent)	Savings Accounts of the Population (million DM)		Share of Savings in Personal Consumption (percent)
		Aggregate	Annual Growth	
1950	72.6	1,270	—	..
1951	77.1	1,446	176	.63
1952	78.0	2,024	578	1.80
1953	79.7	2,536	512	1.49
1954	80.0	3,701	1,165	3.14
1955	82.0	4,927	1,226	3.18
1956	83.3	6,062	1,135	2.90
1957	83.0	8,970	2,908	6.93
1958	84.1	11,244	2,274	5.01
1959	85.5	14,010	2,766	5.62
1960	87.0	17,053	3,043	5.89
1961	88.3	19,654	2,601	4.83
1962	88.3	21,000	1,346	2.51
1963	87.8	23,060	2,060	3.81
1964	84.9[a]	26,596	3,536	6.11
1965	84.6	30,271	3,675	6.18[b]
1966	85.9	35,030[a]	3,755	6.2[b]
1967	..	38,976	3,946	6.3[b]
1968	..	43,319	4,343	6.7[b]
1969	..	48,049	4,730	6.9[b]
1970	..	52,149	4,100	5.8[b]
1971	..	51,721	3,572	4.8[b]

[a]Start of new series.
[b]Author's estimates on the basis of SJ 1972, p. 42.

Sources: Schaefer 1967, pp. 50, 72, 94, 107; 52, 75, 97, 110; SJ 1972, p. 334.

TABLE 9.15

Per Capita Use of Selected Consumer Goods in
East Germany and West Germany

| | East Germany | | | | | | | West Germany |
	1955	1960	1964	1966	1968	1970	1971	1968/69[a]
Cereals and products (kg)	121.6	101.6	99.0	101.0	96.8	97.3	97.2	64.1
Meat and products (kg)	45.0	55.0	58.0	60.1	63.0	66.1	67.8	73.2
Fish and products (kg)	..	..	8.2	8.8	8.7	7.9	8.9	10.8
Liquid milk (liters)[b]	90.7	94.5	93.9	95.7	99.2	98.5	100.2	104.2
Eggs and products (number)	116	197	205	213	220	239	244	254
Sugar and products (kg)	27.4	29.3	30.7	29.3	32.9	34.4	35.2	31.8
Potatoes (kg)	174.6	173.9	155.9	155.7	150.0	153.5	150.4	112.0
Vegetables (kg)	..	60.7	67.7	73.0	73.9	84.8	82.0	64.4
Fruit (kg)	..	80.1	43.2	57.4	59.0	55.5	48.4	92.9
Coffee (kg)	.3	1.1	1.7	1.9	2.0	2.2	2.3	4.1
Tea (grams)	77	88	89	87	84	91	106	..
Cigarettes (number)	1,042	1,069	1,098	1,136	1,201	1,257	1,310	1,849
Alcoholic beverages (liters)[c]	3.9	4.1	4.7	5.2	5.4	6.1	6.5	..
Wine	.2	.4	.5	.5	.6	.6	.6	1.8
Beer	2.1	2.3	2.4	2.5	2.6	2.9	3.1	4.6
Spirits	1.6	1.4	1.8	2.2	2.2	2.6	2.8	2.8

[a] Not strictly comparable due to differences in statistical composition.
[b] 2.5 percent fat content.
[c] 100 percent alcohol content.

Sources: DIW 1971, p. 209.

269

and since the wall produced a psychological climate of accommodation to the existing situation in East Germany.

Table 9. 15 shows changes in per capita consumption of some foodstuffs, cigarettes and alcohol. It can be compared with Tables 5. 19, 5. 38, 7. 8, and 8. 9 in previous chapters. It reveals comparatively high and rising standards of living, the latter documented by a decline in consumption of cereals and potatoes and by increases in the consumption of other products. Consumption of fruits shows wide swings, presumably resulting from variations in domestic fruit harvests. The steady increase in consumption of cigarettes is interesting, revealing that social costs do not loom as large in consumption choices as might be expected in a socialist society. The same may be said about consumption of alcohol and particularly the significant rise in consumption of hard spirits.

The last column in Table 9. 15 provides a partial comparison with West Germany. It suggests that West Germany has a higher standard pattern of consumption. A fuller comparison than that provided also shows that West Germans appear to be more health-conscious* (except in their consumption of cigarettes), consuming substantially more fruit (although slightly less vegetables) and meat and fish, and less sugar and fats, especially less butter. There may be an element of conspicuousness in the East German consumption of sugar and fats, or a desire to make up for past privations (for international East-West comparisons of consumption of foodstuffs per capita, see Schmidt 1968, pp. 67-74). West German consumption of wine is substantially above that of East Germany, about three times as high (tradition and location of main vine-growing areas being main reasons for that difference), while their consumption of spirits and beer is only moderately higher, also showing a shift to a more refined form of consumption (DIFW 1971, p. 209; West Germany produces more and better wine, especially in the Rhineland region).

Official statistics also show steady improvement in the provision of East German households with durable consumer goods, in quantities larger than in other East European countries. A comparison with West Germany, which is not complimentary to East Germany, would be only partially instructive due to qualitative differences in durable consumer goods between East and West. For instance, TV sets in East Germany are smaller and not in color, cars on the average are smaller, and so are the refrigerators. Even so, West Germany shows superior endowment in durable consumer goods (DIFW 1971, p. 211).

Provision with living quarters seems inferior to that in West Germany. The age structure of houses in 1968 showed that only 20 percent

---

*Some West Germans do not share this view, as shown in Sueddeutsche Zeitung, June 4, 1973.

TABLE 9.16

Indexes of Wages, Productivity, and Cost
of Living in East Germany

	Average Income from Work[a]	Average Income from Work in Industry[a]	Index of Labor Productivity[b]	Cost of Living Index[c]	Index of Disposable Income Per Employed Person
1950	..	..	..	189.8	..
1955	100.0	100.0	100	110.4	..
1956	..	..	107	109.0	..
1957	..	..	112	108.1	..
1958	..	..	122	103.2	..
1959	..	..	133	101.1	..
1960	127.1	124.2	141	100.0	100.0
1961	132.3	128.7	149	100.1	104.4
1962	134.2	131.1	159	100.4	104.6
1963	136.2	133.4	167	100.3	107.4
1964	140.3	137.6	178	100.4	109.7
1965	145.8	142.6	188	100.1	113.1
1966	148.7	145.4	200	100.1	116.8
1967	152.4	147.9	213	100.0	121.8
1968	159.5	154.4	224	100.2	125.1
1969	166.3	160.0	238	100.0	131.9
1970	173.6	167.4	253	99.9	138.9
1971	180.4	173.5	266	100.2	..

[a]Including premiums.
[b]Blue- and white-collar workers.
[c]Weights of 1968

Source: SJ 1972, pp. 73, 137, 348, 352.

271

TABLE 9.17

Monthly Income Per Worker in East Germany and West Germany
(respective DM and percentages)

| | East Germany | | West Germany | |
	Gross Income	Net Income	Gross Income	Net Income
1960	555	483	588	476
1970	755	659	1,312	982
Percentage growth of nominal income	36.0	36.4	123.0	106.3
Percentage growth of nominal income*	36.0	36.4	69.7	57.0

*With a 31.6 percent rise in the cost of living in West Germany.

Source: Obst 1973, p. 22.

of housing had been constructed since the war, whereas in West Germany the proportion was 50 percent (DIFW 1971, p. 134).

Table 9.16 provides information on trends in remuneration from work. Official indexes of income from work apparently are in terms of real income, since the money index would have to be raised between 1955 and 1960 by almost 10 percent due to a decline in the cost of living index (see column 4). From 1960 onward, due to near constancy of the cost of living index, the problem of money versus real income became statistically unimportant. A comparison between columns 2 and 3 shows that between 1960 and 1971 workers received in wage increments only 44 percent of the increase in productivity in industry, with the state appropriating to itself the residual 56 percent. A comparison between columns 1 and 5 shows that while average income from work rose between 1960 and 1971 by 41.9 percent, disposable income per capita of employed persons rose by 38.9 percent, indicating an increase in the tax bite from gross incomes, although such a conclusion is not apparent from data on tax deductions from gross incomes, which indicate aggregate deductions of 13.5 percent in both 1960 and 1970 (Obst 1973, p. 23).

Table 9.17 compares monthly income from work in East with that in West Germany, using respective DM in the first two lines of the table. The 1970 consumer purchasing power of the East German DM has been estimated at 0. 88 of the West German DM. * Using that figure, we recalculate East German gross monthly income in 1970 as equal to 664 in West German DM. This compares with the following figures for 1970 average gross incomes of industrial workers, recalculated in West German DM:

US	1, 760	France	870
Sweden	1, 520	Austria	760
West Germany	1, 165	Italy	690
Great Britain	1, 060	Japan	640
Switzerland	1, 050	Spain	400

East Germany thus compared in 1970 with the approximate real wages in Italy and Japan, but ranked lower, or much lower, than other West European countries, outside of Ireland and the southern tier of Europe.

Table 9. 17 also shows that the 1960s saw a widening of the gap between real incomes of East and West Germany. In 1960, real incomes in East Germany were 32 percent lower than in West Germany. By 1969/70, they were 45 percent lower; for households of four persons they were 55 percent lower (DIFW 1971, pp. 205-7). It should be added that these comparisons do not take account of the difficulties of obtaining goods in East Germany, the waiting for some products (such as cars), the difficulties connected with securing repairs, and problems with other services (such as laundry services).

Income distribution became more egalitarian in East Germany between 1960 and 1967. When measured in terms of disposable income of households, the distribution was as shown in Table 9. 18; West German distribution is also shown, for comparative purposes. While West Germany's distribution also became less unequal, it was less egalitarian in 1967 than East Germany's in 1960.

East German households of retired persons received in 1970, according to estimates of the Berlin Institute for Economic Research, substantially less than one-half of the purchasing power of similar West German households (DIFW 1971, pp. 199-200). In view of information from Table 9. 17, and information on the East German DM's purchasing power in relation to that of the West German DM (0. 88), it seems that such treatment of retirees tended to increase the inequality of income distribution in East Germany.

---

*Obst 1973, p. 25, obtained as an average of East and West German market baskets. In 1960 the East German DMs respective purchasing power was 0. 76. See also DIFW 1971, pp. 203-4.

Obst 1973, p. 26. The coverage of Table 9. 17 is different, and hence the figure for West Germany is not the same.

CONCLUSIONS

East Germany has become a political and economic reality, and its population seems to have found a way to accommodate itself to that reality. East Germany can boast of substantial economic achievements, of raising the level of living, and of good prospects for continuing such achievements. It still has serious failures, among them housing and adequate provision of some durable consumer goods, but these failings do not seem so aggravating when set within the relative picture of Eastern Europe. East German agriculture has enabled high nutritional levels to be attained; a high volume of investments has advanced the industrial progress of the country, labor productivity has been growing (even if comparatively inadequately) to make up for absence of growth in the labor force. Foreign trade is active, although its impact on the domestic economy is unknown. Thus there are some foundations for further progress in the field of consumption.

However, when compared with West Germany, East Germany does not measure up to the consumption promises embedded in Communist ideology. Its progress has been slower, more costly, and less efficient than that of its western counterpart. As shown above, it lags more and more in the important sphere of personal consumption, although its comparative achievements in the field of social consumption are more substantive. In view of such relative backwardness of personal consumption, the East German citizenry—though recognizing the fact of their separate statehood—may become disillusioned and

TABLE 9.18

Relative Distribution of Disposable Income of Working
Households in East Germany and West Germany
(percentages)

| | 1960 | | 1967 | |
	East Germany	West Germany	East Germany	West Germany
First quintile	9.8	8.4	10.5	8.7
Second quintile	15.5	12.6	15.8	13.0
Third quintile	19.3	16.4	19.7	17.1
Fourth quintile	23.4	22.8	23.6	23.0
Fifth quintile	32.0	39.8	30.4	38.2
Total	100	100	100	100

Source: DIFW 1972, p. 198.

TABLE 9.19

Relation of East German Personal Consumption
to That of West Germany .
(percentages)

Year	East German Per Capita Consumption Ratio as Percentage of West German
1950	60. 5
1955	71. 8
1956	66. 4
1957	66. 2
1958	70. 8
1959	72. 4
1960	72. 1
1961	69. 2
1962	65. 1
1963	64. 8
1964	62. 9
1965	61. 0
1966	62. 0

Source: Snell and Harper 1970, p. 589.

may find that, after all, "blood is thicker than water," national bonds
stronger than those created by Communist ideology and policies. This
is a turn that Communist leaders of East Germany must do their best
to avoid, and so they will be forced to make increasing concessions
to consumer aspirations.

Our final table, Table 9.19, reproduces findings on the relation
between per capita consumption in East and West Germany. It shows
that, from the time the Berlin Wall was erected, the East German consumer has been progressively worse off in comparison with his West
German brethren, having started from an inferior position in 1960.
This finding is a strong condemnation of the East German economic
system in the age of consumer awareness, even when that system
compares fairly well with other East European countries. One may
well wonder whether the newly found sense of belonging to a separate
East German entity would persevere for long among East German citizens were it not for the Berlin Wall and the mine fields on the border
with West Germany.

PART

III

EVALUATION

International comparisons of consumption experience are inherently difficult for reasons indicated elsewhere (for example, Hanson 1968, ch. 2; see also chapter 3 above). No definitive answers can be expected, and we are condemned to deal only in approximations, tendencies, and possibilities. Nevertheless, the present chapter attempts eclectically to provide a broad setting for consumption comparisons, some comparisons between East Germany and West Germany having been provided in Chapter 9, and some comparative data having been given in Chapter 2. The present comparison is made in three steps: (1) estimates of relative magnitudes of consumption are provided from outside sources; (2) estimates of growth of consumption are compared for the postwar period; and (3) an original method of consumption comparisons is proposed by the author.

RELATIVE LEVELS OF CONSUMPTION

Two independent estimators have provided international comparisons of absolute levels of personal per capita consumption. Their results are reproduced here separately, Maurice Ernst's in Table 10.1 and Vaclav Holesovsky's relevant portion in Table 10.2. Two columns broadly overlap in the two tables, those for prewar and 1960. When those columns are recalculated from Ernst's data to use Czechoslovakia as 100, and from Holesovsky's data to use West Germany as 100, the results are as presented in Table 10.3.

As could be expected, estimates for prewar, not made for the same years by both estimators, show wider disparities, but a general comparability does exist between the two sets of estimates. The picture that emerges from these three tables is one of West Germany forging ahead, after the wartime destruction, and of Hungary and Poland

TABLE 10.1

Comparative Levels of Personal Consumption Per Capita

	Prewar*	1950	1955	1960	1964
West Germany	100	100	100	100	100
Austria	81	82	79	78	79
Czechoslovakia	95	100	71	63	57
East Germany	95	54	68	68	60
Hungary	87	69	52	49	48
Poland	45	60	48	42	40

*1936 for West Germany and East Germany; 1937 for Poland and Czechoslovakia; 1938 for the other countries.

Source: Ernst 1966, p. 887.

TABLE 10.2

Relative Levels of Per Capita Personal Consumption in Czechoslovakia
and Some Other Countries in Selected Years

	1938	1952	1955	1957	1960
Czechoslovakia	100*	100	100	100	100
Poland	56*	71	78	83	75
Hungary	101	68	78	82	82
United States	217	271	291	273	263
United Kingdom	186	156	172	166	163
West Germany	136	111	140	149	154
Italy	75	75	84	85	87

*1937

Source: Holesovsky 1965, p. 632.

TABLE 10.3

Comparison of Ernst and Holesovsky Estimates

	Ernst's Estimates Recalculated to Holesovsky's Basis				Holesovsky's Estimates Recalculated to Ernst's Basis			
	Prewar		1960		Prewar		1960	
	Ernst	Holesovsky	Ernst	Holesovsky	Ernst	Holesovsky	Ernst	Holesovsky
Czechoslovakia	100	100	100	100	95	74	63	65
Poland	47	56	67	75	45	41	42	49
Hungary	92	101	78	82	87	74	49	53
West Germany	105	136	159	154	100	100	100	100

Sources: Tables 10.1 and 10.2.

gaining over the postwar period as a whole on Czechoslovakia, previously the most affluent East European country. Table 10.1 also shows that East Germany has overtaken Czechoslovakia, to become the most affluent East European country. That fact has been widely perceived, as indicated by the following quotation:

> . . . there is no doubt that the standard of living of the average DDR citizen exceeds that of other East Europeans and has become one of the more important sources of the regime's legitimacy. (Baylis 1974, p. 89.)

It also may be noted that East European levels of consumption are lower than those in Western Europe, except for southern European countries. Among the four countries covered in the present study, Poland seems to show the lowest level of consumption.

On the whole, the foregoing comparisons do not reveal much consumption-based success among the East European countries compared to the West, with the four East European countries discussed here showing 1964 per capita consumption levels from 40 to 60 percent of West Germany's; by comparison, the prewar figures were 45 to 95 percent of West Germany, and from 54 to 100 percent of West Germany shortly after World War II. The relative backward slide of East Germany, from near parity with West German territory before the war to only 60 percent of West German consumption in 1964, is thought-provoking.

In discussing his results, Ernst mentioned some not yet quantified problems:

> Among the influences on consumer welfare that the personal consumption statistics do not reflect, some probably favor Western Europe, others Eastern Europe. For example, the range of choice among products and models has been considerably narrower in Eastern Europe than in Western Europe. Recurring shortages of many products and the consequent need to queue up for hours, possibly to go home emptyhanded, also has been a negative feature of the Eastern European scene. On the positive side has been the large increase in the supply of free, or nearly free, social services, such as educational and health services and recreation, which, in contrast to personal consumption, probably was at least as rapid in Eastern as in Western Europe (although to make certain of this would take additional research). (Ernst 1966, pp. 887–88.)

As indicated in Chapter 2, this last thought, if only tentative, seems controversial since West European social services also have risen from prewar levels and have become considerable.

TABLE 10.4

Share of Consumer Goods Production in Aggregate Industrial
Production in Eastern Europe, 1950 and 1969
(percentages)

	1950	1969
Poland	47.4	34.0
Czechoslovakia	50.6	38.3
Hungary	35.0	35.5
East Germany	33.4	29.9
Romania	47.1	30.8
Bulgaria	61.8	46.6
USSR	31.2	26.0

Source: Zebrok 1973, p. 57.

The relatively low per capita consumption levels in Eastern Europe
are the direct result of two factors: (1) low relative level of per capita
GNP, (for example, lower in Czechoslovakia than in Italy, Austria,
and other West European countries) and (2) low share of personal consumption in GNP. In 1966 that share was 64.9 percent in Belgium,
63.7 percent in France, 63.1 percent in Italy, 61.8 percent in the
United Kingdom, 59.8 percent in Austria, 57.1 percent in West Germany, 56.3 percent in Sweden, and 53.4 percent in Czechoslovakia
(Ministry of Economic Planning 1968, cited after Sik 1972, p. 85).
Obviously, both these factors conspire to keep the level of per capita
consumption in Eastern Europe relatively low.

One of several estimates of per capita levels of GNP in 1972,
expressed in 1972 U.S. dollars, was as follows (Alton 1974, p. 268):

Poland	1,640	Romania	1,590
Czechoslovakia	2,820	Bulgaria	1,610
Hungary	1,850	USSR	2,414
East Germany	2,530	US	5,515

The above comparison reveals the potential ability of countries
in Eastern Europe to satisfy consumer needs.

The share of production of consumer goods declined in all East
European countries between 1950 and 1969, except for a small rise in
Hungary. Table 10.4 shows that trend, which exerted an influence
on the situation of consumers in Eastern Europe.

One also can compare changes in the per capita consumption of
various products, shown in Chapters 5 to 9. Table 10.5, a summary,
is produced here since comparisons between countries cannot be

282

TABLE 10.5

Per Capita Consumption of Selected Products in Eastern Europe

	Poland 1971	Czechoslovakia 1970	Hungary 1972	East Germany 1971
Cereal products (kg)	129	150.2	127.0	97.2
Potatoes (kg)	189	103.4	70.0	150.4
Meat and animal fats (kg)	64.0	71.9	61.7	67.8
Fish and fish products (kg)	6.4	5.2	2.3	8.9
Milk and milk products (liters)	410	196.2	114.0[a]	100.2
Edible fats (kg)	18.0	19.9	27.5	14.2
Eggs (number)	193	277	14.3[a]	244
Sugar (kg)	39.6	37.7	35.3	35.2
Vegetables (kg)	107.4[b]	76.3	84.0	82.0
Fruit (kg)	31.4[b]	49.1	72.0	48.4
Spirits (liters; 100 proof)	3.5	5.9	6.0[c]	2.8[d]
Wine (liters)	6.2	14.6	40.0	5.1
Beer (liters)	33.7	139.9[e]	59.0	102.2

[a] Kilograms.
[b] On the basis of domestic production figures.
[c] 50 percent alcoholic content.
[d] 100 percent alcoholic content.
[e] 40 percent alcoholic content.

Sources: Tables 5.45, 7.8, 8.9, 9.15; RS 1973, pp. 551, 265, 266, 66; SR 1972, p. 462; SE 1972, pp. 388, 389; SJ 1972, p. 353.

TABLE 10.6

Production in Selected Sectors in Eastern Europe
in 1968 in Relation to 1950
(1950 = 100)

	Aggregate Industry	Food Industry	Agriculture	Ratio of Growth of Aggregate Industry to Food Industry (Percentage)
Poland	642	302	164	213
Czechoslovakia	430	236	142	182
Hungary	466	350	148	133
East Germany	469	388	190	121
Romania	916	466	213	197
Bulgaria	984	542	228	182
USSR	592	396	209	149

Source: Lewandowska 1972, p. 157.

easily attempted by the reader from Tables 5.3, 5.19, 5.38, 5.45, 7.8, 8.9, and 9.15 in earlier chapters. Table 10.5 brings out some salient points: Poland shows the highest per capita consumption of cereals and cereal products, as well as of potatoes. Czechoslovakia may have the highest consumption of meat, but Hungarian statistics do not include fats with meat so it is impossible to tell whether Hungary or East Germany holds second place. Poland seems to have the lowest per capita consumption of meat, but the highest of sugar. However, it should be stressed that differences in coverage and measures used render precise comparisons difficult. * Hungary and East Germany show the highest per capita consumption of fruits, Poland the lowest. The estimate of vegetable consumption for Poland includes beets and over one-third of it is cabbage, which is used partly as fodder. Since production figures are used to estimate the per capita consumption, cabbage used as fodder may inflate the consumption figure. Consequently, the Polish primacy in vegetable consumption may be spurious.

The form of alcohol consumption differs substantially. Czechoslovakia and East Germany lead in per capita consumption of beer, while

---

*Romania and Yugoslavia show per capita consumption higher than Poland for cereals and cereal products, and for potatoes (cf. Lewandowska 1972, p. 153).

Hungary holds primacy in consumption of wine. Differences in the translation of hard liquors into a common measure make comparisons difficult.

Table 10.6 shows the comparative growth of production in selected sectors between 1950 and 1968, so as to highlight the relative growth of the most important consumption category: foodstuffs. It suggests that agriculture showed the poorest performance in Czechoslovakia, Hungary, and Poland; food industry showed the poorest performance in Czechoslovakia, Poland, and Hungary; while aggregate industry predictably showed the poorest performance in the two most industrialized countries of Czechoslovakia and East Germany, and in Hungary. In all the countries of Eastern Europe shown in Table 10.6, growth of aggregate industrial production overtook by a substantial margin the growth of food industry; the margin was smallest in East Germany, probably because of its competition with West Germany, and in Hungary, probably because of its policy of "goulash Communism," as it was dubbed by Khrushchev. The margin was largest in Poland and, more predictably, in Romania. The last column of Table 10.6 could be, under East European conditions, dubbed "the indicator of relative consumer neglect."

An international comparison of the level of per capita agricultural output may be couched in terms of the USSR taken as 100 to provide a rough measure of relative self-sufficiency of the East European economies and the contribution of their agriculture to consumption levels. Such a comparison for 1970 was as follows (Lazarcik 1974, pp. 380-81):

USSR	100	East Germany	108
Poland	114	Romania	74
Czechoslovakia	92	Bulgaria	105
Hungary	122	US	135

The above quantitative relations refer, of course, only to the direct contribution of domestic agriculture, since Czechoslovakia could replenish its supply of agricultural products by engaging in international trade and supplementing needed foodstuffs. Hungary, it should be noticed, is relatively best supplied in Eastern Europe with domestic agricultural products, while Romania is in the relatively worst position. The relatively small advantage enjoyed by the United States (before the effect of its foreign trade is included) also should be noticed.

Table 10.7 shows the total per capita caloric intake in Eastern Europe in 1958, and the percentage share of foodstuff categories. All the East European countries have a caloric intake above the "norm" for Europe. Bulgaria and Romania have the poorest composition of diet, East Germany and Czechoslovakia the best, as indicated by the share of cereals and root crops in caloric intake. Czechoslovakia used the most sugar, followed by Poland and East Germany (which has

TABLE 10.7

Share of Various Foodstuffs in Daily Caloric Intake in 1958
(percentages)

	Calories*	Cereals and Root Crops	Fruits and Vegetables	Sugar	Fats	Products of Animal Husbandry	Fish
Poland	3,100	58.8	2.8	9.3	10.2	18.6	.3
Czechoslovakia	3,010	52.1	3.9	12.3	12.1	19.3	.3
Hungary	2,925	57.7	5.1	8.8	13.4	15.0	..
East Germany	2,950	50.7	3.1	8.4	15.9	21.2	.7
Romania	2,790	72.8	4.3	4.3	9.1	9.3	.2
Bulgaria	2,780	74.4	6.3	3.3	7.9	8.1	—
Yugoslavia	2,770	..	..	..	..	..	..
United States	3,220	24.2	9.3	15.8	20.4	30.1	.2

*"Norm" for Europe was 2.635 calories.

Source: Lewandowska 1972, pp. 159, 162.

TABLE 10.8

Endowment of Households in Eastern Europe
With Selected Durable Consumer Goods
(per 100 households, in 1971)

	Radios	Television Sets	Electric Washing Machines	Refrigerators
Poland	90.8	77	81	46.6
Czechoslovakia	150	80	80	50
Hungary	76	58	51	39
East Germany	93	72	58	62
Bulgaria*	67.4	17.6	33	8.5

*No date given

Sources: Lewandowska 1972, p. 170; RS 1973, pp. 708, 560.

achieved a good increase in sugar consumption since 1958). East
Germany and Czechoslovakia also show the highest percentage of
calories derived from products of animal husbandry (although far below
the U. S. percentage), while Bulgaria and Romania again show the
diets poorest in quality.

An indication of low levels of living is the high proportion of total
consumption expenditures spent for food, noted in Engel's law. That
proportion in 1964 was as follows (percentages; Ministry of Economic
Planning, Prague 1968, after Sik 1972, p. 88):

Sweden	22.8	Austria	40.4
United Kingdom	33.4	Italy	46.4
France	36.6	Czechoslovakia	50.0
West Germany	36.8		

Czechoslovakia, which is relatively advanced among the East
European countries, shows a very high proportion of expenditures on
food when compared to West European countries. This in itself
indicates a comparatively low level of living.

Table 10.8 shows the endowment of households with selected
durable consumer goods. Czechoslovakia seems best supplied with
radios and TV sets (perhaps physical propinquity to Western broad-
casting stations has been a factor here); Poland, somewhat surprisingly,
with washing machines (East Germany heavily emphasized its public
laundries); and East Germany with refrigerators. One has to remember
that the quality and capacity of many durable consumer goods in

TABLE 10. 9

Work Time Required for Workers in Czechoslovakia and
West Germany to Earn Money to Buy
Selected Consumer Goods
(hours of work)

	West German Worker	Czechoslovak Worker
TV set	133	470
Sewing machine	88	287
Portable typewriter	32	129
Transistor radio	12	117
Pair of shoes	6	17
Pair of ladies' stockings	.8	5.8
17.5 kilograms assorted meat	27.4	53.9
1 kilogram chocolate	1.5	10.5
Can of crab meat	.7	1.4
Can of Nescafe	.5	4.2
Frankfurters (canned)	.4	1.6
Can of strawberries	.3	1.2

Source: Sik 1972, p. 86.

Eastern Europe is lower than in the West, so a comparison might be misleading. Nevertheless, the figures in Table 10. 8 do provide some index of satisfaction of households, some possession and fulfillment of aspirations. No similar information was found in national statistical yearbooks of other East European countries.

Table 10. 9 provides insight into the relative personal cost, in terms of work, of obtaining various consumer goods in West Germany and Czechoslovakia, apparently in the late 1960s. The information is approximate because the quality of goods differs, but the general conclusion that emerges from Table 10. 9 is clear: It takes much more effort in Czechoslovakia to earn enough money to purchase a desired good.

Finally, one should mention the inferior trade and handicraft network in Eastern Europe, compared to that in Western Europe. The number of inhabitants per retail trade employee and per store is substantially higher in Eastern Europe than in Western Europe, contributing to consumer hardships. The same is true of repair and other handicraft establishments (Sik 1972, p. 94).

RELATIVE GROWTH RATES OF CONSUMPTION

Our second focus of interest is on postwar growth rates of personal consumption, shown earlier in the chapters on individual East European countries. Table 10.10 gathers together the independently derived indexes of per capita personal consumption and compares them with some Western countries, while Table 10.11 contains official indexes of per capita consumption. Table 10.10 shows that East Germany suffered most in the area of consumption, as it did in production, as the result of World War II. Hungary was next, then Poland; Czechoslovakia suffered least. Prewar consumption levels on postwar territories were recovered first in Czechoslovakia in 1949; then in East Germany in 1957; then in Hungary in 1959; and last in Poland in 1961. Between 1956 and 1965, the fastest growth in per capita consumption was achieved by Hungary and East Germany (both of them ex-enemy countries, having suffered most, had most to make up); the slowest growth was shown by Czechoslovakia. The East European calculated growth rates of consumption compare favorably with the United States, but they are substantially lower than the growth rates of per capita consumption in West Germany.

Table 10.11 shows the official claims of rise in per capita consumption. While the level of consumption rose by 4.5 times in Poland between 1947 and 1972, it rose by about 60 percent in Poland, Czechoslovakia, and Hungary between 1960 and 1971. Bulgaria claimed an 80 percent rise in current prices between 1960 and 1968, while East Germany and Romania claimed slower, and less unrealistic, rates of growth of per capita personal consumption. On the whole, these results do not seem realistic, both in view of direct observations and when compared with calculated indexes.

Holesovsky's comparison of rates of growth of consumption between 1950 and 1960 indicates that Poland, Czechoslovakia, and Hungary showed a faster rate of growth only compared with those Western countries — like the United States, Canada, Sweden, and Belgium — that already had attained a high level of consumption. Other West European countries, except Ireland, showed higher rates of growth of consumption (Holesovsky 1965, p. 624). Ernst, comparing prewar to 1964 growth of per capita consumption, found Poland (which had changed its territory to substantial qualitative advantage), making a good show, better than Denmark or France but inferior to Austria, West Germany, and Italy. Czechoslovakia, Hungary, and East Germany had a growth performance much inferior to that of West Germany (Ernst 1966, p. 886).

Changes in consumption also can be measured in relation to GNP or national income. Thad Alton provided, among others, statistics on the share of personal consumption in national income at constant

TABLE 10.10

Comparison of Calculated Indexes of Per Capita Personal Consumption
in East Europe with West Germany and the United States
(index numbers)

Year	Poland	Czechoslovakia	Hungary	East Germany	West Germany	United States
1937	114.6[a]	87.3	..	104.4[b]	..	..
1938	64.9[c]	..	107.4	..	..	..
1946	53.3	..	..	37.6	..	90.2
1947	64.0	..	66.3	..	..	87.0
1948	75.3	81.8	73.3	..	..	85.4
1949	81.1	87.3	80.1	46.5	..	86.3
1950	88.0	97.5	80.8	61.4	..	90.2
1951	89.7	96.8	86.3	75.5	..	89.9
1952	88.4	97.3	81.8	83.0	..	90.5
1953	87.3	92.9	81.2	91.2	..	93.2
1954	91.7	94.6	87.2	99.5	..	93.7
1955	95.4	97.3	92.1	100.2	..	98.5
1956	100.0	100.0	100.0	100.0	..	100.0
1957	107.1	102.4	102.1	106.2	..	100.8
1958	110.6	103.7	103.9	113.3	..	99.8
1959	111.1	105.3	111.8	121.3	..	103.9
1960	113.3	110.9	112.3	128.1	100.0	105.0
1961	115.5	109.9	114.8	132.2	105.6	105.4
1962	118.4	110.3	116.8	135.4	109.1	108.9
1963	122.2	111.0	121.5	133.9	112.6	111.7
1964	125.3	112.2	125.2	135.6	116.1	116.3
1965	127.6[d]	114.6	128.5	139.4	122.3	122.9
1966	134.8[d]	..	131.2	143.5	125.5	126.7
1967	137.5[d]	..	137.7	149.0	126.2	129.7
1968	..	..	..		130.2	135.4
1969	..	..	..		139.2	139.0
1970	5.1[e,f]	5.2[e,f]	5.7[e,f]	4.3[e,f]	147.1	139.8
1971	7.0[e]	5.0[e]	5.6[e]	4.3[e]	..	143.7
1972	8.8[e]	4.8[e]	3.7[e]	5.6[e]	..	150.8

[a] Postwar territory.
[b] Rough aggregate consumption index.
[c] Prewar territory.
[d] Continuation of author's index, calculated at the Project on National Income in East Central Europe and grafted onto author's index.
[e] Annual rate of growth.
[f] Average for 1965-70.

Sources: Tables 5.49, 7.12, 8.11, 9.11; Alton 1974, p. 277.

TABLE 10.11

Comparison of Official Indexes of Per Capital Personal
Consumption in Eastern Europe

Year	Poland	Czechoslovakia	Hungary	East Germany[a]	Romania[b]	Bulgaria
1960	100.0	100.0	100.0	100.0	100	100
1961	105.3	101.3	100.7	104.4	103	.
1962	107.6	104.4	103.8	104.6	108	119
1963	111.3	105.9	108.4	107.4	113	.
1964	114.8	108.2	113.9	109.7	115	.
1965	120.4	112.5	115.3	113.1	122	143
1966	126.5	117.4	120.6	116.8	129	150
1967	131.5	123.2	127.9	121.8	133	163
1968	138.2	138.1	133.2	125.1	134	181
1969	143.2	153.1	140.4	131.9	136	.
1970	147.8	156.4	151.2	138.9	146	.
1971	157.0	162.8	159.2	.	150	.
1972	169.1	.	.	.	152	.
1973	186.3	.	.	.	.	.

[a]Per capita real income.
[b]Index of real wages for all employees.

Sources: Piasny 1970, p. 273; SI 1972, p. 352; AS 1973, p. 100; AS 1970, p. 114; AS 1966, p. 105;
SEzh 1969, p. 270; RS 1972, p. 539; RS 1973, pp. 3, 549; RS 1974, p. 144.

prices. Table 10. 12 reproduces the relevant portion of Alton's data. There is an obvious trend to decrease the proportion of consumption in national income in all countries shown in Table 10. 12. Only two major irregularities appear in that trend: one in Hungary in 1960, when personal consumption rose as proportion of GNP from 1955, apparently as the result of Kadar's new policy of winning the population after the Hungarian Revolution; the second in Bulgaria in 1956, when there was a similar interruption of the downward trend of the share of consumption in national income. A slight break in the downward trend also appears in Poland between 1955 and 1960 as the result of the Polish October of 1956.

In a later study, Alton made the following observation on the basis of official figures in constant prices:

> In all countries [of Eastern Europe], over the 1950-70 period, consumption grew at a slower rate than total [net material product] or accumulation (net investment). This conclusion also holds with respect to 1965-72 in all countries except Bulgaria (1965-71), where the index for consumption is slightly higher . . . . In the period since 1970, the consumption categories grew faster than accumulation in all countries except Poland, where an import surplus made possible a high increase in all final uses, but especially of accumulation . . . .
>
> "Other consumption" (variously defined, but comprised mostly of consumption of material goods and services in government, defense, health, education, communal services, etc.) grew more rapidly than personal consumption (also variously defined as that which is financed by households from their own incomes or that which is attributed to households from all sources. (Alton 1974, p. 271.)

Alton also found that average annual rates of growth of GNP per capita in Poland (3. 7 percent), Czechoslovakia (3. 4 percent), Hungary (3. 9 percent), East Germany (3. 4 percent), Romania (5. 3 percent), and Bulgaria (5. 9 percent) for the period 1960-72 were about the same as those of the European Economic Community (4. 1 percent) for 1960-70, but lower than those for Italy, Greece, or Spain:

> Within the group of Eastern European countries, Bulgaria and Romania, the less developed countries, showed the higher rates, while Czechoslovakia and East Germany, the more developed countries, showed lower rates as a rule. (Alton 1974, p. 272.)

TABLE 10.12

Percentage Shares of Personal Consumption in GNP
or National Income in Eastern Europe
(percentages)

	Poland	Czechoslovakia	Hungary	East Germany	Bulgaria
1950	59.6	52.7	55.8	..	70.3[f]
1955	55.0	48.4	51.4	80.5	78.6[g]
1960	55.3	44.2	56.3	76.1	66.0
1965	51.4	44.2	54.3	72.5	65.0
1967	51.2	44.1	50.6	71.7	59.9
1965[a]	63.7	60.3[c]	68.1[d]	71.6	69.2
1970[a]	61.4	57.9	63.2[e]	66.8	66.3
1972[a]	57.7	57.6	68.5	68.0	70.2

[a]Proportion of national income (material product) in "comparable" prices.
[b]Proportion of GNP in constant prices.
[c]1966.
[d]1966–70.
[e]1971.
[f]1952.
[g]1956.

Sources: Alton 1970, pp. 59–60; Alton 1974, p. 261.

If the shares of consumption in GNP were equal between countries, that would allow the less developed countries of Eastern Europe to eventually catch up in per capita consumption with their more developed neighbors (cf. Table 10.12).

As already stated, the shares of aggregate consumption in national income have tended to decline over the longer postwar period while the shares of accumulation showed a concomitant increase, indicating practical application of planners' priorities in those countries (see Alton 1974, p. 261). These priorities also were indicated by rising shares of employment in the capital goods sector of the industry as a whole, and in the decline in the share of capital engaged in "non-material production" in the aggregate fixed capital (Alton 1974, pp. 265, 267).

This may be the story of unfulfilled hopes of the East European consumer as a shareholder in the national development. He saw the value of his shares decline, his dividend reduced because "the management" had decided to plough back the profits for some other use. The shareholder was left only with hopes for future appreciation of the value of his shares. He may have felt a bit let down when he remembered that "the natural aim of social production is . . . consumption" and that "the aim of socialist production is maximum (or optimum) satisfaction of the wants of the whole society" (Miszewski 1972, pp. 68, 70; see also ibid., pp. 67-68 n. 3). In theory, the East European consumer is the sovereign; in practice, he gets a smaller and smaller share of the production arrived at with his own effort and at his sacrifice.

For the general background, I may also mention one of several estimates provided by Thad Alton (1974, p. 268) of the 1972 GNP figures, expressed in billions of U.S. dollars at 1972 prices:

Poland	54.2	East Germany	43.3
Czechoslovakia	40.8	Romania	32.9
Hungary	19.3	Bulgaria	13.8

These comparisons indicate the overall economic importance of individual East European countries, and their ability to fulfill consumer aspirations.

A recent study by Gregor Lazarcik compared expenditures on defense, education, and health in Eastern Europe—defined to include Poland, Czechoslovakia, Hungary, East Germany, Romania, and Bulgaria—with those in other areas of the world between 1960 and 1970. As indicated in Chapter 2 above, health and education constitute the most important elements of social consumption, and they thus may be regarded as representing here that form of consumption. While expenditures on education and health for the East European area as a whole remained constant as a share of GNP during the period 1960-70 (the share of education declined from 3.7 percent to 3.6 percent, while

TABLE 10.13

Average Annual Percentage Rates of Growth
for East European Countries, 1960–70
(in current dollars)

	GNP*	GNP	Defense	Education	Health
Poland	4.9	7.7	10.6	7.4	8.7
Czechoslovakia	3.7	5.4	6.1	6.2	7.6
Hungary	4.3	7.3	12.7	7.4	5.5
East Germany	3.1	5.8	22.9	6.3	6.0
Romania	6.2	9.2	8.1	10.8	9.3
Bulgaria	6.6	9.4	5.0	8.2	7.2
Eastern Europe	4.2	7.3	11.1	7.3	7.6

*In constant 1967 dollars.

Source: Lazarcik 1973, p. 31.

TABLE 10.14

Students in Institutions of Higher Learning in Eastern Europe
(per 10,000 population)

	1950	1960	1972
Poland	50	55	110
Czechoslovakia	36	69	88
Hungary	35	45	88
East Germany	17	59	90
Romania	32	39	69
Bulgaria	46	70	122
USSR	69	121	186

Source: Gospodarka Planowa 1974, p. 34.

the share of health rose from 2.8 percent to 2.9 percent), the share of defense expenditures in GNP rose from 3.6 percent to 5.1 percent, as contrasted with the decline in the share of defense expenditures in NATO countries (excluding the United States) and in the United States (Lazarcik 1973, pp. 29-34; cf. Alton et al. 1974).

Table 10.13 reproduces Lazarcik's table on the average annual percentage rates of growth of GNP and the relevant expenditures for the period 1960-70. For the full assessment of those rates of growth one would need the proportion of the relevant expenditures in GNP, but Table 10.13 concentrates on the relative effort to raise the given expenditure level. It may be noted that East Germany and Romania increased their expenditures on both education and health faster than the growth rate of their GNP, while Bulgaria did the opposite. The relatively steeper increase in defense expenditures by East Germany, Hungary, and Poland pulled the average for Eastern Europe strongly upward and resulted in faster growth of expenditures on defense in Eastern Europe during 1960-70 than growth of social consumption, as represented by education and health.

Relative attainments of social consumption also can be depicted in terms of Tables 10.14 and 10.15, the former showing the number of students in institutions of higher learning per 10,000 of population. Standards of education may differ between countries, and so can the proportion of population in the 18 to 25 age group from which university students are most often recruited. Nevertheless, an unmistakable upward trend is revealed in the table for all East European countries. The high proportion of students in Bulgaria in 1972 is somewhat out of line, while that in Poland is explained by the postwar demographic wave and the consequent high proportion of the student-eligible group in the total population. The Soviet Union shows the highest relative emphasis on higher education, mostly on the applied level.

A recent study of the role of education in the economic growth in Poland and Hungary concluded:

> Because the Socialist countries have developed using
> centralized economic planning, and the need for skilled
> and semiskilled manpower to meet the economic plans
> was recognized, expansion of the educational system
> was an active part of the development program. This
> had the effect of producing rapid gains in educational
> attainment at all levels, but especially the vocational
> secondary level in Poland and the primary level in Hun-
> gary . . . . Emphasis [was] placed on functional edu-
> cation, i.e., that training which provided the vocational
> skills needed in both economies to achieve the goals of
> the economic plans. (Searing 1974, p. 481.)

Table 10.15 shows changes in the relative number of physicians and hospital beds in Eastern Europe. The former shows a steady climb in all East European countries, while the latter seems to have achieved an upper optimal level in East Germany around 1960 and has declined since. In the United States, the number of medical doctors, including dentists, per 10,000 of population was 22.9 in 1971, the number of beds in hospitals per 10,000 of resident propulation was 74.7, and the number of beds in hospitals and nursing homes per 10,000 of resident population was 134 (Statistical Abstract of the United States, 1973, pp. 5, 72, 76, 77). Standards of medical practice and use of medical resources differed between countries, but it could hardly be maintained that the quality of medical care in East Europe is substantially below that of the United States. The virtual absence of a financial barrier to medical services in Eastern Europe also seems important in raising the accessibility of those services.

The share of social consumption in national income has tended to increase in all East European countries — except for Bulgaria until 1965, after which date that country registered also an increase. Wide discrepancies existed in those shares between different East European countries, the reasons being different levels of economic development and probably different practices with respect to statistical coverage of social consumption (cf. Alton 1974, p. 261).

Table 10.16 shows the effort of East European countries in providing housing to the population, roughly in terms of need for new housing. It should be remembered that the quality of housing in Eastern Europe is inferior to that in the West. It appears from the table that East Germany, Bulgaria, and Poland are relatively least adequately providing the housing market with new dwelling units, while the USSR, Hungary, and Romania supply that market much more adequately. Even if we assume that the life of an average housing unit is longer than the life of an average couple inhabiting it, and that consequently some existing housing units can be passed on from older to younger generations, the current supply of new housing in Eastern Europe seems inadequate. In the Soviet Union and Romania, where that supply seems relatively adequate, there is great need for new housing in urban areas due to a shift of population from rural to urban occupations.

The relative contribution of housing to GNP has declined in all East European countries, except for a slight increase in Bulgaria between 1970 and 1972. The growth rates of housing services have been by and large constant and smaller than those of other sectors of the East European economies (Alton 1974, pp. 256-57, 274, 276).

TABLE 10.15

Medical Doctors (Including Dentists) and Hospital Beds in Eastern Europe
(per 10,000 population; end of year figures)

	Doctors			Hospital Beds		
	1950	1960	1972	1950	1960	1972
Poland	5	13	20	51	70	75
Czechoslovakia	10	18	25	62	76	80
Hungary	10	15	23	53	67	78
East Germany	11	12	21	102	119	109
Romania	10	14	15	42	73	85
Bulgaria	9	17	24	39	63	84
USSR	15	20	29	56	80	112

Source: Gospodarka Planowa 1974, p. 34.

TABLE 10.16

New Housing Units Put to Use in Eastern Europe
(per 1,000 new marriages)

	1950	1960	1970	1972
Poland[a]	228	582	693	669
Czechoslovakia[b,c]	285	694	887	850
Hungary	329	656	832	923
East Germany	153[d]	480	582	646
Romania[c]	291[d]	677	1,118	896
Bulgaria	..	722	625	661
USSR	514	1,000	962	954

[a] Without hostels.
[b] Only new houses.
[c] Without housing for students.
[d] 1951

Source: Gospodarka Planowa 1974, p. 35.

INFLUENCE OF PLANNING ON RESIDUAL CONSUMPTION

Under a centrally planned economic system, characterized by a strong growth bias as well as a tendency to increase the share of the government sector in the distribution of national product (Mieczkowski 1960, pp. 76-77), the consumer may find himself in the role of a residual claimant on national product. In view of our discussion in Chapter 4, it seems reasonable to suspect central planners of a high propensity to direct resources toward investment, insofar as the prevalent economic thinking in centrally planned economies attributes economic development primarily to the creation of new physical productive capacities. Additionally, planners' imaginations may be captivated by some conspicuous investment projects; they may find themselves trapped in cost overruns that lengthen the gestation period of projects already under way; and they may simply become victims of their own excessive eagerness to achieve ever higher indicators of success, conceived of in terms of inputs rather than outputs. The results of such tendencies have been described by Raymond Hutchins with reference to the Soviet Union:

> There is a perpetual tendency to over-invest, which is of
> service to the State in facilitating ventures of great size
> and prestige value . . . but which at times gets out of
> hand and is liable, unless checked, to create an over-
> strained and distorted economy. (Hutchins 1971, p. 212.)

The aim of the present section is to provide a measure of one of the possible distortions caused by the workings of economic systems in Eastern Europe. The distortion in question lies in the area of consumption, and is conceived of in terms of variations in a residual left over from the distribution of national product. The residual itself is explained below, and it is defined as used for raising the part of per capita consumption that is not due to greater individual effort or contribution on the part of members of the population, but is a sort of free external gift accrued to the average individual, due to his membership in a productive society that is willing, by virtue of its economic administration over scarce resources, to accord to its members a higher degree of material well-being on an "unrequited" basis. Increased contribution and effort by the population are reflected in the present section only partially, in terms of increased proportion of economically active population and increased labor force participation rates. What is not considered is the rising level of education, possible changes in the incidence of overtime work and upgrading of skills, and their influence on aggregate production.

The present section constitutes a pilot study, and it covers only Poland and Japan. Its methodology can be extended to other East

European and Western countries, although in preliminary efforts to do so for Eastern Europe I have encountered substantial difficulties due to lack of adequate data. The choice of Japan for this pilot study was dictated by the secondary research interest on my part.

The data used in this section* concern the Polish economy for the period 1960-70 and the Japanese economy for the period 1960-69. The basic model assumes that GNP produced is distributed among the following claims: (1) investments, (2) defense and government consumption, (3) net exports, (4) depreciation, (5) provision of consumption for the increments of the population, so as not to decrease per capita consumption as population expands, (6) provision of consumption earned additionally through the part of increases in employment due to increases in the proportion of economically active population, and to increased labor force participation rates, and (7) the residual consumption, taken to represent the actual, true consumption benefit allowed by central planners or by their actions. Residual consumption consists of consumption at the beginning of the period under investigation, before increments to population and changes in the proportion of economically active population had taken place, plus the residual increments of consumption that accrued in successive years. It is the variations in that last, the residual component of GNP, that will be of interest, for those variations reflect either a conscious policy on the part of the planners to allow the population some of the fruits of rising productivity, or reflect planning errors.

The formula used for evaluation of percentage changes in residual consumption was:

$$\frac{C_n}{GNP_n} \left(\frac{C_n - C_{n-1}}{C_{n-1}} \right)$$

where: C_n = consumption in a given year n
GNP_n = GNP in a given year n

Thus the year-to-year percentage changes in consumption were weighted by the given year's proportion between consumption and GNP.

Factors not taken explicitly into account were: (1) the effect of occupational shift from low-productivity employment (as in agriculture) to high productivity employment (as in industry); (2) increased input of labor resulting from improved education and upgrading of skills; (3) possible changes in the incidence of overtime per employed person.

---

*The constant price series used for computations were derived mostly from RS 1971. Some estimates were based on Alton et al. 1965 and on Mieczkowski 1971b. For Japan, the Japan Statistical Yearbook 1970 was used.

It also has been implicitly assumed that the rate of economic growth is a function of planning, which is an obvious simplification.

Results of a computer analysis and additional calculations for Poland are shown in Table 10.16, which focuses on residual consumption as defined above. Column 1 shows percentage changes in weighted residual consumption over preceding year. Of particular interest are the three years during which declines were registered. In 1962, there was retardation of growth within the Comecon region, particularly pronounced in Czechoslovakia. In Poland, agricultural production declined in that year by 8 percent, contributing to a relatively minor rise in national income (see column 5). In 1969, there was a disastrous consumption decline in Polish agricultural production; in 1967, when residual consumption declined least, the rate of growth of agricultural output declined to 3 percent, down from 5 percent registered in the preceding year, and the rate of growth of national income declined by better than 1 percent (see column 5).

Column 2 resulted from a recalculation of the values of residual consumption used to obtain column 1 to show them as percentages of investment undertaken in a given year. The resulting percentages are interpreted as follows: In 1961 a 4.1 percent increase in investments over the level actually achieved in that year would have eliminated all the increase in residual consumption attained in that year. Similarly, in 1962 a 9.2 percent decrease in investments below the level actually achieved would have been necessary to keep residual consumption unchanged. During the period covered, at most a 10.6 percent margin of error in the planning of investments would have produced no change in residual consumption, or perhaps an outside 9.2 percent margin of error in planning of investments might have been committed, resulting in a decline of residual consumption when perhaps none had been contemplated. It also is interesting to observe that the considerable decline in relative residual consumption in 1962 was followed by the offsetting largest increase recorded, while the second largest increase in relative residual consumption followed a small decline in 1967. From this point of view, the year 1970 seems to have been a fiasco in that there was a failure to compensate for the substantial decline in the ratio between residual consumption and investments that occurred in 1969. This shortcoming in 1970 may help explain the December workers' riots of that year.

Column 3 was calculated on the assumption that some of the variation in residual consumption was due to the unpredictable element of change in the level of agricultural production. Consequently, since farm income during the 1960s was roughly one-fifth the total incomes of the population, the same proportion (or one-fifth of changes in national income produced in agriculture) was deducted from total residual consumption and was calculated as percentages of investment

TABLE 10.17

Residual Consumption in Poland, 1960-70

Year	Percentage Changes in Residual Consumption (1)	Changes in Residual Consumption as Percentage of Investments (2)	Percentage Changes in Residual Consumption, Corrected for Changes in Agricultural Production, as Percentage of Investments (3)	Percentage Increases of Investments (4)	Growth Rate of Real National Income (percentage) (5)
1961	1.51	4.1	2.2	7.5	8.2
1962	-3.46	-9.2	-6.4	10.9	1.9
1963	3.94	10.6	9.3	2.9	7.2
1964	1.30	3.6	3.7	4.2	6.7
1965	2.28	6.0	5.5	9.8	6.9
1966	1.52	3.9	3.4	8.6	7.2
1967	-0.34	-.8	-.5	11.4	5.6
1968	4.08	9.9	9.1	8.7	9.0
1969	-2.28	-5.5	-4.1	8.6	2.8
1970	0.45	1.1	.8	4.3	5.2

undertaken in the given year.* In effect, central planners were absolved of part of the blame for fluctuations in residual consumption, namely the part that may more properly be blamed on the vagaries of the weather. However, no adjustment was made for the distribution of a fall harvest's crop partly over the succeeding year. In the calculation, a rough allowance also was made for a normally expected increase in agricultural production, assumed to amount to 1 billion zlotys per year, or about 1 percent per annum.

An allowance for imports, or net imports, of foodstuffs was possible but was rejected. Poland imports mostly grains, while exporting processed foodstuffs. Its imports during the period covered here were fairly constant, as were exports. The latter may be a function of world markets and the need for foreign exchange, rather than of any particular domestic situation. The former depend partly on the availability of credit financing. Rather than make new assumptions to obtain results of probably marginal importance for this study, the foreign sector was disregarded. In effect, changes in net imports of foodstuffs were treated as results of central planners' actions, insofar as they affected the consumer sector.

As might have been expected, the margin of planning errors that possibly may cancel out changes in residual consumption decreases as a result of the allowance made in column 3. While the average variation in investments that would have reduced residual consumption during the period to zero is 5.5 percent in column 2, it diminishes to 4.5 percent in column 3, a reduction of a full percentage point. Thus an average 4.5 percent increase or decrease in investments in a given year, added to the vagaries introduced by the weather and a certain normal growth of agricultural production (assumed here to be about 1 percent) could have eliminated any changes in residual consumption.

The impression left by column 3 of Table 10.16 is that the margin of planning errors affecting residual consumption, as expressed in the form of percentages of the primary planning decisions concerning investment activity, is precariously narrow. It seems that slightly higher increases in planned investments, or miscalculations in connection with those investments, have important results in terms of residual consumption. For this purpose, column 4 was added to Table 10.16, showing actual percentage changes in investments in constant prices from year to year. Except for 1963 and 1968, the changes in investment are larger than the changes in residual consumption in columns 2 and 3. This seems to indicate that relatively small changes in investment plans for a given year could have produced

---

*An alternative adjustment is possible by smoothing out agriculture's contribution to GNP by least square method, and then calculating residual consumption from such GNP corrected for agricultural fluctuations.

substantial changes in residual consumption, and hence in the consumers' sense of well-being.

It can be seen that declines in residual consumption took place in years characterized by large jumps in investment, while during one of the two years with the largest increase in residual consumption (1963) the increase in investment was the smallest of the whole period. There thus seems to be a degree of compensation between changes in residual consumption and changes in investment. To the extent that changes in residual consumption have fluctuated relatively more sharply than changes in investment, it may be concluded that investment plans seem to have been relatively inflexible. Consequently, perhaps also due in part to planning imponderables, residual consumption seems to have taken the brunt of adjustments. This observation is in agreement with one made by Kaser and Zielinski in their recent study of planning in Eastern Europe: "During the fifties, and even subsequently, targets for the consumption sector were the regular victim when goals for capital and defense goods were put in jeopardy." (Kaser and Zielinski 1970, p. 61.)

Column 5 was added to provide a broader picture of a key economic variable affecting residual consumption: the growth rate of real national income.

In the spirit of generosity toward central planners, we may conclude that under a system of taut planning it seems relatively easy to "overshoot the mark" one way or another, and that the vagaries of nature, as reflected in the fluctuations of harvests, compound the difficulties of hitting just the right mix of competing demands on national product to allow for steady growth of what has been termed here residual consumption. Given all kinds of political and personal pressures, the task may seem almost impossible. But the unevenness of what the consumers may well perceive as true growth in their material welfare, or true rewards generated by the operation of the planned system, may of itself breed dissatisfaction, tensions, and maladjustments, for which the planners are likely to take the blame. Consumers, in their evaluation of the functioning of the centrally planned economic system, are unlikely to appreciate the theoretical niceties of Hirschman's unbalanced growth strategy, if its adoption results in frustration of their expectations. On the other hand, instead of having the rate of investments, or of the growth in government programs, absorb planning miscalculations, it may have been decided that consumers should—for the sake of efficiency, intergenerational justice, or even expediency—absorb the frictions produced in the operation of the system, regardless of their possible discontent.

Independently of the above policy choices, the problem of what has recently been named "instrument instability" may be partly responsible for the swings in residual consumption. The tendency toward "instrument instability" is that "attempts to offset completely the cumulative impact of past changes in the policy instrument may

TABLE 10.18

Residual Consumption in Japan, 1960-69

	Percentage Changes in Residual Consumption (1)	Changes in Residual Consumption as Percentage of Investments (2)
1961	. .	9.3
1962	6.63	12.9
1963	5.15	12.2
1964	4.74	11.9
1965	2.29	6.2
1966	3.80	9.1
1967	4.51	9.4
1968	4.25	8.7
1969	4.16	8.2

	Percentage Increases in Gross Domestic Investment (3)	Growth Rate of Real GNP (percentage) (4)
1961	38.7	14.4
1962	-15.1	5.7
1963	31.6	12.8
1964	5.0	10.4
1965	2.0	5.4
1966	21.8	11.4
1967	27.7	13.1
1968	16.5	13.7
1969	16.0	12.6

require ever greater changes in the future value of the instrument."
Thus, "even an omniscient policy maker can be faced with a serious
dilemma due to the cumulative effects of past policy choices" (Holbrook 1972, pp. 57, 63). Consequently, planners may be confronted
with increasingly severe problem of adjustments, necessary as the
result of their past policies. Some of those adjustments may, as
shown above, take place at the expense of residual consumption.

In order to provide a comparative analytical basis, recent Japanese
data were used to derive residual consumption for that country. The
results of computations are shown in Table 10.18. A comparison of

Tables 10.16 and 10.17 leads to the following observations:

1. Residual consumption grew much faster in Japan during the 1960s than in Poland.

2. Fluctuations in the growth of residual consumption were markedly smaller in Japan than in Poland. The main discernible exception for the former country occurred during the Japanese recession of 1965.

3. While no upward or downward trend seems detectable in Poland, the growth of residual consumption in Japan reveals a slowing down, in conformity with the usual assumption about the short-run shape of the consumption function.

4. The proportion of residual consumption to investment was markedly higher in Japan than it was in Poland, indicating the presence in Japan of higher efficiency of investments with respect to consumption, as compared with Poland.

5. While no clear trend seems to exist in Poland in the proportion of changes in residual consumption to investment, the Japanese figures reveal a decline in that proportion.

6. Investments in Japan grew at a substantially faster rate than in Poland, this difference being connected with the faster rate of economic growth in Japan.

7. Investment in Japan fluctuated substantially wider than in Poland.

It thus appears that in Japan investment and other components of GNP, rather than consumption, bear the brunt of adjustment, when such adjustment is called for. On the whole, the Japanese economy seems to show a substantially higher viability than does the Polish economy. It also may appear that the planning system in Japan is more efficient than that in Poland, at least from the point of view of increasing the rate of growth of residual consumption and reducing fluctuations in that rate, as well as leading to faster increases in labor productivity.

These differences may be attributable to differences in the systems of economic planning in Poland and Japan, to different plan priorities and planner attitudes, and to differences in the rates of growth. The result is a considerable superiority in the situation of Japanese consumers over the situation of their Polish counterparts.

CHAPTER 11

Oskar Lange defined economics as the science of administration of scarce resources in the human society. That administration includes making choices between competing goals, with resulting need for compromises. During the period of forced industrialization in Eastern Europe, little was known of compromising since the headlong drive for accumulation of more and more capital goods was accepted by planners as the goal, bar none. Hence, administration of scarce resources was possible only in a relatively narrow sense.

Since the 1960s, however, consumption has been recognized in Eastern Europe as having a valid claim on the attention of planners, who are the administrators of scarce resources. This new limelight on consumption also has brought some, though for the East European area as a whole not uniform, statistical recognition, with the East Central countries providing better statistical coverage than the South Eastern countries. There also have been more publications of consumer-oriented studies, from books and articles on narrow problems (such as time budgets) to comprehensive studies of consumption problems. My research on consumption has utilized many of these sources, and has led to the following conclusions derived from those sources (not all of which were discussed in the present study) and from our explicit analysis:

1. Despite the new emphasis on consumption, East European statistics of consumption so far have been inadequate. The traditional heavy emphasis on production has by and large continued in the statistical coverage, with increasing information on consumption added to that coverage only slowly. Some official statistics of consumption apparently have been tampered with for political reasons.

2. Statistical coverage of consumption tends to be best in Poland and Hungary, with East Germany and Czechoslovakia following behind. It is most deficient in Romania, Bulgaria, and Yugoslavia.

3. Under these conditions, the value of independent estimates quoted in this study is paramount. I have been particularly impressed with the scientific integrity of such estimates.

4. The level of consumption in Eastern Europe is substantially lower than that in Western Europe, and is roughly comparable to that in Southern Europe. The level of consumption in Romania, Bulgaria, and Yugoslavia seems to be in a separate, substantially lower, category.

5. Even the best East European performer in the area of consumption, East Germany, has fallen badly behind the (admittedly remarkable) performance of West Germany.

6. Per capita consumption in Eastern Europe has shown a perceptible improvement during the postwar period, but its growth has been uneven, subject to the influence of political circumstances. During 1971-73, Poland and Romania experienced an acceleration and the best performance in the growth of personal consumption (Crawford and Haberstroh 1974, p. 48). The problem of assessing the degree of that growth remains a subject of controversy and will remain so as long as statistical practices in Eastern Europe are shrouded in official secrecy.

7. The present study has stressed the key importance of some planning decisions with respect to their repercussions on consumption. In particular, those decisions concerned the following areas:

●   Investments: An increase takes away scarce resources from consumption, as during the forced industrialization period. In the long run, however, industrialization that results from such investments has been favorable to the growth of consumption in that it has increased the amount and assortment of available goods. This long-run effect already is being felt in Eastern Europe.

●   Employment: An increase helps raise aggregate production, and hence raise the portion that may be directed for production of consumer goods. This extensive source of economic growth has been prevalent in Eastern Europe, except East Germany. Among topics discussed in this study in connection with employment, it was noted that a change in the structure of employment toward more productive jobs (and in particular the shift of labor from agriculture to industry that has been characteristic of East European experience since the war) increases labor productivity and tends to raise real wages. An increase in labor force participation rates, characteristic for the whole of Eastern Europe and resulting largely from greater employment of women, tends to decrease the number of dependents per employed; thus, given a real wage, it tends to raise the level of consumption attainable by households. A similar trend has been observed in other countries, as, for example, in the United States, where married women in particular have increasingly sought employment (Manpower

<u>Report of the President</u> 1972, pp. 192-96; Booth 1973, pp. 145-46; cf. also Alton 1974, pp. 287-88).

• Agricultural production: To the extent that it is influenced by planning decisions with regard to the supply of fertilizers, agricultural machinery, agricultural education, and so on, agricultural production shows the effect of planning on the most important single component of consumption: food. A rise in agricultural production has been witnessed in Eastern Europe, although on the whole its rate has been rather slow and uneven. An observer of East European agriculture concluded recently that "up to now socialized agriculture in the countries of Eastern Europe has not lived up to the expectations of their Communist governments," and that "comparisons of socialized versus private farming in Eastern Europe show better results for the latter. The inefficiences of socialized agriculture have impeded economic development." (Lazarcik 1974, p. 386.) They have obviously impeded a rise of consumption as well. A partial decentralization of agricultural activity in Eastern Europe shows concern with lagging productivity.

• Industrial production: This has been expanding quite fast in Eastern Europe, although from very low prewar levels in most countries (Czechoslovakia and East Germany being the exceptions); such expansion lays the foundation for production of more consumer goods, and particularly of durable consumer goods, but whether such increased production actually would be attempted has depended largely on changes in the political situation in individual East European countries. Over the postwar period as a whole, the East European consumer has profited from the rise in industrial production.

• Foreign trade: A consistent increase also has expanded consumers' opportunities in Eastern Europe (as for Russian and Polish consumers), both with regard to the available assortment and the total available amount, since individual countries can concentrate on production of commodities in which they enjoy comparative advantage. However, it has been pointed out in Eastern Europe that the structure of regulated prices does not allow a clear picture of who has such comparative advantage in what lines of production. Additionally, foreign trade has allowed the demonstration effect on consumption in other countries to seep into the societies of Eastern Europe, making them aspire for more and better goods; the importance of this factor has increased with the recent rise in the share of non-Communist trade in East European foreign trade (cf. Matusek 1974, p. 28).

8. The changing pattern of expenditures on personal consumption conforms by and large to Engel's law.

9. An increase in personal consumption expenditures has been noted in areas that are of doubtful social value, such as alcohol and

tobacco. This remark is not made on any subjective moralistic ground, but it stems from the Communist insistence on improved quality of life and social values, thus trying to apply to Communist countries their own value judgments.

10. Our study has shown that diets in Eastern Europe improved considerably, contributing to better health and longer life expectancy. It also has shown that the consumption of nonfood items increased, and that the endowment of households with durable consumer goods improved.

11. Not enough attention has been, perhaps, devoted in this study to housing. This is an area where inadequate progress has been made according to East European economists.*

12. Services remain inadequate throughout Eastern Europe.

13. Personal savings have been increasing lately in Eastern Europe, indicating improved levels of living, and possibly dissatisfaction with the quality of available goods. Some savings are made toward later purchase of durable consumer goods or housing.

14. It ought to be emphasized that all the socialist countries have stressed social consumption and its expansion. That stress has resulted in considerable improvement in the quality of life in Eastern Europe through education, improved health and life expectation, vacations, protection of labor, expansion of public transportation, and so on. Health standards seem to have attained the West European level in much of Eastern Europe. There has been considerable investment in human capital, with desirable economic results in the form of increased labor productivity and reduced economic losses of social investment in persons through illness or death. It also should be pointed out that this investment in human capital has not been costless to the East European societies.

15. Social consumption, intended or billed to push toward greater egalitarianism, has in some cases been a vehicle of unequal treatment of people, including unequal access to or use of education and health. It is possible that these, and the administrative aspects of social consumption, may inculcate in some people a feeling of dependency, powerlessness, and inability to direct their own lives. The same point has been made by psychologists about the education process in the United States.

16. I have found during my research that social security was extended in coverage, although there are some doubts as to its adequacy. It does effectively alleviate the insecurity of modern life.

---

*In Poland in 1971, only 653 dwelling units were constructed for each 1,000 newly married couples, this indicator being the lowest in Europe (see Kultura (Paris), 1973, no. 9, p. 145; Gutowski 1969, pp. 104-5).

17. Real wages have increased throughout Eastern Europe, but those increases have tended to be less than the increase in labor productivity, with the state appropriating the residual to itself.

18. Some aspects of socialist procedures, at least as they exist in statute books, may seem superior to actual capitalist practices. Consider, for example, the following rules regarding employment in East Germany: "Arbitrary dismissals are out of question. The management can only give notice with the consent of the works trade union committee." The management is required "to find another suitable employment . . . . Working people can only be dismissed immediately if they have violated state and labor discipline seriously. However, this step can only be taken if all measures to educate the offender have been unsuccessful." (Committee for German Unity 1961, p. 121.) If adhered to in practice, such rules do seem sensitive to human and societal welfare and to the elimination of some kinds of insecurity.

19. Wage incentives, in terms of differentials for greater effort and better work, seem inadequate in Eastern Europe, a state of affairs that affects mainly consumers. Complaints about assortments available in stores, and the quality of goods, are common in the East European press.

20. The importance of consumption as an incentive to work has been by now realized in Eastern Europe (Zduniak 1972, p. 82; Piasny 1971, pp. 10, 12; Lewandowska 1972, pp. 175-79; Beskid 1972, p. 10).

21. It appears that, at least in the short run, an expansion of consumption creates strong incentives toward increase in production, so that overall industrial expansion, including expansion of the producers' goods sector, does not suffer. This conclusion is supported by the experience of East Germany, Hungary since 1968, and Poland since December 1970.

22. The distribution of incomes and consumption has remained unequal in Eastern Europe, with a not inconsiderable proportion of households below the poverty level.

23. Time-budget studies have shown persisting differences between various groups of the population, according to income, type of work, education, and so on. The following is the conclusion from one of such studies:

life style, and more precisely the manner of utilization of time outside work, and especially of free time . . . is still one of the traits of the class and stratum of an individual within the society. While it is a trait secondary to such factors as, for instance, the level of income, localization in the power structure, job qualifications, etc., it still constitutes a rather important criterion of the stratification of the society. (Wnuk-Lipinski 1972, p. 152.) [It ought to be stressed that this work was published in Eastern Europe.]

24. Of the criteria proposed by the United Nations committee of experts, "human freedoms" seem to be least adequately safeguarded in Eastern Europe. This subject may be more extensively treated by a political scientist than by an economist. I may note only that participation in social processes (directly or through democratic representation) and in human freedoms seems very limited in Eastern Europe.

25. Bureaucracy in retail trade seems to affect consumer welfare adversely. Complaints about treatment of consumers by trade bureaucrats are frequent in the East European press (cf. Matusek 1974, p. 27).

26. The same point can be made about the state administrative bureaucracy.

27. Our analysis of "residual consumption" in Chapter 10 leads to a tentative conclusion that the economic results of central planning in Eastern Europe may be inferior to economic results in Western countries, with regard to both overall efficiency and avoidance of fluctuations.

28. Planners' priorities in Eastern Europe may not, and perhaps are not likely to, coincide with consumers' interests. This may be true because of the specific institutional conditions obtaining in Eastern Europe.

29. Planners may, and indeed do, try to influence consumers to adopt certain "socially preferred" patterns of consumption. Whether such preferred patterns tend to increase collective welfare cannot clearly be determined.

30. There has been some tendency to abandon the heavy planners' stress on investments, and to use consumption as an incentive to greater effort, with results that seem satisfactory to everybody concerned. It is likely that this trend toward "consumerism," however limited, will continue.*

31. I have been struck many times and in many contexts by the similarity of problems facing the socialist and capitalist economies. While not a believer in the convergence hypothesis, at least not in the ultimate sense, I have acquired a suspicion that some differences between economic systems may be overemphasized for ideological reasons. There seems no doubt that there are a variety of economic and social factors that affect both types of systems, tending to produce similar responses.

Finally, let me stress that the present study can be regarded only as part of the beginning of comparative discussions in the area of economic systems concerned with consumption, and as an encouragement to independent statistical research. It entails an appeal for more statistical data, greater openness in the official derivation of such

---

*Interest in Western "consumerism," its approval and stress on the need for "social marketing" and market research, are contained in Duliniec and Golebiowski 1973, pp. 207–15.

data, and more studies of those data. It contains a suggestion for integration of independent estimates of personal consumption with those for social consumption to provide a comprehensive index of changing levels of living.

The author would like to see more research on poverty and its distribution in Eastern Europe (by sex, age, and educational level); on discrimination; on housing; urban-rural differentials; wage differentials by skills; and so on. Many more studies are necessary, if only to give the planners an indication of what is needed, of the problems to be faced and tackled. It is with an emphasis on such a spirit of positive contribution to a solution of problems, rather than gloating over them, that this study ends.

Like discrimination, economic and social problems exist everywhere, regardless of the political system in force. It is to the solution of those problems, possible only after an unbiased, objective examination, that thinking people ought to direct their efforts.

For abbreviated references, the reader is advised to refer
to the List of Abbreviations on page xx.

"Agriculture." 1957. In Poland, ed. Oscar Halecki. New York:
Praeger Publishers.

Alton, Thad. 1970. "Economic Structure and Growth in Eastern
Europe." In U.S. Congress, Joint Economic Committee, Devel-
opments in Countries of Eastern Europe. 91st Congress, 2nd
Sess.

_____. 1974. "Economic Growth and Resource Allocation in Eastern
Europe." In U.S. Congress, Joint Economic Committee, Reorien-
tation and Commercial Relations of the Economies of Eastern
Europe. 93rd Congress, 2nd Session.

Alton, Thad, et al. 1962. Czechoslovak National Income and Product,
1947-1948 and 1955-1956. New York: Columbia University Press.

_____. 1963. Hungarian National Income and Product in 1955. New
York: Columbia University Press.

_____. 1965. Polish National Income and Product in 1954, 1955 and
1956. New York: Columbia University Press.

_____. 1974. "Military Expenditures in Eastern Europe: Some
Alternative Estimates." In U.S. Congress, Joint Economic
Committee, Reorientation and Commercial Relations of the
Economies of Eastern Europe. 93rd Congress, 2nd Session.

Annuarul Statistical Republicii Socialiste Romania. Annual. Bucharest:
Directia Centrala de Statistica.

Arrow, Kenneth. 1963. Social Choice and Individual Values. 2nd ed.
New York: John Wiley.

Balassa, Bela. 1959. The Hungarian Experience in Economic Planning:
A Theoretical and Empirical Study. New Haven: Yale University
Press.

_____. 1970. "Growth Strategies in Semi-Industrial Countries."
Quarterly Journal of Economics, February.

314

Bandor, Frank, Laszlo Czirjak, and George Pall. 1970. Hungary: Extension of Growth Indexes to 1967. OP-33.

Barabas, Tamas, and Gyula Nemeth. 1966. "Living Standard." In Hungary, ed. Zoltan Halasz. Budapest: Corvina Press.

Baring, Arnulf. 1972. Uprising in East Germany: June 17, 1953. Ithaca, N.Y.: Cornell University Press.

Baylis, Thomas. 1974. "The consolidation of the DDR." East Central Europe, vol. 1, part 1.

Beksiak, Janusz. 1972. Spoleczenstwo gospodarujace. Warsaw: PWN.

Bergson, Abram. 1968. Planning and Productivity Under Soviet Socialism. New York: Carnegie-Mellon University Press.

Bernasek, Miloslav. 1969. "The Czechoslovak Economic Recession, 1962-65." Soviet Studies, April.

Beskid, Lidia. 1962. System cen detalicznych w Polsce. Warsaw.

_____. 1972. Zmiany spozycia w Polsce. Warsaw: PWN.

Biuletyn Statystyczny. Monthly. Warsaw: GUS.

Bochenski, Joseph, and Gerhart Niemeyer, eds. 1962. Handbook on Communism. New York: Frederick A. Praeger.

Boettcher, Bodo. 1956. Industrielle Strukturwandlungen in Sowjetisch besetzten Gebiet Deutschlands. Berlin: Duncker und Humbolt.

Booth, Philip. 1973. Social Security in America. Ann Arbor, Mich.: Wayne State University Press.

Bozyk, Pawel. 1971. "Nasza przyszlosc—gospodarka otwarta." ZG, no. 48.

Brodzinski, Bohdan. 1965. Stopa zyciowa w Polsce w latach 1945-1963. London: Polish School of Political and Social Science.

_____. 1973. "Dwa lata Gierka." Kultura (Paris), no. 4.

Bronson, David and Barbara Severin. 1973. "Soviet Consumer Welfare: The Brezhnev Era." In U.S. Congress Joint Economic Committee, Soviet Economic Prospects for the Seventies. 93rd Congress, 1st Session.

Brus, Wlodzimierz. 1956. "O placach realnych w okresie planu szescioletniego." Zycie Warszawy, February 2, 3, 5-6, 7, 9.

_____. 1971. "Wlodzimierz Brus o Grudniu." Kultura (Paris), no. 9.

Brzeski, Andrzej. 1964. "Inflation in Poland, 1945-1960." Ph.D. dissertation, University of California, Berkeley.

_____. 1971. "Poland as a Catalyst of Change in the Communist Economic System." The Polish Review, spring.

Brzezinski, Zbigniew. 1970. Between Two Ages: America's Role in the Technotronic Era. New York: Viking Press.

Buky, Barnabas. 1972. "Hungary's NEM on a Treadmill." Problems of Communism, September-October.

_____. 1956. SBZ von 1945 bis 1954. Bonn.

Bundesministerium fuer gesamtdeutsche Fragen. 1966. SBZ von A bis Z. Bonn: Deutscher Bundes-Verlag.

Burks, R. V. 1974. "The Political Hazards of Economic Reform." In U.S. Congress, Joint Economic Committee, Reorientation and Commercial Relations of the Economies of Eastern Europe. 93rd Congress, 2nd Session.

Byrski, Zbigniew. 1971. "Legenda pierwszego sekretarza." Kultura (Paris), no. 3.

Bywalec, Czeslaw. 1972. "Analiza zaleznosci pomiedzy dochodami a wydatkami ludnosci na zywnosc." Zeszyty Naukowe Wyzszej Szkoly Ekonomicznej w Krakowie, no. 53.

Chapman, Janet. 1963. Real Wages in Soviet Russia Since 1928. Cambridge, Mass.: Harvard University Press.

Chelstowski, Stanislaw. 1972. "Wstepny bilans." ZG, nos. 51-52.

_____. 1974. "Utrwalanie — przeksztalcanie." ZG, no. 5.

Chinowski, Krzysztof, and Anna Stepniewska. 1972. "Rola importu w zaopatrzeniu rynku w konsumcyjne artykuly niezywnosciowe w Polsce." GP, no. 3.

Chmara, Michal. 1973. "Przenikanie wzorcow cywilizacyjno-kulturowych z krajow kapitalistycznych a odrebnosc socjalist-ycznego modelu konsumpcji." In Socjalistyczny model konsumpcji, ed. Janusz Piasny. Warsaw: KiW.

Cholinski, T., et al. 1967. Gospodarka zapasami w krajach socjalistycznych. Warsaw.

Ciamaga, Lucjan. 1973. "Rosnaca rola handlu i wspolpracy zagranicznej." ND, no. 3.

Committee for German Unity. 1961. GDR, 300 Questions, 300 Answers. Leipzig: the Committee.

Crawford, J. T., and John Haberstroh. 1974. "Survey of Economic Policy Issues in Eastern Europe: Technology, Trade, and the Consumer." In U.S. Congress, Joint Economic Committee. Reorientation and Commercial Relations of the Economies of Eastern Europe. 93rd Congress, 2nd Session.

Csikos-Nagy, B. 1971. "The New Hungarian Price System." In Reform of the Economic Mechanism in Hungary, ed. Istvan Friss. Budapest: Akademiai Kiado.

Czerwinski, Zbigniew. 1965. "Stopa inwestycji a maksymalizacja spozycia." Ekonomista, no. 1.

Czirjak, Laszlo. 1967a. Growth of Hungarian Domestic and Foreign Trade, 1938 and 1946-1965. OP-11.

_____. 1967b. Hungarian Agricultural Production and Value Added, 1934-38 and 1946-1965. OP-14.

_____. 1968a. Hungarian Investment, 1938 and 1949-1965: Trends in Fixed Capital, Inventories, and Net Foreign Investment. OP-17.

_____. 1968b. Indexes of Hungarian Industrial Production, 1938 and 1946-1965. OP-16.

_____. 1973. Hungarian GNP by Sectors of Origin of Product and End Uses, 1938 and 1946-1967. OP-43.

Czirjak, Laszlo, and Jaroslav Dusek. 1972. Growth of East German Industrial Output, 1936, 1946, 1948, and 1950-1967. OP-35.

Czirjak, Laszlo, and Paul Marer. 1973. Comparison of Hungarian Agricultural and Nonagricultural Incomes in Current and Real Terms, 1938 and 1949-1970. OP-21.

Danecki, Jan. 1972. "Egalitaryzm spoleczny a modele konsumpcji." ZG, no. 51.

Dangel, Jan. 1971. "Budownictwo mieszkaniowe w latach 1966-1970." GP, no. 6.

Davis, Lance, et al. 1972. American Economic Growth: An Economist's History of the United States. New York: Harper & Row.

Denison, Edward. 1962. The Sources of Economic Growth in the United States and the Alternatives Before Us. New York: Committee for Economic Development.

DIFW. 1971. DDR—Wirtschaft: Eine Bestandsaufnahme. Frankfurt am Main: Fischer Buecherei.

DIFZ. 1964. Handbuch der Deutschen Demokratischen Republik. Berlin (?): Staatsverlag der DDR.

_____. Jahrbuch der Deutschen Demokratischen Republik. Annual. Berlin: Verlag die Wirtschaft Berlin.

Djilas, Milovan. 1971. "Wnioski z Polskiego Grudnia." Kultura (Paris), no. 3.

Dlugosz, Zofia. 1972. "Skolatane rzemioslo." ZG, no. 21.

Dolina, Joseph, and Bogdan Mieczkowski. 1957. "Domestic Trade and Finance." In Poland, ed. Oscar Halecki. New York: Praeger Publishers.

Dornberg, John. 1968. The Other Germany. Garden City, N. Y.: Doubleday & Co.

Douglas, Dorothy. 1953. Transitional Economic Systems: The Polish-Czech Example. London: Routledge & Kegan Paul.

Drewnowski, Jan. 1971. "O polskiej gospodarce." Kultura (Paris), no. 4.

_____. 1974. "'Proces Centralnego Urzedu Planowania' w 1948 roku." Zeszyty Historyczne, no. 28. Paris: Instytut Literacki.

Dudzinski, Wladyslaw. 1968. "Polityka spoleczna a ceny." ZG, no. 43.

_____. 1970. "Efektywnosc spoleczna." ZG, no. 3.

Due, John. 1963. Government Finance: An Economic Analysis. 3rd ed. Homewood, Ill.: Richard D. Irwin.

_____. 1968. Government Finance: Economics of the Public Sector. 4th ed. Homewood, Ill.: Richard D. Irwin.

Duliniec, Elzbieta, and Tomasz Golebiowski. 1973. "Konsumeryzm— geneza, zakres i perspektywy." Zeszyty Naukowe Szkoly Glownej Planowania i Statystyki, no. 91.

Dziennik Ustaw. Warsaw. Occasional (journal of laws).

Eckstein, Alexander. 1954. "Postwar Planning in Hungary." Economic Development and Cultural Change, June.

Ekonomista. 1971. "Uchwala krajowego zjazdu ekonomistow." No. 3.

Ernst, Maurice. 1966. "Postwar Economic Growth in Eastern Europe: A Comparison with Western Europe." In U.S. Congress, Joint Economic Committee, New Directions in the Soviet Economy, part IV. 89th Congress, 2nd Session.

Fallenbuchl, Zbigniew. 1974. "East European Integration: Comecon." In U.S. Congress, Joint Economic Committee, Reorientation and Commercial Relations of the Economies of Eastern Europe. 93rd Congress, 2nd Session.

Feiwel, George. 1968. New Economic Patterns in Czechoslovakia: Impact of Growth, Planning and the Market. New York: Frederick A. Praeger.

_____. 1971a. "The Inverse Economic Miracle: Sources of Growth and Retrogression in Postwar Czechoslovakia." Economic Development and Cultural Change, April.

_____. 1971b. Poland's Industrialization Policy: A Current Analysis. 2 Volumes. New York: Praeger Publishers.

Fick, Bronislaw. 1971a. "Na okres przejsciowy: Place i system premiowy." ZG, no. 8.

_____. 1971b. "O systemie bodzcow." ZG, no. 6.

Flakierski, H. 1973. "The Polish Economic Reform of 1970." The Canadian Journal of Economics. February.

Franzl, Karel. 1924. "Industries." In Czechoslovakia: A Survey of
  Economic and Social Conditions, ed. Josef Gruber. New York:
  Macmillan.

Galante, Pierre. 1965. The Berlin Wall. Garden City, N.Y.:
  Doubleday.

Gamarnikow, Michael. 1974. "Balance Sheet on Economic Reforms."
  In U.S. Congress, Joint Economic Committee, Reorientation
  and Commercial Relations of the Economies of Eastern Europe.
  93rd Congress, 2nd Session.

Gibney, Frank. 1959. The Frozen Revolution: Poland: A Study in
  Communist Decay. New York: Farrar, Straus and Cudahy.

Ginsbert, A. 1965. "Rozwoj uslug komunalnych w Polsce i w innych
  krajach demokracji ludowej." Biuletyn Instytutu Gospodarstwa
  Spolecznego, no. 2.

Glowczyk, Jan. 1969; 1970. "Intensyfikacja i konsumpcja." ZG,
  nos. 51-52; 5.

Gmytrasiewica, Michal. 1971. "Ilosc czy jakosc?" ZG, no. 14.

Goldman, Josef, and Karel Kouba. 1969. Economic Growth in Czechoslovakia. Prague: Academia.

Goldman, Marshall. 1971. "More Heat in the Soviet Hothouse."
  Harvard Business Review, July-August.

Gomori, George. 1973. "The Cultural Intelligentsia: The Writers."
  In Social Groups in Polish Society, eds. David Lane and George
  Kolankiewicz. New York: Columbia University Press.

Gomulka, Stanislaw. 1974. "Nowa polityka uprzemyslawiania
  Polski." Trybuna (London), no. 17.

Gospodarka Planowa. 1972. "Program na miare spolecznych
  mozliwosci i potrzeb." No. 1.

_____. 1973. "Plan na rok 1973 — kontynaucja strategii, przys-
  pieszone tempo." No. 1.

_____. 1974. "Rozwoj spoleczno-gospodarczy krajow RWPG." No. 1.

Graszewicz, Henryk. 1973. "Anachronizmy zaopatrzenia rzemieslniczego." ZG, no. 19.

Gurley, John. 1972. "Have Fiscal and Monetary Policies Failed?" American Economic Review, May.

GUS. 1956. Wykonanie zadan planu szescioletniego. Warsaw.

_____. 1957. Dochod narodowy Polski 1954 i 1955. Warsaw.

_____. 1972. Umieralnosc wedlug przyczyn w latach 1951-1970. Warsaw.

Gutowski, Antoni. 1969. "Polska droga do . . ." Kultura (Paris) no. 12.

_____. 1970. "Statystycy i statysci." Kultura (Paris), no. 4.

_____. 1974. "Zblizenie polsko-francuskie." Kultura (Paris), no. 9.

Hangen, Welles. 1966. The Muted Revolution: East Germany's Challenge to Russia and the West. New York: Alfred A. Knopf.

Hanhardt, Arthur. 1968. The German Democratic Republic. Baltimore: The Johns Hopkins Press.

Hanson, Philip. 1968. The Consumer in the Soviet Economy. Evanston, Ill.: Northwestern University Press.

Higgins, Benjamin. 1968. Economic Development: Principles, Problems, and Policies. Revised ed. New York: W. W. Norton.

Hodoly, Andrzej. 1966. Problemy spozycia w Polsce. Warsaw: PWE.

_____. 1970. "Zachowanie sie konsumentow jako przeslanka polityki konsumpcji." Ekonomista, no. 1.

Hodoly, Andrzej, et al. 1971. "Zarys polityki konsumpcji." In collective work, Konsumpcja w gospodarce planowej. Warsaw: PWE.

Holbrook, Robert. 1972. "Optimal Economic Policy and the Problem of Instrument Instability." American Economic Review, March.

Holesovsky, Vaclav. 1961. "Karl Marx and Soviet National Income Theory." American Economic Review, June.

_____. 1963. "Personal Consumption in Czechoslovakia: 1937, 1948." Ph.D. dissertation, Columbia University.

_____. 1965. "Personal Consumption in Czechoslovakia, Hungary and Poland, 1950–1960: A Comparison." Slavic Review, December.

_____. 1968. "Planning Reforms in Czechoslovakia." Soviet Studies, April.

Holesovsky, Vaclav, and Gregor Lazarcik. 1968. Czechoslovakia: I. Extension of Growth Indexes to 1965; II. Personal Consumption Index, 1937 and 1948–1965. OP-25.

Holesovsky, Vaclav, and George Pall. 1968. Personal Consumption in Hungary, 1938 and 1947–1965. OP-18.

Hutchings, Raymond. 1971. Soviet Economic Development. New York: Barnes & Noble.

Ignotus, Paul. 1966. "Hungary 1966." In Ten Years After: The Hungarian Revolution in the Perspective of History, ed. Tamas Aczel. New York: Holt, Rinehart and Winston.

_____. 1972. Hungary. New York: Praeger Publishers.

Japan Statistical Yearbook. Annual. Tokyo: Japan Statistical Association.

Jaroszynski, Wladyslaw. 1973. "RWPG—wymiana artykulow konsumpcyjnych." ZG, no. 1.

Jedrychowski, Stefan. 1974. "Aktualne zagadnienia polityki finansowej w trzydziestym roku Polski Ludowej." Finanse, no. 7.

Kalecki, Michal. 1962. "Akumulacja a maksymalizacja spozycia." Ekonomista, no. 3.

_____. 1964. Z zagadnien gospodarczo-spolecznych Polski Ludowej. Warsaw: PWN.

_____. 1972. Selected Essays on the Economic Growth of the Socialist and the Mixed Economy. Cambridge: Cambridge University Press.

Kamecki, Z., J. Soldaczuk, and W. Sierpinski. 1971. Miedzynarodowe stosunki ekonomiczne. 2d ed. Warsaw.

Kantecki, Antoni. 1972. "Jak ksztaltowac socjalistyczny model konsumpcji?" ZG, no. 41.

Karpinski, Andrzej. 1958. Zagadnienia socjalistycznej industrializacji Polski. Warsaw: PWG.

_____. 1964. Twenty Years of Poland's Economic Development, 1944-1964. Warsaw: Polonia.

Kaser, Michael, and Janusz Zielinski. 1970. Planning in East Europe. London: The Bodley Head.

Kasperek-Hoppe, Maria. 1973a. "Rozwoj spolecznego funduszu konsumpcji w Polsce." In Socjalistyczny model konsumpcji, ed. Janusz Piasny. Warsaw: KiW.

_____. 1973b. "Tendencje rozwojowe funduszu konsumpcji w Polsce." Ruch Prawniczy Ekonomiczny i Socjologiczny, no. 3.

Kawalec, Wincenty. 1969a. "Przemiany struktury spoleczno-gospodarczej Polski." Ekonomista, no. 4.

_____. 1969b. "Zatrudnienie—kadry—kwalifikacje." ND, no. 12.

_____. 1971. "Miejsce Polski w swiecie, Europie i RWPG." ND, no. 9.

Kecsekemeti, Paul. 1961. The Unexpected Revolution: Social Forces in the Hungarian Uprising. Stanford: Stanford University Press.

Kendrick, John. 1961. Productivity Trends in the United States. Princeton: Princeton University Press.

Kierczynski, Tadeusz. 1971. "Problemy dostosowania struktury asortymentowej produkcji do potrzeb odbiorcow." Finanse, no. 8.

Kiss, Sandor. 1968. "Hungarian Agriculture Under the NEM." East Europe, no. 8.

Knab, Julian, and Karol Pach. 1968. "Producent a cena." Finanse, no. 3.

Knyziak, Zygmunt. 1964. Czynniki wzrostu produkcji przemyslowej w Polsce, 1950-1960. Warsaw: PWN.

Korbonski, Andrzej. 1965. Politics of Socialist Agriculture in Poland, 1945-1960. New York: Columbia University Press.

Korbonski, Andrzej, and Gregor Lazarcik. 1972. Polish Agricultural Production, Output, Expenses, Gross and Net Product, and Productivity, 1934-38, 1937, and 1946-1970. OP-37.

Korbonski, Andrzej, and Claus Wittich. 1968. Indexes of Polish Housing, Service, and Government Sectors, 1937 and 1946-1965. OP-29.

Korbonski, Andrzej; Alexej Wynnyczuk; and Wassyl Znayenko. 1973. Poland: Index of Gross Investment. OP-41.

Kosk, Henryk. 1972. "Stare i nowe w handlu zagranicznym." ZG, no. 7.

Kozminski, Andrzej. 1969. "Socjologiczne problemy planowania konsumpcji." Ekonomista, no. 3.

Krawczewski, Andrzej. 1972. "Bledy teorii—korekta praktyki." ZG, no. 49.

Krencik, Wieslaw. 1961. "Niektore problemy obliczania dynamiki plac realnych w Polsce." Studia Ekonomiczne, no. 6.

Krol, Henryk, and Zygmunt Drozdek. 1971. "Problemy spoleczne w planowaniu gospodarczym," ND, no. 9.

Kruczek, Adam. 1973. "W sowieckiej prasie." Kultura (Paris), no. 9.

Kruszewski, Z. A. 1972. The Oder-Neisse Boundary and Poland's Modernization: The Socioeconomic and Political Impact. New York: Praeger Publishers.

Krzyzewski, Remigiusz. 1968. Konsumpcja spoleczna w gospodarce socjalistycznej. Warsaw: PWN.

Kucharski, M. 1964. Pieniadz, dochod, proporcje wzrostu. Warsaw.

Kultura (Paris). 1971a. "Polski grudzien." Nos. 1-2.

_____. 1971b. "Swiadek szczecinski." No. 11.

Kultura-Dokumenty. 1971. Poznan 1956, Grudzien 1970. Vol. 202.

Kuron, Jacek, and Karol Modzelewski. 1966. List otwarty do Partii. Paris: Institut Litteraire.

Kurowski, Lech, and Urszula Plowiec. 1972. "Optymalizacja importu artykulow konsumpcyjnych." Ekonomista, no. 5.

Kurowski, Stefan. 1957a. "Model a cele gospodarki narodowej." In Dyskusja o polskim modelu gospodarczym. Warsaw: KiW.

_____. 1957b. _Szkice optymistyczne_. Warsaw: Pax.

_____. 1971. "Spor o wzorzec konsumpcji w Polsce." _Ekonomista_, no. 6.

Kuzinski, S. 1962. _O czynnikach wzrostu gospodarczego Polski Ludowej_. Warsaw.

Lange, Oskar. 1963. _Pisma wybrane_. Warsaw: PWN.

Lange, Oscar, and Fred Taylor. 1938. _On the Economic Theory of Socialism_. Minneapolis: University of Minnesota Press.

Lazarcik, Gregor. 1963. _The Performance of Socialist Agriculture: A Case Study of Production and Productivity in Czechoslovakia, 1934-38 and 1946-61_. New York: L. W. International Financial Research.

_____. 1968. _Comparison of Czechoslovak Agricultural and Non-agricultural Incomes in Current and Real Terms, 1937 and 1948-1965_. OP-20.

_____. 1969. _Czechoslovak Gross National Product by Sector of Origin and by Final Use, 1937 and 1948-1965_. OP-26.

_____. 1972. _East German Agricultural Production, Expenses, Gross and Net Product, and Productivity, 1934-38 and 1950-1970_. OP-36.

_____. 1973. "Defense, Education and Health Expenditures and Their Relation to GNP in Eastern Europe, 1960-1970." _The American Economist_, spring.

_____. 1974. "Agricultural Output and Productivity in Eastern Europe and Some Comparisons With the U.S.S.R. and U.S.A." In U.S. Congress, Joint Economic Committee, _Reorientation and Commercial Relations of the Economies of Eastern Europe_. 93rd Congress, 2nd Session.

Lazarcik, Gregor, and George Staller. 1968. _A New Index of Czechoslovak Industrial Output, 1937 and 1947-1965_. OP-24.

Lerner, Max, ed. 1948. _The Portable Veblen_. New York: Viking.

Lewandowska, Zofia. 1972. "Proba analizy ksztaltowania sie konsumpcji w Polsce w okresie industrializacji." _Prace Instytutu Nauk Ekonomiczno-Spolecznych Politechniki Warszawskiej_, no. 1.

Lewis, Flora. 1958. A Case History of Hope: The Story of Poland's Peaceful Revolutions. Garden City, N. Y.: Doubleday.

Lipinski, Edward. 1964. "Przedsiebiorstwo socjalistyczne." Ekonomista, no. 3.

_____. 1972. "System wartosci spoleczenstwa socjalistycznego." ZG, no. 28.

Lipinski, Jan. 1969. "System cen srodkow konsumpcji a reforma podatku obrotowego." Ekonomista, no. 1.

_____. 1972. "Ceny a dostawcy." Ekonomista, no. 1.

Lippold, Gerhard, ed. 1970. Das Zeitbudget der Bevoelkerung. Berlin: Verlag die Wirtschaft.

Los, Janusz. 1964. Wstep do polityki zywnosciowej. Warsaw: PWE.

Loucks, William, and William Whitney. 1969. Comparative Economic Systems. 8th ed. New York: Harper & Row.

Magyar Gazdasagkutato Intezet. 1947. A research paper.

Magyar Statisztikai Zsebkonyv. Annual. Budapest: Kozgazdasagi es Jogy Konyvkiado.

Malecki, Stanislaw. 1960. "Przeklenstwo grzechu pierworodnego." Kultura (Paris), no. 11.

Maly Slownik Ekonomiczny. 1958. Warsaw: PWG.

Manpower Report of the President. 1972. Washington, D.C.: U.S. Government Printing Office.

Marczewski, Andrzej. 1974. "Poprawa warunkow zyciowych ludnosci a rownowaga pieniezno-rynkowa w latach 1971-1973." Finanse, no. 3.

Marer, Paul. 1972. Soviet and East European Foreign Trade, 1946-1969: Statistical Compendium and Guide. Bloomington: Indiana University Press.

Marer, Paul and John Tilley. 1974. "Tourism." In U.S. Congress, Joint Economic Committee, Reorientation and Commercial Relations of the Economies of Eastern Europe. 93rd Congress, 2nd Session.

Markowski, Stanislaw. 1968. "Racjonalizacja godpodarowania a struktura spozycia i dochodow ludnosci." ZG, no. 14.

_____. 1972. Spozycie w Polsce Ludowej. Warsaw: Instytut Wydawniczy CRZZ.

Matusek, Ivan. 1974. "Eastern Europe: The Political Context." In U.S. Congress, Joint Economic Committee, Reorientation and Commercial Relations of the Economies of Eastern Europe. 93rd Congress, 2nd Session.

Mazys, Jerzy. 1970. "Kapitalochlonnosc produkcji w Polsce." Ekonomista, no. 2.

Medvedev, Roy. 1971. Let History Judge: The Origins and Consequences of Stalinism. New York: Alfred A. Knopf.

Metera, Jerzy. 1971. "Znaczenie miedzynarodowej wspolpracy naukowej i technicznej." ND, no. 2.

Michal, Jan. 1960. Central Planning in Czechoslovakia: Organization for Growth in a Mature Economy. Stanford: Stanford University Press.

Mieczkowski, Bogdan. 1953. "The Effects of Financial Policy and Direct Controls on the Balance of International Payments, with Special Reference to Post-War German Experience." M.A. thesis. University of Illinois.

_____. 1954a. "Communist Money and Banking: The Polish Case." Ph.D. dissertation, University of Illinois.

_____. 1954b. "The Operation of Communist Banks." Current Economic Comment, November.

_____. 1960. "Na marginesie zapasow, prawa Wagnera i przecietnej sklonnosci do oszczedzania." Finanse, no. 1.

_____. 1967a. "Communism and Morality in Poland." Orbis, fall.

_____. 1967b. "The Unstable Soviet Bloc Economies." East Europe, no. 10.

_____. 1968a. "Bezrobocie w systemie komunistycznym." Kultura (Paris), no. 11.

_____. 1968b. "Poland: Politics vs. the Economy." East Europe, no. 12.

_____. 1969. "The Polish Index of Consumption, 1938-1964."
    Bentley Business and Economic Review, June.

_____. 1970. "The Sinews of Poland's Current Policy of Economic
    Intensification." *The Polish Review*, autumn.

_____. 1971a. "Poland, 1968." In *The Prediction of Communist
    Economic Performance*, ed. Peter Wiles. Cambridge: Cambridge
    University Press.

_____. 1971b. "Recent Discussion on Consumption Planning in
    Poland." *Soviet Studies*, April.

_____. 1972. "Rocznik Statystyczny 1971." *Kultura* (Paris), no. 5.

_____. 1973a. Book review. *Journal of Baltic Studies*, winter.

_____. 1973b. "Ekonomisci krajowi o spozyciu w PRL." *Kultura*
    (Paris), no. 6.

_____. 1973c. "Evaluating Planners." *Co-existence*, November.

Mieroszewski, Juliusz. 1971. "Refleksje grudniowe." *Kultura*
    (Paris), no. 3.

Mikolajczyk, Zbigniew. 1973. "Przemysl ktory nie moze sie
    spozniac." *ZG*, no. 18.

Miller, Margaret. 1965. *Rise of the Russian Consumer*. London:
    Institute of Economic Affairs.

Ministry of Economic Planning, Prague. 1968. *Analyza pricin vyvo-
    jowych tendenci o stavu cs. narodniho hospodarstvi*. Prague:
    the Ministry.

Misiak, Marek, and Ryszard Zabrzewski. 1969. "Struktura kon-
    sumpcji." *ZG*, no. 45.

Miszewski, Bronislaw. 1972. *Postep ekonomiczny*. Warsaw: PWE.

Monitor Polski. Warsaw. Occasional (journal of laws).

Montias, John. 1962. *Central Planning in Poland*. New Haven:
    Yale University Press.

_____. 1974. "The Structure of Comecon Trade and the Prospects for East-West Exchanges." U.S. Congress, Joint Economic Committee, Reorientation and Commercial Relations of the Economies of Eastern Europe. 93rd Congress, 2nd Session.

Mozolowski, A. 1972. "Cichy glos konsumenta." Polityka, no. 33.

Mstislavskii, P. 1961. Narodnoye potreblenye pri sotsyalizme. Moscow: State Publishing of Planning and Economic Literature.

Mujzel, Jan. 1969. "Problemy rynku w systemie planowek gospodarki socjalistycznej." Ekonomista, no. 2.

_____. 1972. "Planners' Preferences and Social Needs." Co-existence, November.

Musgrave, Richard. 1959. The Theory of Public Finance. New York: McGraw-Hill.

Nachtigal, Vladimir. 1970. "Productivity Trends in Czechoslovakia, 1948-1967." Czechoslovak Economic Papers, no. 12.

Nagy, Karoly. 1969. "The Impact of Communism in Hungary." East Europe, no. 3.

Nasilkowski, Mieczyslaw. 1973. "Symptomy intensywnego rozwoju." ZG, no. 17.

Nieciunski, Witold. 1973. "Rola mieszkania i jego ceny w rozwoju spoleczno-gospodarczym i w ksztaltowaniu modelu spozycia." Ekonomista, no. 5.

Niedzialkowski, Otton. 1969. "Roznicowa czy procentowa forma podatku obrotowego?" Finanse, no. 10.

Niewadzi, Czesalw. 1971. "Dynamika i proporcje rozwoju sfery uslug." ND, no. 5.

_____. 1972. "Efekty szybszego rozwoju uslug." ZG, no. 27.

_____. 1974. "Problemy i perspektywy rozwoju uslug dla ludnosci w Polsce do roku 1980." GP, no. 9.

Nowe Drogi. 1967. "Rola rynku w planowej gospodarce socjalistycznej." No. 1.

_____. 1972a. "Sprawozdanie KC PZPR za okres miedzy V and VI Zjazdem." No. 1.

_____. 1972b. "Szerokie mozliwosci wymiany towarow konsumpcyjnych." No. 9.

Obst, Werner, 1973. DDR—Wirtschaft: Modell und Wirklichkeit. Hamburg: Hoffmann und Campe.

The Official Associated Press Almanac, 1974. Maplewood, N. J.: Hammond Almanac.

Osikowski, Eugeniusz. 1972. Budzety gospodarstw domowych 1966-1970. Warsaw: GUS, no. 42.

Pajestka, Jozef. 1969a. "Niektore problem strategii rozwoju ekonomicznego Polski Ludowej." ND, no. 7.

_____. 1969b. "Problemy polityki strukturalnej konsumpcji na obecnym etapie rozwoju." ND, no. 10.

_____. 1973. "Czy beda zmiany w zarzadzaniu?" Zycie Literackie, No. 1.

Pawlowski, Zbigniew. 1971. "System informacji i sterowania konsumpcja." Ekonomista, no. 3.

Piasna, Barbara. 1971. "Powstanie i rozwoj instytucjonalnych form ochrony interesow konsumenta w Polsce Ludowej." Ruch Prawniczy Ekonomiczny i Socjologiczny, no. 4.

_____. 1973. "Przejawy i nastepstwa naruszania interesow konsumenta w obrocie towarowym." Ruch Prawniczy Ekonomiczny i Socjologiczny, no. 2.

Piasny, Janusz. 1970. "Podstawowe zmiany w poziomie i strukturze konsumpcji w Polsce Ludowej." Ruch Prawniczy Ekonomiczny i Socjologiczny, no. 3.

_____. 1971. Konsumpcja w teorii i praktyce gospodarki socjalistycznej. Warsaw: PWN.

_____. 1973. "Przemiany w polskim modelu konsumpcji i jego prognozy." In Socjalistyczny model konsumpcji, ed. Janusz Piasny. Warsaw: KiW.

Pisarski, Grzegorz. 1969. "Koncepcje rozwoju spozycia spolecznego." ND, no. 12.

Pluta, Ryszard. 1971. "Zmianowosc a inwestycje." ZG, no. 48.

Pohorille, Maksymilian. 1966. "Model konsumpcji." Ekonomista, no. 2.

_____. 1971. Model konsumpcji w ustroju socjalistycznym. Warsaw: PWE.

_____. 1972. "Istota sporu o wzorzec konsumpcji." Ekonomista, no. 4.

Polikeit, Georg. 1966. Die sogenannte DDR. Jugenheim: Weltkreisverlag.

Prucha, Vaclav. 1972. "Basic Features of Economic Development in Czechoslovakia in 1945-1970." Czechoslovak Economic Papers, no. 13.

Pryor, Frederick. 1963. The Communist Foreign Trade System. Cambridge, Mass.: The MIT Press.

Przelaskowski, Waclaw. 1960. Spozycie zywnosci w Polsce. Warsaw: PWG.

Przywara, Boleslaw. 1970. "Konsumpcja dzis i jutro." ZG, no. 3.

Ptaszek, Jan. 1971. "Wspoldzialanie w ramach RWPG." ZG, no. 30.

Radio Free Europe, News From Poland.

Radio Free Europe Research. Munich: RFE. Occasional.

Rajkiewicz, Antoni. 1965. Zatrudnienie w Polsce Ludowej w latach 1950-1970. Warsaw: KiW.

Rakowski, Mieczyslaw. 1970. "Maksymalizacja konsumpcji a system cen." ZG, nos. 5, 6.

_____. 1971a. "Makroekonomiczna efektywnosc uslug." Ekonomista, no. 3.

_____. 1971b. "Pozyteczny nadmiar." ZG, no. 11.

Roberts, Eirlys. 1966. Consumers. London: C. A. Watts & Co.

Robinson, Joan. 1965. "Consumer's Sovereignty in a Planned Economy." In On Political Economy and Econometrics: Essays in Honor of Oskar Lange. Warsaw: PWN.

Robinson, William. 1973. The Pattern of Reform in Hungary: A Political, Economic and Cultural Analysis. New York: Praeger Publishers.

Rocznik Polityczny i Gospodarczy. Annual. Warsaw: PWE.

Rocznik Statystyczny. Annual. Warsaw: GUS.

Rogozinski, Wladyslaw. 1962. "Ogolne proporcje ksztaltowania sie dochodu narodowego w latach 1956-1960." GP, no. 4.

_____. 1973. "Dotychczasowe i przewidywane tendencje rozwoju spozycia z dochodow osobistych." GP, no. 7.

Ruminska, Ewa. 1972. "Aktualne problemy handlu Wschod-Zachod." ZG, no. 30.

Rurarz, Zdzislaw. 1972. "Przeslanki przyspieszenia rozwoju kraju." ND, no. 10.

Ryc, Kazimierz. 1968. Spozycie a wzrost gospodarczy Polski, 1945-1970. Warsaw: KiW.

_____. 1970a. "Wzorzec konsumpcji." ZG, no. 8.

_____. 1970b. "Zroznicowanie dochodow—egalitaryzacja spozycia." ZG, no. 12.

_____. 1971a. "Produkcja a konsumpcja." ND, no. 3.

_____. 1971b. "Rownowaga rynkowa." ND, no. 11.

_____. 1972. "Konsumpcja—czynnikiem rozwoju." ND, no. 9.

_____. 1974. "Wzrost gospodarczy a ksztaltowanie struktury konsumpcji." ND, no. 9.

Rychlewski, Eugeniusz. 1970. "Dlugookresowy popyt mieskaniowy." Ekonomista, no. 6.

_____. 1972. "Potrzeby mieszkaniowe w strukturze potrzeb spoleczenstwa." GP, no. 3.

Samuelson, Paul. 1973. Economics, 9th ed. New York: McGraw-Hill.

Sarapuk, Marian. 1972. "Czynniki wzrostu sektora uslug." Ekonomista, no. 6.

Schaefer, Klaus. 1967. "Produktionsdynamik und individuelle
   Konsumtion in der DDR in den Jahren 1950 bis 1965." In Die
   Konsumption im Reproduktionsprozess, Hans Roessler. ed.
   Halle-Wittenberg: Wissenschaftliche Beitraege der Martin-
   Luther-Universitaet.

Schaffer, Harry. 1970. "Progress in Hungary." Problems of Communism, January-February.

Schmidt, Hans. 1968. "Entwicklungstendenzen und Strukturwandlung
   der Ernaehrung." In Planung und Leitung der Volkswirtschaft,
   Beitraege zur Ernaehrungsekonomik, vol. 26. Berlin: Verlag
   der Wirtschaft.

Schoenbaum, David. 1972. "Introduction." In Arnulf Baring,
   Uprising in East Germany: June 17, 1953. Ithaca, N. Y.:
   Cornell University Press.

Schroeder, Gertrude. 1973. "Consumer Problems and Prospects."
   Problems of Communism, March-April.

Schwartz, Harry. 1954. Russia's Soviet Economy. New York:
   Prentice-Hall.

Searing, Marjory. 1974. "Education and Economic Growth: The
   Postwar Experience in Hungary and Poland." In U.S. Congress,
   Joint Economic Committee, Reorientation and Commercial Relations
   of the Economies of Eastern Europe. 93rd Congress, 2nd Session.

Secomski, Kazimierz. 1950. Analiza wykonania planu trzyletniego.
   Warsaw.

_____. 1958. Premises of the Five-Year Plan in Poland, 1956-60.
   Warsaw: Polonia Publishing House.

_____. 1971. "Nowa koncepcja planu 5-letniego." ND, no. 5.

Selucky, Radoslav. 1970. Czechoslovakia: The Plan that Failed.
   London: Thomas Nelson and Sons.

Seume, Franz. 1948. "Organisationsformen der Industrie in der
   sowjetischen Besatzungszone." In Deutsches Institut fuer
   Wirtschaftsforschung, Wirtschaftsprobleme der Besatzungszonen.
   Berlin: Duncker und Humbolt.

Sik, Ota. 1972. Czechoslovakia: The Bureaucratic Economy. White
   Plains, N. Y.: International Arts and Sciences Press.

Silone, Ignazio. 1971. "Oswiadczenie." Kultura (Paris), no. 3.

Smith, Jean. 1969. Germany Beyond the Wall: People, Politics . . . and Prosperity. Boston: Little, Brown.

Smith, Willard. 1973. "Housing in the Soviet Union—Big Plans, Little Action." In U.S. Congress, Joint Economic Committee, Soviet Economic Prospects for the Seventies. 93rd Congress, 2nd Session.

Snell, Edwin, and Marilyn Harper. 1970. "Postwar Economic Growth in East Germany: A Comparison With West Germany." In U.S. Congress, Joint Economic Committee, Economic Developments in Countries of Eastern Europe. 91st Congress, 2nd Session.

Societe d'Edition, Librairie, Informations Ouvrieres. 1972. Pologne 24 Janvier 1971: Gierek Face aux Grevistes de Szczecin. 2nd ed. Paris: SELIO.

Sokolowski, Kazimierz. 1973. "Luksus i postawa konsumpcyjna." Ruch Prawniczy Ekonomiczny i Socjologiczny, no. 4.

Sopinski, Stanislaw. 1973. "Zalozenia i kierunki rozwoju uslug." GP, no. 2.

Staatliche Zentralverwaltung fuer Statistik. 1969. Bilanz unserer Erfolge: 20 Jahre DDR in Zahlen und Fakten. Berlin: Staatsverwaltung der DDR.

Statistical Abstract of the United States. Annual. U.S. Department of Commerce, Bureau of the Census.

Statisticheski Ezhegodnik. Annual. Sofia: People's Republic of Bulgaria National Information Office.

Statisticka Rocenka Ceskoslovenske Republiky. Annual. Prague: Federalni Statisticky Urad.

Statisticki Godisnjak Jugoslavije. Annual. Belgrad: Sovezni Zavod za Statistiku.

Statistisches Jahrbuch fuer die Bundesrepublik Deutschland. Annual. Wiesbaden: Statistisches Bundesamt.

Statistisches Jahrbuch fuer das Deutsche Reich. Annual. Berlin: Statistiches Reichsamt.

Statistisches Jahrubach der Deutschen Demokratischen Republik.
Berlin: Staatliche Zentralverwaltung fuer Statistik.

Statisztikai Evkonyv. Annual. Budapest: Kozponti Statisztikai
Hivatal.

Stolper, Wolfgang. 1960. The Structure of the East German Economy.
Cambridge, Mass.: Harvard University Press.

Strapko, Aleksander. 1970. "Majatkochlonnosc produkcji rolnej."
GP, no. 2.

Strumilin, Stanislav. 1959. Problemy wydajnosci pracy. Warsaw:
KiW.

_____. 1962. Problemy socjalizmu i komunizmu w ZSRR. Warsaw.

Sueddeutsche Zeitung. 1973. "Nach der Fresswelle die Fressflut."
June 4.

Szabados, Joseph. 1968. "Hungary's NEM: Reorganization or Basic
Reform?" East Europe, no. 6.

Szeliga, Zygmunt. 1971. "Jak sie to robi." Polityka, June 5.

_____. 1974. "Handel i strategia." Polityka, March 16.

Szerwentke, A. 1962. "Wykonanie planu inwestycyjnego w latach .
1956-1960." GP, nos. 9-10.

Szulc, Tad. 1971. Czechoslovakia Since World War II. New York:
Viking.

Szyndarczuk, A. 1962. "Dochody ludnosci chlopskiej w latach
1956-1960." GP, no. 4.

Szyndler-Glowacki, Wieslaw. 1973. "Handel zagraniczny 1972-1973:
Wysokie obroty." ZG, no. 7.

_____. 1974. "Wzrost roli handlu zagranicznego." ZG, no. 24.

Trybuna Ludu. Warsaw. Daily.

Tymowski, Andrzej. 1973. Minimum socjalne: metodyka i proba
okreslenia. Warsaw: PWN.

United Nations. 1954. Report on International Definition and Measurement of Standards of Living: Report by Committee of Experts.
New York.

_____. 1961. International Definition and Measurement of Levels of Living: Interim Guide. New York.

_____. 1970. Report of the First Session of the Expert Group on Statistics of the Distribution of Income, Consumption and Wealth. New York.

_____. 1972a. A Draft System of Statistics of the Distribution of Income, Consumption and Wealth. New York.

_____. 1972b. Statistics of the Distribution of Income, Consumption and Wealth. New York.

U.S. Department of Health, Education and Welfare. 1973. Health Insurance Statistics, October 10.

Urbanek, Lida. 1968. "Some Difficulties in Implementing the Economic Reforms in Czechoslovakia." Soviet Studies, April.

Urbanek, Zdenek. 1968. "Development of Consumption and Wages in Czechoslovakia in 1956-1965." Czechoslovak Economic Papers, no. 10.

Wan, Henry. 1971. Economic Growth. New York: Harcourt, Brace, Jovanovich.

Warsaw. 1950. Spoldzielczy Instytut Wydawniczy "Kraj." Warsaw.

Werewka, Stanislaw. 1969. "Ocena nowoczesnosci wyrobow w przemysle polskim." GP, no. 12.

Wheeler, George. 1973. The Human Face of Socialism: The Political Economy of Change in Czechoslovakia. New York: Lawrence Hill.

Wilczynski, Jozef. 1969. The Economics and Politics of East-West Trade. London: Macmillan.

_____. 1970. "Consumer's Sovereignty Under Market Socialism in Evolution." Australian Economic Papers, June.

_____. 1972. Socialist Economic Development and Reforms. New York: Praeger

_____. 1973. Profit, Risk and Incentives Under Socialist Economic Planning. London: Macmillan.

_____. 1974. Technology in Comecon. London: Macmillan.

Wiles, Peter. 1971. "The Planning of Industry." In The Prediction of Communist Economic Performance, ed. Peter Wiles. Cambridge: Cambridge University Press.

Winiewski, Michal. 1969. Fundusze spozycia spolecznego a stopa zyciowa ludnosci. Warsaw: KiW.

Wiszniewski, Edward. 1971. "Pozycja konsumenta." ZG, no. 22.

Wnuk-Lipinski, Edmund. 1971. Gospodarowanie czasem wolnym i zajetym. Warsaw: GUS, no. 35.

_____. 1972. Praca i wypoczynek w budzecie czasu. Wroclaw: Osso-lineum.

Wojcieszak, Aleksander. 1974. "Gierkowska ekonomia w odwrocie." Kultura (Paris), nos. 7-8.

Wszelaki, Jan. 1957. "Industry." In Poland, ed. Oscar Halecki. New York: Praeger Publishers.

Wynnyczuk, Alexej, and Wassyl Znayenko. 1970. Trends in Output Inputs, and Factor Productivity in Polish Industry, 1947-1967. OP-34.

Zarski, Tadeusz. 1972. "Kierunek—wiecej lepszych mieszkan." ND, no. 3.

Zauberman, Alfred. 1964. Industrial Progress in Poland, Czechoslovakia and East Germany, 1937-1962. London: Oxford University Press.

Zduniak, Krystyna. 1972. "Przeslanki aktywnej polityki konsumpcji." Zeszyty Naukowe Szkoly Glownej Planowania i Statystyke, no. 89.

Zebrok, Jozef. 1973. "Kompleksowy rozwoj gospodarczy a miedzynarodowa specjalizacja produkcji panstw socjalistycznych." Zeszyty Naukowe (Wyzsza Szkola Ekonomiczna w Krakowie), no. 58.

Zekonski, Zygmunt. 1969. "Zmiany w strukturze spozycia w latach 1960-1968." GP, no. 11.

_____. 1974. "Z problemow metodologicznych formulowania spoleczno-bytowych celow rozwoju." GP, no. 6.

Zeman, Z. A. B. 1969. Prague Spring. New York: Hill and Wang.

Zielinski, Janusz. 1965. "The consumption Model and Means of Its Implementation." In On Political Economy and Econometrics: Essays in Honor of Oskar Lange. Warsaw: PWN.

_____. 1971. "Planners' Growth Priorities and System Remodelling." Co-existence, July.

_____. 1973. Economic Reforms in Polish Industry. London: Oxford University Press.

Zienkowski, Leszek. 1959. Jak sie oblicza dochod narodowy? Warsaw: PWG.

_____. 1963. Dochod narodowy Polski 1937-1960. Warsaw: PWE.

_____. 1964. "Wzrost dochodu narodowego w PRL." Ekonomista, no. 5.

Zinner, Paul. 1962. Revolution in Hungary. New York: Columbia University Press.

ZG. 1971a. "Place 1966-70." No. 34.

ZG. 1971b. "Zmianowosc." No. 10.

ZG. 1972. "Jubileusz rzemieslniczego stanu." No. 10.

166-67, 176, 179, 180, 181

saving, personal, 3, 4, 56, 57, 108, 129, 177, 237-40, 241, 267, 310
Schmidt, O., 193
Schroeder, G., 188
Schumpeter, J., 76
Schwartz, H., 67
Secomski, K., 176
self-service stores, 56
services, 148, 172, 174, 181, 184-85, 267, 310
shift coefficient, 186
shortages, 281
Sik, O., 192, 194, 213
social benefits, 165
social consciousness of consumers, 55, 58-59
social costs, 164, 165, 270
social preferences, 57
Stalin, J., 14, 154, 213
Staller, G., 204
State Planning Commission, 162
statistics, 19, 22, 47; coverage, 296, 306; falsifications of, 44, 112; lack of, 9, 98, 219, 312; unreliability of 47-48, 104, 106, 145, 148, 201, 206, 216, 224, 231, 261, 264 (See also, independent estimates)
Stolper, W., 256, 264, 267
Strumilin, S., 33
success indicator, 7, 10-11
sumptuary excise taxes, 58 (See also, taxes, excise)
Szulc, T., 191

taxes: direct, 56, 272; excise, 58; turnover, 70, 161-62
television, 29, 46, 142, 164, 170, 270, 287
thefts, 111
Third Reich, 22, 267
time-budget, 311
transport, 22, 151, 157, 167, 208, 233, 236
Trud, 44
Trybuna Ludu, 170
Tymowski, A., 41

Ulbricht, W., 244, 245, 247
United Nations, 3-4, 15, 22, 27, 43, 311
US, 12, 17, 48, 218, 245, 273, 285
UNRRA, 88, 89
USSR, 17, 31, 32, 43-46, 47, 62, 65, 67, 80, 91, 172, 247, 248, 285

Vneshnaya Torgovlya, 182

wages, 33, 41, 56, 64, 66, 76, 80, 85, 86, 91, 93, 94, 99, 108, 110, 111-12, 120, 124, 129, 132, 138, 145, 149, 164, 170, 193, 243, 245, 253, 254, 272-73, 311; incentive; 170, 311, real, 64, 65, 76, 80, 85, 91, 93, 94, 99, 108, 110, 111-12, 145, 149, 171, 190, 211, 219, 220, 253, 308, 311
Warsaw Pact, 92 (See also, defense)
Weber, M., 15
Western Territories, 85, 88,
West Germany, 32, 193, 211, 243, 244, 245, 251, 253-54, 256, 257, 261, 267, 270, 272-75, 278, 281, 285-87, 288, 289, 308
white-collar workers, 36, 41, 76, 80, 85, 129, 149, 151, 153, 213
Wilczynski, J., 35, 187
Winiewski, M., 37, 39, 41
women (See, employment of women)
Writers' Association, 221

Yugoslavia, 15-16, 17, 32, 75, 148, 243 (See also, international comparisons)

Zabrzewski, R., 165
Zaleski, E., 48
Zekonski, Z., 154-56, 157-59, 165, 167
Zielinski, J., 58, 64, 65, 66, 68, 303
Zycie Gospodarcze, 155, 159, 176
Zycie Warszawy, 112

ABOUT THE AUTHOR

BOGDAN MIECZKOWSKI is Professor of Economics at Ithaca College, Ithaca, N. Y. He holds a B. Sc. (Econ.) from the University of London, and an M. A. and Ph. D. from the University of Illinois.

Dr. Mieczkowski is co-author of Polish National Income and Product in 1954, 1955, and 1956, published by Columbia University Press, and he countributed to Poland, Oscar Halecki, ed. published by Praeger (1957) and to The Prediction of Communist Economic Performance, Peter Wiles, ed. published by Cambridge University Press. His articles and reviews on the economies of Eastern Europe and Japan have appeared extensively in the leading scholarly economic and Slavic studies journals in the West and in Poland.

CRISIS IN SOCIALIST PLANNING: Eastern Europe
and the USSR
> Jan Marczewski

MODERNIZATION IN ROMANIA SINCE WORLD WAR II:
> Trond Gilberg

POLITICAL SOCIALIZATION IN EASTERN EUROPE:
A Comparative Framework
> edited by Ivan Volgyes

THE POLITICS OF MODERNIZATION IN EASTERN
EUROPE: Testing the Soviet Model
> edited by Charles Gati

SOCIAL CHANGE AND STRATIFICATION IN EASTERN
EUROPE: An Interpretive Analysis of Poland and Her
Neighbors
> Alexander Matejko

YUGOSLAV ECONOMIC DEVELOPMENT AND POLITICAL
CHANGE: The Relationship between Economic Managers
and Policy-Making Elites
> Richard P. Farkas